THE DEVELOPMENT OF SOCIAL PSYCHOLOGY

The Development of Social Psychology

edited by

ROBIN GILMOUR and STEVE DUCK

*Department of Psychology, University of Lancaster
England*

1980

ACADEMIC PRESS

A Subsidiary of Harcourt Brace Jovanovich, Publishers
London   New York   Toronto   Sydney   San Francisco

ACADEMIC PRESS INC. (LONDON) LTD.
24/28 Oval Road
London NW1

United States Edition published by
ACADEMIC PRESS INC.
111 Fifth Avenue
New York, New York 10003

Copyright © 1980 by
ACADEMIC PRESS INC. (LONDON) LTD.

All Rights Reserved
No part of this book may be reproduced in any form by photostat, microfilm, or any other means, without written permission from the publishers

British Library Cataloguing in Publication Data

The development of social psychology.
1. Social psychology
I. Gilmour, R   II. Duck, S
301.1   HM251   80-40540

ISBN 0-12-284080-1 Casebound Edition
ISBN 0-12-284082-8 Paperback Edition

Filmset by Northumberland Press Ltd.,
Gateshead, Tyne and Wear
Printed in Great Britain by Fletcher and Son Ltd., Norwich

Contributors

Michael ARGYLE, *Institute of Experimental Psychology, Oxford University, South Parks Road, Oxford, England.*
Carl W. BACKMAN, *Department of Sociology, University of Nevada, Reno, Nevada 89557, U.S.A.*
Philip BRICKMAN, *Center for Group Dynamics, ISR, and Department of Psychology, University of Michigan, Ann Arbor, Michigan 48109, U.S.A.*
Steve DUCK, *Department of Psychology, Fylde College, University of Lancaster, Lancaster, England.*
J. Richard EISER, *Department of Psychology, Washington Singer Laboratories, University of Exeter, Exeter, England.*
Robert FARR, *Department of Psychology, University of Glasgow, Glasgow, Scotland.*
Kenneth GERGEN, *Department of Psychology, Swarthmore College, Swarthmore, Pennsylvania, 19081 U.S.A.*
Robin GILMOUR, *Department of Psychology, Fylde College, University of Lancaster, Lancaster, England.*
Rom HARRÉ, *Subfaculty of Philosophy, Oxford University, 10 Merton Street, Oxford, England.*
John INNES, *Department of Psychology, University of Adelaide, GPO Box 498, Adelaide, South Australia 5001.*
Peter KELVIN, *Department of Psychology, University College, London University, Gower Street, London, England.*
William McGUIRE, *Department of Psychology, Yale University, 2 Hillhouse Avenue, New Haven, Connecticut 06520, U.S.A.*
Wolfgang STROEBE, *Psychologisches Institut, Universität Tübingen, Friedrichstrasse 21, D-74 Tübingen, Germany.*

To
RALPH and RUTH PICKFORD
as a token of esteem

And to
A.E.G.
and
S.A.M.
as a token of worth

Preface

Although there is a good deal of debate in social psychology about where we are, what we are doing and where we are going, in our view this potentially healthy activity has not been carried out as constructively as it might.

Our decision to put this book together was prompted by the belief that, to be of real value, such self-questioning must be located against a background or setting and that it must not be seen as an isolated upheaval but as an integral part of the development of social psychology. Such a perspective offers the hope that we can make most sense out of present criticisms, defences, and arbitrations, as well as indicating the more fruitful lines of future progress. As the saw has it: if you seek the future in the present, look for the present in the past.

The title and plan of the book were thus not idly chosen but were intended to emphasize not merely an historical, time-linked view of the subject but also the analytic treatment of social psychology as a dynamic and developing subject. The theme of development will, we hope, provide one version of an integrating framework to the subject which seems so conspicuously lacking elsewhere. Behind this emphasis, also, is a feeling that we may have failed to make the fullest use of earlier workers in our field and that we have not adequately clarified or exploited their potential contribution to the future of the subject. Social psychology (and perhaps other disciplines as well) has not developed in any linear fashion, and progress—in the literal sense—has not been simply cumulative as models of science often suppose; perhaps this also accounts for a felt lack of progress in the evaluative sense. Indeed, it may be more approproate in practice to consider a cyclical model, or at least something like Heinz Werner's spiral model of development. This more circular way of proceeding is well seen in the way that older work suddenly comes back into fashion after a period of neglect. Good examples are to be found in the periodic resurgence of interest in Kurt Lewin's work and in the current interest in attribution theory's links to Heider's more general work on social perception.

An important strand in the structure of the book, then, is the belief that we have, in some significant measure, failed to learn from the past and that this can weaken us both in our present endeavours and for the future. Our existing debate in social psychology and, indeed, the current state of social psychology itself have to be understood in relation to a dynamic, historical and analytic framework. We have tried to avoid at all costs another "crisis/crossroads book" and to provide a positive and constructive perspective on our subject by taking a cool and coherent look at the whole enterprise of social psychology.

As can be seen from the contents page, the structure that we chose for the book is not a simple "past–present–future" *report*, even though we wish to emphasize such a temporal context. Our intentions dictated that we start with the analysis of the present, followed by an analysis of the past explaining how we reached the present. This provides a basis for speculating about the future, once the present is seen to have emerged *from* something, just as the future will. It also provides, we hope, the basis for a fuller use or exploitation of the past in contributing towards a better future than straightforward extrapolation from our current concerns would produce.

Given such a structure, there were certain themes that we wished to emphasize within the historical, analytic context. We wished to have method, theory and application discussed in all three sections, to balance optimism and pessimism about the subject, and to demonstrate the hand of the *Zeitgeist*, as it were, by showing that the *Zeitgeist* is us as social psychologists, not some disembodied ghost in the research machine.

Having clarified our objectives, we selected prominent contributors who have thought deeply about the issues on both a specific and a more general level. We wanted heterogeneity, not uniformity, since we felt that one earlier oversimplification of arguments about social psychology is the representation of it as a subject with a single mind. Social psychology is *heterogeneous*, and we chose contributors to reflect this heterodoxy. We were therefore pleased rather than surprised or dismayed when the contributors produced such a lively, stimulating and varied set of approaches to the topics. We regard it as a sign of health in a discipline when such diversity emerges and is encouraged rather than disparaged, and we feel very strongly that it is something to be fostered in the future. We are not on the side of those who propose only one particular style of research, methodology or theory in the subject.

Accordingly, we have provided a brief introduction for each section in which we content ourselves with describing the aims and rationale of that section without attempting to summarize the content. There is the danger that summaries present too passive a picture, and package information too neatly, whereas our aim is to stimulate and to give fresh impetus to the endeavours of social psychologists. There is also the danger that summarizing puts a distracting and distorting editorial gloss on the original contributions; our contributors speak for themselves, and that much more capably than we could convey.

At this point it is customary for editors to thank various people who have helped on the book (and to mention an anecdote showing that they have actually met Leon Festinger!). We would like to thank our contributors for their efficiency and attentiveness, the secretarial staff at Lancaster for their essential help, and the staff of Academic Press for their support and guidance. Unfortunately, we have never met Festinger, but we have this optimistic fantasy that after reading this book he may want to meet us!

Lancaster ROBIN GILMOUR
May 1980 STEVE DUCK

Contents

Contributors	*page* v
Preface	vii

Part 1 PRESENT CONCERNS

INTRODUCTION
Making sense of the status quo — 3
Steve Duck and Robin Gilmour

1. CAUSES FOR OPTIMISM
A social psychology of human concerns — 5
Philip Brickman

2. CAUSES FOR PESSIMISM
Making social psychology scientific — 27
Rom Harré

3. THEORETICAL STATUS
The development of theory in social psychology — 53
William J. McGuire

4. APPLICATIONS
The development of applied social psychology — 81
Michael Argyle

Part 2 PAST HISTORY

INTRODUCTION
Social psychology: a history or merely a past? — 109
Robin Gilmour and Steve Duck

5. SUNK WITH HARDLY A TRACE
On reading Darwin and discovering social psychology — 111
Robert M. Farr

6. FASHIONS IN SOCIAL PSYCHOLOGY
John M. Innes — 137

7. PROMISES UNFULFILLED
The premature abandonment of promising research — 163
Carl W. Backman

8. PROCESS LOSS IN SOCIAL PSYCHOLOGY
Failure to exploit?   181
Wolfgang Stroebe

Part 3   FUTURE EXTENSIONS

INTRODUCTION
Promises fulfilled: futures for social psychology   209
Robin Gilmour

9. TAKING THE PAST TO HEART
One of the futures of social psychology   211
Steve Duck

10. DEVELOPMENTS IN THEORY
Toward intellectual audacity in social psychology   239
Kenneth J. Gergen

11. DEVELOPMENTS IN APPLICATION
Prolegomena to a more applied social psychology
J. Richard Eiser

12. SOCIAL PSYCHOLOGY 2001
The social psychological bases and implications of structural unemployment   293
Peter Kelvin

ENDPIECE
Valedictory for a young social psychology   317
Robin Gilmour

References   319
Author Index   347
Subject Index   353

Part 1
Present Concerns

Making Sense of the Status Quo
STEVE DUCK and ROBIN GILMOUR

The future development of social psychology will, of course, be a complex mix of present potential, past experience and hopeful aspiration. The first of these—the *inherent* potential of social psychology—is the most familiar and for us, in a sense, the most significant defining feature of the ultimate mixture. Part 1 of the book therefore reviews the present state of social psychology: where we are now, how we got there from the very recent past, and what we seem presently to know or have learned; it contains doses of optimism and pessimism about the present state of social psychology, along with consideration of theory in, and applications of, social psychology. The chapters taken together, then, offer a review of some of the major current foci in the subject.

However, it will be clear that the various authors perceive the present state of social psychology differently and interpret the forces within it in a different fashion. It should also be noted that they focus, as they were asked to do, on the intellectual threads of the subject rather than its social threads. This book subsequently shows that whilst the present state of a subject can be characterized almost purely in intellectual terms, the arrival at that state needs to be understood also in terms of non-intellectual forces. That will be a prime concern of later chapters, where authors explore some of the social and psychological factors—typically overlooked—that have contributed in significant measure to the shaping and development of our subject.

In this part the reader should be ever alert to the question of how we reached the present state, as that is seen by the various authors. What forces could create such a state and what intellectual strands from the past have contributed to it?

In historical *reviews* of the development of social psychology it is customary to emphasize the importance of the contributions of the founding fathers or Great Men. Whilst the Great Man theory of leadership has already decomposed on archival shelves, the Great Man theory of the development of social psychology has not. It is of considerable psychological interest in itself to speculate why subjects choose to elect a founding father: an Origin Myth of a kind that Freud might well have seized upon with interest.

Given that the development of the subject is not to be seen in terms only of the influence of founding fathers, how can the development of a subject be evaluated? One way might be in terms of achievement of goals—but goals are naturally illusory and shift with the perspective of the perceiver. Often it is easier to recognize the magnetic force of a goal after it has been achieved: the vantage point of the viewer is often translated into the goal point.

An important point here is that development is dynamic and continuous, and there is a danger that to make evaluative sense of a sequence we create a kind of arbitrary endpoint and thus underplay the continuity of the dynamics. The present can be seen simply as the place where we have stopped for the moment. The problem is to provide a sensible view of sequence in a developmental model without creating a finalized, static endpoint that minimizes the continuing interplay of creative tensions. Evaluation within a developmental view of the present runs the risk of imputing too much finality to the present, rather than seeing it as a merely temporary node of forces which could more promisingly be viewed as converging on a given point whilst retaining the potential to diverge subsequently in various directions.

This argument seems to lead us to the view that with the adoption of a developmental perspective it might be better to eschew evaluation except in the sense of a temporary summary of the state of the Art as a preparation for improving it. One useful general way, then, of describing the aims of the following part would be to say that it attempts to provide this kind of overview in two different ways. One is in terms of the content of the subject, covering both theory and application; the other is in terms of outlook, of bases for optimism or pessimism. In this way we hope to make useful sense of the present, and to make sense of it in relation to the immediate past as we appear to have learned from that past.

1
A Social Psychology of Human Concerns

PHILIP BRICKMAN
Research Center for Group Dynamics, Institute for Social Research, and Department of Psychology, The University of Michigan

A. What is social psychology? 7
B. What are the enduring sets of human concerns? 14
C. Implications for the development of social psychology 23

Has there been a crisis in social psychology? This can only be decided in retrospect by those people who can see what came after as well as what came before the period in question. The answer will necessitate deciding whether there was a break in the continuity of research or a breakdown in the assumptions governing research. I think it would be at the moment hard to prove that either has occurred. None the less, there has undeniably been a crisis of spirit for at least some researchers. As is usual in crises, there are a small number of active participants and a much larger number of passive ones who lend quiet but vital and often unwitting support to the attack. They include everyone who feels that most research in the field other than their own—and ultimately including their own—is not worth publishing.

Critiques of the fundamental scientific faith of social psychology have all questioned whether laboratory experiments can serve as a trustworthy basis for building a science of human behaviour. Gergen (1973) says no, because history will change the meaning of these experiments. By the time we establish a coherent set of principles for explaining, say, why people like or dislike one another, the things that cause them to like or dislike one another will be different from what they are today. In fact, they could be changed by people's knowledge of the very experiments that discovered them in the first place. Moscovici (1972) doubts whether the principles discovered by American social psychology—especially those that depend on the assumptions that people are basically "nice" or that they "exchange" mutually profitable behaviour like good capitalists—will hold for Europe or other parts of the world. Rosenthal (1966) has discovered that what an experimenter expects a subject to do can unwittingly determine what the subject actually does in the experiment. This means that the results of at least some previous experiments may be due to quite different factors from those the researchers thought they were studying. Finally, Kelman (1968) and others have raised questions about whether experimental research in social psychology is generally ethical. Even if the experiments are harmless, subjects cannot usually be told what their true purpose is until afterwards, since knowing the purpose of the research can make people behave in very unusual and unrepresentative ways. But these are the moral and scientific consequences of research based on situations in which participants cannot be sure whether they are being told the truth or not.

To varying degrees, behind all these critiques is some sense of disappointment that social psychology has not lived up to its early promise. Perhaps it seems strange that so much was expected from a field whose origin cannot be dated much more than forty years ago, with the pioneering experiments on groups by Kurt Lewin (1936). But we forget the sense of excitement surrounding the discovery that experiments could be done with people and groups, just like experiments in biology and chemistry. In its own way, perhaps unrealistically, the demand for social relevance in social psychology was even greater in the early days after World War II than in the socially conscious 1970s. So was the hope that scientifically guided experiences in groups would be a new basis for personal growth. The change in attitude towards social psychology probably parallels the larger change in attitudes towards science in general. We are not sure that science is as powerful as we once thought, nor that we would want it to be that powerful. Those most vulnerable to the idea of crisis in social psychology are probably those who had the highest expectations for a universal science that would transform society, like biology or chemistry.

In part, I think this discontent has been merely a matter of taste for life on an isolated frontier versus life at the centre of the empire. New developments in physics, biology, or chemistry make much more difference to society than new developments in social psychology, just as developments in Europe in the seventeenth century made much more difference than developments in America. Physics, biology, and chemistry are the centre of today's scientific empire, just as Europe was the centre of the seventeenth-century world empire. People who need to be influential need to be at the centre of empire, not in the provinces (where they are invariably unhappy) even though there are some pleasant features to life in an unsettled territory, for instance, more freedom to choose what one does. Perhaps social psychology is just the wrong place to be for someone whose tastes are refined or who sees science as power.

Yet in a curious way, a much more modest way, I see social psychology as very much at the centre of what is happening in our society. This is not how social psychology is thought about either by those who see the field as in crisis or by those comfortable with a traditional model of science. But I think in part the sense of crisis has rested upon a misapprehension of what social psychology has been or can be about. In what follows, I would like to make a preliminary sketch of what this is.

A. WHAT IS SOCIAL PSYCHOLOGY?

Social psychology is, first of all, *a vantage point* on all of human behaviour. If you wish to study birth and death, war and peace, marriage and divorce, poverty and affluence, you can do it all within social psychology. I do not mean that social psychology subsumes economics or anthropology or political science; I merely mean that from social psychology you can see into each of these other disciplines and borrow to the limits of your taste and capacity what seems relevant to the problem at hand. I do not know of any other point where the view of the human sciences is as good. Social psychology is a point of confluence for the human sciences—and could be such a point to a much greater extent than it is. At least some scholars in all these neighbouring disciplines are just waiting to hand certain problems over to social psychologists. Economists would like more research on the psychology of utility, historians on psychological factors in collective behaviour, and literary scholars on psychological and social factors in interpretation. The crisis of spirit in social psychology comes in part from too parochial an identification of the field. If the field is defined as a narrow stretch of laboratory experiments, it is possible to ask whether progress is being made or whether a new paradigm is needed. If these experiments are properly seen as simply one stream into the larger flow of the social sciences, the sense of crisis is quickly seen as a product of a self-centred concern with the stream rather than with the larger flow. The debate over the negative income tax experiment or the general theory of sociobiology are part of what social psychology looks at. Social psychology is special, in part, because its scope is so broad. It is one of the few fields that can be interested in the unique behaviour of an individual, the historically specific behaviour of a particular group of people, or the universal behaviour of all humankind. In this sense, for better or worse according to taste, it is at once art and history and science. As a social psychologist, I am obviously suspect as a judge of whether social psychology is interesting or not, but what baffles me is the question of what else there is to be interested in. If you are tired of social psychology, you are tired of—well, not life, perhaps, but thinking about life.

Secondly, and perhaps most important, social psychology is a *culturally mandated translation* of our understanding of human behaviour from an older language into a newer one. The older language was a language of religion and custom and law and etiquette. In the not too distant past, if we wanted to predict what someone would do or explain why they would do it, we would speak in religious terms or in terms of tradition. This would tell us quite well what kind of occupation a person would follow or what kind of person they would marry. For a variety of historical reasons, people in modern society have more choice in these matters than they once did. The old categories no longer seem to predict or explain very well. Social psychology, and the social sciences in general, emerged to explain how people will make the choices now available to them. (It is a paradox that the social sciences, which arise to explain how people use the new freedoms available to them, are often seen as threatening the very freedoms that have called them into being.) The substance of the new explanations may not in many cases be very different from the substance of the old explanations. After all, religion, like social psychology, talked about rules that people followed and rewards that they expected. But the old language has been discredited in many details and is in any case barely comprehensible to modern ears. We demand an explanation of human behaviour in a language we find compelling, and this is now the language of science.

Interestingly enough, the novel is also a modern invention (earlier stories were not simply created by single individuals or inhabited by psychologically realistic characters), and may since the seventeenth century have played some of the same role as social science in giving people a new explanation of their world (Berger, 1977). But now even the continually recreated language of fiction does not satisfy this need. Varela's (1971) social psychological advice to an executive on how not to upset his subordinates may be no more insightful than Machiavelli's (1950) counsel to his prince five centuries earlier, but it is Varela's language and Varela's kind of evidence that we want. It may even be—as is brilliantly illustrated by the story of Rashomon (Akutagawa, 1952), by the parable of the blind men and the elephant and by Hastorf and Cantril's study (1954) of perceptions of a football game by partisans of each side—that there are elements in the way different people perceive the world that are unbridgeable and perhaps unknowable. We still demand explanation—the best we can find, however inadequate—and the best explanations we can find in our culture are explanations in the language of science. Like it or not, the old truths, the old wisdom—and the old falsehoods—are now in the process of being translated into the variables and hypotheses of social psychology. They will then be played back into the culture through books and newspapers, movies and television. This much is now the historically inevitable mission of the field.

I am not saying that social psychology is nothing but the pouring of old wine into new bottles. I am saying that this is a large part of its current activity and a part that is neither trivial nor dishonourable. Furthermore, the ultimate scientific value of this translation is as yet unknowable. When arabic numbers replaced roman numerals, this was at first merely a change from one system of notation to another. However, arabic numbers made it easier to calculate and to represent various quantities and paved the way for a powerful new mathematics and science. It is quite possible that the translation of past cultural wisdom into scientific categories will eventually do the same.

Translating that mixture of fact and fiction, wisdom and superstition, known as common sense into scientific language has the effect, at least temporarily, of making us as social psychologists less confident than our parents, friends, and children of our ability to explain why a certain neighbour down the street behaved in a certain way. We are more conscious of our ignorance. As Socrates long ago made clear, however, being aware of what one does not know is the first step towards knowledge. In the American expression, it is not what we don't know that hurts us, but what we think we know that ain't so. None the less, the understanding of how little we know, and how much the wisdom and confusion of common sense are inextricably mixed together, is a humbling position.

A scientific language of human behaviour will seem less awkward to future generations than it does to us, partly because its categories will be improved and streamlined, and partly because it will be more familiar and hence more comfortable for future generations. The metric system is awkward at first, especially when continually measured against Anglo-Saxon categories. It is hard at the moment to think of third-person singular pronouns that are neither sexist nor strange. Not only will we get better at these things over time, but as Zajonc's (1968) work on the mere exposure effect shows, we will come to like them. The idea of a culturally mandated translation, however, should also serve as a warning for social psychology. The field may invent new terms, but they should not be so obscure or so cut off from common experience as to be unable to pass, eventually, into the language of common experience.

Social psychology is also a *science*. As the foregoing implies, it has no choice in this status. It has been assigned the task of scientific inquiry and codification by our period in history. Contrary to what is sometimes asserted, science is a question of aim, not method. Science is an effort to make accurate observations and valid causal inferences, and to assemble these observations and inferences in a compact and coherent way. Social psychology aims to do this for the study of human behaviour. The fact that its concepts are still fresh from common sense, its methods crude, and its effects specific to particular times and places has no bearing on the question of whether or not it is a science.

People who have been pessimistic about a science of social psychology, like Gergen (1973), have rested much of their case on the fact that the conditions that give rise to an observation can be changed by the very understanding that grows out of this observation. Gergen has called this an enlightenment effect. For other observers, however, this has been not the problem but the goal of human inquiry. Freud based his slender hopes for the future of civilization on the changes that might occur when people were enlightened by an understanding of psychoanalytic theory. Marx wrote that the point was not to study society, but to change it. Neither man thought these aims incompatible with science. On the contrary, neither thought that the improvement of psychic or social functioning could be achieved on any basis other than a correct scientific understanding of how minds and societies function in the first place.

Marx and Freud, curiously enough, may have made the same error as Gergen: believing that understanding or enlightenment alone would be sufficient to produce change. Leninists and behaviour modifiers arrived with their arsenal of change strategies when these overoptimistic hopes proved false. Increasing people's understanding of a situation will not necessarily affect how they wish or are able to react to it. We still get wet even if we know why it rains; we still get hurt even if we know why people are rejected; we still wonder whether a situation is an emergency or whether anyone else is helping even if we have heard of the murder of Kitty Genovese or read the work of Darley and Latané (1968) on bystander intervention. Once people understand that the presence of other bystanders may cause them to underestimate the likelihood that the situation is an emergency or to overestimate the likelihood that someone else will help, they may be more likely to help (Beamon et al., 1978). Such a change does not invalidate the original discovery of how the presence of bystanders affects helping, but represents an intervention designed to alter the balance of forces known to operate in that situation. It applies, not repeals, the original principles. Since the change in this case is only in how people calculate, rather than in the costs and benefits inherent in the situation (which could be changed by a law that makes people liable for not helping), we should not be surprised that the change is marginal and that newspapers continue to carry accounts of failures to intervene, even in the neighbourhood where the murder of Kitty Genovese took place. Research on an effect can also be of value even when it is quite unable to change the conditions that produced that effect. Research on rejection or bereavement may not keep people from feeling hurt or abandoned, but it can give them an understanding that helps them to deal with their pain and evolve new ways of coping with their environment.

The relationship of social psychology to common sense functions in two ways to make social psychology appear less of a science than it is. First, since common sense contains contradictory wisdom, almost any finding in social psychology is likely to appear familiar from at least some perspective. The idea that mere exposure is a sufficient condition for attraction may seem like common sense, but common sense also contains the idea that familiarity breeds contempt and that absence makes the heart grow fonder. Secondly, since social psychology returns its findings to the general culture, they are apt to become more familiar or more commonsensical over time, like the idea that elections can be predicted from tiny samples of the population. A finding in social psychology cannot remain non-obvious as people hear it again and again any more than a joke can remain funny to people who hear it again and again. More generally, we may propose that discoveries emerge from a region in which we are oblivious to them, pass through a region in which we disbelieve them, into a zone in which we find them interesting, and then a zone in which we find them obvious, and eventually, perhaps, into a further region in which we are again oblivious to them.

Finally, I see social psychology as *a search for wisdom, not knowledge*. This may be the most controversial point. Knowledge is an essential component of wisdom, but it is not by itself enough. Wisdom requires a fusion of moral and intellectual concerns, and also a fusion of direct and indirect experience. We cannot tell people whether something like marriage is good or bad, but we can tell people what leads individuals to get married and what, under different circumstances, are the typical consequences of getting married, so that they are better able to examine their own unique experience and decide whether marriage is good or bad for them, and plan their lives accordingly. We cannot debate values, but we can provide facts that allow people to debate values in a more intelligent manner. And our search for facts should be governed by a specific concern for their moral relevance. Social psychology should be a field that deals with fundamental human concerns. Campbell (1969) has described social psychology as a methodological servant for society, a discipline that will enable administrators and the general public to know whether particular social reforms are really working. I would add to that the idea of social psychology as a conceptual servant for society. This means helping people to think about important things like happiness or power in a way that illuminates what is involved in their pursuit. It means rescuing people from emotional pigeon-holes society has placed them in without putting them into new "scientific" pigeon-holes. It means reminding them, from time to time, of concerns and perspectives they may overlook in the press of living. In turn, it means remaining open, as a field, to being reminded by people of what the enduring concerns of human experience are.

There is a danger that social psychology as a culturally mandated translation of age-old concerns into scientific language will work against social psychology as a search for wisdom, not knowledge. The danger is that the knowledge accumulated by the field will reside entirely in a specialized language known only to a few scientists, making the realities of human experience seem less rather than more accessible to ordinary people struggling to make practical and moral choices in their own lives. If human experience is defined in technical terms, in a language that only a scientific priesthood can understand, it will be the power of this priesthood and the class interests it serves, rather than the wisdom of the species, that benefits. Elite classes have, of course, always governed in part through their control of language or of the symbols of experience. What is new is the coming place of social psychology in this scheme of things. If the field fails to speak a language ordinary people can understand it will make it harder rather than easier for them to make the kind of enlightened choices that will improve their chances for happiness or the species' chances for survival.

It could be argued that by staying close to the ordinary language of human concerns social psychology risks having its findings prematurely popularized and applied. On the contrary, however, it is the mystifying language of science, not the common-sense language of human concerns, that is apt to be uncritically accepted and applied. We are more likely to immunize the lay public against a credulous acceptance of research findings by making it clear that we are addressing issues about which they have some historically accumulated wisdom, not issues about which they are completely ignorant. The ability to understand findings and see their relevance is the ability to reject them as well as to accept them, to be judicious rather than uniformly suspicious or gullible.

Like most of our previous points, the search for wisdom defines social psychology as a field that will be characterized by slow growth and by a continual return to certain fundamental issues rather than by the dramatic paradigm of Kuhn's (1962) theory of science. Social psychology will be less a process of once-and-for-all discovery than it will be a process of continual re-discovery and re-evaluation of received knowledge, including the field's own past research. Past research is a necessary, but not a sufficient, condition for understanding future experience. As new forms of human society and human experience emerge, old problems of coping and old moral dilemmas will take on new shapes and require new research. The primary gain from the accumulation of research is not a set of final solutions but a greater capacity for each generation to ask its own questions and to solve its own emergent problems.

What are the fundamental concerns of human experience, and what would they look like as an orienting framework or agenda for the field? What would their relationship be to current topics in social psychology like attribution, aggression, conformity, interpersonal attraction, sex roles, and altruism? To practical problems like child abuse, alcoholism, or the effects of television? To the central questions of other disciplines like sociology, anthropology, or biology? It is probably not possible, at this point, to provide a list of fundamental concerns that people would find at once concise, complete, and appropriately labelled. Yet it seems to me imperative that we try, if only to give the field an alternative vision that would make it less vulnerable to fads and mood swings, to bouncing from the euphoric sense of remaking society to the depressed feeling of crisis and scientific dead-end. We can take at least the initial steps towards formulating such a list of concerns by considering three things: lists that other social researchers have formulated, issues that have been historically important in Western civilization (note the limitation), and criteria that any such list would have to meet in order to be considered satisfactory.

B. WHAT ARE THE ENDURING SETS OF HUMAN CONCERNS?

A human concern in our sense is not a value, but rather a domain in which people are compelled to hold values. Concerns in this sense are first located in environments, not people. They are problems or issues which people living in these environments must confront, and it is their behaviour in confronting them that determines values. The fundamental set of human concerns are the domains in which all individuals and all cultures are compelled to hold values. It should be noted that the values people hold in these domains are not necessarily idealistic. They may be quite cynical about the possibility that anything of value can be realized in a given domain, or even deny that they care whether anything of value is realized in that domain. They may not even have thought very much about the matter one way or another, simply taking for granted whatever solution their culture offers in that domain. All we require is that there is an issue people must deal with, however they do so and whatever the outcome. The form of this experience may differ, but the fact of this experience is universal. I would argue, for example, that freedom is a universal human concern, perhaps even one that is genetically based in the selfish desire of genes to propagate themselves whatever the demands of the social order (cf. Campbell, 1975). This does not mean that all people feel free, that all people hold freedom rather than duty or discipline as a value, or even that all people have thought very much, or very clearly, about their own freedom. It does mean, however, that all people have somehow come to terms with the competing demands of the social order of which they are a part and their own contrary impulses. And it means that such a concern should be—and in this case is— an enduring focus of social psychological inquiry.

Previous lists of fundamental human concerns in psychology have been of two general types, each with its own distinctive purpose. The first are the lists of needs or motives compiled by personality psychologists like Murray (1938) or Maslow (1954). The purpose of these lists was to provide a systematic basis for studying individual differences, and in particular for distinguishing between healthy and unhealthy personalities. The second are the lists of values or life concerns assembled by social psychologists like Rokeach (1973) or Andrews and Withey (1976). The main purpose of these lists has been to understand the concerns that determine people's feelings about major political, social, and economic issues, like racial equality or the state of national well-being. Both of these aims are tremendously important, and our list too should provide a useful basis for thinking about individual differences and major social issues. But our list must first serve a different purpose that calls for a slightly different language, scope, and focus from previous lists. Our list must articulate, in some coherent and comprehensive fashion, the fundamental concerns of human experience with the major theoretical concerns of social psychology.

The major problem with all such lists, as Allport (1961) stressed, is that the decision as to how many separate items are listed and what they are called is somewhat arbitrary. It should be noted that this is as much a problem when extracting items from a factor analysis as it is when deriving them on some *a priori* basis. Allport himself emphasized that each individual's list of concerns would be slightly different from every other individual's and argued that psychology should emphasize, rather than try to overlook, these differences. But in fact people's lists have a great number of common elements, however different their language and patterning. So, it turns out, do the lists of fundamental concerns compiled by the investigators mentioned in the previous paragraph. It would be perhaps more surprising to find no consensus on fundamental human concerns than to find the degree of consensus that exists. We will present in detail the correspondence between our list of fundamental concerns and only one other list, Erikson's (1963) list of essential choices that confront individuals at different stages of life. Erikson's approach is closer to ours than are many others because, like us, he thinks about issues or problems that face individuals rather than particular needs or values that in fact represent solutions to these problems. Articulating a social psychological agenda with Erikson's developmental agenda has the additional benefit of laying out the correspondence between issues in social and developmental psychology (see also Veroff, 1978). The ability to translate between our list of concerns and Erikson's stages of growth of ego identity or Rokeach's set of terminal values does not, of course, demonstrate that any of these lists are valid. But it is an encouraging indication that certain matters have been recognized as basic for some time in a number of different areas of psychology.

My own sense of what a list of fundamental concerns should contain comes from some thinking about what have been the overriding issues in Western culture over the last 2000 years. The Old Testament, in this light, is about justice, and the New Testament is about love. It seems clear to me that these should be two of the central concerns of social psychology, as they have been for so many people for so long, and it has always surprised me that they have been relatively late and still modest entries among the list of social psychological topics (see Lerner, 1975; Rubin, 1973). The Greeks in a sense originated Western civilization with their ideal of reason and the philosopher's quest for knowledge. Knowledge is clearly a fundamental human concern, perhaps the one social psychology promises to address most adequately with the growth of cognitive social psychology and the theory of science (Campbell, 1970; Nisbett and Ross, 1980). The greatest struggles in human history, both between nations and among classes of the same nation, have been over land or, more recently, over the control of other means of production (Paige, 1975). This is the concern for power. It, too, has played an important part in social psychology in such various guises as the study of authoritarianism (Adorno *et al.*, 1950) or learned helplessness (Seligman, 1975).

The other concerns, it seems to me, are more modern, at least in the sense that their clear articulation in the culture does not come until the time of the Reformation and the Enlightenment. They are, perhaps, more individualistic, though modern conceptions of love and justice are also highly individualistic. The American Revolution claimed the inalienable rights of life, liberty, and the pursuit of happiness, and, in one form or another, these have been the concern of revolutions since. Freedom and happiness, however hard they are to define, belong on any list of fundamental concerns that would claim to represent these centuries. The next I would draw from Freud's legendary reply, on his deathbed, to a disciple's question as to what was the secret of life. Freud's reply was love and work, and work, in the broader sense of work and play, clearly belongs on a list of essential concerns. Work and play have of course always been elements of human existence, though imbued with a special status in the West ever since the Reformation introduced the idea of vocation or calling as a clue to one's relationship with God. Finally, our literature and art and philosophy have characterized identity as the driving uncertainty of a society in which the individual person lives in a measure apart from his or her cultural group. This list of concerns is summarized in Table I. I would not claim it to be either unique or complete, but I would say that it represents considerably more than the opinion of one social psychologist. It represents a set of issues that have been of great moment in Western civilization for a long time.

A question that immediately arises involves the labelling of these issues. We have simply borrowed historic labels. But they differ strikingly from the usual categories of psychological study in that they are positive rather than negative. What difference does it make if we study health and happiness rather than death and despair, power rather than fear or helplessness, love rather than hate, freedom rather than conformity? Substantively, it should make no difference, for in studying any of these we must also study its lack or opposite. In practice, of course, the way we label things often does make a subtle difference to how we think about and present them. The present labels are likely to call attention to the study of healthy or well-functioning individuals

Table I. A social psychology of human concerns.

Concern	Eriksonian polarity	Standard topic in social psychology	Relevant applied area
Knowledge	Basic trust versus mistrust	Attribution	Panic / Persuasion / Television
Power	Autonomy versus shame and doubt	Aggression	Child abuse / Prejudice / Rape
Freedom	Initiative versus guilt	Conformity	Crowding / Communes / Loyalty
Work and play	Industry versus inferiority	Achievement	Creativity / Fantasy / Survival
Identity	Identity versus role confusion	Sex roles	Adoption / Ethnicity / Shyness
Love	Intimacy versus isolation	Interpersonal attraction	Divorce / Homosexuality / Jealousy
Justice	Generativity versus stagnation	Altruism	Parenting / Research ethics / Euthanasia
Happiness	Ego integrity versus despair	Mental health	Alcoholism / Moods / Suicide

rather than unhealthy or unfortunate ones. This is probably an advantage: at present we know more about what it means to be depressed than what it means to be happy, more about what it means to be sick than what it means to be well. The more important advantage is that the labels capture historic concerns in a language familiar to much of the culture. This has, not incidentally, the secondary gain of making it much easier to design a curriculum whose relevance to students is self-evident.

A more serious question concerns the relationships between these concerns and the relationship of each to basic psychological processes like communication and reinforcement. The answer to this is frankly beyond the scope of this paper. It is rather what this paper proposes as the basic agenda for social psychology in the coming years. At this point, in contrast to the essentially uni-motivational theories of Freud (libido), Marx (economics), La Rochefoucauld (vanity), or Adler (power), we do not see any of these concerns as generally and universally primary over the others. There is rather a sense in which all these concerns can be taken in turn as primary over all the others. One could argue, for example, that the ultimate goal of all activity is happiness, and that the pursuit of other concerns is only incidental to the individual's more general pursuit of happiness. One could say that no action is possible without knowledge, or that power is a factor in all other concerns, or that a sense of one's own identity is the guiding determinant in behaviour. I would like to argue, at this point, that there is survival value attached to a satisfactory position on all of these concerns independent of the influence each of them may have on the others. A capacity for love, for example, has demonstrable value in the production and protection of viable offspring (cf. Harlow, 1958). A concern for justice, according to Trivers (1971), would benefit those who possessed it by motivating them to ferret out and punish others who failed in their social obligations and thus to ensure that their own sacrifices were reciprocated. The survival value of happiness follows, curiously enough, from the fact that evolution is conservative. Most evolved behaviours are adaptive, or at least more likely to be adaptive than novel and unselected alternatives. A tendency to feel reasonably content no matter how drastic one's circumstances (cf. Brickman et al., 1978) would thus be selected for since it would serve the predominantly conservative strategy of evolution. Sociobiologist E. O. Wilson (1975) has argued that a major weakness of psychology is that it has failed to pay attention to the functional or survival value of the drives and states it has studied and has thus remained isolated from the other life sciences, for which this is the central question. We have illustrated the argument from survival value for three of the less obvious concerns of Table I. Here too a great deal of work needs to be done, but it seems clear that our lists of concerns can serve as a starting point for building bridges between the theoretical interests of social psychology and the evolutionary concerns of biology, anthropology, and economics.

If there is no general or universal hierarchy among these concerns, it is also true that they are not always equally important. Some are more salient than others in certain cultures (see Hsu, 1971; Kluckhohn,

1965), certain individuals (Kelley, 1955; Atkinson, 1964), and certain periods of life (Erikson, 1950; Veroff, 1978). The extent to which this is true, the conditions that make it true, and the consequences of such differences in salience are also part of our general agenda for social psychological research. Our framework only requires that, whatever the variations in salience, all concerns may be found in all environments, even if only in Erikson's (1963) sense of the anticipation of a future problem or the reactivation of a past one. In some environments, some of these concerns may seem like luxuries, in the sense that people can care about them only when they are sufficiently well off to know where their next meal is coming from and to have some degree of choice in their lives. But they are involved, indirectly, even in people's pursuit of the necessities of survival, as indicated in our previous comments on freedom, love, justice, and happiness. And they emerge as things people consciously care about as soon as their environment gives them the space to do so.

To be significant and practical, any list of human concerns must satisfy three criteria already noted in passing. First of all, *it must relate to current topics in social psychology*. If we are to supply a new set of co-ordinates for the field, we must specify how they relate to the old co-ordinates. Otherwise our map will be unreadable, or at least needlessly difficult for people trying to see where a current topic fits. In fact, a surprising amount—though not all—of current research in social psychology bears upon one or more of these fundamental human concerns. Interesting as it is to see this correspondence, it is equally important to note areas of concern which are not well represented by any current body of literature. Column 3 of Table I lists a series of standard topics in social psychology as they might appear in an introductory text. By comparing the human concerns in Column 1 with the corresponding standard topics in Column 3, we can get a sense of where the field covers and where it falls short of covering these concerns. For example, attribution research is coming increasingly close to studying what we mean by knowledge and the process by which people feel knowledge is acquired. On the other hand, the study of achievement so far comprises only a small part of what people care about around the issue of work and play. When we list a topic in social psychology next to a human concern, we do not mean that this is the only concern the topic is relevant to, nor that only this topic is relevant to that concern. The correspondence is not even intended to be perfect. None the less, it does seem surprisingly good, and it did seem useful to match as many standard topics as possible with that human concern for which they seemed to have primary relevance.

Secondly, our list of human concerns *should relate to major issues in developmental psychology*. This may seem like a less obvious point. I make it in the conviction that the basic concerns of human life are developmental. They involve growing up and growing old. Different themes are most salient to people at differing points in their lives. The mushrooming study of adult development has established this clearly in a way that was somehow not quite possible when developmental psychology was limited to the study of child development. Social psychology and developmental psychology have mostly been familiar strangers and at best linked mechanically rather than organically. A theoretical framework that could establish the interface between social and developmental psychology would have a powerful advantage by that very fact. I think our agenda of human concerns could establish that interface, in part because of the very natural way it relates to the sequence of major issues in the development of identity outlined by Erikson (1963). Erikson's scheme of identity stages is still probably the best known and most comprehensive in developmental psychology, though it would have a close rival in Piaget's stages of cognitive development. At eight different points in the life cycle, according to Erikson, people must make a fundamental decision about themselves. At each point there is either a solution or a failure to reach a solution. Furthermore, people's arriving at a satisfactory identity at a previous stage affects their ability to deal with the issues that will be raised for them at the next stage. Erikson's stages, from infancy to old age, are listed in order in Column 2 of Table I. The human concerns in Column 1 have been arranged to fall adjacent to the Eriksonian stage to which they seem most relevant. The weakest fit would appear to be the first stage, where knowledge is placed next to the question of basic trust versus mistrust. I think this works better if we understand trust at this point to refer not merely (or even primarily) to interpersonal trust but the child's trust in his or her sensory apparatus, ability to perceive the world and make sense of it, and good fortune in having certain external stimuli (a mother's face or touch) reliably associated with good internal states (fullness and warmth). We are really talking about children's trust in their ability to tell what is real, an issue, as I have pointed out elsewhere (Brickman, 1978), which involves recognizing a correspondence between one's behaviour and both internal states and external consequences. Interpersonal trust as we ordinarily think of it is probably more of an issue in late adolescence around the polarity of intimacy versus isolation than it is in the first two years of life. None the less, even if this reinterpretation of basic trust versus mistrust is rejected, the general correspondence of Erikson's stages to our set of human concerns seems worth noting. I take this as further evidence that we have selected an orderly and fundamental set of concerns.

Finally, our list of concerns must deal with *practical and applied problems* as well as abstract ones. Indeed, it should highlight the relationship between the abstract and the general and the concrete and the particular, between things that ordinarily seem unrelated. A set of relevant applied areas is listed in Column 4 of Table I. This set of applied problems was not selected to represent anything in particular. It is simply a sample of problems that interested the teaching fellows in my introductory social psychology class over a period of two years and hence a sample of the problems that were covered in the class those years, in addition to the human concerns and standard topics. (Certain units were required of all students. Beyond that, students chose additional units that they were especially interested in studying.) Here the strength and weakness of our analysis become simultaneously apparent. The strength is that our set of concerns indeed encompasses virtually any problem. Furthermore, deciding what basic human concern is most implicated in that problem is not merely a trivial question of classification but a challenge that helps us to understand the basic nature of the problem. For example, to see that child abuse or rape are fundamentally issues of power is very different from seeing them as fundamentally issues of love or mental health. The weakness, or at least the flexibility, of the scheme is that any particular problem could be seen as involving a number of basic concerns. Sometimes, how that problem is to be approached will determine what concern is most relevant. For example, homosexuality could be seen as an issue of identity or it could be approached with attention to the question of love. Certain broad issues, like the family, might be studied with reference to every single one of the basic themes in Table I. As people become more familiar with this set of human concerns, they will find it easier to see these concerns reflected in different applied problems and to decide which concern or concerns are most relevant to a particular problem. None the less, the fact that most practical problems cannot be simply and unequivocally linked to one of these concerns will, from time to time, leave us uncomfortable with the elegance or completeness of the scheme. The ambiguity at the margins is the price we pay for the scope of its coverage.

C. IMPLICATIONS FOR THE DEVELOPMENT OF SOCIAL PSYCHOLOGY

This framework suggests certain specific directions for research in social psychology. The dominant line of inquiry in social psychology today—and probably more so in the immediate future—is cognitive social psychology. Broadly defined, this is the study of the prototypes, schemas, maps, grammars, scripts, frames, heuristics, and attributions that people carry about in their heads. What we need to know are the kinds of schemas or heuristics that people have for each of our fundamental human concerns; the consequences of having versus not having a well-developed schema for each of these concerns; the ways in which people's ideas about each of these concerns change with age or circumstance; and, finally, the extent to which social interaction or social organization is dependent upon people's sharing an understanding of some or all of these concerns. Addressing these questions in a systematic fashion may be a way of introducing structuralism (Lévi-Strauss, 1963) into social psychology. It should certainly lead us to devote more attention to the study of what people find real and why (Brickman, 1978), and to seek research that makes simple and direct contact with people's experience, like Piaget's (1928) demonstrations of an egocentric bias in children's judgement or Tversky and Kahneman's (1974) demonstrations of an availability bias in adults' judgement. It should help us to be more tolerant of concepts that are fuzzy and not clearly refutable but that have broad heuristic value and ready accessibility to an informed public.

It should not be felt, however, that staying close to the fundamental set of human concerns means closing off the field to new concepts or new directions in research. First of all, we may need to differentiate our understanding of the fundamental concerns themselves in a way that can only be done by the introduction of new concepts, as in French and Raven's (1959) analysis of power or Steiner's (1970) research on freedom. Secondly, new concepts may label modes of functioning that contribute to our understanding of the workings of a concern, as Snyder's (1974) idea of self-monitoring does for identity or Langer's (1978) use of mindlessness does for knowledge. Finally, and most important by far, we must remember that all art and all science advance only by allowing their practitioners the freedom to follow any intellectual stirring, however playful or useless it may seem to outsiders at first or however remote it may appear from fundamental human concerns. It is not our intention to impede any investigator from pursuing any arcane, specialized, or obscure form of inquiry whatsoever. It is our intention to point out, however, that the field also needs a series of integrative specialists who will have an equivalent passion for setting out the relationship between emerging concepts and research in social psychology and the enduring set of human concerns. Some, if not all, of the field must be concerned with the ultimate origin and destination of our concepts, with the completeness or the incompleteness of the map they provide to the range of human experience. We may not be able, at the moment, to provide a very complete map of this experience, perhaps a map no better than the thirteenth-century maps of the world. But we should try, if only to know how far we fall short, if only to gain a better sense of what is known and unknown territory. As the field matures, it will come to include a broader, more representative, more truly universal set of human concerns.

In general, I see this framework less as affecting the substance or the method of social psychological research than as providing a context in which the overall balance of the field's accomplishments and failures can be assessed. As such, it may suggest relationships between certain theoretical and applied areas that were not thought of before, or an expansion of certain traditional areas of research to include more of the human concerns of which they are a part. It may help to prevent the proliferation of studies that have lost touch with their essential concerns, as the studies of risky shift in group decision-making lost touch with the relevant concerns of knowledge and freedom or conformity (see Cartwright, 1973). And, if my own experience is any guide, it can provide a coherent, flexible, and tremendously exciting framework for teaching introductory social psychology. The purpose is not to reshape the field but to obtain a better comprehension of it. This sense of what we can be, and must inevitably be, is the best possible antidote to despair over what we see.

ACKNOWLEDGEMENT

I wish to thank the members of the Group Dynamics Seminar at the Research Center for Group Dynamics for their provocative and searching critiques of an earlier draft of this paper.

2
Making Social Psychology Scientific

ROM HARRÉ
Subfaculty of Philosophy, University of Oxford

A. The persistence of pseudo-science 27
   1. The experimental approach distorts reality 28
   2. The psychophysical approach ignores the social dimension of *all*
      psychological concepts 31
   3. Psychodynamics reifies features of accounts 32
B. The character of natural science 38
C. Linguistics as a model for psychology 40
D. Ethogenics and other psychologies 44
E. The question of empirical concepts 46
F. The return to single case studies 49

Despite the depth and the seriousness of the criticisms that have been made of traditional methods in social psychological studies (Harré and Secord, 1972; Armistead, 1974; Shotter, 1975), it is apparent that the experimental approach still dominates the study of this area in universities. Applications of social psychological understanding in the real world are also unsatisfactory in that the psychophysical approach has some measure of hegemony in hospitals and the medical services generally, while the psychodynamic seems to be the dominant theory in counselling both professional and lay.

A. THE PERSISTENCE OF PSEUDO-SCIENCE

Normal social behaviour is assumed to be that of programmed automata at worst, and of mere human habit at best. Abnormal social behaviour must therefore be due to "mechanical" failure of the organic system or to cognitive malfunction. Even the latter has been treated as an automatic process of repression and the forming up of repressed material into complexes. In none of these pictures are people represented as agents acting in accordance with reason to realize personal projects through social conventions of shared meaning. But to defend a general anthropomorphism in social science it is not enough merely to proclaim it; specific defects of the current psychologies as resources for social psychology need to be pointed out. The standard criticisms of these traditional approaches can be summed up as follows: the experimental approach grossly distorts reality, the psychophysical approach ignores the social contexts of human functioning, and the psychodynamic reifies as entities or components of the psyche certain features of the way people account for their actions to each other. It treats as individual attributes what are, strictly speaking, properties of the local collective.

1. The experimental approach distorts reality

If empirical methods in psychology are conceived in terms of the interaction of dependent and independent variables, they inevitably destroy the very thing they are attempting to study.

Public (social) and private (individual) psychologically relevant entities such as discourses, ceremonies, languages, and so on, are structures, the elements of which are internally related one to another (i.e. are largely determined as to kind and to causal powers by their location in a network of relations to other things). When the physical bearer of the psychological entity is studied in isolation from that structure it ceases to be psychologically relevant. This holds for anything from a chemical reaction in the brain to the phonetic basis of a verbal discourse or the geometry of a design. Illustrations from studies of liking (frequency of meeting) and social facilitation (spatial distance) have become clichés. The destructive effect of trying to study as an entity something internally related to other features of a social event can also be illustrated by "social learning" theory (Bandura and Walters, 1963). The experiment, as classically conceived, is just the wrong method for making an empirical study of psychological processes and products. We shall return to a sketch of more appropriate methods in a later section. They can be borrowed from such sciences as chemistry or linguistics. A useful analogy to bear in mind is the hopelessness of the early attempts to study organic chemistry by quantitative analytical methods. Progress was very rapid in that science once the structural approach had been developed. It grew from the simple Theory of Types of Williamson to the complex geometrical layouts of carbon atoms proposed by Frankland and Kekulé.

Simple quantitative studies of organic reactions had led to an impasse. Many apparently distinct substances had either identical or very similar properties of the very same elementary constituents. It was clear that in following inorganic reactions the type of constituents and their properties were at least an adequate guide, e.g. N_2O_5 was distinct from NO_3, but the vast number of distinctive compounds of carbon, hydrogen and oxygen seemed to be insufficiently distinguished and their reactions inadequately explained by this type of analysis. Why were C_2H_4 and C_4H_8 *so* different? Adopting the structural approach supplied the answer; molecules were seen as having an additional distinguishing characteristic. There were the list of elements (carbon and hydrogen), the proportion of these elements relativized to allow for different atomic masses, and the fact that the structure

$$\begin{array}{c} H \qquad\qquad H \\ \diagdown \qquad \diagup \\ C=C \\ \diagup \qquad \diagdown \\ H \qquad\qquad H \end{array}$$

was clearly and radically distinct from

$$\begin{array}{c} H \qquad H \quad H \qquad H \\ \diagdown \quad | \quad | \quad \diagup \\ C=C=C=C \\ \diagup \quad | \quad | \quad \diagdown \\ H \qquad H \quad H \qquad H \end{array}$$

Borrowing this idea leads to the thought that it is not just the catalogue of elementary externally described behaviours that matters, but the structures into which they enter and the extra dimension of meaning they acquire by virtue of the relations in which they stand. One smile may be physiologically indistinguishable from another, but if differently located in a social event (e.g. in an approach to an attack or in the acceptance of a greeting) it may have a radically different social force.

The second seriously distorting feature of much of psychology is the setting up of psychological "laboratories". This assumes that a clear separation can be made between the sociogeographical *Umwelt* within which a person functions as an active being, and his or her psychological processes and products. It seems now entirely clear that *scenes*—the product of *setting* (physical environment as loaded with meanings) and *situation* (socially defined types of human predicaments whose resolution constitutes the action)—serve as major determinants of which subsystem of skills and knowledge an individual will bring into action. The identification of scene is particularly important in predicting how an individual will present himself as a certain kind of person. Vague ideas (and uneasinesses) about the relation between laboratories and life can be made quite specific by the use of these analytical concepts, and the psychological character of the laboratory itself as a setting and a situation can be precisely defined. When this is done the "laboratory" turns out to be a very odd *Umwelt* indeed. Compared with normal settings like homes, consulting rooms, factories, etc. it is impoverished in meaning. It is essentially ambiguous and under-determined. The situations occurring in laboratories are largely defined as interactions between strangers, and again are grossly under-determined relative to the situations of everyday life, where projects and roles are largely pre-assigned.

The third trouble is more subtle and perhaps more serious. It has "surfaced" recently not only in social psychology but also in perception studies and in the investigation of remembering. It is the question of how far the action, perception, etc. which occur are necessarily dependent on the activity of the person engaged. In social psychology part of the difficulty in dealing with attributions of responsibility for their actions to others (Jones and Nisbett, 1971) depends on how agency is distributed in the system. Gibson (1968) has demonstrated the central role of active exploration in generating adequate percepts. In essence the issue is philosophical and the problems are a legacy of the uncritical acceptance of a positivist philosophy of science. Positivists have followed Hume in treating causes as the regular antecedents of effects. Realists have tended to accept a dynamicist philosophy of science which treats causality as a real relation of production. Events are the effects of the workings of causal mechanisms. In the positivist philosophy it is impossible to distinguish cause-as-"stimulus", that which prompts or triggers a reaction (all the power coming from outside the system, so to speak) from cause-as-release (that which brings about an action by the removal of an impediment to the release of a pent-up or pre-programmed, or charged condition of an agent). The naïve, experimental approach has tended to design its "experiments" on the basis of a stimulus–reaction schema rather than a release–manifestation schema. For example, in a positivist schema the continuous performance of a lecturer is to be explained by reinforcement from the audience, but on the realist schema it is explained by the preformed plan of the lecturer and his continuous determination to fulfil it, provided he is not impeded in the execution of his project.

2. The psychophysical approach ignores the social dimension of *all* psychological concepts

The psychophysical approach to general psychology not only commits all the sins of the naïve experimental approach but compounds the difficulty by introducing one of its own—namely, the tacit elimination of the social element in human functioning. If human beings are created as persons by and in social relations and if their most elaborate forms of activity are found in social ventures, whether co-operative or agonistic, then human life and its unfolding processes are not definable in terms of processes occurring within the physical boundaries of individuals. It is as if an epidemiologist tried to define an epidemic by reference only to the individual responses to infection, without introducing the vector or means of transmission ("Illness as a punishment for sin" is just such a theory). More subtly, a science of psychology has to introduce the physiological machine of human cognitive, emotional and social functioning in accordance with the principle that philosophers call the Taxonomic Priority Thesis (TPT). This requires that for the identification of types of physiological processes, structures, states and products, the psychologist works *from* the conscious identifications and classifications of active people *to* the physiological level, not vice versa. Only from a tacit adoption of this standpoint could such a discovery as Schachter's epoch-making proof of the role of cognitive and social factors in the genesis of emotions be possible. Schachter needed to make three distinct assumptions: that he knew the nature of the physiological manipulation he was performing on his subjects; that the people involved were able to identify the social settings he created for them; and that they were competent users of the emotion vocabulary. It is obvious that the second two assumptions require the priority of the cultural–cognitive system. It is less obvious, but equally important, to realize that the first assumption also requires it. Somewhere in the past history of physiological studies someone had to have experienced a distinctive mode of feeling when physiologically aroused by ephedrine—otherwise the use of ephedrine to produce the basic arousal makes no sense. Once the connection has been made, TPT can be discarded and the physiological ramifications explored independently, perhaps feeding back new distinctions into the cultural–cognitive, conceptual system. The exploration of the consequences of TPT is a very deep matter and surprisingly it turns out to support a generally materialist metaphysics of mind (Jensen, 1972). In brief, if we use cultural–cognitive categories to identify physiological processes, states, structures, etc. relevant to human action (and sometimes this requires a cybernetic network as intermediary), there will be a continuous tendency to fill gaps in our knowledge with hypotheses about hypothetical physiological structures, ensuring a generally materialist grounding for the human dispositions we call "mind".

3. Psychodynamics reifies features of accounts

Finally, I want to mention certain doubts about the way psychodynamic approaches which are being used in the caring professions are currently understood. These approaches are treated as contributions to rival forms of individual psychology. I want to argue that they are nothing of the sort, but rather are social through and through. Further, I believe that, in a sense, they are not contributions to psychology at all, but to our resources for making actions (whether our own or those of other people) acceptable. There are three main ways of interpreting psychodynamics: the Freudian, or the psychomechanism interpretation, the Evreinovian or the dramaturgical interpretation; and the Fingarettian or the accounting interpretation. The latter two are closely related and stand in contrast to the first.

(i) The Freudian interpretation is, I take it, assumed to be a psychology, i.e. an account of the causal mechanisms by which various kinds of human behaviour are generated, and in particular those forms of behaviour of which a person's friends and companions may legitimately complain. On this assumption the Freudian entities are taken to be dynamic or causal factors within the psyche, even in social behaviour. I shall argue that they are better conceived as features of a rhetoric through the use of which social complaints can be handled.

(ii) Evreinov has interpreted the Freudian apparatus as a projection in speech of a fictional world in which aspects of the self are personified as characters in dramatic scenarios which adopt and adapt their plots from commonplace episodes of social life. He called this "monodrama". A Freudian theory, then, is not a causal account of a happening, but a dramatized version of that happening. Indeed, in some contemporary psychotherapies (e.g. psychodrama, T-group therapy, etc.) this interpretation is realized literally in the actual form the therapy takes.

(iii) Closely connected in spirit with Evreinov's idea is Fingarette's notion that a Freudian, psychodynamic account is an addition to someone's resources for accounting for his actions—that is for making them intelligible and warrantable, i.e. justifiable within a certain framework. The effectiveness of the psychodynamic therapy lies just in its amplification of the resources that a person can call upon in explaining himself and his actions to others.

What went wrong? It could be said that a hundred years has been wasted. I shall try to show that at the heart of the trouble was a laudable aspiration—to make psychology scientific. But for reasons too complex to discuss here the aspiration was realized according to mistaken exemplars of the admired natural scientist. The exemplars were really philosophical theories of science, not the natural sciences themselves. Philosophers of a positivistic tradition who promoted their caricature of natural sciences at about the same time that the behaviourist movement in psychology began, have the most to answer for, since to the methodological innocents working in psychology in an atmosphere of growing technologism, the positivist seemed to legitimize the ways of proceeding that came unrecognized from the social forms of the time. At the back of the continuing failure of many psychologists to grasp the sense of the criticisms to which the "experimental" approach has been subjected, is an uncritical (because usually only tacit) assumption of a positivist philosophy of science. This is still very widespread among American psychologists of the experimental persuasion, and it is common even in Britain (for example, the personality research of Eysenck and his collaborators is still entirely within this tradition).

The positivist theory of science can be summed up in two connected doctrines:

(i) On the basis of an alleged identity of logical structure between prediction schemata and explanation schemata, it is argued that it is sufficient for a discourse to be an explanation that it should permit a logical deduction of a description of the phenomena to be explained. Thus, predictive power becomes the prime criterion of good science.

Against this, realists now hold that explanatory power is quite independent of predictive power. In explanations we render a phenomenon intelligible. There are several ways that might be done. One could elicit the nature of a puzzling phenomenon and render it intelligible by assigning to it an existing category (Walker, 1976; Gauld and Shotter, 1977). Complementarily, one might seek to show how the phenomenon in question was produced (Keat and Urry, 1976). In the realist view, explanatory power becomes the prime criterion for good science. Sometimes the methods by which phenomena are made intelligible allow predictions of similar phenomena in similar circumstances; sometimes they do not. Perhaps the most striking example of this asymmetry is Darwinian evolutionary theory. Certainly, in the neo-realist view, scientific studies need not be, and indeed should not be, aimed primarily at the discovery of prediction schemata.

(ii) The anti-theoretical (and indeed anti-intellectual) direction of the positivist doctrine of explanation is matched by a stringent theory of meaning. The significance of an action tends to be restricted to the empirically realizable correlates of symbols, via the quite mistaken criterion of "observer validity". Unless an observer can be presumed to share the interpretative schemata, social understanding, etc. of an actor, then the observer has no firm basis for categorizing an action in any particular way. On this view, theoretical thinking cannot pass beyond what is given in experience (or, as is sometimes said, what is observable) to propose a realm of unobservable but real things and processes whose properties are responsible for the patterns that can be observed, say, in human behaviour. The widespread misuse of the term "construct" by psychologists enshrines just such a theory, suggesting as it does that theoretical concepts are just instrumental, made up for some practical purpose such as predicting. A Kellyan "construct" is always an opposed *pair* of concepts, a powerful instrument of thought. To call concepts "constructs" is not only to misuse Kelly's terminology, but also to reduce the order of cognitive operations from that of theory to *mere* prediction.

Few psychologists today would consciously subscribe to the tenets of the positivistic theory of science. Few would hold that theory can be reduced to a deductive system without consideration of its content—what it could be interpreted to say about human beings and the processes productive of their action. Few would subscribe to the doctrine that their concepts must be reduced in meaning to the merely observable. But while the official philosophy of science still tacitly adhered to in psychological laboratories is expressed in terms of the aim of prediction, and while the setting up of an experimental test is said to require "operationalization" of concepts, it is almost impossible to make the step into real science. As long as people are spoken of as "subjects" and the complex processes of the genesis of action are described in terms of functional relations between "dependent and independent variables", then despite the professions of abjuration of positivism, what is actually done will be as positivistic (and as empty) as ever.

Alternative approaches are all based upon the idea of meaning. To see the force of the principle that human interactions occur through meanings and not through behaviour it is essential to grasp the idea that there is a general disconnection between meaning and vehicle of meaning, which is remedied by only *locally valid* social conventions. Similarities in behaviour, that is, in the production of vehicles of meaning, may conceal differences in interactional pattern if the conventions by which meanings are associated with the behaviours are different—and differences in behaviour may mask similarities in meaning.

This can occur at different levels. There may be a disjunction between physical movement and social and intentional meaning. For example, the widespread practice of shaking hands, a publicly identifiable type of co-ordinated physical movement, can have various social meanings, depending both on shared cultural conventions and individual and personal projects. Technically one may say in the language of logic, an extensionally defined class such as *the handshake*, may comprise many diverse intensionally defined classes. So, though instances of such a type of mutual movement may be very similar in appearance, they may be very diverse in social significance. The same person in different social circumstances may use *the handshake* in greeting, leave-taking, congratulating, betting, and so on.

Bruner (1978) has recently emphasized the point that at a still higher level of publicly displayed cognitive functioning there may be a disjunction between grammatical form, for instance the question-form, and the performative force of a speech. As well as message content an act of speech can have social force such as the power to create commitments, to insult, congratulate, plead and so on. The power of speech to perform these acts is its "illocutionary force". But insults can raise bad feelings; commitments can eventually lead to actions fulfilling them, and so on. The consequences of acts of speech that are mediated by their illocutionary force are called the "perlocutionary effects" of speech. "Shut the door" has the illocutionary force of an order and the perlocutionary effect of getting the door closed.

Bruner believes that small children first acquire an understanding of the question-form as the vehicle for the expression of the illocutionary force of an order or a request rather than as a query requiring an answer. It is apparently fairly standard practice for a mother to phrase a request to finish a meal in the grammatical form of a question: "Won't he eat up his greens then?" Children discover this disjunction and express their delight in it with a characteristic surge of jokes, answering the literal question in circumstances that require compliance with the conventionally associated request or order.

The failure to realize that all human interaction is mediated by meanings, that is, by culturally and historically specific conventional associations, is compounded by the failure to realize that meanings form into structures and are effective in ways quite different from the ways physically defined entities bring about effects. In the physical sciences an investigator can often separate the factors involved in a complex process by treating all but one as parameters, and contrive that they be maintained at a fixed level while he manipulates the remaining factor as a variable. This can be done in a variety of ways, including setting up a parallel "control" study. An essential requirement for this technique to work is that the manipulated factor is not internally related to the parameters. In general this requirement cannot be met for factors which are "internally" related components of structures, that is which are partly defined by the relations in which they stand in the structure. While this is obviously true of social roles, for instance "husband–wife", our concepts of which cannot be defined independently of each other or of the social order with which they have meaning, the "structural principle" has been overlooked for components of social processes for which it is equally true. The structural principle must begin to play a greater part in future psychologies. If a component of a structure is internally related to other components, that is, partly constituted as an item of a certain kind by its relation to the others (temporal, spatial, causal, semantic, etc.), then *it* cannot be detached from the structure and studied in isolation. This very obvious point is still widely ignored in much old-paradigm experimental social psychology in the study of learning and memory and personality investigation. Indeed, the very idea of studying something by treating it as representable by a dependent variable which varies with contrived variation in an independent variable, forces the detachment of the element from the structure in which it was constituted as an element of a type to be studied. For instance, it has emerged that one cannot study "aggressive acts" as such, since their causal powers and social function depend upon the structure and interlocked processual features of the whole interactional episode in which the event occurred. Football hooliganism involves a great many actions which have the general appearance of aggressive acts, i.e. they look just as if they are preliminaries to actual violence to be imposed on a putative victim. However, since they turn out to be ritual acts, at most metonymically related to real attack preliminaries, it is clear that "aggressive act" is not a uniform category for classifying social actions, because the social significance of an aggressive stance depends upon whether it is occurring in a preliminary to a fight or in a male dominance hierarchy ritual.

As I have pointed out in the first section, an analogue of the structural principle is to be found in organic chemistry, the modern development of which depended on the realization that the properties of organic molecules and radicals were not a function of the proportions of the elements involved, but of the structural organization of the atoms of these elements within the molecules. It follows from this that if meanings are local and exist only in structures, then the demand that generality of application should be an immediate desideratum of all empirical work leads to an abstraction from meaning and hence a gross distortion of the reality being investigated. Two grotesque examples of this are the study of mere frequency of presentation as a condition of liking in the study of interpersonal attraction (Zajonc, 1968) and of the use of repetition of nonsense syllables as a way of studying repetition as a factor in learning.

Connected with the illusions which I have been at pains to expose in these introductory criticisms, there is still a reluctance amongst social psychologists to listen to people's talk and to take serious notice of the interpretations and theories it involves. Indicative of a failure to realize that language and other sign systems are devices for conducting co-operative, cognitive operations in public, has been a neglect of the problem of collective psychological phenomenon. This failure has meant that even though there has been a welcome return to cognitive studies they have been vitiated by the practice of imposing or attributing meanings in human actions and merely hypothesizing possible inner cognitive processes. The imposition of meaning is unavoidable while the use of the standard equipment such as rating scales, questionnaires, etc. is continued. These instruments contain a prior conceptual scheme predetermining the possibility of response. They abort, rather than capitalize upon the capacities for people to reveal their cognitive operations in co-operative speech. In part, this is a consequence of a perennial tendency to forget that human action is essentially social.

However, to replace these thought and work patterns with a social psychological science, it is necessary to describe what sort of theory will be appropriate and what sort of empirical practices will be legitimate ways of revealing the way people think and feel and act within the social world. The first step is to get our exemplar right and that means we must look briefly at the way a natural science is put together.

Why, one might ask, is any exemplar necessary? Why not develop a method out of the problems posed by, and techniques developed in, native social psychology practices of interpretation and theorizing? The answer is partly one of mere rhetoric. The moral advantage of the possibility of substantiating a claim of the same sort of authority enjoyed by the natural sciences is surely irresistible, and indeed legitimate. More importantly, the long history of natural science has allowed a good many philosophical options to be tested in both methods and metaphysics.

B. THE CHARACTER OF NATURAL SCIENCE

In the natural sciences an explanatory theory is defined not by its logical form but by its content. For a theory to be explanatory and thus genuinely scientific, as opposed to merely instrumental or technological, it must fulfill certain criteria.

(i) It must make reference to an *agent*, an individual or a substance of such a nature that it has the power to produce the required product. For example, the formation of methane depends on the combining power of carbon atoms, that is, they are of such an electronic structure that they are quadrivalent. The tendency of a body to accelerate towards the centre of the earth is explained by the reference to the gravitational field with field potential G.

(ii) The theory must make reference to a pre-existing template structure which determines the form that the action of the agent takes in generating a product with determinate features. For example, the valencies of a carbon atom act at the vertices of a tetrahedron and it is this fact that accounts for the particular structure taken on by carbon in the form of diamonds. $F = G\, m_1 m_2 d^{-2}$, is the law of the structure of the gravitational field and accounts for the form of the kinematic profile of a falling body. In short, to account fully for a product we need to specify the properties of the agent, the conditions of its action, the material that it acts upon, and the template which determines the form its action will take. All of these are responsible for the properties of the product of that action.

It should be emphasized that, in general, the content of explanatory theories is not arrived at inductively by generalizing similar instances into a law, but rather by imaginative model building. Gaps in our knowledge of the causal agents and mechanisms of production of experienceable patterns have to be filled by imagining a paramorph or material analogue of the real mechanism acting there, an analogue which, if it were real, would produce a pattern comparable to that which we observe in the actual patterns.

The dynamics of theory-construction can be represented in the following principles:

(i) There are unknown generative mechanisms which produce the observed patterns;

(ii) A theory is created by imagining a hypothetical, but real, generative mechanism capable of producing simulacra of the observed patterns, and of such a kind that they could be real.

These two principles reduce to the requirement that there is a behavioural analogy between the imagined hypothetical mechanism and the real but unknown mechanism.

(iii) Conceptions of hypothetical generative mechanisms are based on a suitable general theory of the kinds of materials and general workings of nature. By building his imaginary mechanisms according to this general theory a theoretician ensures that his theory (which describes the nature and workings of a hypothetical generative mechanism) is reasonably plausible as a possible real mechanism. But this again is a relation only of analogy, since the components and modes of working of the imagined generative mechanism are usually only rather like the nature and workings of the real processes upon which it is based. This is the material analogy.

The plausibility of a theory in natural science, such as the atomic theory of chemistry, is by reference to the balance between the formal and material analogies.

If we follow the ideas about the content of theories outlined above, it is evident that we must introduce into science the conception of the real tendencies of an agent—real tendencies to bring about effects in other things. But if theories talk of real tendencies, and experiments and observations reveal only the *effects* of these tendencies, it is evident that theories are never tested directly in natural science. The laws of nature cannot, then, be mere generalizations of the functional relations between observed treatments and manifested behaviour. They must be descriptions of the tendencies of active agents to produce effects in whatever medium they act upon. It follows further that explanatory theories are testable only by reference to their explanatory power, that is by asking ourselves (rather than Nature) whether the interacting tendencies of powers we have supposed relevant natural agents to have, would produce the patterns we experience when observing and experimenting.

The patterns experienced in the laboratory are almost never the same as those experienced in nature, since in the laboratory one tendency is isolated and made to act by isolating the agent which possesses it, because only in this way can individual tendencies be studied. In nature there are no isolated tendencies.

C. LINGUISTICS AS A MODEL FOR PSYCHOLOGY

Even using an accurate picture of the natural sciences as a model for a scientific psychology is not sufficient to generate an exemplar for a psychology. Too many ways of realizing the general format outlined above remain as possible options. To focus in a little closer we can use the protoscience of linguistics as an example. Conveniently it is both a psychological and a social science and is articulated within the natural science pattern, i.e. it proposes hypothetical mechanisms and uses the general structural explanation pattern of agent and template.

Furthermore, it is guaranteed to yield schemata for theories which avoid the covert behaviourism of current "cognitive" psychology. The guarantee of avoidance of behaviourism is a simple consequence of requiring that a scientific linguistics aims at both a competence theory and a performative theory.

The general scheme for a scientific approach to the psychology of any kind of human social functioning requires a distinction between:

Performance. Public, meaning-mediated actions by individuals acting within a certain social identity, accomplishing thereby the construction of an orderly fragment of social life within a specific social milieu.

Competence. The knowledge and skill required for an individual actor to be able to create, sustain and change the orderly, structured flow of social life. Competence in this sense comprises both what has to be done to accomplish a certain social end defined by the projects of persons as social beings, and the means to do it.

Distinct branches of psychology are to be identified by:
(a) the analytical schemata they deploy to discover the elements and structures proper to these two domains;
(b) the form of explanatory theory in each domain, i.e. the appropriate realization of the conceptions of agent and template;
(c) the distinct methods for exploring each of these domains can be devised as a consequence of (a) and (b).

Currently, though psycholinguistics lacks a well-developed performance theory, it has an analytical scheme for performance, part of which we call grammar.

Competence theory in current linguistics—its way of representing linguistic knowledge—is generative rather than taxonomic. It represents an indefinitely large body of linguistic knowledge in terms of one or more base structures from which each surface structure can be generated by transformation according to rule. Each surface structure has its own generative tree. Another way of representing a body of knowledge generatively is the "Euclidean" axiomatic method. Unlike the base structure–transformation scheme, it is hierarchical, with axioms providing a starting point. By applying the rules, new members can be generated without returning to the axioms for each derivation. Linguistic method is based upon people's intuitions of grammatical and categorical propriety rather than explicit knowledge of rules, hence it makes no use of accounts. This reflects the fact that most people have only tacit knowledge of their language.

Ethogenics is a social psychology, consciously modelled on the outline structure of linguistics. As an alternative social and personality psychology, this approach draws upon an elaborated form of the common-sense folk theory of social performance. Social activity is taken to be the actions of agents who form intentions to perform social acts and draw upon the rules and conventions for realizing their act-intentions in public, meaningful actions. Ethogenics recognizes two kinds of performance as essential to social life: act–action performance in pursuit of both practical and expressive ends in recognizably distinct situations and settings; and accounting, i.e., discourse in which the act–action structure is commented upon. It can be made intelligible and warrantable, that is demonstrated to be proper in that setting for people in those realms and exhibiting those personas.

By analysing these performances it is possible to attribute social knowledge and skill to any individual member of the collective in which performances of the specific kinds occur, who shows him/herself competent in them. An analysis, however, requires a conceptual system in terms of which it can be systematically carried through. If we follow the lead of the natural sciences, such systems must be developed by prior theorizing, that is, by developing models of the processes involved.

Ethogenic analysis is structured according to an overall anthropomorphic model, i.e. social action is to be understood as the activities of *persons* as we know and experience them. Ordinary language and folk conceptions become a kind of grounding model, playing the kind of role in social and personality psychology that Atomism played in Newtonian science. Within that overall source model two more specific source models are deployed in the genesis of analytical concepts: the first is that kind of social event in which socially relevant problems are solved by ritual or conventional means; the second is that kind of staged dramatic performance where actor roles and action scripts are fully explicit and defined. Adopting the latter model structures our view of social events, according to the Goffman–Burke actor–action–scene theory (Goffman, 1969; Burke, 1945). The specific source models interact with each other, since sometimes it is helpful to see problem-solving activities as dramatic performances of the scenario "Rational Beings Get Together to Solve a Problem".

On the basis of analysis of action in episodes, attributions of knowledge (competence in the linguist's peculiar sense) can be made to people as social actors. But unlike the exponents of transformational linguistics we have had no success at all in demonstrating any generative structure in this knowledge. We have not been able to demonstrate a few base structures that could be transformed into the structures of performances as we have experienced them in public social life. Ethogenic competence theory is taxonomic rather than generative. Items of social knowledge, such as situation, setting, criteria for and definition of social identity, rules of action and persona presentation, etc., are known as such and cluster around socially distinct situations. Situations seem to be the main taxonomic category with rules, personas and arbiters of propriety dependent upon them as sub-categories of social knowledge.

The upshot of this approach is to highlight the analysis of accounts as a characteristic feature of ethogenic method (Marsh *et al.*, 1978), because it serves both as a source of concepts for analysing performance theory and acts as the prime, initial source of hypotheses about competence. Hypotheses as to individual competence can be further elaborated by the use of the methods of George Kelly. For example, a situation category like "school" is immensely internally complex, since it involves Kellyan constructs relating to such items as teachers, times, curriculum divisions, social groupings in various times and places in the school day, folk theories of schooling, and so on, according to a multidimensional space of polarized evaluative concepts. To reveal the cognitive organization of each general category repertory grids can be constructed based upon constructs, i.e. polarized pairs of concepts, elicited for sets of elements. Kelly's methods are particularly advantageous because they are so designed as to elicit the actor's own conceptual system and then turn that back upon the content of his knowledge. They involve no *a priori* assumptions other than that the actor's knowledge is structured in some fashion or other.

Both psycholinguistics and ethogenics can be compared favourably in their structure with the desiderata for scientific explanatory theories generally. An explanatory theory must:
  (i)   mention an agent to account for the mere fact of the production of a product and a template to account for the properties that the product is found to have;
  (ii) have explanatory power;
  (iii) have plausibility, that is describe or conjure up a representation of processes, mechanisms, etc. that could be in the real world.

These are tested by long-run confirmation of attributions of competence from episode analysis and from account analysis. It should be clear that ethogenics satisfies all three of these desiderata, while linguistics fares not quite so well, lacking a performance theory.

The ethogenic performance theory is based upon the assumption of the reality of the role–rule system, the system which is consciously attended to in ceremonial behaviour and is taken to be structurally identical with a system that is at work when we are acting without immediate awareness of the processes by which we act. This is justified on the grounds that when a check occurs and the processes of action control are registered in consciousness, what surfaces is interpretative of role–rule–action structures. It seems reasonable, then, to hypothesize that hidden mechanisms are similar. For example, we examine diseased people microscopically; what surfaces are bacteria, and it is reasonable to suppose that the hidden causes of all diseases are similar. It was this supposition that lead to the virus hypothesis.

D. ETHOGENICS AND OTHER PSYCHOLOGIES

Ethogenics is not the only non-behaviourist psychology in current use. Two sibling movements must be considered, both for their contribution to truly scientific psychology and for their limitations.

Hermeneutics proposes to treat social life as a text, the meaning of which is to be reached only by detailed interpretative analysis. The idea that social action must be interpreted and the meaning revealed before it can be properly considered scientifically is an important insight, but it can be taken in more than one way. In the ethogenic methodology this insight is realized in practice by seeking for the interpretations that social actors put on their actions and on the actions of others, because it is felt that only as interpreted in this way do actions have specific social and psychological effects. In short, ethogenics works to reveal rather than to impose interpretations. The interpretative schemata are those of the folk. In so far as I understand it, hermeneutic psychology proposes to reveal deeper meanings hidden from the folk. The claim that there are such meanings and that they have social effects is consonant with the ideas of false consciousness in sociology and self-deception in psychology. But the concepts in which this deeper meaning is interpreted are contributed by the analysts rather than extracted from the folk practices of interpretation and judgement of action. What, then, is their status? From an ethogenic point of view they can have only one location. They are rival accounts and as such must survive or perish in day-to-day practical negotiations with folk accounts as useful interpretations of the social activities in which people are engaged. It seems, then, that though they have a legitimate place in psychology, they cannot, as I have so far described their mode of entry, claim any priority over other accounts. Moscovici (1976) has shown how such accounts spread from original academic or medical sources, become part of the accounting resources of a population. In modified form they will then appear in the ordinary accounting techniques of ordinary folk. We have seen something of the sort in the recent Women's Movement, when a political rhetoric was introduced to offer alternative accounting resources for women to deal with marital and other relations and to deploy in the presentation of acceptable selves.

Psychodynamics, while taking the individual's knowledge and mental state seriously, failed to control its construction of possible generative mechanisms which might be a guide to the way action is actually generated. The basic dynamic structure depends on proposing independent agencies within a person which produce actions despite himself. Such a conception is contrary to the fundamental role any psychology must accord to the agency of the persons in normal circumstances.

The limitations of this theory derive in part from Freud's own insistence that it was a non-pathological psychology, a psychology of people who, at worst, were neurotic. Notoriously, Freud refused to treat the mad. If it is anything, psychodynamics ought to be a theory of the psychological functioning of normal people. However by attributing the dynamic sources of action to components of or inclusions within people, rather than to people themselves, it places itself within the realm of the pathological, because it is a central tenet of the ethogenic approach that people are actually or potentially in control of any of the vicariously active components of their cognitive apparatus and even of their autonomic nervous system. Ethogenists have not been the first to notice this curious ambiguity in the psychodynamic approach. It has sometimes been unkindly ascribed to the unusual social conditions of nineteenth-century Vienna, and its subsequent popularity to the perennial human temptation to slough off personal responsibility, even to an inner element of themselves.

This last observation gives a clue to the ethogenic way of rescuing what is valuable in psychodynamic approaches. They are contributions to accounting. A psychodynamic treatment, for example, is a training in accounting, providing a more powerful justificatory apparatus than the person had at his or her disposal prior to the "treatment". But what does it contribute? To see clearly we need to remind ourselves of Evreinov's concept of monodrama. In monodramatic accounting, aspects of an individual are projected as persons and made to seem to engage in a social interaction played out according to some standard scenario of the stage of everyday life. A very simple case is encapsulated in the little imagined playlet between the characters, "I", who is strong and consistent, and "me" who is weak but willing, represented in the accounting sentence, "I made myself do it". A psychodynamic account is *just* a more elaborate version of monodramatic speaking. On this interpretation it can be protected from the damaging charge of introducing vicarious or pseudo-agents into relatively ordinary folk, and can be drawn into the mainstream of scientific, that is ethogenic, *social* psychology.

E. THE QUESTION OF EMPIRICAL CONCEPTS

Examining the latest issues of the journals, one is still horrified by the persistence of the rhetoric of "measures" and other pseudo-numerical indices. Despite all the criticism, from psychologists and from outsiders as diverse as mathematicians and sociologists, the science continues to exhibit a numerological cast. It reminds one of nothing so much as the persistence of alchemy and astrology into the eighteenth century: then, too, there was a blind empiricism with a numerology derived from an exploded theory.

In pseudo-scientific psychology it seems to persist as a part of a rhetoric of "precision". But precision of thought and treatment of a field of studies can come either from devising instruments and scales or from the analysis of the concepts with which the field is described and with the help of which its properties are perceived. Compare the real precision of Goffman's concept pair "with"/"single" for analysing the structure of a social scene with the pseudo-precision which would come from plotting the distances in centimetres people keep apart. The illusion of precision can be achieved by mapping the extension of a comparative concept, more or less "liking", say, on to a numerical scale. Real precision would be achieved only if a stable, translatable (in the mathematical sense) standard or unit of the parameter under study could be devised. Pseudo-precision can usually be achieved. There is hardly ever any discussion of the latter condition because it is widely assumed that a comparative scale is immune from the need to define a translatable unit. Since the problem of standards and units is almost never addressed, the issue of whether pre-tested reliability is an artefact may not even be raised.

In the light of the fact that psychological phenomena are structural through and through, that is, internally related in a multiple network of relations to other phenomena, real and potential, the measurement approach is almost wholly ill-judged. If, as in an application of the semantic differential, the idea of measuring the meaning of a word has been proposed, it is clear that "measure" is a rhetorical device, not a literal usage. Similarly, no non-rhetorical sense can be given to measuring an emotion, since an emotion is the conventional meaning defined with respect to a socially identified situation of a kind of bodily feeling, which Schachter has shown is an ingredient in many very different emotions.

Logical muddles about the concept of a *variable* are very widespread; the word is used in psychology with two distinct meanings with widely different implications. It can mean a property that has or could have different magnitudes at different times in the same individual, or it can mean a property that has different but stable magnitudes in different people. In most studies the two senses are promiscuously lumped together, for example, in the interpretation of statistical distributions as psychological properties. This becomes clear when we distinguish distributively reliable parameters, that is, statistical properties of populations which can be distributively predicated of individual members of a population as likelihoods of *developing* the property under the treatment, and statistically unreliable properties which cannot be so predicated. The common muddle is perhaps the fault of textbooks choosing examples such as "being blue-eyed" and "being a member of the tennis club" to introduce inferences from statistical distributions to probabilities. This lets people come to think that they are related, like treatments and subsequent behaviour. The former is an epistemic relation between prior existing properties; the latter a causal relation between a treatment and a produced property. It by no means follows that there is a probability that *any* member is influenced by working with a companion, from the fact that there is a well-grounded distribution of members so influenced among all members so treated. The most glaring example of such fallacious reasoning occurs in the preface of Milgram's (1974) *Obedience to Authority*, p. xi, "Behaviour that is unthinkable to *an* individual acting on his own *may* be exerted without hesitation when carried out under orders". (My italics highlight here the logical form of the statement of the conclusion of his monstrous experiments.)

Part of the importance of Mixon's reworking of Milgram's experiment (Mixon, 1971) in the morally acceptable atmosphere of dramatic simulation was the demonstration that statistical distribution reflected more or less those who always would and those who never would torment other people with electricity.

In the ethogenic approach, ordinary language is taken as the most refined and precise *technical* vocabulary we possess both for designing and for carrying out psychological and social studies. It is rich in distinctions of the highest precision and abounds in implicit theories of great sophistication. This is not to say that explicit empirical testing of its worth in the field, so to speak, may not lead to its being improved upon in time: its priority is not supposed to be a matter of necessity, but rather a matter of fact. This is shown by the fact that human life is lived according to a cluster of historically and culturally conditioned psychological and social theories as to what sort of people we should express ourselves as being. The ordinary languages of mankind contain these theories. For example, Japanese grammar contains a social theory which, through the use of distinctive language forms in social life, controls perceived position in the social order. Torode (1976) has shown how English grammar contains a theory of discipline represented in the monodramatic uses of pronouns by figures of authority, like teachers and nurses. Consider the social implications and power of the simple sentence "How are *we* today?" addressed to a miserable patient by a jolly, healthy nurse. Then there are the intentional implications of English verbs of action. We can hardly say "I went to the bank" if we arrive there by accident. Not only grammar but vocabulary provide an enormously rich and continually sharpened conceptual apparatus for representing and analysing cognitive and social action. For example, Clarke (1975) has shown that people deploy and routinely recognize four hundred distinct performatives, social actions carried out by speaking, clustering into very complex and highly ordered structures.

Brenner (1978) has shown that in a fifteen-minute conversation there may be hundreds of transitions involving over one hundred recognized rules of transition from one socially distinct form of speech to another, forming an elaborate, nesting structure. Finally, and most important, ordinary language can act as a guardian or filter against artefacts. However it cannot wholly prevent their appearance, because that which cannot be expressed in the most refined descriptive instrument we possess must be treated with suspicion until it can be satisfactorily defended as psychologically or socially real.

F. THE RETURN TO SINGLE CASE STUDIES

There are two ways of seeking knowledge of a type:

The extensive design. A set of individuals is chosen, their common properties are elicited, and from them a type is derived by abstraction. RISK: Although some nomothetic result is certain—that is, some kind of lawful concomitance is almost bound to turn up—it may be trivial, artefactual, or both. In short, a type reached by abstraction may be thin, or absurd, or both. For example, the only trait human beings seem to have, taken in the large, is relative excitability (Mischel, 1968).

The intensive design. A typical individual is chosen and its properties are elicited. From it the corresponding set is constructed by defining it as those individuals who are of that type. Most natural science investigations are based upon the intensive design. RISK: Although an idiographic result is certain, it may be generalizable to very few others, that is, the set of individuals of the highly specified type may be small.

To find out how people come to act we need the intensive design to ensure a context rich enough for the structures (both cognitive and social) to remain undistorted and, in particular, unbroken and unfragmented, because action elements will lose their meaning if removed from the structure within which they are defined. Similarly, people become other than they are in new social environments, particularly in simplified ones. Hence the risk involved in the intensive design must be run to ensure faithful representations of human functioning. The best setting for an intensive design is real life.

This implies a radical change in methodology. No longer can we be content with sloppy investigations using large samples and statistical operations to yield correlative factors. This is the method of agriculture.

We must become like real natural scientists—like anatomists or chemists —who intensively explore particular cases and erect their species and elements by definitional enlargement. Both people and episodes can be subjected to this kind of treatment.

The adoption of either the intensive or the extensive design for empirical studies determines how an investigation is made. However, the aim of the investigation is the same in both cases—the discovery of general principles of human action, organization and functioning. The return to single case studies has made prominent the individuality or uniqueness of some patterns of action and of some people's cognitive and emotional organization. The interplay between individual constitutions and general patterns and principles used to be dealt with in the old pseudo-scientific psychology by trying to "account for the variants", implying that there remained a central tendency. This acquired normative associations in some branches of social psychology, from which individuals are said to deviate. The new psychology suggests the possibility that in certain respects each person has a unique history and way of functioning within which there may be central tendencies and that his uniqueness should not be treated as a deviation or a variance.

At the same time, there is the possibility that the social or collective aspects of psychological activities may also be unique. It may be that each one "develops" human beings in ways different from every other —at least in certain respects. There seems to be good evidence that "personality" is developed in different ways and according to different criteria at different times.

Taken together these considerations suggest that what a person does —that is, the social interpretation of his actions—is likely to be the intersection of two unique processes: the development of his biography as an individual life and the ever-changing historically conditioned social milieu. The way a person's biography develops, particularly his sense of the kind of person he is and the personal worth he accumulates by being of that type (or striving to be of it) is influenced by the historical conditions by which he is living, and particularly of the folk psychology current at that time, which is itself a derivative from the professional psychologies of previous eras. Until it can positively be shown to be otherwise we must work with the assumption that human modes of functioning are so culturally dependent that the introduction of a psychological theory into a culture will sooner or later bring about changes in actual psychological functioning to accord with it. For instance, automata-like conceptions of man, with the emphasis on external control, have quite patently led to a passive attitude to the rules and regulations imposed upon the folk by bureaucrats. This is particularly noticeable in the way the activities of daily life, such as driving cars, selling goods, serving meals, solving problems, and so on, are managed in the United States and is vividly illustrated in the "technologisms" of the MacNamara era. It is my belief that the externalistic psychology predated and partly produced this very distinctive lifestyle rather than that the psychologies are merely reflections of it.

The form of a psychological study shifts, then, to an examination of the interaction and transformation of structures, both personal and social, and away from the treatments imposed upon people in accordance with the conception of an experiment as the manipulation of an independent variable producing changes in a dependent variable. It shifts from a mythical conception of natural science invented by philosophers, usually of a positivistic persuasion, to the adoption of real sciences, like chemistry, as our exemplars.

3
The Development of Theory in Social Psychology

WILLIAM J. McGUIRE
Yale University, New Haven, Connecticut

A. The classification of social psychological theories 55
   1. System theories versus guiding-idea theories 55
   2. Life history of a guiding-idea theory 56
   3. A typology of guiding-idea theories 57
B. Social psychological theory as product: the sixteen views of human nature underlying social psychological research. 60
   1. Four cognitive stability theories 60
   2. Four cognitive growth theories 63
   3. Four affective stability theories 66
   4. Four affective growth theories 68
C. Social psychology theorizing as process 71
   1. Creative generating of theories 71
   2. The role of empirical observation in the development of social psychological theories 74

Theorizing is a form of thinking and is distinguished from ordinary thought by the use of more explicit definitions and more abstract and more formally interrelated principles. As a kind of knowledge, theories share the possibilities and limitations of all forms of thought. Hence, it is appropriate to begin my discussion of the development of theory in social psychology by pointing out that theorizing, like knowing in general, has at its core the tragedy that to cope with reality we must use thought processes to represent reality to us and yet by their nature thought processes inevitably oversimplify and distort reality. The oversimplification derives from a number of sources. The act of knowing breaks up integral reality into arbitrary chunks to make it intelligible (an epistemic process vigorously condemned by Heidegger, 1962), abstracts out a few features of reality while ignoring others, focuses on isolated relationships within an intricately interrelated causal network as if everything else were equal, and so on. More seriously, theorizing, like other thought, distorts reality in a variety of ways. Knowing involves lumping together diverse entities and ignoring their essential peculiarities; it forces observations into available mental categories, however ill-fitting; it allows the knower's values, desires, and expectations to distort his or her observations and inferences. These oversimplifications and distortions cloud even our basic sensory impressions and our everyday concrete speculations. More seriously still, they warp our more formal general theorizing that carries our thinking to high levels of abstraction.

What makes theorizing a tragedy is not that our theories are poor but that, poor as they are, they are essential, for we cannot do without them. The ubiquity of formal and informal theorizing demonstrates its indispensibility. To cope with reality we must reduce it to the oversimplified level of complexity that our minds can manage and distort it into the type of representations that we can grasp. We are reduced to groping for theories that are happy instances of brilliant oversimplification whose elected ignorances and distortions happen to be incidental to the matter under consideration, so that within the momentary situation the theory's apt focusing of our creative and critical appraisal yields gains that outweigh the losses caused by its oversights and distortions. These cautionary notes should serve as a reminder that all the social psychological theories to be described capture only part of the truth and contain a non-negligible amount of falsity. Rather than being contenders from among which the correct theory should be selected, they should be recognized as partial views of the person, whose separate and diverse insights supplement and correct one another, a broad set of them being needed to provoke our creative insights and provide explanatory accounts.

A. THE CLASSIFICATION OF SOCIAL PSYCHOLOGICAL THEORIES

1. Systems theories versus guiding-idea theories

There are two genera of theories used in psychology: systems theories and guiding-idea theories. A systems theory consists of a series of postulates, each one independent of the others in inspiration and together accounting for a broad domain of behaviour. The historic prototype is Euclidean geometry, consisting of a set of axioms from which a vast number of theorems describing spatial relations can be logically derived. In empirical sciences such systems are sometimes known as hypothetico-deductive theories in that their fundamental postulates are induced from observation and then from the postulates numerous hypotheses about behaviour are derived for testing. The prototypical example in psychology is the behaviouristic theory of Hull (1952) as applied to social psychological phenomena by Miller and Dollard (1941, 1950). A narrower example is McGuire's (1968) system for deducing from five postulates and two corollaries a large number of hypotheses about individual differences in susceptibility to social influence.

Some students of social psychological theory (e.g. McGuire, 1972) regard such systems theories as the goal towards which our theorizing must aspire if we are to construct a true science where the name "social psychology" now lies; but while the sensitive optimist may feel some distant rumblings suggesting that such a science is slouching towards Bethlehem to be born, even so sanguine and imaginative an observer must grant that it slouches slowly, slowly.

Hence, our discussion of social psychology theories must deal more with the other genus, the guiding-idea theories. Such formulations focus on one of the multiplicity of tendencies, typically motivational, that underlie the person's behaviour and experience. For example, they may depict the person as a reward maximizer, consistency maximizer, ego defender, or stimulus-hungry organism. Such a theorist then analyses how the person, considered as a consistency maximizer (or whatever), can be expected to behave in the situation under study and how the behaviour will be affected by independent variables in the situation.

of a guiding-idea theory

...g-idea theorist, in his or her better moments, undoubtedly ...es that the person is guided by numerous tendencies whose ...n determining behaviour will differ from situation to situation ...d from person to person. Yet in the initial, heroic age of a guiding-idea theory's life history its pioneer advocates ignore individual differences and situational interactions, using their partial view of the person almost as a "nothing but" depiction. Independent variables whose importance the given guiding-idea theory creatively evokes are selected out for study, while other independent variables that might affect behaviour in the situation but are irrelevant to the given guiding idea are ignored. This elected ignorance may even lead the pioneer to the fallacy of denying that other independent variables, not suggested by his or her new theory, can affect behaviour in the situations. Its initial success in accounting for behaviour in the situation that gave rise to it results in the hubris of extending the guiding-idea theory to new situations where its oversimplifications and distortions may be more damaging, so that other partial views of the person are more apt. While parochial advocates of a given guiding-idea theory tend to reject other theories as adversaries, the more perspicacious social psychologist will utilize several guiding-idea theories to supplement one another.

Guiding-idea theories in social psychology tend to wax and wane in successive waves of about a decade's duration: learning theories dominated in the 1950s, consistency theories in the 1960s, and attribution theory in the 1970s. In the early, heroic stage of its life cycle a guiding idea tends to be pushed pugnaciously in the nothing-but mode described above. Once it evolves to the "normal", tidying-up phase that constitutes the second half of its ten-year life cycle, the wider circle of adherents tend to add interactional hypotheses and definitional refinements and even to integrate its insights with those from other guiding-idea theories. Sub-schools tend to arise and the theory becomes weighed down by forbiddingly arcane complexities and reservations which hasten its demise. The insightful recognition of a partial view of human nature that had previously been slighted by other guiding-idea theories first attracted enthusiasm because of the brilliant aptness of its oversimplifications for the situation to which it was first applied; but as the theory is extended to new areas, the corrections and additions needed to overcome its limitations and distortions multiply until finally its heuristic and explanatory power becomes lost to all but the diminishing rear-guard of faithful followers able and willing to use the cabalistic additions.

Each of the 16 guiding-idea theories described below has inspired a certain amount of creative work in social psychology: some attained popularity as the Establishment viewpoint of a decade (as attribution theories did in the 1970s and consistency theories in the 1960s), while others have been dimly heard voices in the wilderness whose future lies before them. The underlying logic that we used to generate these 16 theories, as described below, suggests that each has equal explanatory potential so that those which have been relatively quiet in the past hold the promise of the future.

3. A typology of guiding-idea theories

A procedure for generating theories. The technique used to identify the 16 basic concepts of human nature underlying social psychological research is of sufficient general utility to deserve description here. It involves "listing and organizing", one of the four dozen creative techniques for generating psychological hypotheses I have described elsewhere (McGuire, 1975). I began by listing the more popular guiding-idea theories which have been used by substantial groups of social psychologists to explain behaviour, for example, the five partial views of human nature—the functional, perceptual, learning, consistency, and information-processing—that underlie attitude change research (McGuire, 1971). I then organized this short initial list of guiding-idea theories by teasing out underlying dimensions which differentiate the theories and used the dimensions to construct a matrix into whose cells the five initial theories fit, with some cells left vacant. Useful descriptors for these empty cells were provided by the dimensional characteristics out of which the matrix was constructed, suggesting additional theories to fill the empty cells. The augmented list suggested new dimensions that generated a broader matrix whose empty cells suggested additional theories. Ultimately, I abstracted four bipolar dimensions and by considering them as orthogonal constructed the 16-cell (2^4) matrix of guiding-idea theories shown in Table I (McGuire, 1974).

The distinguishing dimensions. The four bipolar dimensions shown in Table I as organizing the 16 basic guiding-idea theories that underlie

Table I. Sixteen guiding-idea theories: partial views of human nature that lie behind social psychological research in the 20th century.

		Initiating dimensions					
		Stability				Growth	
		Active	Reactive		Active	Reactive	
Cognitive	Internal	1. Consistency (balance)	2. Categorization (perceptual)		5. Autonomy (control)	6. Problem-solving (utilitarian)	
	External	3. Attribution (epistemic)	4. Induction (observational)		7. Stimulation (exploratory; novelty)	8. Matching (teleological; script)	
Affective	Internal	9. Tension (drive) reduction	10. Ego-defensive (functional)		13. Assertion (dominance; achievement)	14. Role-playing (identification)	
	External	11. Expressive (cathartic; acting out)	12. Habituation (behaviouristic; stimulus–response)		15. Affiliative (empathy)	16. Modelling (social learning)	

End state dimensions: Cognitive, Affective

social psychological research all tend to describe people in terms of some fundamental motivational state towards which their thoughts, feelings, and behaviours tend. Two of the four dimensions have to do with what initiates human action and the other two with the end state that terminates action. The first of the initiating dimensions deals with *active versus reactive* impetus to behaviour. Some guiding-idea theories stress that human experiences and behaviours are actively initiated by forces within the person; contrasting theories regard behaviour more as a reaction to forces coming from the external environment.

The second initiating dimension distinguishing the guiding-idea theories, *stability versus growth*, has to do with whether the economy of human action is depicted primarily as maintaining the present equilibrium or whether the person is viewed as chronically striving to grow to a new level of complexity. This stability versus growth distinction is an ancient one, antedating social psychology in various polarities: being versus becoming, classical versus romantic, Apollonian versus Dionysian, etc. In general, the more "mechanistic" theorists, with natural science or behaviouristic orientations, tend to stress the homeostatic position that the person is best seen as endeavouring to maintain the current equilibrium; the more humanistically oriented theorists stress the person as constantly striving to grow towards a new developmental stage.

The other two dimensions distinguishing these partial views of the person concern the end state towards which human action is postulated to be directed. The third dimension, *cognitive versus affective*, has to do with whether the terminus towards which the person tends is depicted as the establishment of an ideological or a feeling state. The final, *internal versus external*, dimension has to do with whether the end state towards which the person tends is defined more in terms of the internal relations among aspects of the individual's personality or more by the relationships between the person and the external environment.

By considering each of these four dimensions as bipolar and orthogonal to the other three, we can produce the 2^4 matrix shown in Table I, each of whose 16 cells is described by the characteristics furnished by the four dimensions. Each cell of Table I contains the name of a family of guiding-idea theories. The 16 will be discussed in sequence, starting with the four in the upper-left quadrant of Table I, then successively, the upper-right, lower-left and lower-right quadrants. For each of the 16 families of theories, we shall first describe the partial view of the person that it utilizes, then its variants and the theorists who have used it, as well as some of its applications in social psychology.

B. SOCIAL PSYCHOLOGICAL THEORY AS PRODUCT: THE SIXTEEN VIEWS OF HUMAN NATURE UNDERLYING SOCIAL PSYCHOLOGICAL RESEARCH

1. Four cognitive stability theories

This first tetrad of guiding-idea theories (shown in the upper-left quadrant of Table I) views the person as essentially directed towards preserving some cognitive state (rather than as preserving an affective state or as striving towards a cognitive or affective growth as do the other three tetrads). Among these four cognitive stability concepts of the person, we shall first describe the two which focus on stabilizing internal aspects of cognitive states, namely, consistency and categorization theories; then we shall consider two which emphasize stabilizing cognitive states as regards relations to the external environment, namely, attribution and inductional theories. Within each of these two pairs, the first-named member assumes that behaviour is actively initiated from within the person and the second views the person more as reacting to external forces. In discussing the other tetrads in subsequent sections, we shall discuss their four theories in the same sequence.

1. *The consistency theories.* These partial views of human nature depict the person as minimizing incoherence within the person, and between the person and the environment. The person's beliefs, feelings, and actions are depicted as interconnected and tending towards mutual coherence. When incongruities develop, the person acts as an honest broker, adjusting the interconnected system to effect a compromise among the conflicting forces, thus reducing inconsistencies (perhaps tending towards a "least squares deviation" solution minimizing the extent to which any one of the factors is left with a large discrepancy from the others).

Consistency theories were particularly popular within social psychology during the 1960s: there were many variants, including Heider's balance notion, the congruity concept of Osgood and Tannenbaum, Festinger's dissonance formulation (the best known of the consistency theories), Newcomb's symmetry concept, McGuire's probabilogical theory, Abelson and Rosenberg's psycho-logic formulation, Adam's equity theory, and the applications of graph theory to intrapersonal phenomena by Cartwright and Harary and others. A brief review of the consistency theories is found in McGuire (1966), a more extensive compilation in Abelson et al. (1968).

The consistency theorists have made a number of contributions to social psychology, although the advocates of alternative theories have argued that the new findings are not replicable and the replicable ones are not new. Work has focused on such topics as interrelations of behavioural and attitudinal change, information seeking, post-decisional readjustment, modes of inconsistency reduction, etc. A consistency theory that approaches the systems theory level is found in McGuire (1980b).

2. *Categorization theories.* These partial views of the person (sometimes known as "perceptual" theories) depict the person as swamped by stimuli from the internal and external environment and coping with this informational overload by developing a set of categories into which experiences can be classified. The person-as-categorizer oversimplifies the complexities of life by categorizations that allow disregarding many of their aspects. Where one's existing categories do not suffice to accommodate an observation, the person either distorts the new information to assimilate it to a pre-existing category and/or adjusts the category to accommodate the new information. The categories tend to have evaluative tags and interconnections which determine the person's reaction to the event as classified.

The concept of the person-as-categorizer goes back at least to the Würzburg school of Külpe and others and to Bartlett's concept of schemata. Muzafer Sherif's frame-of-reference notion as well as his and Hovland's "assimilation and contrast" theory uses the notion, as does Luchin's work on set and rigidity. Asch is also a proponent of this view in his depiction of the social influence process as not so much changing the person's opinion about an object but rather as changing the person's perception of what object it is that one is giving an opinion about. This guiding idea of the person is also basic to the currently fashionable work of structuralists such as Lévi-Strauss and Piaget.

3. *The attribution theories.* The two cognitive stability theories just described, consistency and categorization, agreed in locating the stability sought among the internal aspects of the person's cognitive system. The other two cognitive preservation theories to which we now

turn, attribution and induction, depict the person as maintaining a cognitive stability relative to the external environment.

The Establishment status within social psychology held during the 1960s by consistency theories was occupied in the 1970s by attribution theories. These formulations stress the noetic aspects of the person, the need to project meaning on the experienced world. One imposes upon the events that one experiences some interpretation which provides sufficient reason for their occurrence and situates them within one's own view of reality. Each person is thus assumed to be, for example, an implicit personality theorist or an implicit physicist, generating explanations of why things happen as they do. Confronted with an event that is surprising or inexplicable, the person generates an acceptable explanation to reduce uncertainty stress.

This notion of the person as a meaning or explanation creator goes back at least to the nineteenth-century Helmholtz theory of unconscious inference. Subsequently, it underlay the thinking of the Berlin branch of the Gestalt School and the related work by Michotte on the perception of causality (early work on the person as implicit physicist which was unfortunately not pursued). The influence of Heider joined with several lesser streams of thought to form the torrent of attributional approaches which flooded social psychology in the 1970s. Of note are the work of Rotter and Phares on individual differences in whether events are perceived as being internally versus externally controlled, the work of E. E. Jones (1979) on ingratiation, and H. H. Kelley's demonstration of the common core underlying these theories. An integration of attribution theory with logotherapy and other forms of existential analysis seems promising but has not yet been undertaken. Harvey and Smith (1977) present social psychology from this viewpoint of the person as attributionist.

4. *The inductional theories.* Similar to attribution theories in stressing the epistemic aspect of the person, but differing in depicting the person as more reactive than active in this need to know, are the partial views of the person as inductively accounting for events if asked. Social psychologists drawing inspiration from this guiding idea see the person as rather deficient in cognitive life, with little spontaneous tendency to generate reasons for events and little reflection on one's own behaviour; however, external events, such as being asked a question or being required to make a decision, may call upon the person to find an interpretation. Then one gropes for some explanatory concept by

looking for regularities in one's own behaviour or in the event in question, or one takes a reading from some comparison group, or whatever, until one can induce an interpretation that provides guidance for coping with the externally induced task. To paraphrase Daryl Bem's creative use of this theoretical orientation, the person may spend a lifetime drinking beer without ever formulating the notion that he or she likes beer until when suddenly asked whether one likes beer, the person, observing that he or she has been constantly drinking the stuff, infers that he or she does.

This notion of the person as a reactive explainer is found in William James's theory of the emotions and in the early behaviouristic conception of thought as implicit speech or other proprioceptive feedback. It is also implicit in the social comparison theory originated by Festinger, work on which has recently been reviewed by Suls and Miller (1977). The most heuristically provocative use of the notion is in Bem's (1972) radical behaviouristic (or self-observation) theory.

2. Four cognitive growth theories

The four partial views of human nature shown in the upper-right quadrant of Table I, like the four considered in the previous section, stress the person as striving towards a cognitive, rather than affective, state; however, these four depict the person as tending towards cognitive growth rather than towards maintaining the cognitive stability stressed in the first four theories. In general, these cognitive growth partial views of human nature tend to be espoused by humanistic theorists, often inspired by Freudian or Marxist notions (though often without their reductionist and materialistic aspects). The order in which the four will be described corresponds to that used for the four in the previous section.

5. *The autonomy theories.* There has been a surge of interest in the past ten years within social psychology in stressing people's need for autonomy and freedom (or at least for the illusion of control). In this theoretical framework people are depicted as striving to maximize the available options and their freedom to choose among them. A situation imposed on one makes one uncomfortable, even when one would have selected that situation if left free to choose, but one is willing to endure rather adverse circumstances if one retains a degree of control within them.

These autonomy notions are contained in the mid-century personality theories of Gordon Allport, Henry Murray, and Maslow, and in Erikson's theory of psychosocial development. In experimental social psychology, research within this framework is illustrated by work on Brehm's reactance theory (Wicklund, 1974) and Steiner's illusion of freedom research. Behavioural medicine and environmental psychology, particularly active fields of applied social psychology in the past few years, have made much use of the concept of the person as striving for control and as suffering physically as well as psychologically when the illusion of control cannot be maintained (Lazarus and Monat, 1977). Marx's stress on alienation places his among these theories also.

6. *The problem-solving theories.* Here we consider the partial view of the person as a coper, approaching life's difficulties with a problem-solving orientation and receiving gratification from acquiring new information or new skills which enhance the capacity for dealing with life's challenges. The guiding idea here stresses the person's pragmatic needs and the gratification afforded by overcoming challenges and enhancing coping ability.

Inspiration regarding this purposive view of human personality derives from Lewin's field theory and Tolman's sign-Gestalt behaviourism. The guiding idea is also represented in the long line of expectancy × values theorizing, employing additive or multiplicative models of how the person behaves so as to maximize utility; for example, the attitudinal research by Smith-Bruner-White and that by Peak and her followers, such as Milton Rosenberg, Raven, Dulaney, etc. A convenient summary of this work is found in Fishbein and Ajzen (1975). This partial view of the person also has been useful to social psychologists working on health problems in analysing responses to stress, particularly in the distinction between evasive versus corrective modes of coping suggested by Lazarus and in the work by Leventhal on attitudinal and behavioural effects of threat appeals in social influence situations.

7. *The stimulation theories.* Here we refer to the guiding idea theories of the person as explorer, driven by curiosity, stimulus hunger, and need for varied experience. These partial views of the person stress the human tendency to seek novelty and excitement, and to be quite bothered by boredom and a bland environment.

The stimulation theories were popular in the 1960s among a wide variety of researchers. While the basic inspiration seems "humanistic", even the behaviourists have recently made use of the notion of a stimulus hunger or exploratory drive in postulating that novel experience and information are intrinsically rewarding to humans and other animals, as demonstrated in work on alternation behaviour in rats and exploratory behaviour in monkeys by Hebb, Kendler, Harlow, Fowler, Dember, and others. Physiological work on the limbic system also participated in this theoretical flourishing. Recognition of human need for stimulation has come from developmental researchers such as the Bühlers, students of experimental aesthetics such as Berlyne, and personality theorists such as Zuckerman (1974), Bieri, and Fiske and Maddi.

Peculiarly, the consistency theories considered earlier, and these stimulation theories flourished simultaneously in the 1960s. Their simultaneity is striking because they are rather opposite views; consistency theories stress the need to maintain the old internal coherence by avoiding new information; stimulation theories stress the positive attraction of novelty. Simultaneous popularity of several rather opposing guiding-idea theories is not unusual in the history of social psychology or in other disciplines: e.g., Adam Smith and then Kant each utilized both the assertive and the opposite affiliative guiding-idea theories (numbers 13 and 15, discussed below). Such simultaneity reveals the complementary rather than adversary relationship of these partial views of the person; that several opposite ones can operate creatively within one thinker's head suggests the superiority of my Constructivism (discussed below) over the older Logical Empiricist paradigm.

8. *The teleological theories*. These theories depict the person as a pattern matcher who has an internal representation of a desired end state and manipulates self and environment to bring about the perception of an external state of affairs that corresponds to this internal representation. In earlier centuries, such a view of the person grew out of theological preconceptions; earlier in this century it came from preconceptions regarding genetically encoded instincts; in the past decade, it has developed out of the information-processing paradigm which uses the computer program or flow-chart as an analog for the person.

Precursors of this partial view of the person can be found in Brentano's act psychology and there are intimations of it in the "liberated" behaviouristic formulation of Neal Miller which describes behaviour in terms of acts rather than muscle movements. The recent re-emergence of these teleological notions have derived from the work of computer-oriented theorists such as Von Neumann and Weiner's cybernetic notions and in the conceptualizations of behavioural scientists such as Ashby's design for a brain or the Miller–Galanter–Pribram notion of plans and structure of behaviour. More recent developments, which promise greater flourishing of this type of guiding-idea theories during the 1980s, include the growing popularity of "script" theory (Tomkins, 1978; Schank and Abelson, 1977) and Powers' (1978) intriguing notion of behaviour as the control of perception.

3. Four affective stability theories

The eight partial views of human nature considered in the previous two sections stressed the person as tending towards types of cognitive states; the remaining eight theories postulate an affective end state. We shall describe first the tetrad of affective stability theories, shown in the lower-left quadrant of Table I, before turning in a final section to the affective growth tetrad in the lower-right quadrant. The four affective stability theories here will be discussed in an order corresponding to that used in the previous two sections.

9. *The tension-reduction theories.* The partial view of human nature posited by the theories considered here is that excitation is aversive, so that the person operates to attain a zero level of arousal. Inspirations as diverse as pantheism and materialism have given rise to this somewhat unexciting depiction of the person. Examples include: the Buddhists' notion of happiness as attainment of nirvana, a state of zero arousal involving the abolition of self-consciousness and desire; Freud's notion, derived from the second law of thermodynamics, of tension release as pleasure; and behaviourists' concept of drive reduction as reinforcing.

The orthodox psychoanalytic view that any arousal of erotic or thanatotic tensions is painful and their reduction pleasurable has been utilized widely among social psychologists studying topics such as person perception and racial prejudice. The various psychoanalytic mechanisms for the release of tension, such as displacement, rationalization, etc., have been useful in accounting for such social phenomena (e.g. Bettelheim and Janowitz, 1964). Some of the more sophisticated behaviourists, especially those in the Hullian tradition (Dollard and Miller, 1950) have utilized this partial view of the person, uniting the conditioning ideas of Pavlov and Thorndike with the dynamic ideas of Freud, to explain imitation, personality development, and psychotherapeutic effects.

10. *The ego-defensive theories.* The theories considered here emphasize the person as functioning to maintain an acceptable self-concept, by selectively perceiving, distorting, forgetting, or fabricating one's past behaviour, the current situation, or future expectations as necessary. These theories also derive their inspiration from psychoanalytic sources (from the later ego-psychologists rather than the orthodox Freudians).

A classic example of the use of the ego-defensive notions in social psychology is the work by Adorno *et al.* (1950) on the authoritarian personality, attempting to account for a syndrome of subservience to authority and hostility to social outgroups in terms of the authoritarian person's Oedipal resolution. To defend themselves against awareness of their hostility to their fathers, such people used reaction formation involving idealizing their fathers and other authority figures in the society, bolstering this apotheosis of those in power with low regard and hostility towards atypical or peripheral groups in society. The ego-defensive concept also lies behind the functional approach to attitude change developed by Katz (1960) and his co-workers (Sarnoff, McClintock, etc.) which suggests the efficacy of self-insight versus informational approaches to changing attitudes.

11. *The expressive theories.* The expressive (cathartic, acting out) guiding idea focuses on the person as obtaining gratification or release through acting out and self-expression. On the physiological plane, physical exertion in the form of exercise, strenuous sport, jogging, mountain climbing, etc., can yield joy and release. On the psychological plane, one can obtain comparable rewards through expressing one's feelings and beliefs. Some existentialists would posit an ontological basis for this acting-out tendency, asserting that being follows acting, so that we must act in order to exist, creating our essence by our choices and actions. Others utilize the expressive theories on a more *ad hoc* basis, pointing out that it is lovely to be in love or that there are those whom we love to hate.

This cathartic view of human nature goes back at least to Aristotle's aesthetic theory of the gratification to be derived from witnessing dramatic tragedies, a position still argued, though rather unsuccessfully (Green and Quanty, 1977), as a social justification for televised violence. The reward value of action is especially apparent in childhood: In their concept of functional pleasure the Bühlers, as well as Piaget, have stressed the pleasure that children derive from exercising their capacities. Comparative psychologists have found it useful to postulate a need for activity in non-human mammals, and the human need for play has been suggested as a foundation of creativity by Peckham and as a basis for normality by Huizinga and Leont'ev. Theorists emphasizing the appeal of arousal and activation are also inspired by this concept of the person, e.g., Arnold, Peak, or Berlyne (1969).

12. *The habituation theories*. The partial views of human nature which we here call "habituation" theories are also known as behaviouristic, learning, stimulus–response, repetition, reinforcement, contiguity, familiarity, etc. theories. Their basic notion is that in any situation the person tends to respond with activities similar to those elicited when the person was previously in a similar situation. Most of such formulations are reinforcement theories: they require that previous performance of the response in comparable situations had been rewarded for its subsequent reoccurrence to become more likely. Unrewarded stimulus–response pairings, far from becoming increasingly probable, tend to extinguish themselves. However, also included within this formulation are the "contiguity" theorists who postulate that a given response becomes increasingly likely with successive performances within a similar cue situation even without reinforcement.

Theorists of this habituation orientation have derived their inspiration from the conditioning research of Pavlov and Thorndike, which was transmitted to the educated laity by J. B. Watson and formulated into relatively intricate systems by Skinner, Hull, Tolman, and their followers. Contiguity theorists derive from Guthrie, Estes, and various mathematical formulations involving one-trial learning or stimulus sampling. Doob's (1947) work on the behaviour of attitudes, the work of Dollard *et al.* (1939) on frustration and aggression, and Miller and Dollard's (1941) work on social learning and imitation apply these habituation notions to social psychological topics.

4. Four affective growth theories

The final tetrad of theories to be considered (depicted in the lower-right quadrant of Table I), like the four discussed above, depict the person as tending towards a satisfying affective (rather than cognitive) state. They differ from the previous four in postulating tendencies towards affective growth and enhancement rather than towards moderation and stability. This final tetrad of guiding-idea theories will be taken up in a sequence corresponding to that used for the previous three tetrads.

13. *The assertion theories.* This set of theories derives inspiration from social philosophers like Hobbes and Nietzsche who stressed the self-aggrandizing needs of the person and concepts such as egotism, power, and mastery. The person is viewed as achievement-oriented and as seeking success, mastery over difficulties, and superiority. Rather than passing peacefully through life, the person is depicted as wanting to make a difference, to give meaning to his or her life by leaving a mark upon the world. Sometimes there is an additional interpersonal aspect of the formulation when it is stressed that the person strives for his or her attainment to be recognized by others, and sometimes there is the competitive note of wanting to outdo others or gain dominance and power over them.

This concept of the person as fundamentally power-oriented was the dominant theme in the most socially oriented of the Viennese analysts, Alfred Adler. Although Adler has not had the impact on social psychology of his colleagues, Freud and Jung, his concepts of inferiority, overcompensation, the need for power, sibling order, etc. seem as deserving of a revival as that experienced by the contemporaneous Jungian concepts. The notion of the person as achievement-oriented has been quite useful in the study of personality and motivation by McClelland (1975), Weiner (1974), Tevan and others. This partial view of the person had also inspired the thinking of Spencer and the social Darwinists, with more recent impact on some of the ethologists such as Lorenz, giving rise to the "naked ape" concept of the person as predatory (much stressed lately by popular writers such as Morris, Ardrey, and Tiger and Fox).

14. *The role-playing theories.* The formulations grouped here essentially represent the person as oriented towards accruing an identity. The person is depicted as acting on a need for self-expansion (or self-creation), enhancing the self by creating a fuller identity through the acquisition of distinctive thoughts, feelings, styles and behaviours. In this way the person acquires a sense of self that gives a feeling of worth and guides behaviour.

This depiction of the person as an identity accruer is a central concept of role theorists such as Linton, Newcomb, Sarbin, and Allen. In recent years it has been popularized by Erikson (1968) in his notion of an identity crisis occurring during the adolescent period of psychosocial development. Reference group theorists such as Hyman and Sherif deal with the human tendency to enhance self-identity through added group memberships. A number of Goffman's concepts, e.g. altercasting and self-presentation, make clever use of this view of human nature; ethnomethodologists such as Garfinkel and symbolic interactionists such as Blumer also make use of this role-playing concept of the person.

15. *The affiliative theories.* Theorists who make creative use of the affiliative concept of the person stress the human yearning to win the affection of others and to be accepted and loved. Although it may be more effective to be feared than loved, it feels better to be loved than feared. The person is viewed as having a gregarious aspect such that simply being with others is pleasant, though further gratification is attained from interacting with people and from receiving from them signs that one is accepted and that one's liking is reciprocated.

This partial view of human nature received considerable emphasis in the early twentieth century from social theorists such as Ribot, Giddings, McDougal, and Sorokin. In more recent years, it has inspired a vast outpouring of social psychological research on interpersonal attraction by Byrne, Berscheid and Walster (1978), Rubin, etc. Extension of the affiliative concept to the further notion of the human as basically altruistic and helping, advocated by Kropotkin, Sorokin, and other social philosophers earlier in the century, has likewise evoked a flood of experimental social research on helping behaviour and other forms of altruism by Berkowitz, Latané and Darley, Rodin, Piliavin, Wilson, Staub (1979), etc. Even evolutionary theorists, in the past more likely to utilize the opposite "assertion" notions (number 13), have recently, in the "sociobiology" movement (Wilson, 1978), been proposing genetic bases for human altruism.

16. *The facilitation theories.* The views included here are also known by other names such as imitative, social learning, modelling, etc. theories. They stress the person as tending to empathize with others, adopting the feelings, styles, and behaviours of those with whom they come into contact. The strong form of this notion is that people (and also social animals) have an inherent suggestibility, a compulsion to imitate and match others' behaviour and to empathize with their feelings. A milder version, advocated by theorists with a behaviouristic orientation, depicts the tendency to match or model behaviour of others as deriving from previous reinforcement experiences rather than from innate proclivity.

This view of the person as imitator was particularly stressed in France at the turn of the century by such social theorists as LeBon, Binet,

Charcot, Janet, and Bernheim. Most considered suggestibility to be a general human trait, though a few regarded it as a special pathological state found primarily in hysterics. By mid-century the notion of imitative behaviour or a modelling tendency as a basic aspect of the social person, was being derived by the behaviouristic theorists from the nature of the organism and the conditions of society, e.g., Miller and Dollard (1941). In more recent years the social learning theorists have become particularly provocative in using this formulation (Bandura, 1977) to develop the mode of treatment known as behavioural therapy (Gambrill, 1977).

C. SOCIAL PSYCHOLOGY THEORIZING AS PROCESS

Theory, like thought in general, involves both process and product, both the act of theorizing and the theoretical representation of reality which it produces. The discussion of the development of theory in social psychology in this chapter should deal with both of these aspects. In the previous section we considered theory as product, first mentioning the "systems theories" (which are unfortunately neglected in social psychology) and then describing 16 commonly used guiding-idea theories. Here we turn to the other aspect, theory as process, describing the two main ingredients in the process of theorizing, creative thinking and empirical observation. As product, research guides theory; as process, theory guides research.

1. Creative generating of theories

Neglect of the creative, theory-generating aspect of research has been a serious shortcoming in discussions of psychological methodology, both in print and in the classroom. Although methodology has received due attention—in many doctoral programmes in psychology the only required courses are in methodology—it is invariably focused on the critical, theory-testing aspects of research, covering topics such as measurement, experimental design, and statistical analysis. Since to test a theory you must first have one, this gives our treatment of methodology the sound of one hand clapping and perhaps the wrong hand at that. We have argued elsewhere (McGuire, 1973) that this peculiar neglect is probably not due to psychologists' failure to recognize the importance of creative hypothesis-generating but rather to a feeling that creativity cannot be taught or even described. Whilst we agree that creativity derives from many sources, some of which are hard to describe and even harder to teach, we argue that one teachable factor that facilitates creativity is having at one's disposal various creative heuristics, in the form of tricks of thought and approaches to inquiry, that lead to the discovery of solutions (and, what may be more important, of problems).

Acquaintance with the wide range of creative heuristics used for theory-generating by other researchers in one's field could well expand one's own level of functioning. We examined the thought processes that lay behind a number of productive lines of research in social psychology and described nine such creative heuristics (McGuire, 1973), a little later expanding the list to over 40 (McGuire, 1975) divided among five types of creative approaches. To stay within present space allowance we shall limit their presentation here to Table II, which shows the five types of approaches to theory generating, listing under each four creative heuristics as illustrative; and to a discussion in the text of several examples of the first listed illustrative heuristic of each type.

Using "analysis of paradoxical incidents" to illustrate the first type of technique (the analysis of naturally occurring events), several examples can be offered of its use as a theory-generating heuristic in social psychology. For example, Bettelheim conceptualized the "identification with the aggressor" psychodynamics (a role-playing guiding-idea theory) to account for the peculiarity he observed in the National Socialist concentration camp at Dachau, where some inmates began to adopt the mannerisms of the guards they hated and feared. Again, Festinger's dissonance theory (a consistency guiding-idea theory) derives in part from his study of rumours in accounting for the oddity that, following disasters, several studies showed that the rumours that sprang up among the victims, rather than being of a type that might bring badly needed hope or solace, tended to predict that further disasters were about to befall them.

As an illustration of the second type of approach (simple direct conceptual analysis) the creative heuristic of extending an obtained relationship to the point where it becomes implausible can serve as an illustration. For example, a positive relationship is usually reported between the amount of eye contact and interpersonal liking, and this holds within the normal range of looking; but

Table II. Examples of five classes of creative heuristics used by social psychologists to generate theories and hypotheses.

A. *Techniques involving analysis of naturally occurring events*
   1. Account for paradoxical incidents
   2. Intensive case analysis
   3. Collect practitioners' rules of thumb
   4. Participant observation
B. *Techniques involving simple direct conceptual analysis*
   1. Project an obtained relationship to a point where it becomes implausible
   2. Account for the opposite of a common-sense hypothesis
   3. Explore the limits
   4. Mentally reduce the factor to zero in a given situation
C. *Techniques involving complex mediated conceptual analysis*
   1. Posit multiple mediators for a known relationship
   2. Generate and organize a list
   3. Analogy
   4. Hypothetico-deductive method
D. *Techniques involving analysing outcome of previous research*
   1. Analyse complex relationships into simpler component processes
   2. Reconcile seemingly conflicting outcomes
   3. Deviant case analysis
   4. Interpret serendipitous interaction effects
E. *Techniques involving collection of new data*
   1. Allow open-ended responses and do content analysis
   2. Multivariate fishing expedition
   3. Add independent variables for exploratory interactions
   4. Mathematical modelling

as eye contact becomes excessive, the relationship reverses and prolonged eye contact is perceived as hostility, suggesting a more complex analysis of the processes underlying this and other forms of communicating intimacy non-verbally.

The creative heuristic we described above as used to discover our 16 types of guiding-idea theories, that is, generating and organizing a list, would serve to illustrate the third type of approach (complex mediated conceptual analysis). But for the sake of a new illustration, we shall use the heuristic of generating multiple mediators for an obtained relationship. Researchers should not stop at one or two explanations of an obtained relationship, though empirical research is typically so demanding as to confine one to examining experimentally the implications of only one explanation. For example, when Hovland and his colleagues discovered a delayed action effect of persuasive communications, while they pursued experimentally only one "discounting cue" mediator, they did discuss at least half a dozen additional theoretical factors that might be involved. Likewise McGuire, in accounting for the paradox that forewarning of an impending persuasive attack may actually weaken resistance to that attack, experimentally examined only his "anticipatory change" explanation but did suggest half a dozen additional possible theoretical mediators.

To illustrate the fourth type of creative approach (examining the outcomes of previous research) the heuristic of analysing complexly shaped obtained relationships into simpler component processes will serve. An example is McGuire's analysis of the nonmonotonic inverted-U-shaped relation between many personality variables and susceptibility to social influence into two underlying monotonic relationships, the personality variable's relationship to reception and to yielding. The fifth type (involving the collection of new data) can be illustrated by the heuristic of approaching the research participant with a lower profile, allowing open-ended responses which are harder to analyse because of the richness of the information they contain. An example is McGuire's content analysis of responses to open-ended probes like "Tell us about yourself" to elicit information about the self-concept that structured response alternatives would have lost; or Piaget's free-response tasks that allow analyses of the type of techniques used or errors made by the participants, rather than simply counting the number of correct responses.

2. The role of empirical observation in the development of social psychological theories

For over a decade I have been arguing (McGuire, 1967, 1969, 1973) that a drastic change is needed in the Establishment view of the social psychological research process, particularly as regards the interrelation of theoretical hypotheses to the empirical observations brought to bear upon them. The Logical Empiricism paradigm stemming from the Vienna circle was a useful corrective when first formulated and served social psychology well during the middle half of the twentieth century, but it has outlived its usefulness and is now distorting research and hence should be replaced with a new approach which I call "Constructivism." We shall first mention three earlier paradigms that preceded

Logical Empiricism regarding the role of observation in the validation of theory, then discuss Logical Empiricism itself, and finally describe the new Constructivist approach that we are proposing for the 1980s.

Three earlier paradigms: Dogmatism, Rationalism, and Positivism. Despite my criticism of the Logical Empiricism paradigm as having outlived its usefulness, it should be appreciated as an intellectual triumph, a great leap forward over predecessor paradigms, as was each of the three paradigms that preceded it in dominating Western theorizing since the Classical period. For roughly the first thousand years of the Common Era a paradigm that might be called "Dogmatism" prevailed among the intelligentsia. A Paul of Tarsus or Augustine of Hippo would evaluate the truth of a theory by examining the extent to which the hypotheses derived from it coincided with the accepted doctrines derived from Judaeo-Christian scriptures or the teaching office of the Church. Dogmatism still prevails in some ecclesiastical circles and perhaps also among Marxist-Leninists and Freudians of the strict observance. It should be appreciated that Dogmatism does not ignore empirical observation; on the contrary it asserts that the dogmatically asserted doctrines are in accord with the nature of observed reality.

About a thousand years ago there began to develop a new "Rationalism" paradigm regarding how theories and hypotheses are to be evaluated. Perhaps Abelard's *Sic et Non* serves as a marker event in the emergence of this new view, in having demonstrated that the Scripture and tradition contain mutually contradictory assertions about the same issue. The medieval Schoolmen developed the Rationalism paradigm of constructing an organized body of knowledge consisting of self-evident or firmly established inductive postulates from which were deduced theorems bearing on the significant aspects of human experience. In this Rationalistic period, theories and hypotheses were evaluated in terms of their deducibility from elaborate systems of thought such as the *Summa Theologica* of St Thomas Aquinas, an intellectual Gothic cathedral as flamboyant and beautiful as its contemporaries in stone.

Three centuries ago the opening of the European mind produced by voyages of discovery, geographic and speculative, gave rise to the dramatically different "Positivism" paradigm. Long before, some thinkers, like William of Occam, repelled by the rococo embellishments of medieval Rationalist systems, had already begun to wield their razors against the unnecessary multiplication of being, but it was only in the seventeenth century that thinkers like Francis Bacon turned Duns Scotus on his head and replaced the deductive Rationalistic paradigm with the inductive paradigm of Positivism. By the nineteenth century, thinkers such as the British empiricists, Comte, and Spencer had established that theories should be developed inductively. The scientist should observe phenomena with an open mind, note regularities, and induce a general principle that described these regularities, broader theories then being developed to integrate these inductively derived principles.

Logical Empiricism. Fifty years ago in the disturbed but creative social environment of post-Habsburg Vienna, a group of physical scientists, mathematicians, and philosophers hammered out the new Logical Empiricism paradigm regarding the relation between theory and observation; scarcely a decade after its formation, the brutal fist of National Socialism crashed into the Wienerkreis, scattering its members and insights into more hospitable intellectual circles. By the 1940s Logical Empiricism had become the Establishment paradigm for psychological research, an hegemony which persists to the present day.

In this thousand-year evolution of the understanding of the relationship between theory and observation, Logical Empiricism constituted a particularly significant advance. Whereas its Positivistic predecessor had radically parted company with the Rationalism that preceded it (reacting to the Rationalists' extreme deductivism with its own radical inductivism), the Logical Empiricist revolution deftly integrated the insights of the two previous paradigms. Logical Empiricists accept the Rationalist notion that the hypothesis (and the broader theory from which it is derived) precedes and guides the design and conduct of the empirical confrontation. But if they give deductive theory the first word, the Logical Empiricists give empirical observation, so stressed by the Positivists, the last word in holding that the theory has validity, and even meaning, only insofar as its derived hypotheses are testable and the predicted relationships between operationally defined variables survive the jeopardy of an empirical test.

Since the acceptance of Logical Empiricism, the teacher has taught and the student learned that social psychology progresses when we have a theory from which we derive a testable hypothesis, which is then put to a test and the theory accepted or rejected depending on the outcome of this test.

The Constructivist Approach. The new Constructivist position that I am advocating as a replacement for Logical Empiricism agrees with the latter (against an extreme inductivist positivism) that a guiding-idea or systems theory should precede the empirical work and direct the observations. Constructivism and Logical Empiricism also agree that in science the theory must be subjected to empirical confrontation, as contrasted with artistic or humanistic undertakings that are more concerned with depicting or analysing the theoretical insight. These latter endeavours are not without value, but scientific studies require that we go beyond formulating our theories to developing them through interaction with empirical observations.

Where Constructivism differs from Logical Empiricism is in the function ascribed to this empirical confrontation: Logical Empiricism asserts that the purpose of the empirical work is to test the theory; Constructivism asserts that its purpose is to construct the theory by making its meaning, limitations, hidden assumptions and implications clearer to oneself and others. Logical Empiricism contends that some theories are right and others are wrong and that the function of the empirical work is to test which of the opposed theories is right; Constructivism asserts that each of the different theories is right and that the empirical work reveals the conditions under which each is true.

The difference between the two paradigms can be clarified by an example. Let us suppose that the social psychologist is studying interpersonal attraction. If the researcher is either a consistency theorist or a reinforcement theorist (1 or 12 in Table I) he or she could derive the hypothesis that one's liking for others is a direct function of the other's similarity to oneself. According to Logical Empiricism, the researcher then puts the hypothesis to an empirical test, measuring the participants' similarity to each of their acquaintances and their liking for each acquaintance; if a sizable positive correlation is found between similarity and liking, the theorist gains confidence in the hypothesis; if a significant positive correlation is not found, the researcher rejects the hypothesis and presumably the theory from which it is derived.

While the researcher, brought up as a Logical Empiricist, may claim and even believe that he/she proceeds in this manner, the actual process is (and deserves to be) quite different. More typically, the social psychologist who has formulated the hypothesis that people prefer those who are most like themselves then proceeds by doing thought experiments and perhaps some prestudies to "get control over the variables";

that is, the scientist mulls over the hypothesis and tries out empirical test situations until he or she gets the conditions right. If, after these efforts, one still gets "negative results", one does not reject the hypothesis, much less the theory from which it is derived; nor does one publish these disconfirmations (receiving more than a little help from unenthusiastic editors in this silence). Rather than abandon the hypothesis or the theory, the scientist typically concludes that something is wrong with the empirical test and either tries again or gives up the line of work until more suitable procedures come to hand. In describing the actual scientific process I am not being critical; on the contrary, I think that this general procedure is the one that should be followed. The error and loss of information result from our failing to admit and to exploit our following this investigatory procedure, due to our being embarrassed by its sounding sloppy and in violation of the Logical Empiricist rules of the testing game.

The alternative Constructivist paradigm can be introduced by the outrageous assertion that it supposes that all hypotheses are true: in Blake's words, "Everything possible to be believ'd is an image of truth". That is to say, if a reasonable person guided by some plausible theory formulates the hypothesis that people like best those most similar to themselves, then it should be accepted that *ipso facto* the hypothesis is true. But so would the opposite hypothesis be true if it also could be derived by a reasonable researcher from a plausible theory. For example, in the case of the relationship between interpersonal similarity and attraction, the opposite prediction, that people most like those who are dissimilar to themselves, could be derived from a number of the other guiding-idea theories shown in Table I (such as 7. Stimulation, 13. Assertion, or 14. Role-playing).

The assertion of Constructivism that the two opposite predictions are both true, that interpersonal attraction increases both with similarity and dissimilarity, is not denying the principle of contradiction. Rather, it is a recognition of the limitations of knowledge, whether informal or formalized in theory, such that any depiction of the interrelations among variables will be an imperfect oversimplification, which obtains only partially and under limited circumstances. Hence, considering the derivation of each prediction from plausible guiding-idea theories, it is almost surely true that under some circumstances a person will like acquaintances more because they are similar to oneself in certain ways; while the same or another person will, under other circumstances or in other ways, show the opposite tendency of liking better those most dissimilar to oneself. Of course, one of the opposed formulations may have a wider range of ecological validity than the other. According to the Constructivist paradigm, the role of the empirical side of science is not to test which of the opposite formulations is valid but rather to explore and discover the range of circumstances in which each of the opposite formulations holds.

Hence, it is quite appropriate that the scientist proceed in the "sloppy" manner described above, doing thought experiments, exploratory studies, trying out different kinds of subjects, procedures, response tasks, etc., until it becomes clearer under what circumstances each of the opposed relationships obtains. The present fault lies not in proceeding in this open-minded way but rather in not proceeding strenuously enough in this way and in not having the courage to report the process fully, exploiting adequately the valuable information so obtained. Within the Constructivist paradigm, whenever one derives a certain hypothesis from one's theoretical position, one should also posit the opposite hypothesis and grasp the alternative theoretical position from which this opposite hypothesis can be derived (a procedure urged and used creatively by Simone Weil). The thought experiments and the prestudies should be appreciated for their true worth and elevated to a formal series of investigations that would make clear the different sets of circumstances under which the one and the opposite hypotheses obtain. In publishing one's research, one would report this more catholic thinking and bilateral series of investigations, not to establish which of the opposite hypotheses is valid but rather to describe the circumstances under which each is valid.

Maintaining the fiction of Logical Empiricism rather than the reality of Constructivism has deleterious effects on publication and morale. As regards publication, the sanitized journal articles now prescribed by the Logical Empiricist paradigm require suppressing the most informative part of the research, namely, those initial "explorations" (in armchair or laboratory or field) that uncover the information as to when a specific hypothesis "works" or does not work. If the implications of Constructivism were better appreciated, the researcher and the editor, rather than engaging in this suppressive *folie à deux*, would conduct and publish systematic investigations that clarify the meaning of the opposite hypotheses and the conditions of validity for each. There would also be a gain in research morale, since the corrupting need to describe the work as if it followed the Logical Empiricist prescription (and, worse still, to believe that it does) would be obviated. The social psychologist, rather than being forced into the current alienating position, could put aside guilt and proceed with zest in giving full reign to theoretical insights into the complexities of reality. More confident and centred in our work, we could better appreciate and make more productive use of the full information contained in our alternative theories and of their vicissitudes when exposed to concrete observable confrontations.

ACKNOWLEDGEMENT

The writing of this chapter was greatly facilitated by support received from the Social Science Section. Behavioral Science Research Branch. National Institute of Mental Health (Department of Health, Education and Welfare).

4
The Development of Applied Social Psychology

MICHAEL ARGYLE
Department of Experimental Psychology, University of Oxford

A. The history of applied social psychology	82
B. The importance of applied social psychology	85
C. Examples of applied social psychology	87
1. Industry	87
2. Intergroup contact and racial attitudes	89
3. Mental health	90
4. Attitude change via the mass media	91
5. Training teachers in social skills	93
6. Video-mediated communication systems	93
7. Environmental design	94
8. Everyday life	95
D. Research which could be applied, but which has not been	96
E. Wrongly applied research	97
F. The different routes from research to application	99
G. Summary	106

By applied social psychology I mean the adoption in real-life settings of new or modified practices which are based on social psychological research, methods or ideas. In this chapter I shall concentrate a subdivision of this—new or modified practices which have been shown to be beneficial and I shall give examples of this kind of research from a number of fields. I shall also discuss research which could be applied, but has not been, and research which has been applied, but should not have been, because the changed practices have not in fact been beneficial. Finally I shall discuss how research comes to be applied, and the routes from research to its application.

A. THE HISTORY OF APPLIED SOCIAL PSYCHOLOGY

In the period before World War II, social psychology in the U.S.A. was often carried out in field settings and was addressed to social problems—racial identity in black children, racial prejudice, resistance to propaganda, and job satisfaction, for example (see Hollander, 1978). During World War II, Lewin and his students introduced a number of new ideas and methods to the subject: important strands here were the fusion of theory and research, and the idea of action research. However, during the period 1950–1970, in the U.S.A., a split developed between academic social psychologists and those concerned with T-groups, industrial consultancy and other social problems. The academics saw themselves as pure scientists who could best study social behaviour in laboratory experiments, and they did not recognize the less precise work done in field settings (Deutsch and Hornstein, 1975).

Meanwhile a steady stream of research continued to be done in field settings into the causes and treatment of mental disorder and delinquency, a variety of industrial and educational problems, and the effects of the mass media. *The Handbook of Social Psychology* (Lindzey and Aronson, 1968) contained a whole volume on *Applications of Social Psychology*. However, most of this work fell outside what was regarded as mainstream social psychology, since it was not done by people who called themselves social psychologists and their findings were not reported in textbooks of social psychology. The only applications commonly mentioned in the textbooks were racial prejudice, the effects of mass media, and the effects of different kinds of leadership. On the other hand social psychologists have often believed that social psychology is capable of being applied, and have justified it on this basis.

"Mainstream" social psychology during this period was very definitely not about applied problems. It consisted mostly of rather artificial, sometimes rather absurd, laboratory experiments, testing hypotheses derived from dissonance theory, balance theory, exchange theory and similar theories. Typical experiments were about risky shift, the prisoner's dilemma game, and various forms of social influence. The American textbooks of the period contained no reference to applications of the subject (e.g. Jones and Gerard, 1967; McClintock, 1972; Insko and Schopler, 1972).

The strength of the work in this period was the skill and sophistication of the experiments and the precision with which carefully refined hypotheses were tested. It was extraordinary, however, that very similar experiments were repeated, with minor variations, so many times with no attempt to discover whether the phenomena (of the risky shift for example) held in the real world.

In 1970 Leo Meltzer tried to produce a book of readings on applied social psychology and wrote to 600 American social psychologists asking for suggestions for articles which might be included. His criteria were (1) the work should actually have been applied, (2) the changes effected must have been adequately evaluated by appropriate measurement, (3) the study must have been empirical, not exclusively theoretical or hortatory, and (4) the relation to theoretical or well known experimental paradigms in academic social psychology must be clear. However, of the 20% who replied three-fifths said that there was no such work in social psychology, e.g.

Renato Tagiuri: Professor of Business Administration, Harvard University: "No work I know of meets your well chosen criteria."
Fred L. Strodtbeck: Professor of Sociology, University of Chicago: "At the moment I'm at a loss to identify interventions made by social psychologists which had produced clear results predicted from sound theory."
Guy E. Swanson: Professor of Sociology, University of California, Berkeley: "I wish I could think of things that were obvious candidates for inclusion, but I can't. It seems to me that hardly anyone is doing the kind of things you have in mind."

(Meltzer, 1972).

Perhaps Meltzer's criteria were too stringent in that he demanded a clear relation to a theoretical or well-known experimental paradigm. I think that the explanation lies also in the kind of social psychology which was regarded as mainstream and which was reported in the textbooks at that period in the U.S.A.

In the 1930s the Society for the Psychological Study of Social Issues and the *Journal of Social Issues* were founded. Still an asymmetry remained: mainstream writers ignored this work, while applied social psychologists looked to and quoted the ideas of mainstream writers whenever they could find inspiration there. Some of the most widespread applications of American social psychology have been in the application of methods and measuring instruments, like the Semantic Differential and the Repertory Grid.

Since 1970 there have been a series of "crises" in social psychology.

In the U.S.A. one of the main concerns was the lack of external validity of much social psychology. Sociologists, students, and now social psychologists themselves were pointing out the triviality of much research, and more important, the possibility that the findings were actually wrong. This has led to a growth of research in field settings, e.g. on helping behaviour, aggression, and friendship-formation, but this was still of a rather trivial kind, for example research on helping people who collapse on the Métro, while no research was done on helping aged relatives or others in real need.

Social psychology in Europe developed later than that in the U.S.A., on a smaller scale, and largely based on it. The first systematic research in Britain was done shortly after World War II by the Tavistock Institute of Human Relations, into joint consultative committees and sociotechnical systems in industry (e.g. Jaques, 1951). This research was partly inspired by the University of Michigan group and involved the combination of theoretical research and application. However, when university-based social psychology developed in Britain, the work of the Tavistock was rejected on the grounds of being too psychoanalytic and not using acceptable research methods. Much of the university social psychology has been on applied problems, like the work on the effects of TV on children at the London School of Economics (Himmelweit et al., 1958) and the occupational research at Sheffield (e.g. Wall and Lischeron, 1977), or it was directly relevant to practical issues, like the inter-group relations work at Bristol (Tajfel, 1978) and the social skills work at Oxford (Argyle, 1978). The crisis in social psychology in Britain was partly about external validity and partly about the over-behaviouristic model of man which had been adopted (Harré and Secord, 1972). While this emphasis on conscious planning and verbal accountability provided a useful corrective to the earlier model of man offered by many social psychologists, it did not lead to any obvious form of application. It could be argued that the practical use of an idea provides a kind of second verification, not so much of its truth as of its importance. The "new paradigm" approach did, however, result at a later stage in the discovery of some practically useful findings in the field of rule-following.

Social psychology in continental Europe developed in a similar way. In Holland there was a lot of interest in industrial problems from the beginning; the main applied interest has now shifted to T-groups and clinical applications, and the crisis has focused on the relevance of social psychology. In Germany and Belgium social psychology has followed American ideas of the 1950–1970 era fairly closely, with relatively little interest in applied research, although in Germany there has been some criticism of this by Marxists. In France, too, American ideas have been followed, together with some rebellion against them on the grounds of external validity, and an infusion of ideas from Marxism. Moscovici and others have been interested in the application of social psychology to life, rather than more specific applications; examples are the study of the influence of minorities (Moscovici, 1976) and the role of social representations.

B. THE IMPORTANCE OF APPLIED SOCIAL PSYCHOLOGY

Many social psychologists went into the subject because of their concern for social problems; for them no justification of applied social psychology is needed. Governments and foundations also like this kind of social psychology and offer research funds to do it, because of the need to solve pressing social problems. Some of these problems are very pressing indeed—international conflict, industrial conflict, racial prejudice, delinquency of various kinds, mental disorder and falling standards of education, for example. These problems appear to fall to some extent into the sphere of social psychology, partly because relevant research methods now exist, and the problems are not being solved by anyone else.

Other social psychologists went into the subject because they wanted to understand social behaviour better, or because they wanted to develop a scientific analysis of it. Success has been achieved, on a rather limited scale, in the analysis of a very limited class of behaviour—that which can be observed in the laboratory or in the course of short encounters in public places. However, laboratory research may fail to include important variables. Hovland (1959) observed that laboratory and field studies of the effects of propaganda had produced rather different results. The percentage who were influenced by the propaganda in field studies was of the order of 5%, while in laboratory studies it was $30-50\%$. This was because in the field there are further processes operating, such as selective exposure and group pressures, and because less trivial attitudes are involved. The results of laboratory studies can be quite simply, wrong. Argyle and McHenry (1970) showed that the well-known effect of spectacles on perceived intelligence did not work if those judged were heard talking briefly.

Why, then, have most social psychologists avoided applied research? Why have textbook writers overlooked applied research? In the first place it is more difficult to do than laboratory research. It may be very hard to obtain permission from the various interested parties to do the research; this can take a lot of time and effort and may be unsuccessful in the end. It is difficult to find properly equated groups for comparison; uncontrolled variables are usually present. It is usually impossible to do experiments like those in laboratories. Campbell and Stanley (1963) have devised a number of quasi-experimental designs for research which enable statistical inferences of causal influence to be made without the manipulation of variables by the investigator. The most widely used of these has been the method of cross-lagged correlations in which correlations are calculated between pairs of variables measured at different times. This has been used in a number of industrial studies to disentangle the pattern of causation between variables such as style of supervision, job satisfaction and output (Clegg et al., 1977). Another of Campbell's methods is a way of analysing the effect of naturally occurring events by study of variations over time before and after them. Ross et al. (1970) found that the introduction of the breathalyser in Britain reduced the number of deaths on the road, especially during the four months after it was introduced. A different kind of field study is done with the collaboration of administrators, and it may be possible, as part of regular administration, to manipulate more important variables than a laboratory investigation can control.

Another factor which has kept some social psychologists from doing applied work has been concern with values. During the 1960s many psychologists were influenced by the student revolution and were simply not prepared to do any work for government or industry—or were under strong social pressures from students not to do so. This is no longer the case in the U.S.A. or Britain, or in most European universities. Some psychologists have felt uneasy about helping to "manipulate" other people, although education and therapy, of which they approve, could also be regarded as forms of manipulation. Others have been concerned about the goals which applied social psychology would help to realize. Most would be happy about preventing accidents and reducing crimes, but not all want to help with industrial problems, if this involves helping management or reducing industrial conflict. Some are even unwilling to improve mental health, since they regard this as adjusting people to an unjust social order. If one is going to be a consultant in some field of application, it becomes very difficult to pick and choose the acceptable cases. I have myself declined to help certain industrial firms with social skills training because I thought that their particular product was socially harmful, but for a professional consultant this kind of strategy would probably not be possible.

C. EXAMPLES OF APPLIED SOCIAL PSYCHOLOGY

In this section a number of examples of applied social psychology as defined above will be presented briefly. Some indication will be given both of the extent to which application has been made and of its effects on dependent variables where this is known. No attempt will be made to review the fields in question; this would require an entire book. (I produced a small book, at an earlier stage of the subject (Argyle 1964) and there is the *Handbook of Social Psychology*, vol. 5. Lindzey and Aronson, 1968).

1. Industry

Skills of first-line leaders. Research into this topic arose out of the early work by Lewin on boys' clubs. The original studies were carried out by Katz *et al*. (1951) and Halpin and Winer (1952) and were replicated and extended by others in many industries and cultures, including one by myself (Argyle *et al*., 1958). The basic findings were that certain supervisory skills produce more output, more job satisfaction, less absenteeism, and less labour turnover. These skills are (i) initiating structure—planning, scheduling, instructing, checking, etc., but with a light touch; (ii) consideration (employee-centredness)—looking after the needs of subordinates; and (iii) democratic-persuasive skills. The main revision which has been needed is that more account needs to be taken of specific work-flow systems in defining the optimim skills (Thurley and Wirdenius, 1973). These skills have been widely, indeed universally, applied, via training courses for foremen and managers, throughout North America, Britain, Europe and beyond. The effects of using these skills have been shown in a number of studies. The effects on output are very variable and fairly small if work is machine-paced, but work can stop altogether under the worst skills. Absenteeism and labour turnover can drop to a fifth under the best supervisory skills (Argyle, 1972).

Increasing achievement behaviour of managers. McClelland had previously carried out a lot of laboratory research into the nature, origins, and effects of achievement motivation. He also found a relationship between the rate of economic growth in a country and measures of the level of achievement motivation in its children a few years earlier. He applied these findings in attempts to raise economic activity in under-developed countries by stimulating the achievement motivation of managers. The best documented case is India, where McClelland and Winter (1969) held a number of ten-day courses for managers. These courses trained managers to recognize achievement thinking; they practised creative problem-solving, risk-taking, and the setting of realistic goals, in the context of business games and in connection with their own lives. A variety of achievement-oriented exercises were used. Measures were obtained for the two-year period before the course and the two-year period after the course for 76 managers who were trained and 73 who were not.

The results are very striking. The trained managers started more new businesses after than before (22% v. 4%), while the controls did not (8% v. 7%). The trained managers invested more capital in their businesses after than before (24,030 v. 6680 rupees), while the controls did not (12,190 v. 16,240 rupees). There was a greater percentage increase in the number of workers employed during the 2 years after the course than before (5·86% v. 1·46%) but not much for controls (2·74% v. 1·14%). The trained managers also worked longer hours, and the gross incomes of their firms were greater.

It is reported that more courses of this kind continue to be run in India, but there is no information about the wider consequences. Similar courses have been run in Indonesia, but it is reported that these have been less successful (Jaspars, personal communication).

"Industrial democracy". There have been many studies of the effects of introducing joint consultative committees of various kinds. Recent studies at Sheffield have shown that increased participation results in improved relations between managers and workers, in better decision-taking, and in less absenteeism and lower staff turnover (Wall and Lischeron, 1977). Earlier studies had shown increases in productivity.

Various forms of industrial democracy have been introduced in Yugoslavia (where it is universal), West Germany (introduced by the British in 1947, with worker-directors), Israel, Norway, and in many American and British firms. Although positive results have been reported in a number of studies in different parts of the world (Blumberg, 1968), some observers of the scene are critical of these results. Mulder (1971) argued that there was no real increase in the participation in decisions of lower status members of organizations, since the managers had greater expertise.

However, research has found that the benefits of industrial democracy are most likely to be obtained under the following conditions. Management should be in favour of the scheme, take it seriously, see that issues are properly discussed on the committees, and should not just rush through their carefully prepared plans. The committees are taken more seriously by management and workers if they have real power and are more than advisory bodies—as they have been in most of the British schemes. It is interesting that in two of the most successful schemes—the Yugoslav one and the American Scanlon plan—the committees decide the level of bonus payment. All levels in the hierarchy should be represented, not just the top and the bottom. Supervisors need to be of a higher calibre, since they are likely to be short-circuited by complaints to committees. Their formal power is slightly reduced, and they need additional skills of persuasion and consideration. Representatives should sit on committees which deal with matters that they are able and willing to discuss. A number of studies have found that employees are keener to participate in decisions about their own departments than about company affairs. Where there is a strong trade union it should be closely involved, for example by shop-stewards serving as representatives. Otherwise the new committee structure can act as a substitute for the unions, as in Yugoslavia (Argyle, 1972).

2. Inter-group contact and racial attitudes

A number of experimental field studies have shown that increased social contact with members of a minority group will lead to reduced prejudice under certain conditions. In one of the earliest studies, mixed black and white companies were formed in the American Army during World War II. Although many of those involved were initially opposed to this practice, up to 80% were in favour afterwards, especially in the more closely integrated units, and were found to be much less prejudiced towards members of the other group (Star *et al.*, 1950). This led to numerous other American studies, of the effects of mixed black and white groups at work, on housing estates, and elsewhere. Desegregation leads to reduced prejudice under the following conditions: (a) equal status contact, (b) co-operative relations, e.g. at work, (c) a common threat, e.g. in the Army, (d) social norms in favour of friendly relationships between the groups, (e) minority group members who are helpful in the situation, and who do not fit stereotypes, e.g. of laziness or aggressiveness. In the U.S. Army research only 80% were pro-black afterwards, and it has usually been found that a minority are unaffected by the experience, or are more prejudiced (Cook, 1970). This kind of research has been one of the influences behind desegregation, especially in the U.S.A., in education, work, housing, and elsewhere. It is impossible to say what the effects have been on a national scale. The racial attitudes of white Americans were becoming much more favourable over the period 1950–1964, when black politics suddenly took a more militant form, and there was widespread separation of blacks and whites, especially in housing, accompanied by the rather aggressive adoption of black styles of speech and appearance.

3. Mental health

Social skills training (SST) for neurotic patients. The British version of SST arose out of social interaction research, e.g. into non-verbal communication, person perception, analysis of conversations, etc. It was found that about a third of neurotics had inadequate social skills and could be trained by role-playing and related methods (Trower, Bryant and Argyle, 1978). There are several American versions of SST which have been used with patients. The most widely used is assertiveness training, in which patients are encouraged to take the initiative, in making friends and dealing with other situations (Rich and Schroeder, 1976). SST is now widely used in North America for neurotic patients and prisoners. It is increasingly being used in British hospitals, prisons, and in adolescent units. Follow-up studies show that SST is somewhat more effective than any other form of treatment for socially inadequate patients, though the difference is not very great.

Therapeutic communities (milieu treatment) for psychotics. Maxwell Jones (1952) designed these communities to avoid the "institutionalizing" effects of ordinary mental hospitals in which patients may become completely dependent on the hospital and lose touch with the outside world. It was planned, in addition, to give patients some preparation for life outside by providing them with regular work and giving them some responsibility. The usual ingredients are a sheltered workshop, daily meetings at which reports are made about the previous twenty-four hours and community decisions are taken, and nurses and doctors out of uniform who adopt a similar status to the patients. Expeditions are encouraged, and the hospital is frequently open to visitors. These general principles have been extensively followed in other hospitals, though usually in a rather watered-down form.

There have been a number of experimental comparisons of milieu therapy and more traditional regimes, showing that milieu treatment is somewhat more successful than traditional methods, for emotionally disturbed children, delinquents, psychotics and geriatric patients (e.g. Fairweather *et al.*, 1969; Rapoport, 1960). However, not all communities have been equally successful, and in some cases the results have been disastrous.

It has also been found, in a number of studies, that for psychotic patients the most effective form of treatment is a combination of drugs and milieu treatment (e.g. May, 1968).

4. Attitude change via the mass media

This must be one of the most extensive fields of application of social psychological research—in commercial advertising, political propaganda, government persuasion, and elsewhere. There is a great deal of research, and the main principles of mass persuasion as found in laboratory and field experiments are now familiar, e.g.

1. Gain and keep the attention of the audience;
2. Repetition of the message increases the effect; this, however, quickly reaches an upper limit;
3. It has usually been found that anxiety arousal produces more attitude change;
4. Emotional appeals have often been found to be more effective than logical ones;
5. The message should show how the product or desired action will gratify a need which has been aroused; this includes offering a new self-image;

6. Drawing conclusions is more effective than leaving this to the receiver;
7. Refuting counter-arguments inoculates the receiver against later attempts to change his attitudes;
8. The order of the message should be: attract attention and establish confidence, arouse motivation, present positive case, deal with objections, and draw conclusions, e.g. for specific action wanted;
9. Use of non-verbal messages, which assert, for example that a certain kind of person uses the brand being promoted;
10. Use a speaker who is apparently expert, credible, or attractive in other ways (cf. Jaspars, 1978).

In addition to the application of these principles, various research techniques are widely used in the design of persuasive messages. One of these is the use of Semantic Differentials or Repertory Grids to discover the "brand image" of the product, revealing the negative features that need to be modified by the message. The same methods followed by factor analysis show the main dimensions and concepts used by consumers, and hence the words which should be used in the message (Lunn, 1968). The messages are then tested either with invited audiences in cinemas or by comparing the effects of different advertisements in different parts of the country (Brown *et al.*, 1966).

There have been numerous follow-up studies of the effects of applying these principles. A number of specific advertising campaigns have been very successful. In 1959 the British Conservative Party used an advertising company for the first time; the campaign focused on changing the brand image of the party from being primarily a middle class party. This brand image was changed, as later surveys showed, and there was a very large shift to the Conservative party, which won the election (Butler and Rose, 1960). However, this degree of success is unusual, since there is usually a lot of effective propaganda on both sides in an election. Indeed some authorities on attitude change are unimpressed by the evidence for the effects of the media. "The outcome (of this research) has been quite embarrassing for proponents of the mass media, since there is little evidence of attitude change, much less change in gross behaviour such as buying or voting." (McGuire, 1969, p. 227.) It follows that much of the $20,000,000,000 spent in the U.S.A. (in 1960) was wasted. It is recognized, however, that the media may work in other ways—such as solidifying existing preferences and operating at second-hand on the acquaintances of recipients.

5. Training teachers in social skills

Research on teaching skills has shown that certain kinds of teacher behaviour are regularly associated with higher levels of learning and academic achievement on the part of pupils. The most effective teacher behaviours are:
1. Warmth;
2. Use of praise, approval, or other rewards;
3. Use of criticism (negative);
4. Enthusiasm;
5. Use and development of pupils' ideas;
6. Illustration of principles with examples;
7. Clarity of explanation;
8. Asking higher-order questions, requiring explanations, reasons, and problem-solving;
9. Structuring of lesson, i.e. explanation of plan of lesson at beginning or end;
10. Efficient organization of lessons;
11. Teacher being task-oriented, businesslike, achievement-oriented, encouraging focus on intellectual growth;
12. Flexible, varied style of teaching, variety of classroom materials and activities.

(cf. Rosenshine, 1971).

These principles are now incorporated in "microteaching" programmes in many teacher training colleges. The procedure is as follows: (a) one of the areas is explained and a demonstration given, or a videotape is shown ("modelling"); (b) the teacher teaches a prepared lesson of 5–10 minutes to 5–6 children ("role-playing"); (c) the video tape recording of this session is played back and discussed with the trainee teacher ("feedback"); (d) the lesson is repeated ("reteaching"). This method of training has been found to be very successful; it is equivalent to a much longer period of classroom practice and is better at getting rid of bad teaching habits (Brown, 1975).

6. Video-mediated communication systems

Research on the design and value of video-mediated or "picturephone" systems has been carried out by social psychologists in the Bell Telephone Labs in the U.S.A. and by the British Post Office. The design of equipment has been influenced by research on gaze. The sets are now designed to give the impression of mutual gaze; the camera, by means of mirrors, in effect shoots through the monitor on which the other person's image appears. Research on effectiveness has compared video with telephone and face-to-face. It is found that the telephone is just as good as face-to-face for conveying factual information (without diagrams) and for problem-solving. However, in face-to-face and video, people get to know one another better and like each other more. Bargaining and negotiation take a rather different course—in face-to-face and video conditions the person with the weaker case often wins, since he becomes concerned with the other's good opinion; this does not happen over the telephone (Short et al., 1976).

These systems are now commercially available in several countries. They could be very useful in improving the telephone and reducing travel. However, so far, both in Britain and in the U.S.A. there has been rather little adoption of the videophone.

7. Environmental design

Design of hospitals and similar buildings. Trites et al. (1970) compared the effects of three kinds of hospital ward plan—single corridor, double corridor, and radial, with the nursing station at the centre. It was found that the radial design was superior in that staff spent less time on travel and more with the patients, the level of absenteeism was least, as was the number of accidents. Most patients and staff said that they preferred it, and said that it produced a higher quality of patient care. A number of other studies in hospitals, mental hospitals and old people's homes have shown the effects of creating sociable areas like sun lounges with comfortable and attractive furniture, and chairs placed round coffee tables: passive and isolated behaviour is reduced and social activity increases (Ittleson et al., 1964; Sommer, 1969). Principles such as these are now widely used by architects.

Escaping from fires. Canter, Breaux and Sime (1978) have analysed behaviour at fires in hotels and elsewhere and found the conditions under which people do and do not escape. They found that people often misinterpret the sounds accompanying a fire—shouts, alarm bells, breaking glass—and do not realize that there is a fire; staff in particular need to be trained to recognize these sounds, and better fire alarms need to be installed. People often waste time returning to their rooms (in a hotel for instance), or investigating the place of the fire, and may get stuck in the building; signs and instructions should tell them to leave the building at once by the best route. Some people are less likely to escape, for example older people, and those who check in at a hotel in a large party; in some hotels a computerized index of fire risk is obtained for each guest, and those with a high score are placed in safer rooms. It was found that very few people use fire extinguishers or fire escapes; they tend to go out the way they came in; so less money is being put into such equipment in government buildings, and more emphasis placed on making normal routes into effective escapes.

8. Everyday life

One of the most important areas of application of social psychology is surely everyday life. There are many areas of research for which the most obvious clients are the general public, for example, avoiding errors in person perception, understanding what happens in groups, using non-verbal signals correctly, following the principles of sequences in conversation, and knowing how to influence people. We shall pursue another example here a little further—how to make friends. Among clients for social skills training in Britain, this is the most common problem. Gorer (1955) in an extensive survey in England found that on average it took ten years or more after a family had moved into a town before they considered that their best friends lived near them, and they formed few friendships during the first few years.

Social psychology has a lot to say about how to make friends. (a) Friendship results from frequent interaction with those of similar background, values and interests, for instance, in clubs based on leisure, religious, political or professional activities. (b) Popular people are rewarding; unpopular people are not. People who are rewarding take an interest in other people, help them, are cheerful, interesting and amusing; they are not dominating, boastful, aggressive, and do not constantly try to get others to do things for them. (c) People like those who like them. Liking is signalled non-verbally, by facial expression, tone of voice, bodily proximity and orientation, gaze, and—within limits—by bodily contact. These skills are regularly taught as part of social skills training but can probably be learnt from books to some extent.

D. RESEARCH WHICH COULD BE APPLIED, BUT WHICH HAS NOT BEEN

There are many reasons why research findings fail to be applied; probably the most important is that those who might apply them simply do not know about the findings in question. In this section a few examples are given of well-established results which as yet seem to have had little or no application.

Working groups. There is a great deal of research comparing working groups of different designs, and it is clear that certain kinds of group do more work, have lower levels of absenteeism and labour turnover, and have higher levels of job satisfaction. Working groups should (a) be small, ideally of 4–5 members, (b) be cohesive (created by supervisory skills, incentive arrangements and proximity), (c) be functional, i.e., should co-operate over the completion of common tasks, (d) minimize status differences, (e) work in the same area, with easy communication between them, (f) preferably be paid under shared rather than individual incentives (Argyle, 1972).

Disruption in schools has become a very serious problem in some cities, yet in principle this problem should be soluble by familiar research methods. One approach is to understand better the point of view of the disruptive children. Rosser (in Marsh *et al.*, 1978) interviewed a large number of them, and discovered that they had "rules" to which they expected teachers to conform, e.g. not having favourites and not setting too much work; if teachers broke these rules, they were "punished". A second approach is by means of sequence analysis, determining the precise sequence of events leading up to disruption, in order to find the point in the sequence at which it could be diverted. This is being pursued by David Clarke and colleagues in Oxford. A third approach is to compare the skills or other properties of teachers who do and do not experience disruption.

New models of personality—implications for selection. The new models emphasize the importance of the situation in behaviour. The interview is totally unlike most situations which will be met on the job, so behaviour during the interview should not be used to predict behaviour on the job. The interview should be used solely to find out about behaviour in other situations which are more similar to the job situation.

Ideally prediction should be made from behaviour in situations which are as similar to the job situation as possible. For example performance at third-year projects in British universities can be used to select research students. What is needed is much more information than is normally available about the situations which will be met on the job, together with an assessment of which of these are the most important. Predictions of success at these situations can then be made from (1) testimonials, giving ratings of success in similar past situations, (2) interviews about these situations, or (3) test situations, embodying key features of such situations.

The analysis of social situations: implications for situational modification. It is now known that situations are at least as important as personality for the prediction of behaviour, and that P × S interaction is more important than either alone (Endler and Magnusson, 1976). We also know a great deal about the features of situations which affect behaviour (Argyle, 1976). If we want to deal with some form of problem behaviour, it therefore follows that we should do something about the situation in which it occurs, as well as the kinds of individuals who do it. Some examples of changes in furniture and buildings were given above. It should be possible to modify situations in a variety of ways, such as changing the rules, the repertoire of elements, the role-structure, and so on. Delinquency could be tackled by modifying the situations in which it takes place—shops, buses, football grounds, tenement blocks—in one way or another. Social psychologists have already modified a number of situations; for example brain-storming groups are the result of a small change in the repertoire of behaviour in discussion groups, i.e., the elimination of disagreement and criticism.

E. WRONGLY APPLIED RESEARCH

A number of areas of social psychology have been widely applied, although there was inadequate evidence at the time, and later research showed that the application did not lead to desirable results.

T-groups and encounter groups. I referred above to the split between the academic and applied followers of Lewin. The latter developed T-group training, which became widely used for training industrial managers in North America and Western Europe; in some firms it was compulsory. At a later stage, encounter groups were developed at the Esalen Institute, and these also became very popular, though more with the middle-class public outside industry. The only follow-up research to be carried out initially simply showed that many who went on these groups, though not all, felt they had benefited. Later and more careful studies produced rather different results. One extensive study was that by Lieberman, Yalom and Miles (1973) of 206 Stanford students who attended a variety of groups, and 69 who did not. Careful "before and after" measures were taken, and it was found that 13% of those attending the groups dropped out, 8% were casualties (i.e., had to seek psychiatric help) (0 for controls), 8% showed other negative changes, 38% were unchanged, 34% improved (17% for controls). The figure of about 10% being adversely affected has been obtained in a number of other studies. In my view the consistently high casualty rate outweighs benefits obtained by other people attending such groups.

Methods of persuasion over the media. A number of techniques of persuasion have been adopted for advertising which have no sound research basis and which almost certainly have no effect at all. Subliminal advertising was quite widely used for a time, usually by showing verbal messages for very short exposures. It is certainly possible to find an exposure time for an individual such that the message is below his conscious threshold, but above his perceptual threshold. However, these two times vary greatly between individuals, and are quite close together for older people. In any case there is no evidence whatever that "Eat X" has any great effect when delivered subliminally than when presented for longer periods.

Another advertising technique, which is still employed, is the use of phallic and other Freudian symbols, mainly in cinema advertising. Again there is no evidence that this has any effect, apart from causing such mirth in some cinema audiences that the adverts had to be withdrawn.

The popular use of non-verbal communication (NVC). There are a number of popular books on NVC, and at least one commercial system of personnel selection, which suggest that non-verbal signals reveal personality traits. "Does her body say that she is a loose woman?" or "Does her body say that she's a manipulator?" (Fast, 1970). In fact the correlation between facial expression, posture, or other NV signals is extremely small, and there is no evidence whatever that personality can be assessed or job performance predicted from NVC.

Other writings on NVC, by psychoanalysts, suggest that unconscious motivation can be discovered from postures and gestures. Thus a female who crosses, or uncrosses, her legs is said to be flirting; a female who folds her arms is said to be protecting her breasts; a woman who removes her wedding ring is protesting about her husband. In fact there is no solid evidence whatever for such assertions (Argyle, 1975).

The use of personality traits for selection. For many years the dominant model of personality was the trait model, and its main manifestation was the personality questionnaire. Such questionnaires were widely used for selection purposes, especially in the U.S.A., until it was discovered that they were useless. At first it was believed that this was because they were so easily faked (Whyte, 1957), but now we know that such questionnaires give extremely poor predictions under all circumstances, because the trait model itself was wrong (Mischel, 1968). Later models of personality incorporate the effect of situation and personality–situation interaction.

F. THE DIFFERENT ROUTES FROM RESEARCH TO APPLICATION

Something is known about how medical and agricultural research finds its way to being used. There are two routes from medical research workers to doctors—the media (journals, pamphlets, free samples, etc.), and a continuous chain of personal contacts. It is found that a doctor will generally contact a more senior doctor before actually using a new medicine which he has heard about through the media (Coleman et al., 1957).

Deutsch and Hornstein (1975) suggested that there are three kinds of relationships between social psychologists and the organizations who may use their results: the expert relationship, where the psychologist is a consultant; the collaborative relationship; and the advocate relationship, where the psychologist tries to persuade people or organizations to make use of his findings. In this section I have taken a broader view of the situation, and identified six main routes from research to practice. The increased number is partly because I regard members of the general public (as well as governments) as potential users of our research and I regard doctors, teachers and social workers as very important users of social psychological knowledge.

1. The collaborative relationship: sponsored research

The difference between this and consultancy is that here the organization is more seriously committed to the research. It pays for research to be carried out so that certain problems can be solved. The research worker is usually allowed to pursue more purely scientific goals at the same time, and in many cases this may be necessary in order to solve the problem. The work of the Tavistock Institute of Human Relations at the Glacier Metal Company (Jaques, 1951) was a case of collaborative research. Here an enlightened general manager brought in an outside research group, hoping to solve certain internal problems and also to make a more general contribution to industrial relations. A somewhat similar case was the Coch and French (1948) study of the use of group decisions in groups of workers. Here the collaboration was brought about because the managing director had a Ph.D. in psychology and was able to collaborate in the study. The work on prediction tables in delinquency by Mannheim and Wilkins (1955) was rather different, since they were working for the Home Office Research Unit, and thus had a special relationship with borstals and prisons already.

This form of research has a great advantage over university-based field research, in that it is far easier to obtain access to the data and to elicit co-operation from those concerned. It has a great advantage over consultancy in that it is more likely that the findings will actually be used.

2. The expert relationship: consultancy

Here the social psychologist is paid a fee by an organization to study some problem, offer advice on its solution, and perhaps advise or direct operations in setting up the necessary procedures, e.g., for training or selection of staff. An example is a study of a large oil firm in which the author was involved (Sofer, 1970). One of the problems with which we were presented was discontent among middle management. The methods used were group interviews and discussions with groups of managers, followed by a carefully piloted social survey among the managers in question. The causes of the trouble were quickly identified —insufficient delegation and consultation on the part of senior managers, combined in some parts of the firm with poor promotion prospects for the large number of very able people at lower levels of management. The work so far consisted of the use of familiar research techniques combined with prior knowledge of the likely variables.

Finding the answer to the problem is only the first stage, however. The second and often more difficult part is getting something done about it. Following the oil company study described above, as far as we know, no action was ever taken as a result of the consultancy. If the management are willing to take action, this may be fairly straightforward, such as putting in selection or training schemes. Broader organizational changes are much harder to produce, but several American social psychologists have devised methods of doing it. Mann (1957) for example has developed a combination of group discussion and feedback from social surveys of an organization. Often when consultants present such survey material, the findings are quietly filed and no action is taken. According to Mann's system, feedback sessions are arranged in which the managers of each section discuss the results with a view to doing something about them. Each group discusses the problem at its own level and receives reports of the discussion of more detailed problems at the next level below. Mann has found that this method leads to changes in employee attitudes and in supervisory behaviour.

Blake and Mouton (1965) have reported a scheme for changing the pattern of relationships (not the organizational chart) within an organization. There are six stages: group laboratory sessions are used to demonstrate interpersonal phenomena and skills, such as the use of power in supervision and ways of dealing with conflicting ideas about how work should be done; trainees are helped to analyse the working of their own work teams; lateral links between colleagues are strengthened; diagonal-slice groups discuss new organizational goals; help is given with the detailed implementation of the changes; and there is consideration of further areas where changes are needed. This approach in a firm of 4000 employees, including 800 managerial and technical staff, over a five-month period produced increases in productivity and profits, together with better ratings by subordinates of managers' performance. There also appeared to be improvements in supervisory skills and in managers' relationships with subordinates.

The main difficulty with the consultancy relationship is that often not all sections of the organization are in agreement with inviting the consultant. In the case of industrial firms it is likely to be the personnel department who want to consult a social psychologist, while the production department may be strongly opposed. It is not uncommon for the consultant to find that he is being used in a battle against another department, and that the suggestions he produces had already been thought of by the section which invited him; all they really wanted was some outside support for their policy (see Klein, 1976).

3. Writing books

Social psychologists usually publish their findings in journal articles; if they want a wider audience, they have to write in a more popular form, usually books. This is true if the intended audience is the general public, or managers and administrators, teachers and social workers, or the government, although rather different kinds of book are needed in each case.

Books for the general public. There has never been a book by a social psychologist which has been as popular as Spock's *Baby and Child Care* (1957), which has sold 28 million copies. This book is a model of its kind, although the contents may be criticized and were indeed modified in the second edition. However, the book contained a great deal of expert detailed information, presented in a very readable form. Dale Carnegie's *How to Win Friends and Influence People* (1936) was also a bestseller, this time in the field of social psychology, though making no use of social psychological research. Again this book met an obvious need and was very persuasively written. However, thousands of books on health, child-rearing, how to be more effective and better adjusted, etc., have had a far more modest success, and no book on social psychology proper has found a mass market on this scale. Probably the most widely read books in social psychology are textbooks for first-year students. It is interesting that both of the above books were American, since the American book-marketing scene is rather different from that elsewhere. In many towns there are few bookshops, but many outlets for paperbacks. (Popular non-fiction subjects are health and diet, meditation and yoga, adjustment and personal effectiveness), and the buying and reading of popular books on social psychology is part of the American way of life.

Books for managers and administrators. A consultant who wants to drum up business may write a book, but he is more likely to write articles in professional journals read by potential clients. He will also prepare "packages" or "kits" which explain his ideas in short words and in large writing with diagrams, rather like children's books. What they usually fail to mention is the results (if any) of follow-up or validational studies or the claims of rival schemes. It is rather disturbing to meet managers who have acquired a simple-minded faith in "Herzberg", "Theory X and theory Y", or the "Management grid". In each case there is extensive research about the techniques in question, but this is apparently not mentioned to potential clients.

It is generally agreed in management training circles that "Managers don't read books", presumably because they are too busy. Even on management courses the prescribed reading is often limited to a few semi-popular articles. There are a number of good books, which give a useful account of relevant findings in social psychology: the effects of incentives, organizational structure, working groups, selection techniques, and so on. These are studied by people on the longer management courses, and one hopes by a few actual managers and administrators.

4. TV and radio

The mass media have the advantage of reaching a wider audience than any other form of communication. Furthermore they often reach people who do not wish to be reached, since TV sets in particular are often left on regardless of the programme. Can the mass media be used for communicating the results of social psychological research?

Instructional films are regularly used for training in interviewing and in other social skills, but these are rarely shown over the media. An interesting example from another area of psychology is the use of TV for mass behaviour therapy (to combat cigarette smoking, obesity, etc.) which has been successfully practised by the Max Planck Institute for Psychiatry in Munich. The BBC quite often presents the results of social psychology research in *Horizon* and similar programmes. Such programmes are addressed to the intelligent layman, and may reach a number of practitioners. It is reported that in 1978 Mr Callaghan (then British Prime Minister) watched a BBC-TV Horizon film about micro-processors, and that this led to the Government investing £100 million in the industry; evidently rather influential people can be reached via the media.

We have mentioned one great advantage of the media—the large number of people who are reached. Even more people may be reached at second-hand, by being told about the programme by those who saw it—as described by the two-step model of communication. Furthermore social psychology lends itself very readily to presentation on radio or TV—more so than most other branches of knowledge—because of the nature of the material.

There are, however, difficulties about using the media. Special skills are needed to use them effectively, and access is difficult to obtain. The answer to both problems lies in the need to collaborate with a producer, who has the skills and controls the access. Producers have their own ideas about what it would be interesting to show on their programmes, and they tend to design programmes around dramatic themes which appeal to them. The presentation of scientific research tends to be rather peripheral to such themes, except in the case of serious scientific programmes.

5. Education and training

This is one of the main routes from research to its application.

Schools. Psychology, including social psychology, is slowly coming into schools, as an examined or unexamined subject. Social psychology is also affecting the curriculum in other ways. In the U.S.A. in particular a lot of effort has been taken to eliminate racially biased materials, and in a number of schools carefully designed exercises and activities have been introduced with the intention of reducing racial prejudice. In some British and American schools social skills training has been introduced, and several good textbooks and sets of classroom materials have been produced (e.g. McPhail *et al.*, 1972, 1978).

College. In the U.S.A., Australia, and elsewhere, psychology is now one of the most popular subjects, and very many students take it, in the first year at least. This means that many of those going into a wide variety of professions have some idea of what social psychology has to offer and may remember some of the actual findings.

Teachers and social workers are some of the main users of social psychology. Teachers need to know how to handle classroom situations, how to motivate children to learn, and how to deal with difficult children; social workers have to cope with delinquents and problem families and need to know about the effects of socialization on personality and the functions of groups of adolescents. Training courses include a substantial amount of social psychology, especially in the case of social workers. In addition there is usually some social skills training; micro-teaching is very widely used for teachers.

Doctors can also profit from social psychology, in mastering the social skills of handling patients, and in understanding the effects of psychosocial stress on health. Awareness of non-verbal communication is helpful, in understanding the gestures which patients use to describe internal pains (Miller, 1978). During 1978–80 a number of courses were set up in Britain by social psychologists, to train medical students and general medical practitioners in doctor–patient skills.

6. Influencing government

How can governments be persuaded to act on the findings of social psychological research? Some of the routes described above can lead to government action.

Sponsored research. This is the main route for research in physics, medicine and agriculture, where governments usually have large official research establishments. This has scarcely developed at all in Britain in the case of social psychology, with the exceptions of the Home Office Research Unit into criminology and the Civil Service Research Unit. Government departments also give short-term grants to university social psychologists to investigate practical problems, and in these cases it is likely that the results will be used.

Consultants and advisors. Economists are extensively used as advisers to Government departments and political parties. Social psychologists have not been used very much in this capacity, though they sometimes serve on advisory committees. Civil servants, unlike managers, do tend to read books and often know personally the research workers in their field of interest. However, they are usually not trained social scientists themselves, and their judgement of the merits of research are not always based on the same criteria as those used in the profession. It would therefore be very desirable if more social psychologists were appointed as senior advisers to Government departments.

Books, TV, etc. We gave the example of Mr Callaghan seeing a TV programme on microprocessors. The media provide an important way of influencing government policy independently of the official channels mentioned above. Prison reformers for example have written books, describing conditions in prisons, and the film by Zimbardo on his prison experiment is in this tradition. Books and films on racial prejudice, bad housing and homeless families are other examples.

G. SUMMARY

Social psychologists have always hoped that their work would be used in the real world, but for a lot of mainstream social psychology this has not happened. Much of the criticism of the subject in recent years has been of its lack of application or its lack of external validity. A number of examples have been given here of the application of social psychology. In some cases this has been extensive, and follow-up studies have been clearly positive, as in the case of improved skills for supervisors and teachers, and increased intergroup contact. In some cases the application has been less extensive, but the results positive, as in the case of social skills training for neurotic patients, improved environmental design, and new communication systems. In some cases there is some doubt over the benefits, as with the use of the mass media, industrial democracy, and therapeutic communities. One of the most important potential areas of application is everyday life, and we gave the example of making friends.

There are other areas of social psychology which have scarcely been applied at all, though they could well be, such as the optimum design of working groups. Furthermore, some ideas have been applied which should not have been, because the applications produced either no effect at all or effects which were on the whole undesirable.

Six different routes from research to its application were discussed. Each of these routes has special problems and requires special skills, of communication and persuasion. Each in fact raises problems of applied social psychology.

ACKNOWLEDGEMENT

I am grateful to Dr J. M. F. Jaspars for his comments on this chapter.

Part 2
Past History

Social Psychology: A History or Merely a Past?

ROBIN GILMOUR and STEVE DUCK

The present comes out of the past in a more than trivial sense because the past has contributed to the present in a number of significant ways. However, one curious and important characteristic of social psychology —and, indeed, of many other subjects—is that we fail to learn from the past or overlook features of it that could still be useful to us now. The future development of social psychology can be well served by looking again—perhaps more carefully, constructively and analytically —at the past. Part 1 considered what we have learned from the past, but this alone is not enough; we must also consider what we have failed to learn. In Part 2, therefore, contributors explore different aspects of the past and disinter what they regard as the (unrealized) potential contribution that could have been—and could still be—made to the present and future. It is significant that two contributors focus on the *social* features of the past's development into the present whilst the other two explore our failure to recognize the *intellectual* thrust of some earlier work which they feel has continuing potential and which is at present unrecognized or inadequately exploited. Intellectual history develops in a dynamic social context, and recognition of this enables two lessons to be drawn from the past. First, separation of intellectual and social threads alerts us to the need for two parallel analyses of our past development (viz. of the ideas that have predominated and the means by which they did so); secondly, such separation creates two distinct forces that should be fully employed in the future development of social psychology.

The reader is faced in Part 2 with the intriguing question, *not* of whether we would have got where we are now without the elements of the past that we have actually made use of, but of where would we now be if we had made better use of that past. Inevitably our particular past was a necessary component of our development to the present state; it is also possible that a different past would have led us to the same present, but by a different route. However, it is important to recognize that in significant ways our past constrains us to rely on particular methods and theoretical styles of approach to our subject's present. Nevertheless, we are not complete prisoners of our history; even within the contraints mentioned we still have some scope to modify approaches, to reconstruct a past we can draw on for a different present and thence to construct a different future.

As a further point, it would be naïve to assume that we have had *one* past. This is a vast oversimplification—perhaps a necessary one, but an oversimplification all the same. Perhaps we should see ourselves as having several different theoretical pasts, to which hindsight lends a specious coherence.

Equally, social psychology does not have merely one future but a diversity, not only of *possible* futures, but of actual futures, a theme we shall consider in Part 3.

5
On Reading Darwin and Discovering Social Psychology

ROBERT M. FARR
University of Glasgow

A. Darwin's *The Expression of the Emotions in Man and Animals* (1872) . . 113
   1. Blushing and the social psychology of shyness 114
   2. Human emotion in evolutionary perspective 117
   3. Sources of error in the observation and reporting of human emotions 117
   4. The perception of emotions in self and others 119
   5. Attitude as gesture and behavioural orientation 121
B. Wundt's folk psychology 123
C. The social behaviourism of G. H. Mead 129
D. Summary 135

There were many early ventures in social psychology which came to nothing and of which there is little or no trace today. Many of these early ventures deserved the oblivion which is their current fate and are not now worth recalling, but there were a number of very promising developments in the past which seem to be undervalued at present. If the contemporary explorer of the past is equipped with a good historical knowledge he may be able to pinpoint fairly accurately where there may be hidden treasure which is worth salvaging. My own instincts lead me to single out Darwin's *The Expression of the Emotions in Man and Animals* (1872) as deserving the attention of serious historians of social psychology as a discipline. The book itself is not, of course, a work of social psychology. It is, rather, the impact of this book on two persons—Wilhelm Wundt and George Herbert Mead—who were developing their own versions of social psychology which I wish to trace in the present paper.

Wundt was much influenced by Darwin in developing his *Volkpsychologie* or "folk psychology" in which he attempted to write a psychological history of mankind. This involved him in speculating about the origins of man. It was the origins, in the remote past, of contemporary patterns of human behaviour which primarily interested him. This had been the precise nature of Darwin's interest in *The Expression of the Emotions in Man and Animals*. What were the origins of the mainly facial expressions of emotion in man? Darwin's interests were here more explicitly behavioural than in his other writings. In terms of the evidence available, it is obviously easier to trace man's skeletal past than it is to trace his behavioural past since behaviour leaves few, if any, historical traces. From the perspective of an evolutionary biologist, behaviour constitutes "soft" data and stands in contrast to the more "objective" evidence which can be derived from skeletons and fossils. The distinctiveness of Wundt's contribution resided in his treatment of culture as a human product on the basis of which inferences could be made about the mind of primitive man. For Wundt the study of culture (language, myth, magic, religion and cognate phenomena) was an important source of evidence concerning the early development of man. Darwin had described the movements and gestures associated with the expression of different human emotions and Wundt developed these ideas by situating the human gesture in its social context and by focusing on the evolution in man of the vocal gesture in the direction of speech. For Wundt language was a distinctive characteristic of man as a species. Wundt thus helped to develop Darwin's work in the direction of an explicit social psychology: it is a characteristic of man as a species that he has a social and cultural inheritance *in addition* to his genetic inheritance.

Mead developed the whole of his social psychology starting from Wundt's concept of the human gesture which in turn derives from Darwin. Indeed, his entire philosophy, as well as his social psychology, was based on a close reading of Darwin. He believed that Darwin's book *The Expression of the Emotions in Man and Animals* was the single most important text in the psychology of his day. He thought that it contained the key to an adequate understanding of the nature of language, and language plays a critical role in Mead's social behaviourism. There is thus little doubt about the seminal influence of Darwin's book on both Wundt and Mead. Each of the two men then went on to establish their own distinctive tradition of social psychology. For further details of the neglect of Wundt's and Mead's theories see Farr, (1978, 1980). Both Wundt and Mead discovered social psychology on the basis of reading Darwin but Darwin's influence on the development of social psychology waned with the passing into obscurity of Wundt's *Volkpsychologie* and with the fact that Mead's influence has been much more extensive in the development of American sociology than it has in the development of American psychology. Thus, although I shall attempt in this chapter to show how Darwin had a significant influence on the development of modern social psychology, there are other, historical reasons why, today, there is little or no trace of this influence.

A. DARWIN'S *THE EXPRESSION OF THE EMOTIONS IN MAN AND ANIMALS* (1872)

Darwin published this volume the year after his *Descent of Man* appeared in print. Like all Darwin's books it was based on a great wealth of observations, both of man and of other animals. Some of the observations which he reported on the expression of the emotions in the human infant were based on the diaries which he kept on the development of his own children, starting with the birth of his first child in 1839. In keeping a diary of the development of his own children Darwin set the fashion for later specialists in the study of child development e.g. the Swiss biologist, Piaget. Darwin's original intention was to incorporate his observations on the expression of the emotions in man and animals in the *Descent of Man*. Referring to *The Expression of the Emotions in Man and Animals* in his autobiography, Darwin wrote: "I had intended to give only a chapter on the subject in the *Descent of Man*, but as soon as I began to put my notes together, I saw that it would require a separate treatise" (quoted in Ralling, 1979, p. 174).

In keeping with the context for which he originally envisaged it, Darwin traced the natural origins of the expression of human emotions. He focused mainly on human facial expressions, and his introduction to the volume contains three highly detailed diagrams of the muscles of the human face, one of which is reproduced from the work of Sir Charles Bell. His final substantive chapter before the concluding summary is devoted to a discussion of these uniquely human emotions of self-attention (shame, shyness, modesty) which are reflected in the act of blushing. The significance of the human face as an important source of information concerning human emotion is one of the unifying themes in Darwin's treatise.

1. Blushing and the social psychology of shyness

Darwin treats the human blush as an explicitly social phenomenon.

> Blushing is the most peculiar and the most human of all expressions ... it is not due to the action of the heart that the network of minute vessels covering the face becomes under a sense of shame gorged with blood. We can cause laughing by tickling the skin, weeping or frowning by a blow, trembling from the fear of pain, and so forth, but we cannot cause a blush ... by any physical means,—that is, by any action on the body. It is the mind which must be affected. Blushing is not only involuntary; but the wish to restrain it, by leading to self-attention actually increases the tendency. (Darwin, 1872, pp. 309 et seq.)

George Herbert Mead, on the basis of a close reading of Darwin, traced how mind and self emerge in social interaction with others. Mead thus argued for the purely social antecedents both of mind and of self—the two concepts which Darwin made central in his analysis of shyness. If we accept Mead's argument (which will be elaborated at a later point), then we have here, in a nutshell, both the observations and the theory necessary for understanding shyness as a purely social phenomenon.

Darwin himself was fully aware of the social nature of shyness. He regarded shyness as the most efficient cause of blushing. He noted that

> The young blush much more freely than the old, but not during infancy, which is remarkable, as we know that infants at a very early age redden from passion ... Many children, at a somewhat more advanced age blush in a strongly marked manner. It appears that the mental powers of infants are not as yet sufficiently developed to allow of their blushing. (Darwin, 1872, p. 310.)

Mead might have observed that the sense of self is insufficiently developed in infancy for shyness to be a common phenomenon. Darwin then went on to note that women blush much more than men and that the tendency to blush is inherited. In noting that the blind also blush Darwin commented: "The blind are not at first conscious that they are observed, and it is a most important part of their education, as Mr. Blair informs me, to impress this knowledge on their minds;

and the impression thus gained would greatly strengthen the tendency to blush, by increasing the habit of self-attention" (Darwin, 1872, p. 311). In the majority of cases the face, ears and neck are the only parts of the human body which redden with blushing. Darwin discusses the possible physiological reasons for this. He reports various observations, mainly from medical persons, as to how far down the body the blush extends. He then discusses the form which the blush takes in the various races of man depending upon the colour of their skin and which parts of their bodies are habitually clothed as protection against the weather. He notes the movements and gestures which often accompany blushing.

> Under a keen sense of shame there is a strong desire for concealment. We turn away the whole body, more especially the face, which we endeavour in some manner to hide. An ashamed person can hardly endure to meet the gaze of those present, so that he almost invariably casts down his eyes or looks askant. (Darwin, 1872, p. 321.)

In discussing the nature of the mental states which induce blushing Darwin listed shyness, shame and modesty: "the essential element in all being self-attention" (p. 325). He thought that self-attention was directed originally towards personal appearances "in relation to the opinions of others" (p. 325) and that this subsequently became associated with self-attention in relation to moral conduct. "It is not the simple act of reflecting on our own appearance, but the thinking what others think of us, which excites a blush" (Darwin, 1872, p. 325).

In discussing shyness Darwin stated:

> This odd state of mind ... appears to be one of the most efficient of all the causes of blushing. Shyness is, indeed, chiefly recognised by the face reddening, by the eyes being averted or cast down, and by awkward, nervous movements of the body ... Shyness seems to depend on sensitiveness to the opinion, whether good or bad, of others, more especially with respect to external appearance ... The consciousness of anything peculiar, or even new, in the dress, or any slight blemish on the person, and more especially on the face—points which are likely to attract the attention (even) of strangers—makes the shy intolerably shy. (Darwin, p. 329.)

It is clear from these extensive quotations that Darwin analysed shyness in terms of human consciousness and more particularly in terms of a person's awareness of self in the presence of others. Mead described this state of consciousness as "awareness of self as object" i.e. a person's awareness that he is an object of interest to others. This rather precisely captures Darwin's characterization of shyness as an acute state of self-attention. One needs a social model of man in order to understand the phenomenon of human shyness. I have argued elsewhere that Mead provides just such a social model of man (Farr, 1980a). It is part of my argument that the models of man which prevail in contemporary psychology (especially those in social psychology) are, in fact, non-social models. I regard it as a striking confirmation of my views that a distinguished biologist (Darwin, 1872) and a distinguished sociologist (Goffman, 1969) should each have a better understanding of the social psychology of shyness and embarrassment than any contemporary psychologist. Goffman belongs to that tradition of social psychology at Chicago which derives its inspiration from the work of G. H. Mead.

It is significant, I believe, that both Darwin and Mead approach the individual *from the outside*, even when they are describing his states of consciousness or awareness. This is the antithesis of relying on introspection as a valid source of information concerning states of consciousness. It is, however, a strategy which is often misunderstood by orthodox psychologists. Mead's description of the state of awareness which he characterizes as *awareness of self as object* has recently been borrowed by Duval and Wicklund who have introduced into contemporary experimental social psychology the somewhat misleading term "objective self-awareness" (Duval and Wicklund, 1972; Wicklund, 1975). The term is misleading because "objective" appears to describe the state of awareness rather than referring to what the individual is aware of, i.e. himself as an *object* in the social world of other persons. The alternative state of awareness, for Mead, was *awareness of self as subject* or agent; this is equivalent to a completely unselfconscious state of awareness where the individual is so task-oriented that he ceases to be aware of himself as a person. To call this latter state "subjective self-awareness", as Duval and Wicklund do, is to further invite confusion, because "subjective" appears to describe the state of awareness rather than referring to what the individual is aware of, i.e. himself as *subject* or agent. Whilst I regard the experimental studies of Duval and of Wicklund as being of critical importance to any laboratory investigation of the phenomena of shyness and embarrassment, I find their translation of Mead's theoretical terms to be confusing. If the purity of Mead's theoretical formulation is retained, it should be possible, thanks to Duval and Wicklund, to test Darwin's theory of shyness under laboratory conditions.

2. Human emotion in evolutionary perspective

Darwin treated the blush as a uniquely human expression of emotion. Many of the other expressions of emotion in man which Darwin discusses in his book have analogues in the behaviour of species lower than man in the evolutionary hierarchy. It is, after all, the descent of man which provides the unifying theme of the volume. Many of the strong emotions in man are no longer of adaptive significance, although they would have been at some point in man's long evolutionary past. Darwin treats, for example, the human snarl as now having only a purely communicative function. It is an expressive movement which developed out of the motor habit of actual biting. As a means of aggression, however, biting has practically disappeared in the human species. In his valuable preface to the 1965 University of Chicago edition of Darwin's work Lorenz brings out Darwin's awareness of the fundamental principle which now is often regarded as the starting point of ethology

> This fact, which is still ignored by many psychologists, is quite simply that behavior patterns are just as conservatively and reliably characters of species as are the forms of bones, teeth, or any other bodily structures... The conservative persistence of behavior patterns, even after they have outlived, in the evolution of a species, their original function, is exactly the same as that of organs; in other words, they can become "vestigial" or "rudimentary", just as the latter can. (Lorenz in Darwin, 1965, p. xii.)

Darwin was concerned with the bodily expression of the emotions in man and animals. His book was, therefore, based on the careful observation of behaviour, and the evidence which he adduces is thus behavioural rather than structural (i.e. based on skeletons and fossils).

3. Sources of error in the observation and reporting of human emotions

Darwin was very aware of the possibility of error in the observation of emotional behaviour. In the main he depended on the observations of professional men, e.g. zoo keepers, physicians, surgeons, directors of lunatic asylums and of institutions for the blind, animal breeders, missionaries, etc. He insisted that those supplying him with evidence should report actual observations and not rely on memory. He circulated questionnaires concerning the expression of certain emotions in the various races of mankind, and also made use of photographs of persons exhibiting various emotions. Sometimes these photographs were shown to samples of respondents who were then asked to identify which emotion was portrayed, the interest here being man's ability to identify particular emotions in the faces of others. Darwin often obtained a high degree of consensus among his respondents in the identification of certain emotions but, despite this, respondents were often unable to specify the precise cues on the basis of which they reached their judgements. Darwin was fully aware of the difficulties of observing the everyday expression of emotions in humans when the cues are so dynamic and often highly evanescent. He refers to sympathy as a possible source of error in the accurate perception of emotion in others. "Our imagination is another and still more serious source of error; for if from the nature of the circumstances we expect to see any expression, we readily imagine its presence" (Darwin, 1872, p. 13).

Schachter has since cogently demonstrated how the experimental manipulation of circumstance can result in the identification of different (and often quite disparate) emotions (Schachter, 1964). In similar vein film directors have been known to prefer stars who do not exhibit much emotion in their facial expressions. By clever splicing in the cutting room (experimental manipulation?) they are able to provide a suitable context which enables the viewer to "perceive" the appropriate emotion. Actors on the live stage, however, do need to be able to encode the appropriate gestures and facial expressions in their portrayal of a particular emotion. Indeed Darwin employed actors (and photographers) in order to portray, for example, the emotions of disgust, indignation and helplessness, as illustrations for his treatise. In treating the more complex human emotions of jealousy, envy, revenge, suspicion, deceit, slyness, guilt, vanity, conceit, ambition, pride, humility, etc., Darwin doubted whether there was any fixed expression sufficiently distinct to be described or delineated for each of these feelings. He thought that some of these emotions might be visible to the naked eye "but we are often guided in a much greater degree than we suppose by our previous knowledge of the persons or circumstances" (Darwin, 1872, p. 261).

Whilst Darwin was primarily concerned with the recognition of emotion in others on the basis, mainly, of facial expressions, Schachter was more directly concerned with how an individual comes to label his own states of emotional arousal. In a sense Schachter is more genuinely sociopsychological than Darwin in his approach to the study of human emotion. In his experiments Schachter seeks to demonstrate how the individual, when physiologically aroused (due to the effect of a drug with which he has been injected), uses the behaviour of others whom he believes to be in the same situation as himself as a cue in the appraisal of his own emotional state. Whilst Darwin treats the behaviour of others as furnishing the observer with the necessary evidence for inferring their emotions, Schachter treats the behaviour of particular others (whom the observer believes to be in the same situation as himself) as furnishing the observer with the necessary evidence for inferring *his own* emotional state. In his experimental studies Schachter has sought to extend Festinger's theory of social comparison processes (Festinger, 1954) to the study of the emotions (Schachter, 1959). Darwin and Schachter are both behavioural in their approach to the study of human emotions and neither fell into the trap, which ensnared Wundt in his experimental studies, of using introspection to try to capture the nature of emotion. Darwin only very occasionally indulged in the luxury of referring to his own emotional responses—he more often referred to the responses of his own children as babies, of his dogs, or of a horse he was riding. I hope later in this chapter to demonstrate how Wundt used Darwin's work in the *development* of his own social psychology (or folk psychology as he preferred to call it). For Wundt this folk psychology was a quite distinct enterprise from the experimental science of psychology, based on introspection, which he had earlier established in his laboratory at Leipzig in 1879.

4. The perception of emotion in self and others

Darwin's pioneering work on the expression of the emotions is still acknowledged as authoritative in those areas of research in social psychology directly concerned with the study of non-verbal behaviour and with person perception. Classically the field of person perception is concerned with the perception of other persons. The centenary of the publication of Darwin's book was marked by the publication of a volume edited by Ekman and entitled *Darwin and Facial Expression* (Ekman, 1974).

The inter-relationship between perception of self and perception of others is currently a topic of lively controversy and of theoretical interest within social psychology. Bem, a radical behaviourist, claims that when a person makes inferences about his own opinions, beliefs, attitudes and motives, he uses the same cues that are available to any observer of his behaviour (Bem, 1964, 1972). Bem first developed this provocative thesis as a rival explanation for interpreting the evidence supporting Festinger's theory of cognitive dissonance. Festinger had earlier postulated dissonance as a state of arousal having drive properties (Festinger, 1957). Bem sought to treat Festinger's theory in the same manner that Skinner had earlier treated Hull's theory, i.e. to demonstrate that the concept of drive was superfluous. In his self-perception theory Bem obviates the necessity of postulating a drive state to account for dissonance phenomena. He substituted, in effect, a perceptual theory for what was essentially a motivational theory. Whilst Bem claims that his theoretical perspective is that of radical behaviourism he might more appropriately be classified as operating within an information-processing perspective.

Darwin's study of the expression of the emotions in man ought to pose problems for Bem's overall theoretical perspective. The human emotions which were the object of interest to Darwin are much more forceful and stirring states of arousal than the purely "cognitive drives" first formulated by Festinger. For Darwin, as we noted above, the face was the most important part of the human body in the expression of emotion.

> Of all the parts of the body, the face is most considered and regarded, as is natural from its being the chief seat of expression and the source of the voice. It is also the chief seat of beauty and of ugliness, and throughout the world is the most ornamented. The face, therefore, will have been subjected during many generations to much closer and more earnest self-attention than any other part of the body; and in accordance with the principle here advanced we can understand why it should be the most liable to blush. (Darwin, 1872, p. 327.)

The individual, of course, is on the wrong side of his own face when it comes to utilizing the same cues that are available to an outside observer. Whilst individuals do observe their own faces in mirrors and keep photographs of themselves in albums, these carefully selected images are rarely ones of themselves when they are emotionally aroused. In observing himself in a mirror or in responding to the presence of a camera, man seeks to bring his facial expression under voluntary control. However, as Darwin so amply demonstrated, not all facial expressions can be brought under voluntary control. Goffman—that impresario of the art of impression management—showed that impressions are "given off" as well as created (Goffman, 1969), referring to the involuntary "leakage" of information, usually through non-verbal channels, which the "actor" would prefer to withhold if only he could bring it under voluntary control. How aware, then, are individuals of their own states of emotional arousal? The researches of Schachter suggest that an individual might, on occasion, be only dimly aware of being physiologically aroused without having any clear conception of which particular emotion he might be experiencing. Typically, however, individuals become "aware" of their own emotional arousal from the way in which observing others react to them: and it was G. H. Mead in his social behaviourism who first developed and extended Darwin's work in this direction.

Darwin deals with the strong emotions, i.e. those which readily find bodily expression. In his treatment of the strong emotions Darwin virtually anticipates the famous James–Lange formulation of the emotions and identifies the emotion with its bodily expression. "Most of our emotions are so closely connected with their expression, that they hardly exist if the body remains passive ... So a man may intensely hate another, but until his bodily frame is affected, he cannot be said to be enraged" (Darwin, 1872, pp. 237–238). Emotions typically find expression in certain gestures and bodily postures, which latter Darwin terms "attitudes". For Darwin "attitude" was a behavioural orientation; as such it furnished evidence of emotions which was readily available to any observer. This is so different from the use of the term "attitude" in contemporary social psychology that it deserves a section to itself.

5. Attitude as gesture and behavioural orientation

Fleming (1967) rightly treats attitude as a unifying theme in Darwin's treatise on the emotions while noting that Darwin does not himself make this explicit. Fleming accordingly assigns Darwin a place of honour in his historical account of attitude as a concept (Fleming, 1967). For Darwin attitude was an overt physical posture—often an exaggerated whole-body orientation. It was a general posture of readiness to respond to objects of aversion or craving by attack, flight or seizure. With reference to the erection of the dermal appendages in hens and swans in driving away intruders Darwin comments: "... they might have wished to make themselves appear larger and more terrible to their enemies, by voluntarily assuming a threatening attitude and uttering harsh cries; such attitudes and utterances after a time becoming through habit instinctive" (Darwin, 1872, p. 103). In human anger, Darwin notes: "Such gestures as the raising of the arms, with the fists clenched, as if to strike the offender, are common" (p. 239). In contrasting the attitude of attack in cats with that in dogs Darwin remarks: "We can understand why the attitude assumed by a cat when preparing to fight another cat, or in any way greatly irritated, is so widely different from that of a dog approaching another dog with hostile intentions; for the cat uses her fore-feet for striking, and this renders a crouching position convenient or necessary. She is also much more accustomed than a dog to lie concealed and suddenly spring on her prey" (p. 126). In differentiating indignation from anger Darwin observes: "Instead of the frantic gestures of extreme rage, an indignant man unconsciously throws himself into an attitude ready for attacking or striking his enemy, whom he will perhaps scan from head to foot in defiance" (p. 245). In his portrayal of scorn—"He listened silently and scornfully to the accusation; his attitude erect, chest expanded, mouth closed, lips protruding, eyes firmly set and penetrating" (p. 247)—Darwin demonstrates how the actions and attitude of a helpless man are in most respects the exact antithesis to those of an indignant man.

It is a pity that Darwin's behavioural formulation of attitude was not adopted within psychology. The concept has instead become much too "psychological" and hardly at all behavioural. It is conceptualized as an "intervening variable" or even as a "hypothetical construct", i.e. it is not something which can be directly observed. In this respect it stands in stark contrast to the way in which Darwin used the concept. Learned articles are written on how, in theory, there is a link between "attitudes" and "behaviour" even though in practice the link might turn out to be a highly tenuous one. Attitudes are, at best, only probabilistically related to behaviour. Campbell (1963) traces how the "view of the world" approach to the study of attitude came to predominate within psychology over the "consistency in response" approach. Even though attitude is now a highly "cognitive" term it still retains some vestiges of its behavioural past, e.g. an attitude is always "towards" some significant aspect of one's environment (in the vestigial sense of a general behavioural orientation towards). "Attitudes" tend to be "for" or "against" some issue or object: they represent a "tendency to respond" in a favourable or unfavourable way towards the object of the attitude. This positive/negative dichotomy is all that remains of the conflicting behavioural responses of approach/avoidance. The distinctive component of an "attitude" still remains the affective component i.e. the emotional tone. It is this affective tone which differentiates attitudes from what would otherwise be "opinions", "beliefs" or "cognitions". This affective overtone is a very dilute version of the strong emotions that were the original objects of Darwin's interest over a hundred years ago.

B. WUNDT'S FOLK PSYCHOLOGY

Wundt is justly acknowledged as the "founding father" of psychology as a laboratory science. In his laboratory science he was concerned with the analysis of the contents of consciousness by means of introspection. In Wundt's day, consciousness was assumed to be a characteristic of individuals and so his experimental laboratory science was inherently non-social. He was clearly aware of the limitations of the laboratory science that he had helped to establish. He believed that man's higher cognitive processes were not amenable to study by means of introspection within the confines of the laboratory, and considered it necessary to supplement his laboratory science with the study of mind in society outside. His voluminous writings in folk psychology, however, have been ignored by the official historians of psychology; they remain, for the most part, unread and unappraised. My own remarks are based mainly on a reading of those volumes of Wundt's social psychology that have been translated into English, but much of Wundt's folk psychology is still only available in the original German. Subsequent links between certain forms of folk psychology and the ideology of National Socialism may further have helped to ensure that Wundt's social psychology remained a closed book, especially, perhaps, amongst social psychologists. This is a theme which I have treated at greater length elsewhere (Farr, 1980a, b).

A further feature of Wundt's folk psychology is worth commenting on at this stage. It is quite explicitly a collective psychology and thus stands in marked contrast to the psychology of the individual, which was the focus of his laboratory research. Folk psychology was the study of those collective mental phenomena—language, culture, religion, customs, magic and cognate phenomena—which were the products of a folk community. These collective phenomena were also independent of, and existed prior to, the consciousness of each individual who comprised the community. The task Wundt set himself in outlining the scope of his folk psychology was highly ambitious; it was no less than that of writing a psychological history of the development of mankind. Indeed this was the sub-title of his *Elements of Folk Psychology* which appeared in English in 1916 (Wundt, 1916).

Wundt had read and had been influenced by Darwin's *The Origin of Species* (Darwin, 1859). In his autobiography Darwin had this to say concerning the inter-relationship between his *Descent of Man* and *The Origin of Species*.

> My *Descent of Man* was published in February 1871. As soon as I had become, in the year 1837 or 1838, convinced that species were mutable productions, I could not avoid the belief that man must come under the same law. Accordingly I collected notes on the subject for my own satisfaction, and not for a long time with any intention of publishing. Although in *The Origin of Species* the derivation of any particular species is never discussed, yet I thought it best, in order that no honourable man should accuse me of concealing my views, to add that by the work in question "light would be thrown on the origin of man and his history". (Barlow, 1958—this is the first unexpurgated version of Darwin's Autobiography; quoted in Ralling, 1979.)

'It was Darwin who made the history of man into a topic of serious scientific interest and this was the topic to which Wundt—and later Mead—addressed themselves. Mead was particularly concerned with understanding the natural origins of mind. The theory of evolution entailed a whole new theory of time and of history. In the Platonic and Aristotelian scheme of things, forms were logically prior to the things which took on that form. Hence forms or species had no history. (It is interesting to note that Mead continued to use the term "form" as being equivalent to "species".) That a departure from the true form (i.e. a variant) might actually be the basis for a new species would have been inconceivable in the Aristotelian scheme of things. With Darwin time took on a new meaning: it now made sense to speculate about the origins of man, and Wundt in his *Lectures on Human and Animal Psychology* expressed the belief that Darwin's principles of natural selection were as valid for the evolution of man's mind as they were for the evolution of his body (Wundt, 1894, p. 385).

In his outline for a folk psychology Wundt set out to write a history of mankind from a psychological point of view, and he did this in two different ways. In his more extensive treatment, he traced the history of, for example, speech, or myth or religion. In his briefer *Elements of Folk Psychology* (Wundt, 1916) he put all this together and presented a synchronous account of the history of mankind divided into such epochs as those of primitive man, the totemic age, the age of heroes and gods and culminating with the development of what he called humanity. It is clear from *Totem and Taboo* that Freud had read Wundt's account of the totemic age and was provoked into responding.

Darwin's impact on Wundt is thus reflected in the latter's social psychology, not in his experimental laboratory science. This calls for an assessment of Wundt's status as a social scientist, a perfectly legitimate enterprise in a volume devoted to the *development* of social psychology. Wundt's contribution to the development of social psychology is, at present, inadequately appreciated, for reasons to which I have alluded above, and is treated at greater length elsewhere (Farr, 1980a). He did separate his experimental psychology from his social psychology and this has had some unfortunate consequences, but he did regard both these enterprises as equally legitimate concerns. One could argue that his folk psychology was too "collective" and his experimental psychology too "individual" for social psychology to emerge as a viable synthesis between these two contrasting levels of analysis. Indeed it is important to appreciate that it was precisely because the two levels of analysis were contrasting that Wundt felt compelled to separate them.

Wundt influenced many distinguished social scientists e.g. Malinowski, Boas, Thomas, Durkheim, Mead, Freud, etc.; a fact which is little known within purely psychological circles. We noted above how Wundt considered those collective phenomena which were the focus of his folk psychology to be independent of, and to exist prior to, the consciousness of each of the individuals comprising the community. Wundt insisted that these collective phenomena could neither be reduced to, nor explained in terms of, individual consciousness. Durkheim was later to establish this as a fundamental principle of sociological explanation i.e. that "social facts" cannot be explained in terms of concepts at an individual level. Here we have the introduction of an over-sharp distinction between sociology and psychology to which, in part, Wundt contributed; and one consequence of this is that there are now several different traditions of social psychology, some of which are sociological and others of which are psychological, but they have little or no inter-relationship to each other (see Farr, 1978).

The inter-relationships between the various social sciences were much closer in Wundt's day than they are today. Social psychology, together with developmental and physiological psychology, then formed part of a truly comparative psychology. It was the comparative method which Darwin, more than any other single person, helped to introduce into scientific circles. This was the natural complement to an experimental approach. Rather than bringing variables under experimental control within the laboratory, it was instead necessary to study the range of phenomena existing in nature. This applied just as aptly to studying the varieties of human nature to be found in different societies as it did to the study of different biological species. It was necessary to study the correlations which existed in nature; indeed the whole theory of evolution emerged from just such a study of correlations.

One cannot create new nervous systems experimentally although one can interfere with the operation of a nervous system by surgical or chemical intervention. Nature, however, has spontaneously produced a great diversity of nervous systems, and Darwin showed just how prodigal nature was in this respect. To study the relationships between the nervous system and behaviour it is helpful to adopt a comparative perspective. This is why, classically, there has always been such a close relationship between comparative and physiological psychology.

In order to study the effects of culture on personality it was similarly necessary to adopt a comparative perspective. The extent to which social psychology was at one time part of a much broader comparative psychology can be readily ascertained by considering the scope of the contents of the first *Handbook of Social Psychology* edited by Murchison and published in two volumes in 1935 (Murchison, 1935). There were separate chapters devoted to insects, birds, bacteria; the social history of the white man, of the yellow man, of the black man, and of the red man and so forth. Social psychology, then, was very broadly concerned with the study of social aggregates (whether of birds, insects or even bacteria) as well as with studying the varieties of human nature resulting from growing up in widely differing cultures. Amongst the authors of the various chapters were several distinguished anthropologists and biologists. Perhaps the 1935 *Handbook* represents the high-water mark of the influence of Darwin and Wundt on the development of social psychology. Certainly when the next *Handbook of Social Psychology* appeared, in 1954, under the editorship of Lindzey, it was scarcely recognizable as referring to the same discipline (Lindzey, 1954). In the Murchison *Handbook* only one of the 23 chapters had been based on the findings of experimental research carried out in the laboratory (this was Dashiell's chapter on social facilitation effects which came at the end of the second volume). By 1954 all had changed: social psychology was by then an experimental discipline and the new *Handbook* clearly reflected this change both in methodology and status.

The growing importance of the laboratory and the increased use of experimental methods inevitably led to a decline in the influence both of Darwin and of Wundt on the development of social psychology. The great virtue of the laboratory in the eyes of many of its exponents was that it represented an arena of research which was independent of its location in time and space within a particular culture. The a-historicity of the experiment as a method of research was similarly hailed both as a virtue and a strength. Many of these assumptions are now being questioned. The independence of a laboratory from its location in space/time within a particular culture has been challenged, most notably in Gergen's highly seminal article on social psychology as history (Gergen, 1973). The dangers inherent in an undue reliance upon such an a-historical method of research as the experiment are brought out in Campbell's rather remarkable address as President of the American Psychological Association (Campbell, 1975). The articles by Gergen and Campbell may presage a return to a more evolutionary perspective within social psychology. They certainly both treat history as an important, though neglected, dimension in social psychology. The influence of Darwin on Wundt had previously led to an appreciation of the importance of the history of man in the writing of any worthwhile social psychology, but this failed to make a continuing impact on the development of the subject.

In this section on Wundt, I have so far concentrated on the general influence of Darwin on the development of Wundt's folk psychology. The influences referred to above related to *The Origin of Species* and the *Descent of Man* rather than to the treatise which is the specific focus of interest in the present chapter. In several important respects Wundt extended and developed the ideas which Darwin expounded in *The Expression of the Emotions in Man and Animals* and helped to prepare the ground for the development of the seminal social behaviourism of George Herbert Mead. These highly significant developments appear in the first two volumes of his *Volkerpsychologie*, in which he deals with the development of human speech (Wundt, 1904). Darwin had dealt with the strong emotions, several of which involved quite dramatic changes in the human respiratory system; for instance under strong emotion man is often left speechless. That the emotions which were of interest to Darwin were often highly disruptive of normal functioning can be inferred from an interesting observation which he made. He had hoped to find in the writings and works of painters and sculptors a mine of information about the bodily expression of emotion in man. In this respect he was disappointed. "The reason no doubt is, that in works of art, beauty is the chief object; and strongly contracted facial muscles destroy beauty. The story of the composition is generally told with wonderful force and truth by skilfully given accessories" (Darwin, 1872, p. 14). In his discussion of emotional expression Darwin from time to time depicted particular gestures as characteristic of a given emotion. It is the *gesture* which Wundt picked out and developed much further than Darwin had done. He also set the human gesture in a more explicitly social context than Darwin had done. It is from Wundt's concept of the human gesture that the social psychology of Mead takes off and develops.

Wundt believed that the most significant gestures for the development of men were those vocal gestures which underlay the development of human speech. Darwin was aware of the role of voice in animal communication: in mating-calls during the breeding-season; how social animals often call to each other when separated; the musical singing of certain birds, etc. He noted that: "We can plainly perceive, with some of the lower animals, that the males employ their voices to please the females, and that they themselves take pleasure in their own vocal utterances; but why particular sounds are uttered, and why these give pleasure cannot at present be explained" (Darwin, 1872, pp. 87, 88). Wundt sought for the origins of language in the development of the human gesture. In gesture language

> It is not sounds, but expressive movements, imitative and pantomimic, that form the means by which man communicates his thoughts to man ... This mode of communication is not the result of intellectual reflections or conscious purposes, but of emotion and the involuntary expressive movements that accompany emotion. Indeed it is simply a natural development of those expressive movements that accompany emotion. Indeed it is simply a natural development of those expressive movements of human beings that also occur where the intention of communicating is obviously absent. (Wundt, 1916, pp. 58, 60.)

For Wundt and Darwin, expressive movements were involuntary and served no special purpose. Impulsive actions, on the other hand, were regarded as voluntary actions i.e. as serving a specific purpose or as being goal-oriented. For Wundt and Darwin, expressive movements were the rudiments of what at some time in the evolutionary past of a particular species had been impulsive movements. The distinction approximates to that which is sometimes drawn between the involuntary and the voluntary nervous systems and which may be further reflected in the differences between classical and operant conditioning.

Wundt speculates on how language may have evolved from the vocal gesture; Mead treats the transition in an altogether more profound, and characteristically social, way. Wundt did at least highlight the importance of language in human development and was aware of the intimate relationship between language and thought. In this respect he extended Darwin's own thinking. Wundt believed that man's higher cognitive processes could only be studied in the wider social world outside of the laboratory: they were not amenable to exploration by means of introspection. Language was not an accidental discovery of an individual "it is the product of peoples, and, generally speaking, there are as many different languages as there are originally distinct peoples. The same is true of the beginning of art, of mythology, and of custom" (Wundt, 1916, p. 2). Wundt's point here is that language, and religion were *in origin* the creation of a folk community even though by his day most of them had become universal, having long since transcended the limits of a single people.

For Wundt (and hence also for Mead) there is both a phylogenetic and an ontogenetic continuum between non-verbal and verbal aspects of communication: he pointed to the purely behavioural origins of language as a mode of communication and noted how gesture languages were often restricted to indicating aspects of the world which were directly observable. Indeed his various discussions of the psychology of the sentence sound refreshingly modern.

C. THE SOCIAL BEHAVIOURISM OF G. H. MEAD

Mead set out in his social psychology, as Wundt had done in his, to account for man's higher cognitive functions. His social behaviourism was based on a very close reading both of Darwin and of Wundt's folk psychology. Mead effectively developed the whole of his social psychology from Wundt's conception of the human gesture. For Mead a gesture was a part-action which *others* completed. An "attitude", for Mead, was the beginning of an act—it was, thus, a behavioural term (as it had been for Darwin). Mead argued that the *meaning* of an action was to be found in the response which it elicits from others: his psychology was clearly, then, a *social* psychology. An individual's behaviour comes to acquire the significance for himself which it originally had for others with whom he interacts. Mead directly challenged Wundt's assumption that consciousness is a uniquely individual phenomenon: he showed how man's self-awareness (i.e. his awareness of himself as an object in the world of others) arose from interacting with others in the course of growing up. In this way he demonstrated the purely social antecedents of individual consciousness.

The whole of Mead's social psychology arose from the study of events at the level of social interaction. He thus occupied the middle ground between the "individual" and the "collective" psychologies of Wundt such that if one adopts Mead's perspective then neither of Wundt's contrasting psychologies can be considered to be genuinely social. It was on the basis of a close reading of Darwin's *The Expression of the Emotions in Man and Animals* that Mead was able to focus so clearly on the behavioural interface between organisms engaged in the process of responding to each other. The whole of Mead's social psychology is based on an analysis of the events involved when organisms respond to each other. If Wundt's work can be considered a development of Darwin's in highlighting the importance, in man, of gestures, Mead went a stage further by showing how gestures acquire meaning in the course of social interaction.

As a major pragmatist philosopher, Mead set himself the task of refuting the Cartesian dualism of mind and body which had bedevilled the birth of psychology as an experimental discipline. His arguments against Descartes' dualism of mind and body were based on a close reading of Darwin. In the thinking of Mead mind and self are intimately interlinked: "The body is not a self, as such; it becomes a self only when it has developed a mind within the context of social experience" (Mead, 1934, p. 50). The self, for Mead, becomes linked to the very structure of language.

> The self does not exist except in relation to something else. The word "itself", you will recognise, belongs to the reflexive mode. It is that grammatical form which we use under conditions in which the individual is both subject and object. He addresses himself. He sees himself as others see him. The very usage of the word implies an individual who is occupying the position of both subject and object. In a mode which is not reflexive, the object is distinguished from the subject. The subject, the self, sees a tree. The latter is something that is different from himself. In the use of the term "itself", on the contrary, the subject and object are found in the same entity. (Mead, 1936, p. 74.)

Wundt's conception of individual consciousness, which was the basis of his experimental laboratory science, reflected the Cartesian inheritance; there was no theory of self implicit in his conception of consciousness. For Mead, then, this was a non-social conception of individual consciousness, since for him mind emerges out of social interaction. Here, Mead was much more consistently Darwinian than Wundt had ever been, and he used Darwin in order to banish Descartes' ghostly conception of the human mind. Had Mead's social behaviourism been available to Wundt, there would have been no need for the latter to have separated his "collective" from his "individual" psychology; his social from his experimental psychology. Mead solved the mind–body problem by arguing that mind emerged from bio-social behaviour. His account of mind was thus a behavioural one. Unlike Ryle's much later formulation of this perspective, Mead's argument was based on the work of Darwin: he looked to scientific evidence for his views rather than depending, as Ryle was later to do, on a purely philosophical analysis of linguistic usage (Ryle, 1949).

For Mead gestures and meanings are inseparable. For an act to be a gesture it must be perceived by, and evoke a response from, another organism. Mead discussed the "conversation of gestures" involved in the dog and cat fights which Darwin had described so vividly in his book. Darwin had confined himself to careful observation of the expressive movements of each animal and did not venture into any analysis of the fight as a fight. Mead on the other hand was more genuinely interested in analysing the fight than in attending to the physiological responses of each of the protagonists. Animals engaging in such "conversations" (as Mead called them) strike postures and adopt attitudes towards each other.

> The act of each dog becomes the stimulus to the other dog for his response. There is then a relationship between the two; and as the act is responded

to by the other dog, it, in turn, undergoes change. The very fact that the dog is ready to attack another becomes a stimulus to the other dog to change his own position or his own attitude. He has no sooner done this than the change of attitude in the second dog in turn causes the first dog to change his attitude. We have here a conversation of gestures. (Mead, 1934, pp. 42–43.)

In the social behaviour of lower organisms gestures do not have the same meaning for the individuals engaged in the social exchange, i.e. there is no shared meaning. The hiss of the snake may evoke the response of attack by the dog. The snake is not conscious or aware of the response which its own behaviour may elicit. For a gesture to become a *significant* gesture it must evoke the same response in the organism making it which it evokes in the other who responds.

The vocal gesture becomes a significant symbol ... when it has the same effect in the individual making it that it has on the individual to whom it is addressed or who explicitly responds to it, and thus involves a reference to the self of the individual making it. (Mead, 1934, p. 46.)

Language is a good example of an important class of such significant gestures. It is also distinctive of man as a species. "The conscious or significant conversation of gestures is a much more adequate and effective mechanism of mutual adjustment within the social act—involving, as it does, the taking, by each of the individuals carrying it on, of the attitudes of the others towards himself—than is the unconscious or non-significant conversation of gestures" (Mead, 1934, p. 46). It is the capacity to participate in significant conversations that is the hallmark of man as a species. This further illustrates the profound influence of Darwin on the development of Mead's thought.

Two profoundly different psychologies emerge as a consequence of whether one stresses either the continuity or the discontinuity between man and other species. In his bio-social approach Mead stressed those emergent evolutionary properties which set man apart from other species, e.g. the relationship between the hand and the development of the human brain and, above all else, the development of language from the vocal gesture. In Watsonian behaviourism the stress was on the continuity between man and other species. Mead developed his social behaviourism in conscious opposition to the behaviourism of Watson. They were, for a time, at the University of Chicago together, and Mead was thoroughly familiar with Watson's work. They also knew each other socially and were on friendly terms. Both Mead and Watson were influenced by Darwin, but Mead stressed the emergent properties that set man apart from other species and Watson adopted a more explicitly reductionist stance.

The revolution in psychology which Watson spearheaded was essentially a methodological one. It had more to do with the nature of science than with the nature of man. Watson argued that the methods of observation which had proved successful in studying the behaviour of animals and small children should now be extended to the study of adults. Reliance on introspective reports had no place in an "objective" science. Behaviourism *within psychology* became a systematic programme for ridding the discipline of such "mentalistic" concepts as mind, consciousness, self, thought, self-awareness, etc. Psychologists are only now beginning to appreciate that behaviourism was a heavy price to pay for ridding their discipline of the ghost of Descartes. It was Descartes' ghostly conception of the human mind which behaviourists sought to banish. Behaviourism was a reaction against the experimental laboratory science based on introspection which Wundt had inaugurated in Leipzig and which Titchener had helped to establish in America. We briefly noted above how this new laboratory science was born within the false dualism of mind and body which was part of the Cartesian inheritance. The proper antidote to Descartes, however, is not the behaviourism of Watson or of Skinner but the evolutionary theory of Darwin. What is required is a naturalistic account of the origins of mind. This is precisely what both Wundt and Mead set out to develop on the basis of a close reading of Darwin.

It is interesting that Watson should have cited the success of observational studies of animals and of small children in his clarion call for a new methodology in scientific psychology. Charles Darwin made significant contributions to both of these fields and was a pioneer in each. Yet, as we have had occasion to note in the course of this chapter, he was not averse to referring to the mind of man or to man's awareness of himself in the eyes of others. This was particularly true of his analyses of the peculiarly human emotions of self-attention, such as shyness, which I treated at some length in the first third of this chapter. The essence of good observation is fidelity to the phenomenon under observation. If the phenomenon is a highly social one and is mental in nature, these aspects should be salient features in the report made by any competent observer. In this respect Darwin was a more "objective" scientific observer than Watson.

Mead's opposition to Watson comes out clearly in his strongly anti-reductionist stance in the interpretation of evolution. He thought that Watson's main fault was oversimplification. The emergence of novel characteristics in the course of evolution required, in Mead's estimation, the creation of a new past in order to account for their emergence. Novel characteristics could not have been predicted on the basis of the past that existed prior to their emergence. Mead treated mind as emerging in the course of human evolution. He was therefore committed to identifying the mechanisms of its emergence. His account was a naturalistic one and as such represented a further development and refinement of the work of Darwin. Mead was quick to appreciate the significance of Wundt's identification of language as providing the key to an understanding of human development. For Wundt, as we noted above, language was the creation of a "folk community" and as such was a cultural product. Language is also distinctive of man as a species. Wundt was able to add culture as an important component that was missing from Darwin's earlier analysis of human gestures. Mead's distinctive contribution, as we saw above, resides in his identifying how gestures acquire meaning in the course of social interaction. His social behaviourism is generally superior to the much narrower and more doctrinaire behaviourism of Watson. Yet, curiously, the latter has had a greater impact than Mead on the development of psychology (for an account of how this came about see Farr, 1980a).

In this chapter I have sought to trace the influence of a single book, Darwin's *The Expression of the Emotions in Man and Animals*, on the *development* of social psychology. I believe that both Wundt and Mead developed Darwin's thinking in ways which were highly significant for the development of social psychology and that their ideas are of considerable contemporary relevance. In many research laboratories the study of behaviour is on the way out, and the study of mind (or "cognition" as the more cautious may prefer to call it) is on the way in. The theoretical rationale for making this dramatic switch has not yet been made explicit, even though a cogent rationale can be found in the work of Mead. Language is now acknowledged to be of central significance in understanding man's higher cognitive processes; both Wundt and Mead, however, had come to this conclusion well over half a century ago. As an experimental laboratory science psychology has been based *either* on the study of consciousness *or* on the study of behaviour. Both of these foundations have proved to be too narrow and restrictive. The conceptualization of each has been inherently non-social. A social conceptualization *both* of consciousness *and* of behaviour can be found in Mead. Mead also offers a theoretical understanding of how consciousness and behaviour are inter-related to each other. His work thus opens up the possibility of adopting a "both/and" approach to succeed the "either/or" approaches which to date have characterized the historical development of psychology as a science. My own interests in the history of psychology arise out of a concern with the new directions which psychology might take in the future, and which are reflected in the present volume. The development and the quality of thinking from Darwin through Wundt to Mead is of a sufficiently high calibre, in my opinion, to deserve our serious attention.

D. SUMMARY

An exposition is given of Darwin's treatment of the expression of the emotions in man and animals. His emphasis on the importance of the face in the expression of human emotion is noted, and his analysis of blushing in humans is treated at some length for the richness of its insights into the social psychology of shyness and of shame. His treatment of attitude as a whole-bodied orientation of the organism with respect to some feature of its environment is made explicit and the implications of this for modern social psychology are briefly discussed. There is thus much for the contemporary social psychologist to discover on the basis of a close reading of Darwin; indeed Darwin continues to be an important source of inspiration to those experimental social psychologists concerned with the facial expression of emotion in man (Ekman, 1974). Historically, however, Darwin was an important though neglected figure in the development of social psychology. The seminal influence of his work on the development of Wundt's "folk psychology" is traced. Wundt extended Darwin's treatment of gestures in man by singling out, as particularly significant in the evolution of man, the development of vocal gestures in the direction of human speech and language. By treating language as the product of a "folk community" Wundt added the significant dimension of culture as a form of inheritance in man which acts as a supplement to the genetic inheritance which was the primary focus of interest to Darwin. Mead similarly develops the work both of Darwin and of Wundt in that the whole of his social behaviourism takes off from Wundt's analysis of the human gesture. Mead makes language central to the whole of his social psychology. There is thus an important progression in thinking from Darwin to Mead, through Wundt. This line of thought is not only of historical importance but is also of significance now: it is to be hoped that the realization of this will exert a beneficial influence on the development of social psychology.

6
Fashions in Social Psychology

JOHN M. INNES
University of Adelaide

A. Characteristics of fashions	138
B. Sources of research developments in social psychology	139
1. Intrinsic factors	140
2. Extrinsic factors	140
C. Structural characteristics affecting diffusion of research developments	143
1. Differentiation of references	144
2. Time perspective	147
3. Author networks	149
D. Fashion and changes in social psychology	150
1. Testing substantive hypotheses	151
2. Methodological development	155
3. Recurrence of themes	157
E. Conclusions	161

It is quite clear that social psychology is growing rapidly, and whether one derives satisfaction from such growth or is pessimistic about its worth, the growth itself cannot be denied. One common interpretation of such rapid growth is that it is due to "fashion", to some non-rational tendency for people to follow others. However, such a statement does no more than label the phenomenon without explaining it, and a researcher within the field may, in any case, interpret it as the result of a rational use of resources to solve an important problem with new methods and tools. The goal of this chapter is to analyse some aspects of the current state of social psychological research and to examine to what extent developments in the discipline may possess characteristics that either can be labelled as truly fashionable or can be seen as the result of rational responses to internal and external factors in psychology and in society. To facilitate the discussion of the growth characteristics of social psychology we shall first consider briefly those features which sociological analysis suggests are important for any phenomenon to be labelled as a fashion; we shall then turn the arguments inward—to the development of social psychology itself. These features have been collated from a number of sources (e.g. Crane, 1969; Katz and Lazarsfeld, 1955) and seem to be critical although they may not be exhaustive.

A. CHARACTERISTICS OF FASHIONS

Many events in society influence the opinions and habits of people for predominantly rational reasons but "fashion" is a term which seems most appropriately retained to apply to the case where a number of models or styles compete for adoption and where there is no test or appeal to logical consistency or external, observable criteria that can enable a choice to be made. Fashion applies to the case where conformity or appearance are the dominant causes of adoption or where the criteria are vague and dependent upon external (social) rather than internal (logical) factors, e.g. the influence of an elite (Crane, 1969).

In general, it may be difficult to identify the true *source* of a fashion, but two sets of features seem important: intrinsic factors (e.g. a gadget may be adopted because it fulfils some need or practical requirement, because of a new design, or because of its novelty, even though these characteristics are not related to its usefulness) and extrinsic factors (e.g. availability of finance, climate, the threat of war, or political instability, Sales, 1973).

A second characteristic of any fashion is its *rate of diffusion* throughout a population. The process can be understood in social psychological terms as based on a network of contacts between individuals, these networks varying in the types of relationships which enable the transmission of information or influence to spread through a population. The speed of diffusion will then depend upon the density of the particular network, i.e. the number of links between pairs of individuals, which in turn depends upon the nature of the criterion being used for adoption of the fashion (e.g. on the basis of friends' or professional colleagues' choices). The spread of adoption may also be facilitated by the presence within a network of "fashion leaders" or individuals who are in contact with many other individuals, i.e. who have proportionately denser networks, and who are also more open to influences from outside the particular network (Katz and Lazarsfeld, 1955). A fashion need not of course diffuse throughout an entire population: the links for such complete transmission of information may not exist, or the criteria necessary for acceptance may not be satisfied for certain individuals or groups (Glassman, 1973). Also, notwithstanding any deficiency of links to allow an "excitatory" event to pass through, there may actually be active "inhibitory" features of a network, especially if an idea or event is of an extreme or revolutionary nature. Indeed, the relationship of fashion to extremity may take another form: even if the initial event is not of an extreme nature and does not engender strong resistance, the diffusion of the fashion may itself bring about changes in its characteristics, with a movement towards more extreme values on some attributes (perhaps as a result of the need that people may have, even while conforming, to differentiate themselves from others; Fromkin, 1972). Alternatively, changes may be due to social, structural factors, such as the adoption of some behaviour enabling people to assess their relative position on some dimension and thereby allowing them to remove inhibitions.

A final feature of fashion which has been noted is that particular *themes reappear after a time* (e.g. styles of dress may be adopted again thirty years after they last "died"). In the present context this is a particularly interesting feature of the analysis, since the introduction of new areas in social psychology is often accompanied by a recital of perceived theoretical antecedents that go back some considerable time.

B. SOURCES OF RESEARCH DEVELOPMENTS IN SOCIAL PSYCHOLOGY

Given this background, we may now attempt to consider the present state of social psychology and the process whereby it reached that state and see the extent to which internal structure of the discipline and the internal or external influences upon its growth have fashion-*like* characteristics. It is crucial to such an analysis to differentiate between non-rational, conformist influences and the development of rational processes in the determination of the state of social psychology. However, there seems to be considerable evidence that both the kind of research and the way it is executed are, like a fashion, affected by factors which are extrinsic as well as intrinsic to the actual inquiries.

1. Intrinsic factors

The particular theories current in a discipline dictate the problems which are tackled, the solution of which inevitably exposes other problems. It has been argued that such ideas arise from empirical evidence, or on the other hand that the intellect can transcend empirics and create a system which will determine what is looked for as supportive evidence. A third view sees as crucial the availability of observational data which are given substance by the development of a theory which in turn generates predictions for the gathering of new data. Once established, a theory dictates what further studies need to be done as new perspectives and limitations are perceived. The task then becomes one of solving those problems and is largely immune from outside influences.

Kuhn's (1962) view of the development of scientific knowledge emphasizes the intrinsic factors within a discipline. He postulates the development of scientific disciplines through periods of "normal" science (where a range of specific problems are studied by workers in the field) followed by crises (when the dominant theory cannot account for all of the observed anomalies). These precipitate a revolution in which a new theory emerges to account for the anomalies and provide new predictions. One obvious intrinsic factor which nevertheless seems essential for the development of a field of inquiry is the availability of particular methods. Indeed, the available theories will often specify the "appropriate" types of instrumentation and "the ways in which accepted instruments may legitimately be employed" (Kuhn, 1962, p. 40). Who can tell how psychology would have developed had not the analysis of variance been developed by Fisher and promulgated by Lindquist?

2. Extrinsic factors

A consideration of the role of methods can lead us to see that the development of a discipline, both in the formation of a theory and the testing of that theory, can be dependent upon extrinsic forces, i.e. forces not logically related to the process of thought and experimentation. The developments of technology have influenced psychology by creating new problems, new ways of looking at old problems, and new methods of solving those problems or new metaphorical bases for theoretical work. For example, automation and computer development have required the creation of man–machine studies, to fit men to tasks and tasks to men. Automatic machines also influence psychologists by making them think of men as limited information processors: for example, we have the in-basket, filing cabinet, and waste-paper basket theory of man (Broadbent, 1971). A non-bureaucratic society would have difficulty conceiving of man in such terms.

Non-intellectual extrinsic factors. In addition to such indirect extrinsic influences, other social changes affect the development of social psychological theory by affecting both the way in which a social psychologist studies a problem and what he perceives to be a problem. It may be said quite confidently that in this sense social psychology follows fashions in this way often by tracking the kinds of problems which arise from time to time in society. Fashionable research of this type can be identified in the sense that many people will begin to work on a problem because it is at that time a salient one to the society as a whole. External research funds may become available to examine a problem in society and personnel follow the funds, or particular subject populations consequently become available and easy access leads to the production of lots of data (Barber, 1968). In social psychology it is possible to identify at random many such flurries of research generated by some salient social event. For instance, initial work on communication and attitude change was strongly influenced by the war propaganda studies (Hovland, Lumsdaine and Sheffield, 1949). The work on bystander apathy (Latané and Darley, 1970) was the upshot of concern expressed about the possible decline of urban civilization following a particularly bizarre episode in New York. Again, work on stereotypes and its relationship with prejudice has been continually correlated with American social concerns about the integration of minority groups, and there has been a whole range of studies to examine the structure of the images of foreign groups held by sections of the community (Katz and Braly, 1958). As a final example, the work on the "risky shift" grew from a particular concern about the extent to which groups concerned with decisions of national security could move in the direction of making a risky choice rather than going for safety (Kogan and Wallach, 1964).

Most of the research on topics such as these has sunk with hardly a trace as the social problem which engendered the awareness (and the funds) has been replaced by another. Nevertheless, some of the research on the topics has lasted because the work has forged links with other research traditions in social psychology and so generated a somewhat more intrinsically motivated development, with new data being related to older problems.

There is a rather more subtle way in which fashionable social concerns may influence the nature of research. As an example we may take the theory of cognitive dissonance (Festinger, 1957), *par excellence* a dominant theory in social psychology where empirical evidence has simply fed back and been used to modify the theory. On the face of it, this theory (which by its own intrinsic developments has influenced many social psychologists) seems to have a straightforward intellectual genealogy arising from Lewinian field theory, through interpersonal dynamics in groups, to the need for an individual to substantiate his beliefs through comparison of them with others, leading to the manner in which the person resolves incongruities between beliefs (Festinger, 1954; 1957). A deeper, more symbolic, analysis has however been made by Rosenberg (1970). Cognitive dissonance experiments may dramatize a dominant theme in contemporary life, namely the inauthenticity with which we perform many of our actions. Because of the numerous roles which we play we come to adopt as private convictions many of the beliefs we espouse in public action. The theory can thus be seen as "emphasising our troubled sense that inner self is being gradually eroded and transformed to suit the inauthentic behavior into which we have been seduced without full awareness of the seduction process" (p. 184). It is possible to see many theories in social psychology as having such appeal to fashionable doubts and troubles in this way, even if the growth of a theory can apparently be readily attributed to its intrinsic, rational characteristics.

While some such examples may be seen as having a non-intellectual component, the existence of societal themes determining the appeal of particular theories and methods of research has other forms, particularly exemplified in the influence of *ideology* upon the nature of psychological theory and the kind of problems which are studied. However, it is not sensible to enter here into the detailed analysis of the role of ideology due to the complexity of the issues and the variety of primary sources that already exist (e.g. Innes and Fraser, 1971; Hogan and Emler, 1978). In general terms, the role of an ideology can be construed as similar to that seen by Kuhn as being played by the paradigm, or at least by identifiable components of the paradigm. Indeed, in so far as views of a problem may develop along ideological lines without strong contact with reality, involvement with a paradigm may lead to a set of internally consistent, unreality-based, ideas and theories (McDonagh, 1976).

Over and above these more abstract influences there is a set of factors which affect the direction and style of social psychological research quite directly which, while not related *logically* to the problem-solving process, are inextricably tied to the practicalities of doing research. These are the characteristics of the profession (who is doing the research and what kind of network links the practitioners) and the communication infrastructure (the way in which the results of research are selected and communicated to others). Both are subject to fashionable influences.

While the characteristics of those who do research would seem logically precedent, it is none the less more convenient to examine the characteristics of what is published and then look at the population of authors who use it. In this way the role of journal and author networks may be identified as sources of fashionable influence along with the diffusion of those ideas and the individuals who use them.

C. STRUCTURAL CHARACTERISTICS AFFECTING DIFFUSION OF RESEARCH DEVELOPMENTS

The primary method of communication in science is by journal publication. There are two characteristics of scientific journals which seem to be crucial if one hopes to identify how a discipline is developing: the differentiation of the field (as evidenced by the extent to which articles refer fairly systematically to articles published in a limited range of other journals), and the time perspective of the discipline (as indexed by the age of articles cited as important precursors of the work presently reported, Price, 1970).

1. Differentiation of references

The differentiation of social psychology is observable in several ways. Xhignesse and Osgood (1967), for example, show that in psychology generally there is a considerable degree of self-citation, i.e. the citation in current papers published in a journal of previous papers from that journal, and in addition a reliance upon a very small number of other journals for citation. Xhignesse and Osgood (1967) show a tendency for social psychological journals to depend upon a reducing number of other journals, with increasing dependency upon a small number of psychological as against sociological and philosophical journals.

The *Journal of Abnormal and Social Psychology* (*JASP*) sampled predominantly from the psychological network, but particularly depended upon citations to itself. An examination of the 1970 volumes of *Journal of Personality and Social Psychology* (*JPSP*) (which continued as the social psychological specialization of *JASP*) shows that the reliance upon the core network had increased: 35% of all references were to a small core of journals, but 74% of citations within this network were self-referrals. When it does use psychology the *JPSP* uses itself, indicating an "introspective" approach to the development of research. Furthermore, examination of the bibliographies of articles in *JPSP* reveals that fully 50% of citations are made to only nine sources, namely *JPSP* (and *JASP*) itself, the *Journal of Experimental Social Psychology* (*JESP*), *Journal of Personality* (*JP*), *Journal of Social Psychology* (*JSP*), *Human Relations*, *Advances in Experimental Social Psychology*, *Sociometry*, the *Handbook of Social Psychology* (Lindzey and Aronson, 1968), and *Theories of Cognitive Consistency* (Abelson et al., 1968). Such an analysis suggests that the influences upon social psychological research are not wide, although a citation count of *JPSP* in 1977 reveals that the literature base in social psychology may be broadening. (The self-citation count was down to 20% and the reliance upon the nine sources was down to 33%.) Sadly, there is considerable evidence that the journals with broader citation patterns are also more peripheral to the development of the discipline. Analysis of the impact of journal articles (the use made of particular articles in influencing future developments) suggests that the *JPSP* and *JESP* are considerably more important, especially the latter, than the *British Journal of Social and Clinical Psychology* or the *JSP* (Garfield, 1975).

Thus, analysis of the material used to establish or substantiate the direction of research suggests that for the central journals in social psychology there are few influences outside that of social psychology itself. In this respect, at least, then, the development of social psychology is open to influence in a number of ways that are characteristic of fashions.

(a) *Narrowness of influence*. Any innovation which does occur will be likely to emanate from some previous development in the field rather than to stem from a discovery or innovation outside. There will be a *reduced* probability that other influences will make a contribution to the direction of thinking about the problem, although outside influences will not be entirely absent, even if they may be subtle (Rosenberg, 1970). The example of the theory of cognitive dissonance is a case in point. A highly cited development was the introduction of self-perception theory with its lauded dependence upon a radical behaviouristic tradition (Bem, 1965, 1972). While at one time the supposed conflict between the cognitive and behaviourist influences in the theory was thought to be the source of a creative development in the field (Child, 1973), more recently the theory has been seen either to be wholly assimilable into the cognitive tradition of attribution theory or to be perceived as concerned with a minor set of problems (Greenwald, 1975).

(b) *Recurrence of themes*. The narrow range of influences may render the recurrence of themes more likely. It could be that a small number of problems will be considered as central to the field and therefore over a fairly brief period of time they will reappear for analysis by the new set of theories and methods which become available.

In cases where a flurry of new papers occurs simply because of the influence of social events, the research does not seem to have a great impact unless it can be linked to developments in theory. For example, the work on the "risky-shift" seemed to spiral in on itself in terms of citations (Cartwright, 1973). Two things happened, however. First, the shift to risk was perceived as a special case of a more general movement to polarity in group discussion (Moscovici and Zavalloni, 1969) and this lengthened the "report life" of the phenomenon. Secondly, attempts were made to set the work within the more general framework of group problem-solving (Burnstein, 1969), persuasive argument (e.g. Burnstein and Vinokur, 1977), and social comparison processes (Sanders and Baron, 1977). While work on the group process which leads to risky decisions may still be overly dependent upon a particular method—and the number of papers published per year has declined significantly—nevertheless the research is beginning to take its place in the corpus of knowledge and has not been forgotten or relegated to footnote status. But the field continues via a rediscovery of other, earlier, work and a linking with theoretical concerns of a general nature, not with the *ad hoc* theorizing indulged in by the early workers.

(c) *Inhibition of development.* Few outside influences may result in the failure of inhibitory forces affecting the diffusion of an idea to develop, to counteract the excitatory impact of a "new" theory whilst enthusiasm leads to hopes that it may account for a wide range of phenomena, provided that close ties are seen with work in the same tradition. Amongst such influences, however, is an awareness of the limitations that are perceived by other disciplines. For example, the belief that cognitive dissonance theory could integrate under one rubric the phenomena of cognitive and group processes may have been invalidated by a broader knowledge of sociological analyses of group activity and of informational analyses of cognitive processes. An awareness of research from a somewhat broader time span than is common in social psychology could also have helped—a feature to be considered shortly below.

It is, of course, possible to take a different view of the state of social psychological research from the one here expressed and draw different inferences from it. Shulman and Silverman (1972) argue that social psychology is a "markedly heterogeneous discipline", on the basis that very few single sources are cited frequently. It is true that if viewed from the perspective of the psychologist concerned with the individual and his contribution to the development of a scientific discipline, then there are very few "creative" psychologists who publish a lot and have many citations. Shulman and Silverman show that very few journal articles are cited frequently: only books attract moderate attention. If viewed from a more structural perspective, however, it is clear that the discipline is concerned with a narrow range of problems and that the published papers are extremely closely related to each other. The fact that one paper is cited instead of another does not indicate that the former is more important theoretically, and one must look for other reasons for its citation. For example, one could argue that the inter-observer agreement (about importance of problems, style of approach, etc.) which is possible in social psychology does not appear to be high, even when it is examined in areas over which there is supposed to be consensus, including the choice of an appropriate methodology (Scott, 1974). The lack of consensus on value may then result in emphasis on continuity with previous work (as indicated by familiar citations) as a means of gaining credibility and therefore being accepted for publication, since the way in which the social sciences may develop is through the medium of argumentation, of dispute to convince an opponent (Phillips, 1973). Thus the dominance of certain figures may be due, paradoxically, to the essential similarity of the research literature from which only familiar names are cited, but this may in reality be merely a fashionable path to the inhibition of the development of social psychology.

2. Time perspective

If there is a narrowness of the network of citations which are the foundation of later research and if this is a symptom of a tendency to concentrate on particular problems and solutions, then—like the effects of time on other fashions—it might be expected that a narrowing of the time perspective of research also exists. That is, with a predominance of research on particular problems, there might be a tendency to cite immediately recent papers as they will be of greater relevance to a possible solution. A longer span of citation, stretching back over a number of years, is likely to be indicative of a less cumulative growth of knowledge, with a concern with problems and approaches to problems which have a longer-lasting, less fashionable existence (Price, 1970).

Xhignesse and Osgood (1967) have shown that on average 68% of all citations in the core American psychological literature including social journals are to papers and books less than ten years old and only 11% are more than twenty years old. The picture is complicated by the fact that the literature being cited is increasing exponentially and therefore it is to be expected that any single paper will have a lower chance of being cited the older it becomes. Price (1970) does demonstrate, however, that the older literature is cited at the appropriate rate and that any dramatic spurt (attributable to the "immediacy effect" of a research front) can be mapped fairly accurately by the proportion of references which are less than five years old. (For example, Innes (1973) found a typical figure of 40% for the *Journal of Experimental*

Psychology at three separate years of sampling, and the *JPSP* also shows a similar figure in 1970, 1976 and 1977.)

Such a figure would not indicate strongly a discipline which is heavily committed to activity in a "research front". There are, however, differences within the discipline which would suggest that the pattern of activity varies markedly and significantly from area to area, and from sector to sector within any area.

Evidence that there are indeed research fronts within social psychology comes from an examination of literature on the risky-shift. The overlap in citation by three major reviews of the literature was examined for the proportion of their bibliographies less than five years old. The range was from 31% to 86% with a mean of 65%. Such a figure puts this sub-area of social psychology well into the sphere of research fronts characteristic of which Price calls the "hard" sciences. Certainly these papers on the risky-shift seem to cite each other heavily to the exclusion of earlier literature. This can be accounted for in terms of the easy availability of a test device to measure any effect and is thus comparable to the literature on anxiety (Levy, 1961; Innes, 1973) and the authoritarian personality. As suggested earlier, however, the extent to which a published paper is acknowledged as important may be a function of the extent to which it may make links with other literature of a broad nature.

An analysis of such time perspective and lasting influence seems in order. There are areas in social psychology which bear all the hallmarks of heavily researched scientific disciplines with the importance of wider ranging and older literature minimized. It may of course be the case that these publishing practices in turn influence the style of research which is carried out. It may be that what could be termed a spatial and temporal "myopia" in the perception of ideas and theories has been reinforced by the kind of books and papers which are read in the discipline. A lack of awareness of what has gone before may also make a field more prone to fashionable influences, as there is not the strong context against which any new method or idea may be considered. To paraphrase a saying, "The field which forgets its founding fathers (or archival literature) is lost" (or at least may be more likely to become subject to the whims of fashion and change).

3. Author networks

The growth of research in science typically shows the S-shaped curve which is observable in the spread of fashion (Price, 1962) and social psychology seems no different. Not all social psychologists contribute actively to the growth of the discipline, however, and the people who publish are certainly a minority. Garvey and Griffith (1971) show that only 10% of *authors* (not of all members of psychological associations) publish as much as one paper per year over a five-year period. Those who do publish frequently are also those who are cited frequently by others (Myers, 1970) and hence have a disproportionate influence upon the direction research may take in a discipline. The work that productive individuals do is likely to be read more and perhaps attended to more, thereby leading to a greater effect. When a new paper appears written by someone already known there may be a tendency to read it and cite it rather more than a similar paper by a less well-known author (named by Merton, 1968, the "Matthew Effect").

Merton (1957) and Campbell (1973) have both argued that such eponymy, whereby particular individuals are associated with a number of ideas and papers, may play a valuable role in facilitating the development of research. Given that multiple discoveries are frequent in science, the role of the productive person, who is associated with several multiple discoveries is to direct attention to important ideas; his or her authorship increases the value of the "signal" against the background "noise" of scientific communication. The rapid diffusion of fashionable new ideas may thus be heightened by the existence of productive authors in ways predictable from Katz and Lazarsfeld's (1955) analysis of fashionable influence. (It may be, however, that the predilection to cite the familiar may also inhibit attention to the adoption of innovative material which may be published by an unfamiliar individual. Eponymy may retard progress as well as facilitate it, cf. above and Chapter 8.)

Such prolific producers also seem to play a role in maintaining the rapid growth of new areas, since eminence and influence are associated with collaboration where the people who are prominent in an area tend to have associated with them a large number of research workers and hence the opportunity for more research to be done and for the field to grow.

Price and Beaver (1966) suggest that any group of people working on a related set of problems consists of a core of active researchers with an associated large floating population of other workers who appear on one or two papers and then disappear. In Price and Beaver's data the active researcher may appear to produce up to 28 papers in a five-year period, with as many as 34 collaborators, compared with those who collaborated with only one other person and produced a maximum of four papers in the same period.

Price and Beaver have shown this effect through their use of "fractional productivities" whereby an author is assigned $1/n$ of a point for the occurrence of his name among n authors of a single paper. Such a score is found to be normally distributed, with few highly productive individuals. As many as 50% of contributors have fractional productivity scores of less than 0·5, i.e. appear as second author on one paper or less. (Although Price and Beaver's data came from a group of collaborators in biology, a similar picture emerges in an analysis of published papers in social psychology, Innes, 1978.)

At present nothing can be said about the creativity or ability of people at the centre of research fronts. While it is unlikely that major contributions are made by uncreative people, there are data in other areas of science to suggest that the level of ability of productive scientists may not be all that high. For the moment, however, the structural fact can be identified without an account in terms of individual differences being available.

Such analyses indicate that research networks may exist in the social as well as the natural sciences and may have a facilitative effect upon the growth of research both by making certain developments more salient and by facilitating growth by providing centres for the development of research networks. Leaders in science may thus be viewed as akin to leaders in other social networks. All that these analyses can show, however, is the effect—which may *appear* fashion-like—they do not show that the growth is due to non-rational adherence to fashion.

D. FASHION AND CHANGES IN SOCIAL PSYCHOLOGY

What are the developments in social psychology which may show the characteristics of fashion in their growth? Earlier (see Section 2) I noted the intrinsic and extrinsic forces that acted to develop social psychology;

it is now necessary to distinguish further, viz. between those developments that arise primarily from the testing of substantive hypotheses and those that are generated primarily by methodological concerns and innovations. By focusing first on consistent concerns of social psychology (attitudes, small-group behaviour) it is possible to point to a number of factors that link development with the "fashion forces" that have been considered so far. Subsequent examination of methodological developments in terms of such "fashion forces" amplifies this—and hence we will arrive at a deeper analysis of the major theme determining the study of social behaviour.

1. Testing substantive hypotheses

(a) *Attitudes*. The dominant role played by the study of attitudes in the history and development of social psychology can be accounted for in several ways (McGuire, 1969a), some of which fit neatly with the present analysis (especially in the influence of extrinsic facilitating factors).

The statement of Thurstone (1929) that attitudes could be measured (applying the methods of psychometrics and psychophysics) inaugurated one stage in the growth of research on attitudes and created an interest which continues to the present day (Fishbein and Ajzen, 1975). Also at about that time Sherif's classic work on the formation of norms was published (Sherif, 1936) and demonstrated that it was possible to create systems of interpersonal dependency experimentally in the laboratory. Whilst the classic work of Thurstone and of Sherif generated research in its own right, a major extrinsic factor, the Second World War, also affected social psychological development at that time, and a major outcome of this was the study of attitude *change* using methodology of such a nature that large numbers of people could be studied. The extrinsic need that large numbers of soldiers had to be indoctrinated and have their morale boosted led to vast development of work on norms and attitudes leading to work on mass communication (e.g. Hovland, Lumsdaine and Sheffield, 1949). The major concern here was change and the manipulation of independent variables which would be likely to maximize such change. As McGuire (1969a) has pointed out, the emphasis was upon the manipulated variables and there was less concern with precision of measurement of the dependent variables, as had been the object of Thurstone's work. As such, then, the research was influenced by another extrinsic factor which had entered the consciousness of psychologists, the development of experimental design and the analysis of variance. The lesser concern with precise measurement led to lower reliability and greater error so there was a need for powerful statistical techniques which would reveal statistically significant effects and enable large numbers of subjects to be used. Analysis of variance methods enabled this to be done and led to a strong and continuing preference for "factorial" designs.

However, as the work on changing attitudes continued to develop right through the 1960s and 70s, all the characteristics of fashionable growth became evident. The original concern with societal needs faded, and the area assumed all the characteristics of growth dependent upon structural, endogenous factors, although the growth of the mass media gave some extrinsic impetus to research on characteristics of the message and the medium of communication.

At least one other development occurred during the late 1940s and added to the factors stimulating the growth of attitude work: the rise of fascism led to an attempt to understand the reasons for its growth. The combination of psychoanalytic thinking and attitude measurement methodology led to the publication of *The Authoritarian Personality* (Adorno *et al.*, 1950) and that event had a profound impact upon social psychology. Although severely criticized on methodological and substantive grounds (e.g. Hyman and Sheatsley, 1954), the work influenced research because of the easy availability of measures of attitudes and personality. The ethnocentrism (E) and political-economic conservatism (PEC) scales were popular, but not nearly as much so as the Fascism (F) scale, or potential for anti-democratic beliefs. As demonstrated by others in the field of anxiety research (Levy, 1961) the availability of a test leads to a big upsurge in research, even if the construct validity of the measure is extremely suspect (Pagano and Katahn, 1972). The F-scale was shown to have severe methodological flaws, with problems of response set, complex and varying factorial structure and population specificity (see Brown, 1965, for a clear analysis); nevertheless the work burgeoned.

(b) *Small-group movement in social psychology*. The study of people in groups has naturally been central to the field of social psychology. Early research was more typically concerned with the effect of the presence of others upon the behaviour of the individual. (Dashiell, 1935); interest in the structure of groups was not central to social psychology for a long time, and may be traced to Sherif (1936) and of course to the impact of Lewin. Lewin's interest in the structure of fields in the understanding of personality (Lewin, 1926) was transferred to the study of groups on his emigration to the United States and the development of the work on group dynamics and leadership had a profound impact on the course of social psychological research—partly in ways predictable from our analysis of fashion in terms of networks. For example, Mullins (1973) has examined the development of small-group work, starting with the work of Lewin and charting the movements of the principal investigators from Iowa to Massachusetts Institute of Technology, to Michigan and to Harvard. He identified four stages: the *normal* stage, with individual effort and little co-ordinated activity; the *network* stage, perhaps following some particular breakthrough or exciting publication, with collaboration and the beginning of a differentiation of associations; the *cluster* stage, with the formation of strong groups at particular institutions and with strong teacher–student relationships; and finally the *specialty* stage, with the necessity to establish journals and more formal communication systems to maintain the programme after individual members have left the original small group of research centres.

One other reason for the growth of work on groups is that in the social sciences generally there is the perennial concern with the question of holism versus individualism, whether social behaviour is a function of something more than the sum of the social behaviour of the individuals in society, or whether an understanding of individual behaviour will be sufficient. In social psychology there is a concern with the individuality of the person and the way in which he will be modified by the group or will act to differentiate himself from the group, and indeed act to modify it. Festinger's work on informal social communication within groups (Festinger, 1950) and the influences brought to bear upon people deviant from the modal position in the group exemplify this. Social comparison theory (Festinger, 1954), emphasizing a person's use of the social to calibrate the cognitive, developed and showed the movement towards still more emphasis upon the individual within the group. While not itself a very fashionable field, at least initially, the theory appeared in studies of emotion (e.g. Schachter, 1959; Schachter and Singer, 1962) and research in that area was readily linked to the developments in attribution and self-perception theory (Bem, 1965; Kelley, 1967), developments from separate radical behaviourist and gestaltist traditions but which were rapidly seen to have crucial features in common.

The development of a theory of cognitive consistency, whereby the interactions of cognitions within an individual could be seen to mediate changes in behaviour and (also important) could be affected by changes in behaviour, led to a further rush of activity. Social variables and manipulations which could be thought to induce inconsistency were also likely to result in a change in attitudes and opinions and the work stemming from the original group dynamics tradition merged readily with that which, eponymized by Carl Hovland, had developed from a stimulus response learning theory tradition (Hovland and Rosenberg, 1960).

The development of cognitivity consistency was aided by developments in other areas, especially Osgood and Tannenbaum (1955) and Heider (1946). The latter case is especially interesting: we seem to have here a clear case of a premature discovery (a statement of a cognitive consistency viewpoint) which was largely ignored until other developments showed the value of such an approach. In 1946 social psychology did not appear ready for a view of cognitive processes which was dynamic, and other work continued without attention to such a view suggesting the existence of processes of fashion. So developments begun within the small-group research movement contributed in no small way to the growth of research on attitude change!

Homan's (1961) attempt to reduce social processes to a form of economic exchange theory, based indeed upon operant research in psychology, has also had important outcomes and led to research bearing all the hallmarks of fashion. The major theoretical statement was that by Thibaut and Kelley (1959), but the work in psychology has been very much concerned with the study of behaviour in particular small-group or dyadic games, most commonly the Prisoner's Dilemma Game (PDG), although other matrices have been used. Hundreds of studies have been done on such games, with a person's choice of behaviour being seen as the result of his perception of the joint outcome determined by the matrix presented to him by the experimenter. While Thibaut and Kelley's analysis has implications far beyond the particular matrices used in the laboratory, the work on the PDG and variants has been almost solely concerned with the manipulation of small features of the situation and, like the work on consistency theory, deals with somewhat peripheral features. The research that grew up was very much the study of behaviour in a game setting, and few generalizations beyond that were attempted.

Groups do exist, of course, for all kinds of reasons and psychologists have not been able to ignore them: it is just that they have analysed them very much as though they were collections of individuals. Group problem-solving, however, has not been to any extent a fashionable area of research; the growth of work on how individuals combine efforts to arrive at a group solution to a problem has taken a linear form. One problem with work on group problem-solving is that there are so many variables which may plausibly affect an outcome that it will be difficult to summarize the results (Hackman and Morris, 1975).

2. Methodological development

Kuhn's (1962) analysis of the development of paradigms within the natural sciences has emphasized the importance of consensus about methods in the determination of research. The availability of new measurement techniques has been shown to change considerably the prevalent views of a phenomenon (Rescher, 1978), and the "crises" in development of a discipline conceived by Kuhn to be important can arise from new methods showing the inadequacy of previous theorizing. While many would argue that social psychology does not have a paradigm in the Kuhnian sense and only behaves as though it does (e.g. Briskman, 1972), a concern with methodology has been a central reason for the developments of some fashionable areas. Indeed, the very existence of a complex methodology may establish the respectability of a discipline. Precision of measurement supposedly enables precise prediction, with a clear outcome apparently enabling a choice to be made between competing theories. The development of methodology in social psychology has not tended to take that form, however. Theories are stated very vaguely, in imprecise language (Harris, 1976), and crucial experiments to enable a clear dominance of one theory over another are rare. Methodology in social psychology has taken the form of identifying plausible reasons why experimental data have not unequivocally supported a particular theory and then conducting experiments to identify such reasons (Meehl, 1967). Research has been more the search for artefacts.

In its own right, the social psychology of the psychological experiment has obviously been a very fashionable area in social psychology.

Riecken's (1962) early statement has been highly cited and obviously provided a grounding for concern. An earlier paper by Rosenzweig (1933), in which many points were raised, seems another example of prematurity, coming at a time when psychologists were concerned with other things. The possible existence of demand characteristics (Orne, 1962) was intended to provide a better understanding of phenomena created in the laboratory, but eventually it became a factor studied in its own right. A subject's conception of what was required of him and how he decided to accede to that role or rebel against it, was studied almost without concern for other substantive issues in social psychology. As Meehl (1967) has indicated, it has been possible to follow a trail of possible artefacts and establish a reputation as a methodologist without at any time establishing the original substantive point which stimulated the line of inquiry.

A good example of social psychologists' possible over-concern with methodology can be seen in the development of work on perceptual defence. The early papers (e.g. McGinnies, 1948), suggesting that people could respond to stimuli without their being "aware", drew a responsive flurry of papers and demonstrations of artefacts. When the work was originally done, there was little concept of levels of processing of stimuli and the concern was to show that methods were inappropriate. Frequency of words used, response biases, and even demand characteristics (although not labelled as such) were invoked to account for the data. While such "artefacts" themselves became the subject of considerable substantive concern, the original concept fell into disrepute. It can be considered a premature discovery and later information-processing views in general psychology have redeemed the respectability of the topic (Erdelyi, 1974), and indeed today a fashionable development in social psychology is the study of social behaviour which is "mindless" or out of awareness (Nisbett and Wilson, 1977; Thorngate, 1976).

The concern with artefacts in laboratory settings has produced a repeated call for the execution of research in applied settings (cf. Chapter 11). Such calls have not apparently had much impact upon the actual research done although it has led to debate about the numerous problems of inference and induction which follow from experimental research. The work of Campbell (e.g. Campbell and Stanley, 1966; Cook and Campbell, 1975) has been invoked on numerous occasions, as indexed by the very high citation count Campbell receives (Garfield, 1978). The practical and technical problems of doing evaluation research are such, however, that it will never likely become fashionable.

In the context of artefacts and field research, we should point out here that this is but one sub-set of a very fashionable area in social psychology at the moment (one of which this very volume is part), namely a critique and defence of social psychology. While obedience research for example has not been a fashionable research topic, numerous analyses of the ethics and generality of the work and debates about the value of alternative methodologies have been published. And this is only one small aspect of the "sky is falling" syndrome endemic in social psychology research.

3. Recurrence of themes

Fashions die with time. Work on cognitive consistency for example has virtually reached an asymptote in growth and has been replaced by work on attribution, a related concept but one with a somewhat different set of determinants. In some cases activity ceases because a problem is solved or because the concern of society passes and there is not the motivation (or funding) to continue work. However, given the above (especially the arguments about the imprecision with which social psychology experiments attempt to test hypotheses, Meehl, 1978) it could be argued, quite simply, that social psychology may not be in a position to decide that any problem has been solved. All that may happen is that interest fades with time and researchers move to a different field. Change may be due to change in extrinsic motivation rather than to solution of the intrinsic problem.

It has for example, been suggested that there is a reconsideration of problems from time to time, with social psychologists looking again at particular content areas. Sometimes this may be because new methods become available which make possible a new approach to a problem. To take one example which has been considered to date, work on stereotypes was either concerned with the demonstration that in some sense the holding of a stereotype was pathological (in which case attention was directed towards the dispositions of the individuals considered to possess them (Hogan and Emler, 1978) a feature of social psychological research concerned as it is with the individual and less with the normative, as we have mentioned before and away from the cognitive processes underlying stereotypes) or there was a dependence upon a particular method (Katz and Braly, 1958), producing a succession of papers (e.g. Sigall and Page, 1971) which were extremely difficult to incorporate into mainstream psychology. The developments in attribution theory, and especially those which have linked that work with general information-processing biases (Ajzen and Fishbein, 1975; Tversky and Kahneman, 1974), have enabled social psychologists to consider stereotypes as a special case of general processes within a theoretical framework. An intrinsic development can thus help to organize disparate studies. Newer theories and measures may help to render predictions and data more precise and help solve a problem rather than shelve it.

(a) *The lure of historical antecedents.* One point needs to be made in considering possible rediscoveries of problems or even solutions. It is very tempting to go back in time and identify possible anticipations of a theory made many years before (Sarup, 1978). From the context of the present arguments, for example, one can apparently find anticipations of Festinger's views of cognitive dissonance many years previously. Whether there actually was such a direct or indirect influence on his thinking is almost impossible to discover: theorists may well be open to all kinds of influences on their thinking of which they are unaware. There is in any case little to be gained through such apparent scholarship. That Trotter (1919) could be said to have anticipated a biological analysis of human altruism or attribution theory is to indulge in no more than labelling. Trotter had neither the data nor the method to make any statement likely to generate new data. Equally, it may be tempting to note the links between the development of the contemporary theory of objective self-awareness (Duval and Wicklund, 1972) and the earlier theorizing of G. H. Mead (1934), to show continuity and anticipation. However, the theory arose from a need to understand data and has had an influence upon research because it can be linked readily with developments in attribution theory. Newer ways of conceiving social interaction have resulted from the kind of approach of which self-awareness theory is an example (Snyder and Swann, 1978), and Mead has had little to do with that either directly or indirectly.

Each age, or cohort, has to be looked at in the context of its own time: retrospective analyses will either be used to demonstrate how clever we are now to have got where we are (Young, 1966) or to distort the ideological basis upon which we base our research (Samelson, 1974).

Theories may be reasserted, but theories, and the methods and views we base upon them, change. Historiography has usually been abused in presenting the history of psychology, in suggesting continuity where in fact discontinuity and change exist.

(b) *Themata and scientific paradigms.* I have already considered the possibility that various central themata may help to determine the progress of research in the sciences. Social psychology may share with other sciences a theme of evolutionary development, so that a recurrence of concern with biological determinants and the evolution of social structures is likely from time to time. (The mind–body problem consistently reasserts its existence, for example.) One of the characteristics of contemporary research in attribution theory is the role played by the awareness of one's physiological behaviour in the determination of emotion. Schachter's early work (e.g. Schachter and Singer, 1962) played a critical role in the development of thinking along the lines of attribution and self-perception processes, and there has been a gradual movement to a more biological and less cognitive position in some of this work (e.g. Schachter *et al.*, 1977). A likely fashionable development in social psychology will be the role of social and cognitive processes in the prevention of illness and the promotion of health (e.g. Innes, in press), and the delineation of the role of cognitive and somatic responses will be crucial and will necessitate a clear consideration of the theme.

Sampson (1978), like many others, has pointed to the development of a scientific paradigm which examines the cultural and historical context of research. The changes in society which have produced an awareness of such possibilities will tend also to produce a change in emphasis in the problems of social behaviour which are thought worthy of research, and the concentration upon the individual may dwindle.

(c) *Cohort analysis.* The reasons for an original change in emphasis and for further changes are usually ascribed to the hand of the *Zeitgeist*. This, of course, is no explanation: psychologists do the changing. One can examine the culture, the technological developments which make certain approaches more attractive at particular times (war, a belief in individual responsibility, rapid development of man-machine systems, can all be conceived as determining the direction of research), but such influences must still influence individuals and not all individuals are associated with change. Change in approach takes place over generations. The way in which one generation may see a need to look at a problem in a different light from a previous one has to be explained.

Mannheim (1952) was concerned with the problem of generations and their implications for the development of a culture. Any member of society is only exposed to a narrow range of social and intellectual events and will view problems in the context of those experiences. These experiences may be different from those of another generation and therefore there may be a change in the emphasis given to aspects of any problem. To ensure continuity of culture there is a continual need for the accumulated culture to be transmitted to new members, but they will be assimilating the old against a set of new experiences.

The experience of a cohort will be a function of a number of social events, e.g. Simonton (1975, 1976) has shown the creativity of generations to be a complex function of social and technological events, including the form of education members had in common. The appearance of particular cohorts, with salient experiences different from that of previous generations, will make likely a rediscovery of certain problems and the forgetting of others. Problems will be seen with a fresh eye and new techniques will be seen as relevant. While it is absurd to argue that an entire generation has everything in common, it is quite feasible to conceive of social psychologists (who have a more homogeneous social and educational background than an entire cross-section of a population) bringing a fairly coherent approach to bear on a problem (Innes and Fraser, 1971). Particularly innovative methodological and technological developments may require a cohort change before they may begin to influence the major direction of research. While innovations are produced by particularly talented individuals, one group may need to "pass away" before there is a significant switch in the proportion using the new methods. In fashion terms, new methods may be adopted readily, but they may have a long gestation period before there is rapid diffusion.

A number of implications follow from the concept of cohorts as an agent of change in social psychology research. Since a cohort is an abstraction of the demographer there must be debate about how long any cohort may be (Berger, 1960). But one can begin to identify educational and social events experienced by a group likely to influence its ability to solve problems in social psychology. If cohorts are identifiable in terms of shared experiences, it may follow that with rapid social change the age-range required to encompass any particular cohort will need to be reduced. This could imply that there will be a more rapid change in the future in the approach to particular problems. Problems and methods may go "out of date" more rapidly, so recycling will be more rapid. The long protracted period at present set aside in graduate education for the assimilation of previous work in the social sciences which is thought necessary before the creation of knowledge can begin (Campbell, 1973) may come to be seen as an outmoded concept. And while the need for gestation of ideas over time in order to produce creative work in psychology would continue, the relationship between teachers and students in the formation of the research groups referred to earlier would seem likely to change.

Against this picture of accelerated change, one must put the point made by Buss (1974) that reduced funding in universities may provide fewer opportunities for new cohorts to establish themselves in positions where they will be able to do research. More rapidly changing cohorts may coexist with more slowly changing research. At the same time there may be a flow of people into externally funded, applied positions, with a substantial change in the balance of theory and research in social psychology. Predictions about the future, however, will only come about based upon a knowledge of demographic work on cohorts. It seems likely that the characteristics of research in social psychology will show considerable change.

E. CONCLUSIONS

Whether there is fashion in social psychology cannot be established. Certainly there are changes in emphasis and growth in particular areas which bear a similarity to the growth of a fashion. There are also indications of a narrowness of perspective and a tunnelling of vision which might suggest that some less than rational forces act upon the social psychologist attempting to carry out his research. Failure to agree about value and use of the past as a crutch for doing something today may also hint at the use of fashionable criteria to guide research. But the intrinsic development of a field, with experiments executed to fill a gap or highlight an inconsistency, also drives research. The very developments of theory and method that are criticized as distracting attention from the salient and pressing social needs of the day may provide the continuity that prevents a mindless following of the funds to "solve" immediate social problems and thus may enable an accumulation of knowledge whereby the results of research on some novel social experience may be integrated with some other and be seen in a context.

7
The Premature Abandonment of Promising Research

CARL W. BACKMAN

Department of Sociology, University of Nevada, Reno

A. Factors influencing the development of social psychology . . . 164
   1. Faddism and the premature abandonment of promising research . 165
   2. The gulf between psychological and sociological approaches . . 167
B. The hidden promise of prematurely abandoned areas 172
   1. The study of interaction 173
   2. Socialization 174
   3. Normative structure 175
   4. Group research 176
   5. Applied social psychology 177
C. Comment 178

In this chapter I shall suggest a number of reasons for faddism in social psychology research, discuss some trends that perhaps portend a change in this characteristic of our field, and note signs of a return to a number of areas of investigation which were prematurely abandoned. The major reasons for the topical fickleness of the field include the quest for relevance, the ever-increasing reliance on the social psychological experiment as the principal data-generating mechanism, and the appeal of the counter-intuitive.

Underlying these tendencies has been the reward structure of the discipline, which has emphasized rapid and frequent publication, and a lack of sufficient theoretical structure to provide direction to the field. Harbingers of change include growing dissatisfaction with experimentalism, the emergence of a methodological stance more conducive to alternative methods and theorizing more commonly employed by sociologically trained social psychologists. In passing, I shall note a number of examples where insights from sociological theory have added greater breadth and depth to areas of social psychology research. In the context of these developments, signs of a revival of a number of the topical areas will be noted. These areas include studies of ongoing interaction, socialization, small-group processes, social structure, and personality, together with a renewed interest in applied social psychology.

A. FACTORS INFLUENCING THE DEVELOPMENT OF SOCIAL PSYCHOLOGY

In the plethora of recent assessments of the field of social psychology, a number of authors have noted that the focus of social psychological research has been characterized by an element of faddism. McGrath has traced the ebb and flow of research topics on the small group in the decades from 1920 to the 1960s. In the 1920s, research interest centred on social facilitation; in the 30s on prejudice, attitude formation, and change. Leadership was a major preoccupation in the 40s, conformity in the 50s, and research on conflict and its resolution in the 60s. The history of the 1970s is yet to be written, but one can be fairly confident that various applications of attribution theory will be seen as constituting the dominant focus.

If anything, this topical fickleness appears in recent years to be increasing and has led some workers (Katz, 1967; 1972; Riecken, 1965; Ring, 1967) to conclude that this has resulted in increasing fragmentation of social psychology and a lack of the accumulated knowledge typical of other fields of science. Kenneth Ring commented on this in his now classic critique of experimental social psychology:

> Social psychology today, it seems to me, is in a state of profound intellectual disarray. There is little sense of progress; instead, one has the impression of a sprawling, disjointed realm of activity where the movement is primarily outward, not upward. We approach our work with a kind of restless pioneer spirit; a new (or seemingly new) territory is discovered, explored for awhile, and then usually abandoned when the going gets rough or uninteresting. We are a field of many frontiersmen, but few settlers. And, to the degree that this remains true, the history of social psychology will be written in terms not of flourishing, interlocking communities, but of ghost towns. (pp. 119–120.)

In this chapter, I would like to explore the reasons for this characteristic of our field, suggest possible remedies, and along the way point out some of the unfinished business that remains as a result of prematurely abandoning many lines of research for the latest fad. A variety of factors influencing the direction of social psychology research appear to account for the faddish character of our endeavours, where once-promising lines of research are abandoned before fruition only to be succeeded by new interests whose days soon also become numbered.

1. Faddism and the premature abandonment of promising research

One major influence has been the quest for relevance. Concern over the social relevance of social psychology research has been a theme of the recent period of soul-searching in the field; however, the review of the dominant topics decade by decade previously described by McGrath suggests that social psychologists have long been greatly influenced in their choice of topics by concerns of the time. The interest in attitude measurement and change arose in response to involvement of social psychologists in the development of training programmes for the military forces during World War II. The interest in leadership and small-group functioning was stimulated in part by interest in these areas by the armed forces as well as by the anticipation during the 1950s that social psychological knowledge would be increasingly used by industry. Interest in intergroup conflict and its resolution was heightened by concern for peace during the heyday of the Cold War and later by the turbulence of the 1960s. More recently, the spates of interest in bystander intervention, the effects of media violence on aggression, learned helplessness, and sex stereotyping all appear to have been stimulated by popular concerns. Inevitably, as social psychologists have responded to these concerns, they have had to put aside work on problems prompted by previous interests.

Another major influence on the choice of research topics has been the increasing reliance over the years, particularly by psychologically trained social psychologists, on the laboratory experiment as the principal data-generating procedure. The increasing use of the laboratory experiment along with the reliance on readily available subjects, typically college students, led to the abandonment of many topics that could not be studied in the context of this method. Armistead (1974) and Hendrick (1977) have cited the abandonment of the earlier interest in human development as an example of how creeping experimentalism has influenced the topical focus in social psychology. Another example quickly comes to mind: the investigations of the effects of various social structural and cultural variables on psychological processes. Not only is it impossible to manipulate these variables in the typical experimental fashion, but, given the homogeneity of the college samples typically employed, statistical analysis of these effects is precluded.

A second way in which the increasing reliance on the laboratory experiment has contributed to the topical fickleness of social psychology is through the trivialization of many lines of research to the point where they are abandoned for lack of interest. Such trivialization has taken two forms: either the original substantive problem is transformed into a methodological one, or, more often, into a substantive problem quite different from and almost invariably less significant than the phenomenon of initial interest. The latter tendency is often exacerbated by the emergence of a simple research paradigm. This is typically an attempted analogue of the situation of interest which unfortunately departs from its nature in one or more important respects. Recent examples of this tendency include the choice dilemma questionnaire to study the risky-shift phenomenon, the prisoner's dilemma game to study competition and co-operation, and the bogus stranger technique to study the attraction–similarity relationship. As Smith (1972) in his review of the first five volumes of *Advances in Experimental Social Psychology* notes when commenting on the chapter by Dion *et al.* on risky-shift research, on the similarity–attraction work of Byrne, on research using communication nets, and, in passing, on the research employing the prisoner's dilemma:

> As the authors point out, research in this tradition has paid a high price in substantive relevance for its concentration on a particular type of risk-taking task and a single type of experimental design.
>
> The risk of a similar strategy seems apparent in Byrne's approach to exploring the empirical relations between attitudinal similarity and interpersonal attraction (Vol. 4) where he makes a virtue of his weddedness to a single instrument rather than to a single theoretical concept variously indexed.
>
> I have my doubts, too, about the research on communication nets reviewed by Shaw (Vol. 1). Like the much more extensive work on the prisoner's dilemma (blessedly not reviewed in these volumes) what was initially an inventive methodological device for getting a hold on theoretical concepts and issues originating in observations of real social life became

a functionally autonomous specialty in its own right, an area for the development of arcane knowledge of possible interest only to the priestcraft. (p. 92)

Research using these paradigms has been largely abandoned, in part at least because of the increasing conviction that the findings bear a dubious relationship to the phenomena of original interest.

The appeal of the counter-intuitive and the related attempt where possible to enhance the relative significance of social psychological variables in the explanation of human behaviour have also played a role in generating research along certain lines rather than others. The long series of studies employing the forced compliance paradigm serves as a prime example of this influence, as do many other lines of work stemming from dissonance theory.

Ring (1967) has suggested that these tendencies underlie the fun-and-games style of much experimental research in social psychology as well, which in turn encourages the tendency for social psychologists to search for new topics before they have adequately dealt with old ones. Partly reflecting these influences and partly contributing to them has been the reward structure of the profession. The use of the laboratory experiment, particularly where it involves a standard and widely used experimental paradigm, facilitates rapid and frequent publication which in most major institutions has a strong determining influence on promotion and tenure decisions. In addition, as a recent study by Diamond and Norton (1978) suggests, status in the field in general rests in good part on having opened up new areas of investigation rather than systematically completing research on old ones.

A final source of empirical fragmentation and loss of direction is the lack of a larger theoretical structure that goes beyond those theories that are limited to a particular empirical domain. Such a structure would, as Smith (1972) has suggested, put problems and models in their place, so that the frontiers of progress in the discipline could be identified and promising lines of research distinguished from blind alleys

2. The gulf between psychological and sociological approaches

It is possible that some of these tendencies might have been moderated had not an increasing gulf emerged between the psychological and sociological traditions in social psychology. While some sociologists have confined themselves to experimental methodology, most sociologically trained social psychologists recognize the validity of other methodologies, such as those of survey research and participant observation. Furthermore, compared to their psychological counterparts, they have been much more involved in theory construction and conceptual analyses.

Although examples of the fruitful combination of sociological theorizing and psychological research are not as numerous as might be desired, one can point to a number of instances which provide examples of the benefits from such a mix. Scheff (1967), employing such concepts as definition of the situation, role taking, and intersubjectivity from the symbolic interactionist and ethnomethodologist traditions in sociology, developed a theory of social co-ordination which relates consensus, communication, and co-ordination in a manner that handles a good many empirical results of the research on mixed-motive games done primarily by psychologists. For instance, the general finding that communication increases co-operative choices is explained in terms of the existence of higher levels of consensus characterized by agreement, understanding, and realization. That is, where two game players are in objective agreement on a co-operative choice and communication makes it possible for each to be aware of their agreement and to realize that the other is aware of their agreement, co-ordination of their choices is maximized.

Similarly, drawing on symbolic interactionist theory, Alexander and Knight (1971) have provided a theoretical framework (situated identity theory) which throws considerable light on the responses of participants in psychological experiments. Essentially, the theory suggests that a person responds to situations in such a way as to communicate to other people information concerning the kind of person he presumes to be in that situation—a favourably situated identity. In an interpersonal simulation of the insufficient justification paradigm first employed by Festinger and Carlsmith (1959), they gathered data on the attributions made by observers to subjects in the various incentive (high or low monetary rewards for lying) and encounter conditions (face-to-face or essay writing). The predicted responses in the simulation, which paralleled the actual responses in experiments reported by others, were consistent with the assumption that such responses were selected to maximize favourable attributions in the particular experimental settings.

More recently, Sagatun and Knudsen (1977) have been able to demonstrate on the basis of situated identity theory that whether persons make internal or external causal attributions for success or failure on their part or that of others depends on the identity implications of doing so in the particular experimental condition. Discussing their findings that observers attribute another person's success to internal causes and his failures to external ones, and that actors make external attributions to both success and failure, they note:

> Different attribution norms exist for different people in different contexts. For observers, the cultural demand is one of person orientation and concern for others. Attributing another person's success to internal factors, and his own failure to external factors, fits this model. By attributing the person's success to outstanding abilities and inner motivation, the observer shows himself as a generous person and is likely to be well received because of his explanations. By excusing the other's failure as being caused by circumstances, the observer again shows his concern for others. Similarly, the social expectations for self-explanations of success and failure lead the actor to make external attributions in both situations. In success, the objective fact of success is already there, and the actor will make a good impression by appearing modest and attributing his success to external influences. At the same time, an actor is supposed to believe in his own abilities and not be thwarted by failure. Hence, external attribution of one's own failure will help maintain a favorable impression of the actor. The fact that actors tend to give external attributions in both success and failure conditions, then, does not mean that actors are immune to social pressures. Rather, attribution norms for actors point in the same direction for both success and failure. It appears that ego-enhancement motives are indeed powerful influences on attributions, but that social norms dictate that different techniques must be used for actors and observers in order to make the right social impression. (Sagatun and Knudsen, 1977, p. 12.)

Attribution theory can increasingly be expected to benefit from the impact of another set of ideas developed by sociology: labelling theory. Prus (1975) has criticized current psychological versions of attribution theory for ignoring the social context of attributions. In particular, he suggests that the attributions one person makes of another occur in the context of interaction in which the target person, as well as others in the situation, may influence the attributions made. They may actively contest a particular attribution, or just their presence as an audience may (as the previous comments by Sagatun and Knudsen suggest) affect attributions through their effect on self-presentation. Prus emphasized in particular that the target of the attributions is rarely inert in the process. He may affect the attributions made, either through controlling the information presented to the attributor or by successfully challenging the attributions made concerning his conduct. The latter response is the focus of a general theory which extends attribution theory into a context of negotiation where the target person is seen as playing an active role. I hope these somewhat briefly described examples will serve to illustrate the potential advantages of greater contact on the part of psychologically trained social psychologists with the sociological literature.

As we shall note below, there are some signs that the gap between the two traditions may be narrowing, but it is unfortunately still considerable (Blank, 1978). Those changes that are occurring in this respect seem more in response to internal developments within the psychological tradition, rather than through increased contact between the practitioners of the two approaches, although there may be some feeble increases in this direction as well.

Recent developments within psychological social psychology not only presage a movement in the direction of a more sociological social psychology but should serve to counter some of the influences that we have argued have led to a lack of accumulated knowledge in the field. A number of leading psychologically trained social psychologists have advocated changes in focus and methodology that would shift their discipline in the direction of the sociological tradition in the field (McGuire, 1973; Smith, 1974; and Gergen, 1973). Stryker (1977), a sociologist, also has commented on this shift. Not only has this involved the advocacy of a change away from the heavy reliance on the laboratory experiment and simple unidirectional causal explanations but there has been a gradual erosion in practice if not in theory of some of the basic philosophical premises that in the past have separated the two traditions. The idea of man as agent, the emphasis on meaning, and the importance of situational determinants of behaviour, long a part of the sociological tradition, particularly that of symbolic interactionism, are consistent with what psychological social psychologists are actually doing in their research. As I have suggested elsewhere (Backman, 1979a):

> The idea that man is an active agent rather than exclusively a product of natural forces impinging upon him has become increasingly accepted in social psychological circles. For some, their model of man was never otherwise. Others have had to undergo a conversion to a view of science

different from that of positivism to enable them to accept this view. Still others, less bothered by the philosophers' concern for consistency, may continue to view themselves as behaviorists in a positivist mold, but at the same time have developed theories and conducted research that makes sense only if man is construed as having some degree of freedom. For example, one could hardly argue that persons actively create an interpersonal environment to support their self-conceptions without losing confidence in a view of man as a billiard ball whose behavior is simply a function of externally applied forces. The same is true for an investigator who does research on how persons attempt to maximize their outcomes in games or take or avoid risks, or for a researcher who learns that subjects may choose to confirm or disconfirm an experimental hypothesis.

Accompanying the spread of the point of view of man as agent has been the cognitive revolution in social psychology which has made the construction of meaning a central focus. Foreshadowed in the early work on social perception, later in the work of dissonance researchers, and now reflected in the dominance of attribution theory, this development surely has underscored the importance to an understanding of social life of the meanings which people attribute to their own behavior, as well as to that of others. Again, it can be argued that social psychology has moved further along this dimension than many of its practitioners realize, particularly those who still avoid looking into the black box when carrying out their experiments.

Much the same can be said concerning the third theme, situationism. While we have a good way to go in explicitly dealing with the meanings of situations and particularly their rule-governed character, the move away from intra-individual variables to situational ones is unmistakable. While the movement has been well documented in the field of personality studies, one need not look any further than more traditional areas of social psychology for striking examples of this shift. While this trend was acknowledged two decades ago in the study of leadership, a history of the research on attraction would show the same trend. Whether one examines the early days of the sociometric movement or the early studies of mate selection and marital success, the trend of research on attraction was first to emphasize characteristics of the individual, later those of pairs, and now the current emphasis is on situational and process variables (Huston and Levinger, 1978). Another striking example of the move in social psychology from the individual to the situation has been the dramatic change in the treatment of social motives. Aggression, altruism, and to an increasing degree achievement are being explained in situational terms, rather than as the intra-individual residues of early experience. In addition, whole new areas of research have emerged within social psychology and closely related fields which start out with a situational focus. Examples are proxemics and environmental psychology. Finally, one can point to a number of metatheoretical movements within both the sociological and the psychological traditions in social psychology, including a heightened interest in symbolic interactionism, the emergence of ethnomethodology in the U.S., and a somewhat independent but clearly related movement, ethogenics, in England. All of these are heavily situational in orientation. C. W. Backman—Epilogue: an new paradigm. *In* G. P. Ginsburg (ed.) "Emerging Strategies in Social Psychological Research." © John Wylie 1979. Reprinted with permission.

Hendrick (1977) also sees a move away from the heavy reliance on the laboratory experiment in the direction of methods more typical of the sociological tradition in social psychology. Commenting on the results of the recent crisis in social psychology, he notes:

> It is sufficient to state here that one result of the crisis has been a broadening of the scope of respectable methods and the active pursuit of applied concerns. Lambert and Weisbrod (1971) dared to speak of a revolution in comparative social psychology, which remained underground for many years but which has now emerged as respectable company. The *Journal of Applied Social Psychology* was launched in 1971, an undertaking probably not possible a decade earlier. In part due to the influence of McGuire (e.g., 1967), research in natural settings (e.g., Bickman and Henchy, 1972; Sandowsky, 1972) has become more common. The seminal work by Webb, Campbell, Schwartz, and Sechrest (1966) also contributed to this movement. Sales' (1973) use of archival data to study the relation between threat and authoritarianism was also an interesting innovation in method. (pp. 20–21.)

Although this trend is only feebly reflected in the older social psychological journals (Fried *et al.*, 1973), March *et al.* (1976) note that one of the newer journals, the *Journal of Applied Social Psychology*, contains significantly more non-laboratory studies, and another recently published journal, *Personality and Social Psychology Bulletin*, appears to this writer to be similar in this respect. An examination of the contents of the latter journal, together with the appearance some years ago of the *Journal for the Theory of Social Behavior* suggests that the atheoretical orientation that has characterized much of the journal literature in psychological social psychology is also changing. Accompanying the move away from the laboratory experiment has been the publication of a number of volumes concerned with alternative research strategies (Lofland, 1976; Brenner *et al.*, 1978; Ginsburg, 1979).

B. THE HIDDEN PROMISE OF PREMATURELY ABANDONED AREAS

Given these changes, it might be as well to look back upon a number of areas of research that may have been prematurely abandoned when they could not be accommodated within the old thought ways of experimental social psychology, or, when forced into this framework, were subsequently abandoned because they had been transformed into something of little intrinsic interest.

1. The study of interaction

A combination of the difficulties of dealing with interaction in the laboratory, lack of fresh theoretical insight, and disappointment as a number of lines of work seemed to turn into blind alleys led social psychologists away from the study of interaction. However, several developments suggest a return to this topic. First has been the emergence of the ethogenic movement among psychologists in the U.K. and a highly similar approach, ethnomethodology, in American sociology, both of which focus on interaction and particularly on the underlying structure of interaction. Accompanying this has been a renewed interest in, and the further development and application of, a number of data-generating procedures particularly appropriate to the study of interaction, including cinematic and video procedures for recording interaction, role-playing techniques, techniques of biographical reconstruction, as well as computer simulation procedures and other methods for the study of conversation.

Some of the current work of Argyle (1979) and his group at Oxford is illustrative of ethogenic research. Rather than focusing on the individual and his behaviour, they emphasize the interaction of persons as guided by role–rule frameworks inherent in situations and episodes. Similarly, Garfinkel (1972) and other ethnomethodologists have studied what is "taken for granted" in interaction: the background understanding and tacitly known rules that make the smooth co-ordinated flow of interaction possible. These developments have been accompanied by a renewed interest in a variety of processes that underlie interaction. These processes include self-presentation and impression management, the negotiation of social reality in general and social identities in particular, and the underlying processes of attribution and selective use and retention of information.

Blumstein's (1973) work on identity bargaining and the innovative experimental work of Snyder et al. (1977) on how a person evokes in another behaviour that confirms his initial beliefs about that person (i.e., the processes underlying the self-fulfilling prophecy) are instances of this new interest in interactional processes. Also in this category are the previously mentioned works (Prus, 1975; Sagatun and Knudsen, 1977), as well as that of Shields (1977), which place attribution processes within an interactional context where those cognitive processes become subject to the influence of such interactional processes as self-presentation and identity negotiation. It is rather odd that these developments have been accompanied by the increasing use of methods other than the psychological experiment, when the latter is in many ways an ideal setting to study these interactional processes. As Hendrick (1977) has noted, social psychologists have inevitably been involved in the process of role-taking and role-playing in the design and execution of psychological experiments. Only by doing so could they effectively manipulate their variables by creating a particular social experience for their subjects.

Unfortunately, when it comes to assessing the validity of the conclusions drawn from many experiments, it has become increasingly clear from the literature on the social psychology of the experiment that subjects, too, have engaged in role-taking and role-playing; and they have been actively involved in the negotiation of reality in this situation, so as to achieve their goals in general and in particular to create and maintain favourable identities (Alexander and Knight, 1971). In some ways, the laboratory experiment is a strategic social situation for studying these interpersonal processes. Even the use of the ubiquitous prisoner's dilemma game informed by appropriate theory can provide useful information on self-presentation or impression management, processes of identity negotiation, role-taking, role-playing, etc. (Backman, 1976).

2. Socialization

The new focus on interaction and the greater methodological flexibility of social psychologists are beginning to encourage a revival of interest in another area which social psychologists prematurely abandoned—the study of socialization. The work of Scaife (1979) and Brunner (1975) suggests that language development and early patterns of infant–caretaker interaction are closely linked, that linguistic structures cannot be understood simply in cognitive terms alone but mirror structures inherent in early interactional experience. These developments, together with the interest displayed by the ethogenic and ethnomethodology schools of thought in language, may well stimulate increasing interest in communication. It is curious that, except for a brief flurry of research on communication networks in small groups and the more recent interest in non-verbal communication, this highly significant social process has been largely ignored by social psychologists. The recent work of Clarke (1975, 1979) and of Kent et al. (1978) on the structure of conversations and the work of Rommetvelt (1976) on intersubjectivity, are hopeful signs of a reversal of this neglect.

3. Normative structure

The focus on interaction, particularly its role–rule structure, may, in addition, stimulate a revival of interest in the normative structure and in role theory. Interest in those inter-related topics, popular in the late 1950s but largely abandoned since then, appears to have been a result of a somewhat oversimplified and faulty conceptualization, as well as the retreat of social psychology from what appeared to be the obvious to more esoteric and non-intuitive topics, or those of more timely relevance. Yet, in a rather serendipitous fashion, the findings on a number of these topics served to underscore the importance of norms as a source of structure in social behaviour, and have also led to an expanded and much richer conceptualization of normative phenomena.

Thus the work on non-verbal communication, proxemics, and that broad area which Goffman has described as behaviour in public places underscored the importance of rules (often only tacitly known by participants) in guiding their behaviour. The seeming ineffectiveness of norms in the studies of harm-doing and bystander intervention, while leading some (Latané and Darley, 1970) to question the usefulness of normative explanations of behaviour, has led others (Backman, 1979b; Schwartz, 1968) to a more complex and realistic conception of the normative regulation of behaviour. In this new view, which combines normative theory with accounting theory (Scott and Lyman, 1968), norms are seen to operate against a background of shared understandings concerning the conditions under which adherence is either required or can be safely avoided.

Recent successful empirical attempts to study processes of role and identity negotiation (Blumstein, 1973) and the developments of theoretical models of these processes (McCall and Simmons, 1966;

Secord and Backman, 1974; Prus, 1975) may well encourage the adoption of the symbolic interactionist's version of role theory (Maines, 1977), which emphasizes a much more dynamic and fluid conception of role structure than that which dominated role theory during the 1960s.

Similarly, the empirical work of those in the ethnomethodological and ethogenic traditions has demonstrated that, although a good deal of the role–rule structure of everyday social situations is but dimly experienced by persons in interaction, methods are available to study this empirically; with the increasing methodological flexibility in social psychology a significant expansion of research in this area can be expected.

4. Group research

It is too early to tell whether the conditions that sparked the abandonment of much of small group research have sufficiently abated, but a number of recent developments suggest that Steiner's (1974) prediction of its eventual revival may be borne out. First has been the recent publication of Janis and Mann's (1977) work on decision-making and the earlier work of Janis (1972) concerned with the phenomenon of group-think. It was unfortunate that at about the time a firm theoretical base had developed for the assessment of group effects on decision-making and problem-solving (Steiner, 1972) many social psychologists abandoned the topic or were diverted to what became largely a pseudo-problem, that of risky shift. Janis and his colleagues have not only focused on a problem of particular social significance, but by bringing to bear on this topic the results of studies employing a wide range of methods from that of the laboratory experiment to case studies employing largely archival materials, they provide an excellent example of how the use of a variety of methods can increase both the internal and external validity of social psychological research.

In addition to Janis' work, Steiner cites the revived interest of Aronson (1972) in the group in therapeutic settings and that of Zimbardo (1973) on group influences in simulated prison settings as further signs of a return to group studies. Aronson's recent work on group effects in educational settings might also be mentioned (Aronson et al., 1978). The spate of research on conversion processes within religious groups can be cited as additional evidence of this trend

(Richardson, 1977). In this connection it is encouraging to see that this renewed interest in the group involves ongoing groups in everyday contexts rather than *ad hoc* laboratory groups. Lieberman (1976) has also noted a movement in the direction of the study of group effects involving natural groups in everyday settings, in his recent review of the literature on change-inducing groups. Again, the recent upsurge in tolerance for the use of less rigorous non-laboratory research procedures may play a role in hastening this trend back to the study of groups.

The revival of interest in the small group may be accompanied by an interest in larger groups as well. House (1977) has recently called for a revival of interest in topics on a more macro-level, which in earlier times were investigated under the rubric "social structure and personality". A number of developments may facilitate a renewal of research in this area. These include, in addition to greater methodological flexibility (including increased willingness on the part of many social psychologists to use survey procedures), the emergence of critical social psychology in Europe and, more recently, in the U.S.A., and a revival of interest in comparative social psychology (Lambert and Weisbrod, 1971; Triandis, 1976). The recent concern raised by Gergen (1973) and Jahoda (1979) that social psychology knowledge may be largely inapplicable to the behaviour of persons at other times and places should also stimulate more research on topics at this level.

5. Applied social psychology

Finally, if the increasing concern for relevance along with the shrinking academic market for social psychologists leads to a continual expansion of applied social psychology, interest may be revived in this area, too. As House has noted, the greatest developments in studying the relationship between position in the social structure and other social psychological variables have occurred during periods where applied concerns brought about interdisciplinary efforts between psychologists and sociologists, such as those that occurred during and shortly after the Second World War.

It is to be hoped that such collaboration will result in a fruitful combination of psychological and microsociological theory that will help explicate the relation between social structural and other macrosociological variables and psychological ones. It has become increasingly clear that the effects of such structural variables as race, sex, or social class or of such an ecological one as population density do not bear any simple and direct relationship with individual characteristics such as attitudes and personality traits. Rather, the relationships between these sets of variables are moderated by a host of interactional processes which determine how a given social environment is experienced and a variety of psychological processes that determine the individual reactions to these experiences (House, 1977).

The possibility of a revival of a number of areas of applied social psychology should not be discounted. It is true that the analyses of research trends, using the content of major journals in social psychology, including the *Journal of Applied Social Psychology* (Helmreich, 1975), do not provide strong support for hope in this direction. Yet it is possible that these analyses are somewhat deceptive for several reasons. First, while a number of leading social psychologists have in recent years been engaged in applied research, many such studies result in publications in other than the traditional social psychology journals. Second, we have yet to see what the long-term effects will be of the shrinking academic market and changing pattern of research funding. While, as is noted below, the short-term effects of the job situation may be to increase publication pressure and intensify the emphasis on experimental research, the long-term effects may be to force many young social psychologists in to new career lines where the emphasis will be on applied concerns. The full effect of changing patterns of research support has not yet been felt. The growth of research funding in applied areas and a slowdown in the growth of the support for basic research should increasingly have an effect. Finally, while the methodological revolution frequently alluded to in this chapter is upon us, the conservative nature of most graduate training programmes can be expected to delay its full effects for some time to come, although even here there are signs of change.

C. COMMENT

A chapter that combines a discussion of the faddish character of social psychology with predictions concerning the future focus of research necessarily must end with a caveat. The various influences on the choice of topics in social psychological research are still very much with us. If, as has been suggested, they derive in good part from structurally induced achievement pressures within the profession, these influences may well increase in intensity, at least in the short run, when the supply of social psychologists exceeds demand in the academic marketplace.

The retreat from experimentalism, while perhaps the most encouraging sign of change, is a modest one—certainly not a rout. Similarly, the greater preoccupation with theory and trends which suggest a narrowing of the gap between the psychological and sociological traditions in social psychology are only modest in nature. It still could happen that, after a decade of soul-searching on the part of social psychologists, there could be a return to the business of social psychology as usual.

8
Process Loss in Social Psychology: Failure to Exploit?

WOLFGANG STROEBE
University of Marburg, Germany*

A. Critical rationalism and scientific progress 183
   1. The validity of theories 183
   2. The falsificationist position 184
B. Critical rationalism as a model of group problem solving . . . 187
   1. The model 187
   2. Threats to progress 188
C. Group processes and actual productivity 190
   1. Organizational processes 190
   2. Group norms and paradigms 193
   3. The value of subgroup formation 194
D. The costs of consensus 195
   1. Methodological biases 195
   2. Theoretical biases 196
   3. The interdependence of methodological and theoretical biases . . 200
   4. The consequences of scientific biases for research . . . 201
E. Summary and conclusions 203

Challenges to the scientific status of psychology have a long tradition. However, due to the widespread discontent with the state of our discipline, such criticism (e.g. Gergen, 1973; Harré and Secord, 1972; Holzkamp, 1977; Israel and Tajfel, 1972) has recently received increasing attention in social psychology. Although efforts have been made to defuse some of these arguments (e.g. Schlenker, 1974, 1977), even the defenders of the scientific status of social psychology have had to admit to the nagging feeling that the accumulation of knowledge in

* Now at the University of Tübingen, Germany.

this area is not quite progressing at the rate one would expect (e.g. McGuire, 1973; Smith, 1972).

According to the most widely accepted model of scientific discovery, Popper's (1959, 1963) "critical rationalism" or "falsificationism", science should develop from an interplay of conjectures and refutations, where theories are invented, severely tested, and then—typically after an accumulation of theory-divergent facts—replaced by new ones of higher empirical content. These new theories should not only explain all the facts accounted for by the old theories, but also those facts which were inconsistent with the old approach. In addition, they should make some novel predictions.

It is quite obvious that this model does not give a very accurate description of actual research performance in social psychology, where various dominant mini-theories seem to be periodically replaced by other mini-theories in a process which is best described as an interplay of "novelty" and "satiation". Although attempts at "crucial" experiments are frequently made, their outcomes never seem to be very crucial. In one typical case, after a ten-year battle of pitting dissonance theory against self-perception theory, Bem and McConell (1970) drew the following discouraging conclusion:

> If the past history of controversies like this is any guide, it seems unlikely that a "crucial" experiment for discriminating between [dissonance and self-perception theory] will ever be executed. At this juncture each theory appears capable of claiming some territory not claimed by the other and one's choice of theory in areas of overlap is diminishing to a matter of loyalty or aesthetics. (p. 30.)

Janis' (1968) "biased scanning" hypothesis is also still unrefuted, offering an alternative explanation for most of the "forced compliance" research; Insko et al. (1975) have recently made a similar claim for balance theory. Thus, as Holzkamp (1977) argued, social psychology seems to be plagued by the existence of a great number of competing theories, which, though based on incompatible principles, claim to account for identical phenomena.

However disappointing the actual performance of research may be in social psychology, this does not *necessarily* justify the rejection of the hypothetico-deductive model guiding the research process. The community of social psychologists can be conceived of as a group or social organization engaged in a process of group problem-solving. Critical rationalism is essentially a normative theory of the research process which describes what should happen under certain ideal conditions and thus gives an indication of the outcome *potential* or potential productivity. In analysing the logic of scientific discovery, critical rationalism examines the task demands of scientific research and the relationship between task demands and outcome, given the optimal employment of human resources. It is thus comparable to the social psychology models of group problem-solving (e.g. Lorge and Solomon, 1955; Thomas and Fink, 1961; Steiner, 1966, 1972) developed to predict potential productivity. However, as Steiner (1972) pointed out, in practice human resources are rarely optimally employed. There is always some loss due to "faulty process" and *actual* productivity must be expected to fall short of potential productivity. In this paper some of the causes of process loss in the conduct of social psychological research and their consequences for the development of our science will be analysed. The paper will consist of four sections. In the first section the question of the validity of theories will be discussed and Popper's (1959, 1963) falsificationist position will be described. In the second section a model of group problem-solving will be derived from the falsificationist position, in order to isolate the factors which should affect the rate of scientific progress. In the third section the group process of conducting research will be analysed, paying particular attention to factors which may be responsible for a "process loss". Finally in the fourth section a number of biases in social psychological theorizing and research, which may be the result of the particular group dynamics in the community of psychological researchers, will be discussed.

A. CRITICAL RATIONALISM AND SCIENTIFIC PROGRESS

1. The validity of theories

Popper's (1959) dictum that theories cannot be verified or even demonstrated as probable, but only falsified, has become a sub-cultural truism among research scientists, yet it is hard to live by. As Gadenne (1976) pointed out recently, even such a stout defender of falsificationism as Campbell (Campbell and Stanley, 1963) developed with the theory of internal and external validity a framework which is much more compatible with an inductivist rather than a deductivist methodology. If, Campbell and Stanley (1963) implied, one took great care to eliminate all threats to internal and external validity, one should be able to pass from a singular statement, such as the account of the result of an experiment, to universal statements, such as hypotheses or theories. For example, one could take the experimental observation (singular statement) that student subjects who were exposed to a communication recommending a change in dental care showed more attitude change when gory slides of diseases due to neglect were shown than when the communication was given without such slides, as *proof* for the hypothesis (universal statement) that fear arousal leads to attitude change. This, however, would be an inductive inference and thus logically not permissible. It would be inductive because one can never be certain to have eliminated *all* threats to validity. Even if we replicated the above results in a dozen well-conducted experiments using different communications and subjects each time, we would still not be justified in considering the hypothesis *verified*. There is no way of moving from singular to universal statements. To use the quaint example of traditional logic books, even if we inspected all swans on earth and all were white, we still would not have proven the universal statement "All swans are white". We could never preclude the possibility that a black, green or even red swan might be hatched the minute we ended our search.

Acceptance of this argument puts the empirical scientist in a somewhat awkward position. If research will never allow him to demonstrate the truth of his theories, how can he justify doing research? Strangely enough, it was mainly the philosophers who worried about this problem, while scientists went about their business unworried because largely unaware. Finally Popper (1934) solved the riddle by pointing to an asymmetry in the relationship of singular and universal statements. While millions of white swans can never prove the universal statement that all swans are white, it only takes one black swan to disprove it.

2. The falsificationist position

Progress in science is achieved by trial and error, or "conjectures and refutations", as Popper entitled a collection of his papers. We hope to approach the truth by continually putting our theories to stringent empirical tests. We retain *provisionally* the ones for which empirical evidence can be found and replace those which cannot be corroborated by new theories of *higher empirical content*. All our knowledge remains tentative knowledge only. We will never know whether we have reached the truth with a given theory and must always be prepared to abandon an apparently good theory in the light of a better one.

The question of how theories are developed and why researchers are more interested in certain areas than others is of no concern to the philosophers of science. Theories are "free creations of our minds, the result of almost poetic intuition" (Popper, 1963, p. 192) and their emergence can therefore be no subject of logical analysis. Epistemology is interested only in the logic of theory testing and especially in the question of when a given theory or hypothesis should be considered falsified. Unfortunately, the task of developing criteria for refutation poses more complex problems than might be anticipated. Naïvely, one might suggest that a theory should be rejected as soon as there was good evidence (e.g. by a well-conducted experiment) which was inconsistent with one of its major hypotheses. However, if this criterion were applied, we would probably have to reject every theory in social psychology and in most other sciences too. Thus, dissonance theory should have been abandoned when Rosenberg (1965) observed more attitude change with high rather than low incentives in a forced compliance study, and when Freedman and Sears (1965) could report no evidence for the "selective exposure" hypothesis. Similarly, balance theory should have been dropped when Jordan (1953) and Rodrigues (1967) found that balanced situations in which p disliked o were rated as being as unpleasant as all the unbalanced situations. Nevertheless both theories are still going strong.

One reason for this reluctance to abandon theories is obviously that theory-divergent evidence can always be challenged with the argument that the inconsistency was due to the presence of confounding factors in a given study; and indeed, Linder et al. (1967) could show quite convincingly that Rosenberg's (1965) finding of a positive relationship between incentive and attitude change was due to his unwittingly lowering subjects' freedom of choice. Also Brock and Balloun (1967) and Mills (1968) made a good case to discredit most of the studies on which Freedman and Sears (1965) based their argument, and Aderman (1974) and Insko et al. (1974) found a convincing explanation for the inconsistencies in the Jordan (1953) and Rodrigues (1967) studies.

A second reason is probably that social psychologists sometimes rely as much on their intuition as on experimental evidence in evaluating theories. Since most of the social psychological theories derive from some researcher's intuition in the first place, their predictions are frequently consistent with what one would expect and thus not easily abandoned in the face of contradictory evidence. A case in point is Winch's (1958) "complementary needs" hypothesis, which has only been supported once (Kerckhoff and Davis, 1962) in more than two dozen attempts to test it (Stroebe, 1977), and this result could not be replicated (Levinger et al., 1970). Despite this devastating record, the theory is still presented in most attraction and social psychology textbooks. It just makes too much sense, that, for example, somebody who loves to push people around should get along better with a spouse who prefers being pushed to pushing. The major reason, however, why scientists tend to stick to established theories in the face of some contradictory evidence, is typically the existence of empirical results which can best be explained by this particular theory. For example, if social psychologists had followed Rosenberg's (1965) call to abandon dissonance theory, there would have been quite a few experimental results which could no longer have been accounted for. Rosenberg's (1965) alternative explanation in terms of "evaluation apprehension" and "self-persuasion" had a very *ad hoc* character and, furthermore, could only explain the "forced compliance" findings, but not the results of "free choice" (e.g. Brehm, 1956) or "forbidden toy" (e.g. Aronson and Carlsmith, 1963) studies. The failure of Rosenberg's (1965) attack on dissonance theory was therefore not due to problems with his experimental results, but to the weakness of the theory he offered as an alternative. This is consistent with the falsificationist position that "no experiment ... alone can lead to falsification. There is no falsification before the emergence of a better theory" (Lakatos, 1970, p. 119).

If inconsistent evidence alone is not sufficient, how do we decide, then, that a new theory T' is better than the established theory T? The major criterion suggested by Popper (1959, 1963) is that T' should have greater *empirical content* that T. Lakatos (1970) recently summarized the falsificationist criteria for deciding between theories as follows:

> For the sophisticated falsificationist a scientific theory T is *falsified* if and only if another theory T' has been proposed with the following characteristics: (1) T' has excess empirical content over T: that is, it predicts *novel* facts, that is, facts improbable in the light of, or even forbidden, by T; (2) T' explains the previous success of T, that is, all the unrefuted content of T is included (within the limits of observational error) in the content of T'; and (3) some of the excess content of T' is corroborated. (p. 116.)

B. CRITICAL RATIONALISM AS A MODEL OF GROUP PROBLEM SOLVING

1. The model

A translation of critical rationalism into the language of group problem-solving suggests the following model. Research is a process of group problem-solving, where the group of people (i.e. the community of research social psychologists or that section of the community which is concerned with a particular problem) searches for a solution to a problem (i.e. to find a theory which fits all the known facts and in addition makes some novel predictions). The problem will be solved, if one member of the group comes up with a correct solution (i.e. a better theory), if and only if the correctness of that solution is recognized by the other group members. Such a task, where the potential productivity of the group is determined by the resources of its most competent member, has been called a "disjunctive task" (Steiner, 1966, 1972). Lorge and Solomon's (1955) "Model A" predicts the potential group productivity for such tasks on the basis of information about the proportion of people in a given population who have the ability to solve the problem.

One apparent oversimplification of this model is that it does not take account of the division of labour among scientists. Any scientist works only on one small aspect of the total structure of science and it is due to their *joint* efforts that progress is achieved. Thus, social psychology, which itself is only a branch of psychology (which again is only a branch of human sciences, etc.) is usually broken down into sub-areas such as attitude change, small groups, and person perception. Different scientists are working in each of these areas and each contributes to the progress of social psychology as a whole, which is thus achieved by division of labour. However, any divisible task finally consists of a number of unitary tasks, which cannot be profitably broken down into further sub-tasks. Most of the specific problems in social psychology can be considered as unitary tasks. For example, the question why Rosenberg (1965) found a positive relationship between incentive and attitude change, when Festinger and Carlsmith (1959) and Cohen (Brehm and Cohen, 1962) had observed a negative relationship was attacked by a number of people (e.g. Aronson, 1966; Carlsmith *et al.*,

1966; Janis and Gilmore, 1965; Linder et al., 1967), who suggested different solutions, one of which was finally accepted as most appropriate ("freedom of choice", Linder et al., 1967). At the level of specific problems, research can be considered as consisting of unitary and disjunctive tasks with the potential productivity of the "community of social psychologists" being determined by the work of its most proficient member.

A second oversimplification of this model is that it assumes a criterion for a *correct* solution, while according to critical rationalism such a criterion is not and cannot be available in science. All we can do is to distinguish better from less good theories on the basis of their relative empirical content. However, while this alters the status of an accepted theory, it does not make much difference to the rejected ones. While a corroborated theory will only be accepted as "correct" for the time being, a theory which has once been considered falsified will not easily be reconsidered. It is therefore as important in science as in group problem-solving that the best solution is recognized as such by one's fellow group members.

2. Threats to progress

If we accept this model as an appropriate description of scientific research, we will be able to identify the major factors which determine the actual productivity of a scientific community. Since we are mainly interested in whether a given community makes the best uses of its resources, we will neglect factors which determine the availability of resources. It should be obvious that an area which can attract the best brains and provide them with excellent working conditions should do better than an area which can only attract the mediocre and offers poor conditions. Although these are important determinants of productivity, they are usually not dealt with by research on group problem-solving, which focuses on the discrepancy between potential and actual group productivity. Actual productivity may fall short of potential productivity (1) if some aspect of the group process prevents the most proficient members from achieving their true potential and (2) if the group does not recognize the best solution and instead chooses an inferior one.

Restrictive evaluation criteria. One important factor which may prevent a group from achieving its true potential is the existence of an unnecessarily restrictive group consensus about what is a good or bad solution. Obviously, some such consensus is necessary, for example a "demarcation criterion" to distinguish scientific from non-scientific solutions. However, progress of science depends on the free competition of theories, and philosophers of science (e.g. Albert, 1975; Feyerabend, 1975; Popper, 1959, 1963) have always stressed the importance of theoretical pluralism, that is the freedom to consider any kind of solution for a given problem. If that freedom is restricted, some of the best solutions for a given problem may never be considered, because they appear unscientific, untestable, or unpromising, according to the dominant opinion of the research community. It will be argued that social psychology, with its theoretical fixation on individualistic explanation and its methodological fixation on experimentalism, developed such an overrestrictive group consensus that it prevented researchers from even considering whole classes of promising solutions.

*Low verifiability of solutions.** A group can only work at the level of its best member if it recognizes the correct solution once it has been proposed. This requires either a "high verifiability of the solution for all persons in possession of the original facts of the problem" or, alternatively, that the "solution has plurality support at the outset" or "is attained by members with reputations of high competency" (Kelley and Thibaut, 1969). The lower the verifiability of the solution, the more important become the social factors like plurality support or the prestige of the solution finder (Kelley and Thibaut, 1969). It is well known that scientific procedure places great emphasis on verifiability. Any report of an empirical study should contain sufficient detail to enable the reader to verify all conclusions for himself or even to replicate the study. However, as we argued before, it is not the theory-divergent results alone, but these in conjunction with a better theory, which lead to the rejection of the old theory. Thus, it is not the verifiability of the experimental conclusions, but of the decision that the

---

* The groups studied in group problem-solving research typically work on the solution of logical problems, and a solution is considered highly verifiable if the correct solution is easily recognized as such once it has been suggested by a group member. To maintain the analogy to group problem-solving, the term verifiability has been kept on in the discussion of decisions between theories. This is not to imply that a given theory can be empirically verified (i.e. proven as true) but that decisions can be made between competing theories which will be accepted with near unanimity by the members of the scientific community. The degree of verifiability of a decision between theories depends on the testability of the theories involved in the comparison.

new theory is better than an existing theory which determines whether a scientific community reaches the level of its best member. It is here that a researcher in social psychology finds himself faced with unusual difficulties. If one tries out Popper's (1959) criterion of empirical content on social psychological theories, one soon realizes that it is not all that helpful. It will be argued that due to the problems in verifying decisions between social psychological theories, these decisions will be strongly affected by social processes operating in the community of social psychological researchers.

C. GROUP PROCESS AND ACTUAL PRODUCTIVITY

In this section the group process of conducting research will be analysed. The community of social psychologists can be conceived of as a social group or organization with the goal of furthering knowledge in social psychology. The functioning of this organization can be analysed in terms of four inter-related social processes: *socialization, recruitment, social control* and *communication*. It will be argued that each of these processes contributes to a uniformity of theoretical and methodological perspectives, which in turn serves as a basis for the social validation of social psychologists' beliefs in the correctness of their theories. Since this consensus is undermined by deviant theoretical and methodological opinions, scientists are not very kind to critics, particularly if they are members of their in-group. The expectation of negative sanctions for radical innovation should serve as an additional discouragement for unconventional theorizing and research. Thus, the social organization of the research community, by discouraging theoretical and methodological pluralism and rewarding conformity to a uniform perspective, creates exactly the kind of situation which should be detrimental to the progress of a discipline.

1. Organizational processes

Socialization. Anybody involved in teaching introductory psychology will know the intense feeling of anger and annoyance when students react with boredom to the presentation of some exciting theoretical controversy or novel theoretical approach. What one tends to forget is that it took years of training to get interested in the dull things which now excite us. While the finding that subjects who had access to peanuts and Pepsi-Cola while reading a message were more persuaded than those exposed to noxious odours (Janis *et al.*, 1965) will, at best, amuse the uninitiated, it constitutes striking evidence for the "affect hypothesis of distraction" to the connoisseur of the attitude-change literature. Similarly, Rosch's (1976) controversial statement that the world contains "intrinsically separate things" is only controversial to people who have been brought up on the Whorfian (1956) notion that categories are essentially arbitrary. As Hagstrom (1965) pointed out in his classic analysis of the scientific community: "The socialization of scientists tends to produce persons who are so strongly committed to the central values of science that they unthinkingly accept them.... These comitments are the outcome of a prolonged training process, lasting well into adult life ... in which he [the student] is extremely dependent on his teachers" (p. 9). During this period he learns most of the skills of the trade and internalizes the criteria that distinguish a good piece of research from a bad one. Since his own self-evaluation as a student will be dependent on the evaluation by teachers and peers, he will learn to judge his own work according to these standards.

Recruitment. Apart from in rare periods of expansion, university jobs are scarce and only the best students manage to enter a scientific career. However, competence alone is not sufficient. The teachers who write the recommendations which are essential for a successful application must be convinced that their student is likely to do research and to do good research. They are therefore most willing to recommend someone with whom they themselves have worked well and who has a similar methodological and theoretical orientation. Thus, the system of recruitment will not only help to enforce the internalization of criteria, it will also contribute to the homogeneity of the group.

Social control. The scientific community has two major instruments of social control: journals and granting boards. Scientists are motivated not merely by curiosity but also by a need to be recognized by other members of the scientific community (Hagstrom, 1965). This accounts for some of the aggressiveness of the conflicts over priorities in scientific discoveries (Merton, 1957). To achieve recognition, a scientist has to reach a wide audience of colleagues. The best way to do this is to publish in recognized journals. However, journals are very selective in what they publish: most journals in social psychology reject about 80% of their manuscripts. In order to be allowed to publish, one's research has to meet the criteria put forward by these journals. Editors and members of editorial boards are typically selected from a small group of well-known and well-recognized scientists who form the elite of a scientific community. In an analysis of the membership of the editorial boards of two major social psychology journals, the *Journal of Personality and Social Psychology* and the *Journal of Experimental Social Psychology*, over a five-year period (1971–1975), Morawski (1979) found that 61% or more of the combined editorial board members belonged to the Society of Experimental Social Psychology (SESP), a small, élite society whose members are chosen by peer nominations. At any time, between 6 and 11% of the editorial members held positions in both *JPSP* and *JESP* in addition to their membership of SESP. It is very likely that Morawski would have met some of the same people, had she analysed the membership of the boards of research foundations. Thus, even if a scientist were motivated only by curiosity, he would have to meet established standards in designing his research if he needed a research grant to conduct his studies.

Deviants in science are members of a scientific community who reject the accepted ways of theorizing and, more importantly, of doing research. What happens to deviants depends to some extent on whether they are aspiring or well-established members of the group and how discrepant their novel approach is from the establishment position. Aspiring members who favour a very discrepant approach typically have little chance of changing the field. They will find it extremely difficult to get their ideas or empirical results published in recognized journals or to find financial support for their research. Unless they are part of some radical minority and form a small subgroup with their own means of communication, they will either have to shape up or drop out. In the U.S.A., where getting tenure is linked to publishing in recognized journals, young innovators are likely to end at small teaching colleges or completely out of academia. The fate of a respected member of the field who develops deviant scientific views is similar to that of a member of any group who deviates from the majority opinion on an important issue (Schachter, 1951). At first he will find himself the centre of attention with other members arguing with him to change his opinion. If he does not budge, he will soon lose status in the group; he is likely to be dropped from editorial boards, committees, etc., and to find himself stripped of most of his former power and influence. However, on account of his past merits, the other members of the group will find it hard to completely disregard his novel views, and it is possible that his attack may lead to some innovation in the field.

Communication. The consensus about theoretical and methodological standards which typically exists in a scientific community is maintained not only by normative social influence but also by informative social influence. In analysing the causes for the uniformity of opinions and values in groups, Festinger (1950, 1954) recognized the importance of social comparison processes. People have a need to validate their opinions and one way of achieving this is by social comparison. If one finds that a given view is shared by important reference persons, one will be more confident of its validity and less willing to change it than if such reference persons disagree. As Sherif (1935) demonstrated in his classic study, such social comparison processes lead to a convergence of opinions, at least under conditions where the physical reality is very unclear. Once such consensus has been reached, group members are relatively confident that their views are correct. Thus, the group consensus should help to satisfy the scientists' need for truth and certainty, for which there seems to be no objective basis.

2. Group norms and paradigms

Due to the informational and normative social influence group members exert on each other, there are strong pressures in a group for members to develop or maintain a consensus (Festinger, 1950, 1954). These pressures are the stronger, the more important or central a given topic or activity is for a group (Schachter, 1951). If we accept the notion that a scientific community can be conceived of as a social group or organization with the goal of furthering knowledge by developing theories and conducting research, it seems only reasonable, to assume that they should develop a consensus about the best way to go about these activities. In his *Structure of Scientific Revolutions* Kuhn (1962)*

---

* It is perhaps worth noting that the distinction between potential group productivity and actual performance may help to resolve the apparent contradiction between the models of scientific research presented by Popper (1959) and Kuhn (1962). Whereas Popper's (1959) *Logic of Scientific Discovery* could be considered a model of potential group productivity, Kuhn's *Structure of Scientific Revolutions* is oriented towards actual research performance.

introduced the concept of "paradigm" as the specific beliefs and values shared by a scientific community. Although his discussion of the nature of paradigms is less than clear, paradigms seem to reflect the consensus of a scientific community on what kinds of theories to develop and what methods to use for testing them. "Men whose research is based on shared paradigms are committed to the same rules and standards for scientific practice" (p. 11). In aquiring a paradigm, Kuhn (1962) argues, "a scientific community aquires ... a criterion for choosing problems that, while the paradigm is taken for granted, can be assumed to have solutions. To a great extent these are the only problems that the community will admit as scientific or encourage its members to undertake" (p. 37). There thus appears to be some affinity between Kuhn's (1962) view of the functions of paradigms and our discussion of the effects of group norms on scientific research. It should be noted, however, that Kuhn's concept of paradigm implies more than a mere group consensus about best ways of conducting research in an area (see Masterman, 1970, for a description of the 21 ways Kuhn uses the concept of paradigm). Furthermore, our discussion emphasizes the negative effects of such consensus on the development of science, while Kuhn considers mainly its positive aspects.

3. The value of subgroup formation

Consensus and conformity pressures are by-products of group formation and are essential for the functioning of a group. No group could survive without some norms and the power over its members to reward conformity and sanction deviance. Since the strictest norms typically develop in areas of particular importance to a group, scientific communities are likely to have a body of norms regulating the conduct of research. These norms should tend to reduce or even eliminate the theoretical and methodological pluralism which is essential for scientific progress. From this it would seem to follow that a free competition of paradigms can be assured only if a given discipline is split up into several scientific communities, e.g. competing schools or relatively independent subgroups in various countries. It can be argued that this has not been the case for an important time in the development of social psychology, which until recently developed in one country, stimulated by one school of thought. It is only during this decade that a fragmentation has begun to occur.

D. THE COSTS OF CONSENSUS

According to critical rationalism (Popper, 1959, 1963), science develops from an interplay of conjectures and refutations in which theories are invented, severely tested, and finally replaced by new ones of higher empirical content. Progress in science thus thrives on theoretical and methodological pluralism. It is our argument that, due to the monolithic structure of social psychology, the competition of paradigms has been severely restricted and that for some time methodological and theoretical biases have been operating in social psychology, leading to an *uncritical* preference for certain methods and certain classes of theories. These preferences were uncritical because alternative solutions were not seriously considered. One of the positive results of the so-called crisis of social psychology is that some of these biases have now been recognized.

1. Methodological biases

For a long time, there was agreement among social psychologists about the superiority of the experimental method. The normative character of this consensus can be seen from the practice of élite scientific societies to use experimentalism as a criterion in member admission. Thus, the Society of Experimental Social Psychology and the European Association of Experimental Social Psychology adopted the label "experimental" originally quite intentionally to keep out unwanted colleagues. Some social psychological journals and series started during that period also described themselves as experimental. While it is understandable that social psychologists wanted to distinguish themselves from more philosophically oriented social thinkers, limiting their methodological arsenal to only one empirical method is exceedingly restrictive. It has been recognized only recently that our complete reliance on experimentation may have severely limited our understanding of social phenomena. Smith (1972), for example, remarked that in "building an experimental social psychology, we do well to recognize a certain incongruity between experimental method and the interactive phenomena with which social psychology is supposedly concerned. When pressed, most of us will agree that social behavior involves interactive systems in which feedback loops are more characteristic than linear causation.... With its independent and dependent variables, experimental design inherently produces a unidirectional snapshot" (p. 94). In his analysis of the reasons for the rapid decline of small group research during the 1940s and 1950s, Steiner (1974), too, argued that the experimental methodology with its emphasis on ever stricter controls was partly to blame. This experimental tradition is epitomized by the laboratory facilities of that period, which typically consist of a number of tiny cubicles designed to prevent any contact between subjects. Although I have always argued (e.g. Stroebe, 1979) that the reciprocal and circular nature of social processes should first be reflected in our theories, before we need a different methodology, there might be some merit in the reverse argument as well. After all, theories are developed with empirical tests in mind, therefore it is quite likely that a laboratory experimenter will entertain only theoretical notions which can easily be tested with his usual experimental procedures.

It is not the use of the experimental method *per se* which is at fault, but the *exclusive* reliance on that method. The average researcher in social psychology appears not even to consider the possibility that some hypotheses could be tested as well or better by using observation schedules, content analyses, surveys or epidemiological data, although some of these methods could even be used in conjunction with experimental designs. The reason for this abstention is probably quite simple. Every change in research methodology requires costly investment in training, time and effort, which nobody will be willing to make as long as there are less costly alternatives. There may therefore be some merit in the suggestion of an exasperated colleague who was in favour of imposing a two-year moratorium on doing experiments to force social psychologists to get used to alternative empirical methods. As a firm believer in the economic model, I feel the human subject committees at U.S. universities and APA's ethical rules will do as good a job in the long run.

2. Theoretical biases

While our methodological bias led to an uncritical preference of one empirical method over others, our theoretical biases have led to similar preferences of certain classes of theories over potential alternatives. As with our criticism of the methodological bias, the issue here is not one of right or wrong but of competition versus monopoly. If the progress of science requires theoretical pluralism, dogmatism must slow down the development of an area. Although, like beauty, dogmatism is always in the eye of the beholder, there are some signs that social psychologists have unduly emphasized environmental factors over genetic determinants and individualistic factors over social-structural influences.

The neglect of genetic factors. There appears to be a great deal of consensus among social psychologists that social psychological man is fully determined by his social environment. As McGuire (1969) expressed the common sentiment in his classic chapter on attitude change "A man of this writer's generation considers the possibility that there may be a genetic component in attitude determination only with trepidation" (p. 161). Fortunately, these trepidations did not prevent him from giving the idea some serious consideration and although he had to conclude that the "important topic of possible genetic determination of attitudes has been so neglected by researchers that this section has of necessity been very conjectural" (p 163), he came up with quite a bit of supportive evidence. However, he could have saved his ink, since, unlike other parts of his chapter, his section on genetic determinants of attitudes seems to have had no detectable impact on social psychology. Campbell's (1975) presidential address, in which he discussed the evolutionary roots of many aspects of social behaviour, seems to be destined to suffer the same fate. There were hardly any letters by social psychologists in the collection of comments contained in the 1976 issue of the *American Psychologist* and, to judge from recent "crisis" sessions at social psychological conferences, the subject seems to have been lost without trace on social psychological thinking.

There is reason to believe that this neglect of genetic influences on social behaviour is at least partly ideological. The notion that man's abilities and skills are to some extent genetically predetermined runs contrary to the idea that all men are equal and therefore have equal access to social, political, and economic opportunities. The political implications of environmentalism, on the other hand, are more consistent with the liberal views predominant among social psychologists, since "it allows for man's behavior to be modified or controlled by environmental determination, over which theoretically he has control, rather than inborn predispositions" (Wispé and Thompson, 1976, p. 346). It need hardly be pointed out to an audience of social psychologists that some of the proponents of a genetic view are even more ideologically biased than their opponents and that bad hereditarianism can do—

and actually does—more harm than bad environmentalism. The question is however, whether this is reason enough not even to *consider* the possibility of a genetic basis of behaviour.

If one rejects the notion that innate mechanisms may play some role in the determination of social behaviour, one should also have little use for the ethological literature as a source of hypotheses. It is not surprising, therefore, that most textbooks on social psychology fail to discuss ethological studies. Nor do social psychologists view kindly attempts by ethologists (e.g. Lorenz, 1966; Eibl-Eibesfeldt, 1973) to interpret human social behaviour on the basis of animal observations. Furthermore, the analyses of the evolution of some forms of social behaviour by sociobiologists (e.g. Dawkins, 1976; Wilson, 1975) seem to be generally disregarded by social psychologists.

Some further evidence for the suspicion that the predominance of environmentalism among social psychologists may bias the acceptance of inconsistent information comes from the area of emotion. Here most social psychology texts exclusively discuss Schachter's (Schachter and Singer, 1962) theory of emotions, which assumes that emotions are the joint result of an unspecific physiological arousal and the cognitions derived from an interpretation of the situation in which the arousal is experienced. Recent works by Izard (1971) and Tomkins (1962, 1963), which strongly suggest that emotions are also shaped by innate mechanisms, seem to have done little to undermine the monopoly position of Schachter's cognitive theory as social psychology's theory of emotion.

It should be emphasized that social psychologists' apparent disregard for information supporting the notion of innate mechanisms may be due to ignorance rather than active avoidance. However, even without that evidence, nobody can deny that there are normative pressures in social psychology against *considering* the possibility of genetic determination of social behaviour. With the recent developments in ethology and sociobiology, social psychology may no longer be able to afford the luxury of cutting itself off from promising areas of scientific development on account of noble sentiments.

The neglect of social-structural variables. The emphasis on individualistic factors and the complete neglect of social-structural variables has perhaps been the most crippling, but certainly the most criticised (e.g. Pepitone, 1976; Sampson, 1977; Steiner, 1974; Stroebe, 1979), bias of social psychological thinking. Although lip service has been paid to the fact that individuals function in a social context, individual behaviour is typically explained by relating it to other elements of the individual system such as attitudes, motives, or needs. Berkowitz (1962) expressed the individualistic sentiment perhaps best, when he stated: "... the present writer is still inclined to emphasize the importance of individualistic considerations in the field of group relations. Dealings between groups ultimately become problems of the psychology of the individual. Individuals decide to go to war: battles are fought by individuals; and peace is established by individuals" (p. 167).

One may doubt whether there would be many wars if the decision to go to them was really left to the individual. However, Berkowitz (1962) is not completely wrong in stating that individuals decide to go to war, he merely neglects to mention that in times of war, this decision often boils down to the choice between being shot by the enemy and being shot by one's fellow countrymen. There seems to be therefore some merit in the position taken by Pepitone (1976), who feels that practically all social behaviour of interest to social psychology is normatively determined and that "underlying normative social behavior are dynamics, structures, or conditions that are part of, and generated by the collective system of interdependent individuals" (p. 649). Thus, as sociologists have been stressing all along, one cannot fully account for social organizations (e.g. family, small group) in terms of the attitudes and motives of the individuals forming that organization. Consequently, one cannot *fully* understand interactions between members of such organizations in terms of their individual motives. Pepitone (1976) then goes on to argue that most major theories of social psychology deal with processes that are conceptually located within the individual and are therefore completely inadequate for the explanation of social behaviour.

The implications of this analysis for social psychology are rather grim. If most social behaviour of interest to social psychologists is normatively determined and if social psychological theories cannot account for normative behaviour, social psychologists have led rather useless lives during the last decades. However, as much as one has to agree with Pepitone that social behaviour cannot be sufficiently explained by individual motives, it seems doubtful whether adopting the opposite extreme is really the right answer. Tajfel (1978) has recently developed an intermediate position, arguing that social interactions can be placed on a continuum ranging from *interindividual* to *intergroup* behaviour. At one extreme, interaction between individuals is almost fully determined by their individual relationships; at the other extreme, the interaction is almost fully determined by their respective memberships of various groups or social categories and not at all affected by the inter-individual personal relationships between the people involved. However, if social behaviour is sometimes determined by individual factors and sometimes by normative variables, social psychology theory should identify the conditions which determined the adoption of forms of social behaviour nearing one or the other extreme of this continuum (Stroebe, 1979). Some of these conditions have been analysed by Tajfel (1978) and co-workers who argue that intergroup conflict forces members of opposing groups to behave to each other in terms of their respective group memberships rather than in terms of their individual relationships. However, instances of inter-role behaviour provide similar examples of personal relationships being overcome by powerful normative prescriptions, which typically cannot be accounted for by intergroup or interpersonal conflict. Thus, other determinants of such "inter-category" behaviour will have to be identified.

3. The interdependence of methodological and theoretical biases

Critics of the experimental method (e.g. Smith, 1972; Swingle, 1976; Steiner, 1974) have blamed the predominance of the experimental methodology for the neglect of social-structural variables in social psychology. For example Steiner (1974) argued that the experimental "controls instituted during the 1950s and 1960s prohibited the study of full blown group process. They legislated *mutual* responsivity of participants out of existence" (p. 100). More recently Swingle (1976) has warned that in "its extreme form, the causal fixation gives rise to complete myopia with respect to the reciprocal and circular nature which, as one moment's reflection must indicate, characterizes all social processes" (p. 103/104).

A similar point could be made regarding the neglect of genetic factors. A social psychology which, for methodological reasons restricts itself to the study of the effects of variables manipulable in experimental settings, is likely to develop an environmentalist bias. After all, social environments can be varied at will in social psychology experiments, whereas the genetic equipment of human subjects is yet beyond the control of the social psychology experimenter.

Although I have always been reluctant to blame the predominance of experimental methodology for all that is bad in social psychology (Stroebe, 1979), these arguments seem quite persuasive. It is not unreasonable to assume that experimental social psychologists have frequently interpreted the requirement to develop testable theories more narrowly as a demand for theories that can be tested experimentally. After all, experimental evidence was, for a long time, considered the only proper empirical support for a theory. Such a restriction would go a long way towards accounting for the individualistic and environmentalistic bias observed in the social psychological theorizing of the last few decades.

4. The consequences of scientific biases for research

According to our model of group problem-solving in science, the existence of strong methodological or theoretical biases in a discipline is likely to have two effects. First, it prevents members of a scientific community from exploring potential avenues of theory and research, because they appear unpromising according to common consensus, and at the same time motivates them uncritically to expend a great deal of effort on certain avenues of theory and research which happen to be "in" at the moment. Secondly, it increases the probability that theories which are consistent with certain biases will be accepted, while lowering the probability that inconsistent theories will be accepted by a scientific community.

Effect on the choice of problems. Since the decision to choose a given research problem is usually taken in private, it is difficult to demonstrate that theoretical or methodological biases of the scientific community prevent researchers from approaching certain research areas. Nevertheless, the assumption has a great deal of face validity. Research ideas are rarely developed in social isolation: one is usually stimulated by some colleagues, either directly or indirectly through the literature, and once a problem has been formulated, one is likely to discuss it with others. It is probably during these early stages that positive or negative comments by colleagues are of particular importance. Because ideas which are not in tune with their biases are unlikely to be received with great enthusiasm, they are also less likely to be followed through. With the many claims on the time of an academic teacher, it takes a great deal of determination to go ahead with a research idea which has been unanimously derogated. It is here that the splendid isolation of the European social psychologist, who is typically the only one at his department, may have its advantages (Stroebe, 1975).

The same factors which prevent people from theorizing or conducting research in areas which are commonly considered unpromising, also encourage them to follow the fads and fashions of the field. Thus, the excesses in the research on experimental games, attitude similarity, or choice dilemmas, are probably due to such consensus effects. Once the consensus has worn off, these research decisions are often hard to understand. While too much research seems less damaging than too little, it should be kept in mind that research time is a scarce resource. Therefore, the over-employment of forces in one area is bound to lead to shortages in others.

Effect on acceptance of theories. It has been mentioned earlier that the probability that a group works at the level of its most proficient member is higher the more verifiable the solutions. Thus, the few instances in the group problem-solving research, in which groups generally managed to accept the first correct solution suggested by one of the members (e.g. Shaw, 1932), involved so-called "eureka-problems". Eureka-problems have solutions which are easily verifiable for other members of the group. As soon as the correctness of solutions becomes less easily demonstrable, acceptance becomes dependent on social factors, such as the status of the solution finder or the majority view on the problem. Thus, the lower the "verifiability" of decisions between theories in a discipline, the more the probability of acceptance of theories should be affected by theoretical biases of the scientific community.

Although the author lacks the expertise to judge whether the "verifiability" of decisions between theories is lower in social psychology than in natural sciences like physics or chemistry, there are some indications that this may be the case. For example Harris (1976) has recently criticized the "uncertain connection between verbal theories and research hypotheses in social psychology" (p. 210). Using a number of well-known social psychological theories as examples, Harris demonstrated that it was frequently difficult to decide which hypotheses did follow from these theories. In each instance Harris translated the verbal postulates of a given theory into mathematical symbols and equations and then demonstrated that one or more verbally stated research hypothesis typically assumed to "follow from" these postulates did not necessarily follow from them at all. Obviously, such ambiguities will seriously diminish the testability of social psychological theories and thus the "verifiability" of decisions between these theories.

A further difficulty in testing social psychological theories has been discussed by Greenwald (1975), who complained about the uncertain connection between conceptual definitions and operational definitions in social psychology. Although the connection between conceptual and operational definitions is always an uncertain one, it is probably more uncertain in social psychology than in other disciplines. In social psychology there are hardly any established operational definitions linking theoretical concepts to research procedures. Researchers typically make up their own operations and even such procedures as counter-attitudinal advocacy are less standardized than they might appear. The individual researcher will still have to select an attitude issue and invent a setting in which the advocacy is perceived as involving negative consequences by the actor. With such lack of standardization it is reasonable in the case of theory-divergent data, to question the construct validity of the experimental manipulation (or the dependent measure) before doubting the theory.

E. SUMMARY AND CONCLUSIONS

Deficiencies in the accumulation of scientific knowledge in social psychology are often used as evidence of the inadequacy of the hypothetico-deductive model (e.g. Gergen, 1973; Harré and Secord, 1972; Holzkamp, 1977). However, disappointment with the actual performance of research in social psychology does not necessarily justify the rejection of the model guiding the research process. Such models, like Popper's falsificationism, are essentially normative theories, describing the potential productivity of a scientific community. As we know from research on group problem-solving, human resources are rarely optimally employed in practice, and the actual productivity of a group is typically lower than its potential productivity. In this paper I have explored the argument that such a "process loss" in the conduct of social psychological research could account for the apparently unsatisfactory accumulation of knowledge in our discipline.

On the basis of falsificationism a model of research as a unitary and disjunctive task was derived. Research is a process of group problem-solving, where members of a scientific community search for a solution to a problem (i.e. for a new or better theory). The problem will be solved if at least one member of the group develops a "correct" solution *and* if all other members (or an overwhelming majority) recognize the solution as "correct" (i.e. as better than previous solutions). The major criterion for this decision is the relative empirical content of the theory.

The important determinants of the productivity of a research community, according to this model, are the degree of methodological and theoretical pluralism and the degree of "verifiability" of the theoretical decision. In actual practice, the free competition of theories and methods will always be restricted by the convergence of opinions and the development of norms in groups. These norms, which provide members with standards for evaluation, are essential to group functioning. The competition of ideas is likely to be restricted within groups, and it is therefore important for progress that a number of competing subgroups (i.e. schools) develop in a discipline to create a free competition of methods and theories between groups. It was argued that due to historical conditions, such subgroups did not develop in social psychology until very recently.

The existence of an over-restrictive consensus about the right way of theorizing and conducting research should be particularly damaging to a discipline if the "verifiability" of theoretical decisions is low. If the criteria for recognizing a new theory as better than the old one are very clear-cut, a better solution should be easily recognized, even if it violates some of the biases of members of the research community. The lower the "verifiability" of theoretical decisions, the higher should be the probability that theoretical or methodological biases strongly influence the acceptance of a solution. There is reason to believe that the "verifiability" of theoretical decisions is particularly low in social psychology. While this social psychological model of the research process may help us to understand a number of puzzling aspects of the recent development of social psychology, unfortunately it does not help us to overcome the low "verifiability" of theoretical decisions, which seems to be one of the major causes of our problems.

ACKNOWLEDGEMENTS

The author is greatly indebted to Professor J. H. Davis, Dr S. Duck, Professor G. Fleischmann, Dr V. Gadenne, R. Gilmour, Professor K.-D. Opp, Professor L. H. Strickland, Dr M. S. Stroebe and Professor H. Tajfel for their comments on an earlier draft of this chapter. It should be emphasized, however, that the views expressed in this chapter were not always shared by these colleagues and that the author takes sole responsibility for them.

Part 3
Future Extensions

Promises Fulfilled: Futures for Social Psychology

ROBIN GILMOUR

Part 3 is intended to add the last element to the developmental sequence and discuss what kind of futures social psychology might face. This reflects the general structure and the whole thrust of the book's intention by drawing from the previous sections before extending consideration into the future.

In Parts 1 and 2 we have tried to provide a better basis, or launching pad as it were, for the journey onwards by extracting what was seen by the different authors as being of most value in the present and from the past. Now the general question concerns where we can get to from the present, given, one hopes, an understanding of the past that is improved both in terms of deriving more use or value from past work and also in terms of deriving the benefits of a clearer understanding of the effects of historical context and of social and psychological factors on the way we develop as a discipline.

In keeping with our concern for a wider, rather than narrower, approach to the whole subject, the authors in Part 3 have given very different treatments of the theme of the section: two of the chapters maintain the strand of content focus running through the book and project developments of theory and application in social psychology into the more immediate future; a third chapter seeks to encapsulate and extend the threads of self-examination and self-improving examination to develop a more usefully reflexive social psychology; and the fourth chapter, adopting yet another approach, attempts to provide a rather longer and more general look farther into the future. Taken as a whole Part 3 can be regarded as asserting that there *is* a future for social psychology and suggesting where and what that future might be, at least in some important respects.

We must emphasize again that to speak of only one future is unnecessarily limiting: we can project a number of possible futures and we should really consider multiple futures for social psychology. Accordingly, not only should the reader ask himself whether the directions mapped out here by the contributions are feasible, or worth while, or desirable but also—and perhaps more importantly—he should consider what other, better, futures might await us.

9
Taking the Past to Heart:
One of the Futures of Social Psychology?

STEVE DUCK
University of Lancaster, England

A. Crisis? What crisis? 212
   1. Attacks on method 213
   2. Other types of crisis 215
B. When prophecy succeeds: some lessons of the past and present . . 217
   1. The place of social psychology in "the world" 218
   2. The place of social psychology in the academic system . . . 220
   3. The structure of the profession and its outlets 221
   4. Influences and constraints upon individuals 223
   5. Fashionable influences on social psychology 226
   6. The nature and functions of decisions about social psychology?. . 228
C. Not in our subject but in ourselves? 230
   1. Crisis of theory?. 230
   2. Developing a data base: crisis of utility? 231
   3. Looking at ourselves: crisis of identity? 233
   4. Relating to other departments: crisis of intellectual isolation? . 233
   5. The sound of the wrong hand clapping: crisis of practice? . 235
D. Concluding remarks 236

It has recently been claimed that social psychology is ailing in a variety of ways that present themselves as dissatisfaction with the progress of the discipline and, more fundamentally, with the nature of social psychology and its possible role in society. However, just as medical crises may be reflections of true inherent structural weakness, created out of or intensified by anxiety, or exacerbated by poor diet or lack of useful exercise, so too social psychologists in crisis manifest symptoms and behaviours that may indicate true ailment, complex effects of anxiety, or consequences merely of unwise practice or thoughtless process. The thesis of this chapter is that the future development of social psychology depends on a clearer discrimination of "the crisis" into true ailment and other features with a fuller analysis of the human and social forces in the discipline as well as the assumed intellectual themes and undercurrents.

Ideas, approaches or outlooks can grip people's attention for many reasons, not all of which are related to the richness or power of the ideas themselves. It is too often overlooked—by social psychologists of all people—that what is popular at any time (and even the present state of the discipline) is the result not only of intellectual activity but also of the social processes by which ideas are moulded and communicated to other people. Such processes combine the diverting effects of the social pressures that inhere in the structure of the discipline with the distracting influences of psychological processes that occur in and between social psychologists as human beings. Their consequences thus reflect less on the true nature of the discipline than on those who practise it and are therefore alleviated by different means: by a social psychological analysis of the conduct of the discipline rather than by a logical or philosophical analysis of its principles. A logical or philosophical analysis might simply miss the real reasons for the present state of affairs. This is not, of course, to deny the value of that type of analysis; it is merely to say that a logical or philosophical analysis alone is not enough—especially for social psychologists. Nor is it to fall into the trap of circularity, unless one asserts that the study of human behaviour by human beings is itself circular, such that the study of social psychology is itself logically impossible. Logical circularity must be distinguished from constructive reflexivity and the ability to explain one's own behaviour in terms of one's own theoretical principles. But it does raise the intriguing question of whether our own research (into, say, actor–observer differences) would lead us to expect that we, as social psychologists, actually examine or explain our own behaviour in the same terms as are used to explain *other* humans' activity. This will be the focus of the present chapter.

A. CRISIS? WHAT CRISIS?

To perform an analysis of the crisis using social psychology itself, it is first necessary to identify and define the crisis—and this is surprisingly difficult to do, rather as it is with so many other concepts in social psychology. Different critics take different views of what the crisis in social psychology is, and the first problem is to account for this diversity. To anticipate the argument a little, it should be remembered that the attitudes held or expressed by individuals can serve several functions independent of their "true content": attitudes that seem to the owners to be purely rational assessments of the facts can also serve to defend the ego, to create balance, resolve unacceptable social tensions, and so on (Katz, 1960; Heider, 1958; Festinger et al., 1952).

1. Attacks on method

The confusing ambiguity about the nature of "the crisis" is often concealed by the fact that many critics attack the same target: methodology. Thus Gergen (1978a, p. 507) asserts that "psychological enquiry into social phenomena has become virtually indistinguishable from controlled experimentation" and proceeds to question the value of experiments in furthering knowledge. However the question is misconceived unless one expands the concept of experimentation to include all the theoretical and logical analysis that precedes an investigation (Turner, 1980), distinguishes the different analytic or creative heuristics used to generate theories independently of the method of testing them (McGuire, 1980a), and considers the wide variety of techniques that are loosely collected under the umbrella of "controlled experimentation" (Hendrick and Jones, 1971). Equally, one can distinguish at least seven different arguments about experimentation, each with different consequences:

(i) The philosophical basis of experimentation (i.e. logical positivism) is wrong (e.g. Harré and Secord, 1972). Consequence: await a rethinking of some aspect of philosophy.
(ii) Irrespective of the philosophical value of logical positivism it is now no longer useful as the model for social psychology (e.g. McGuire, 1980a). Consequences: account for experimentation in a different way; construct and test theories differently.
(iii) An experimental method is fundamentally misconceived as a tool of the social psychologist (e.g. because it is bound to cultural or historical context; Gergen, 1973, 1978b). Consequence: change to a new method of research.

(iv) An experimental method gives a distorted or incomplete picture of Man and omits or trivializes normal behaviour (e.g. Gauld and Shotter, 1977; Harré, 1977). Consequences: retain experimentation but add other sorts of study to the general approach; develop and add different levels of analysis of behaviour.

(v) Experiments have potential value but are fundamentally misunderstood or misinterpreted (e.g. Israel and Tajfel, 1972). Consequence: retain experimentation but encourage more careful critical scrutiny and analysis of experimental design and interpretation.

(vi) Experiments and the experimental method are relatively satisfactory but the fault lies in exclusive reliance on that method (e.g. Stroebe, 1980). Consequences: retain experimentation but test its findings in a variety of different contexts and settings; use other sorts of study.

(vii) Experiments are valuable and usually correctly interpreted but are very difficult to do properly (e.g. Hendrick and Jones, 1971). Consequences: research the difficulties of experimentation; train researchers more adequately; attempt to increase competency in experiments.

Since these arguments are very different, it is unwise to attack or defend experimentation in any generalized way. It is not only unwise but also bad logic to point to bad experiments and weak areas in order to establish a generalized case against either experimentation in particular or social psychology as a whole. However, this frequently occurs, notwithstanding its logical fallaciousness. As psychologists observing *other* humans doing similar things, we would no doubt be quick to talk in terms of selectivity of exposure to information (Zadny and Gerard, 1974), stereotypy in attribution (Marston, 1976), and even possibly groupthink (Janis, 1972). Equally, when we observe psychologists selecting familiar, but unreplicated studies to make their case, or (worse) selecting unrepresentatively poor studies from the vast array available, then we should immediately think of Tversky and Kahneman's (1974) analysis of people's failure to deal competently with statistical information, especially the evidence that single familiar instances exert a disproportionate influence over beliefs in the face of statistical evidence about the general pattern (Tversky and Kahneman, 1973). We may even find ourselves thinking of Ross's (1977) powerful analysis of motivational biases in attribution—or we may feel that our failure to think of our own activities in such terms is itself an intriguing example of, say, actor–observer differences or even self-serving bias in explanation!

2. Other types of crisis

Attacks on method are partly, it will be argued, manifestations of other sorts of crisis: crises of theory, of utility, of intellectual isolation, of practice, and of identity. Indeed, Totman (1979) has argued that experiments and experimental reports are, in fact, not the basis upon which theories are tested for rejection and acceptance, nor are they the grounds upon which given areas come into and go out of prominence. Attacks on methodology, then, are not striking at the processual roots of the development of the subject and, I would argue, other crises must be considered.

Crises of theory have taken the form of doubts about metatheoretical orientation (is it a science with a scientific method? Harré, 1980); internal theoretical style (too behaviourist, not anthropological enough; Harré and Secord, 1972); general orientation (too experimentally reductionist, too American, too "nice"; Israel and Tajfel, 1972); inherent models of persons (omitting subjects' plans and contexts; Gauld and Shotter, 1977) or ability to generate and test hypotheses (McGuire, 1980a).

Crises of utility amount to doubts about social psychology's capacity for social impact (Gergen, 1973, 1978b), a criticism with two distinct heads: first, doubting the ability of social psychology to solve major social problems (e.g. war, prejudice, class and sex conflict); secondly, doubting its ability to be useful at any level (e.g. even by clarifying factors in the decision to stop smoking).

Crises of intellectual isolation centre on the view that we have ignored the valuable contributions of colleagues in sociology (Backman, 1980), or other academic disciplines (House, 1977; Stryker, 1977). Occasionally it is also claimed that we pay too little heed to, and learn too little from, the lessons taught by other colleagues in our own psychology department or even by social psychologists in areas other than our own chosen field (Elms, 1975).

Crises of practice are often presented in the form of accusations of artificiality and triviality in the laboratory study of human social behaviour, often expressed in the view that what happens inside the laboratory tells us *nothing* (yes, it is usually in italics, cf. Harré and Secord, 1972, p. 52) about behaviour outside the laboratory (usually reverentially termed "the real world"). In addition to the points made above to distinguish the different and confounded forms of this point, I would make one further observation. The above criticism rests on two possible views about the relationship between any presumed lawfulness of subjects' behaviour outside the laboratory and any observed lawfulness inside (Duck, 1973). Either lawfulness in the real world is entirely different from the lawfulness manifested inside the laboratory, or the behaviour outside the laboratory is not fully explicable in terms of the laws generated from within the laboratory. In the first case, there is simply no evidence to support the view that humans act in *essentially* different ways inside and outside the laboratory, although one might speculate that the emphases of their activities might be slightly different in the two places (in which case some social psychologist ought to be able to say precisely what these differences might be). But it is none the less clear that the laboratory is in the real world in a very real sense. In the second case, one needs reassurance that the laboratory is not simply a special case of the real world—after all, no-one goes so far as to deny that the laboratory is in and is a part of the real world—and hence that one should research its special properties and its differences from other special instances. There would be nothing odd about this: we spend much of our research time exploring other special cases in search of a more general understanding of underlying principles (e.g. courtship as an example of personal relationships, but distinct from other examples, like work relationships). This seems a more productive and mature response than attempting to give up using a special case because it is difficult or not fully understood.

The nearest we, as a profession, have ever come to exploring these issues is, interestingly, usually phrased much more narrowly in terms of the similarities between experimenters' and subjects' behaviour in the laboratory, psychologists (except Kelly, 1955) having been shocked and amazed to find that subjects, too, may come into the laboratory attempting to explain what they find (Orne, 1962). Too often, however, such work on demand characteristics is misunderstood as a mere critique of the experimental method. Clearly it should rather be understood as an important insight into the general social psychological processes that take a particular form in a particular set of circumstances. It could thus be used as the basis for exploring the rich social psychological activities that take place once two (or more) persons enter the special relationship defined as a experimenter–subject relationship. It is, however, indicative of the present status of such work into laboratory activity that although everyone is aware that it both exacerbates and illustrates specific human emotions like suspicion, no-one ever uses this observation as the basis for generalization to real-life instances of those same emotions as in, for example, police work.

In analysing the above it will be argued that the crisis that remains when processual errors are explained is a crisis of confidence or crisis of identity that centres on role conflict and role strain.

B. WHEN PROPHECY SUCCEEDS: SOME LESSONS OF THE PAST AND PRESENT

Social psychological processes can illuminate our understanding of social psychology itself, and I shall give a limited number of examples, perforce giving less attention to the areas already covered by other writers in this volume (e.g. Innes; Stroebe; and Backman). I shall consider briefly some influences upon social psychologists that derive from:

(a) the place of social psychology in the world (real and political);
(b) the place of social psychology in the academic system;
(c) the structure of the profession and its communication systems;
(d) influences of an individual sort (e.g. those ultimately accountable to career and work pressures on "stars");
(e) influences (perhaps fashionable influences) on research topic selection;
(f) the functions of conflict in an academic discipline.

Before looking at these in detail, however, it is worth spending a moment to revisit Goffman's (1959) notion of "teamwork". Goffman (1959) argued that one social process which emerges often in social behaviour (particularly behaviour in public places) is the use of a complex system of rules for preserving the face and public front of a pair (or more) of persons under some apparent threat. Since some of what I will say may be seen as threatening and since I am about to argue that social psychologists themselves are subject to all the general human social processes, I am made rather uncomfortable by my memory of Goffman's work. It makes me none too sanguine about the reception of any analysis of social psychology by a social psychologist in terms of social psychological principles—the ultimate betrayal of the team.

1. The place of social psychology in "the world"

The thrust of many early cogent critical analyses of social psychology (e.g. Tajfel, 1972) was that the people in social psychological experiments are members of the real world and are therefore subject to its pressures and influences—a fact that, at the time, was rarely given much attention in experiments. Turning this on its head, it is easy to see that social psychologists, as members of that same real world, are themselves subject to its pressures and influences, some of which can affect the development of the discipline through non-intellectual means. For one easy example, the most important influence on the development of social psychology was not some new intellectual yeast within the discipline but the distinctly warm, fertile and proving atmosphere provided by the Second World War (Cartwright, 1979). A wide range of topics, problems and issues were brought forward for scrutiny and illumination by social psychologists—and this led to a growth in scope, theories and methods of the discipline as well as to an influx of workers (Innes, this volume).

Since then the discipline has suffered numerous small tremors rather than large eruptions, whilst one gradual shift in the outside world has been a greater emphasis on technology, a development that Kelvin (1980) sees as having significant implications for the work, interests and future development of social psychology. In the past decade, the pressure has come from a generation more concerned than previous generations with large social questions and with self-growth or self-insight. Introductory texts in social psychology soon marched in step with the tune of these pipers, and introductory chapters elaborated the ways in which social psychology could improve self-understanding or gave almost ritual justification of social psychology's value to society in the most optimistic terms. Social psychology, we learned, was just short of explaining and preventing war, prejudice, anti-feminism, Watergate, loneliness and unsatisfactory sexual relations; it could increase happiness, wealth, wisdom, and so on. The complaints against social psychology that were made in those times were also phrased in the same language, with the assumptions of such a background: social psychology was castigated not for having unrealistic aims, but for failing to attain them.

However, it is important to recognize, as Turner (1980) was the first to point out, that social problems are rarely defined as problems solely on the basis of purely social psychological criteria and that, consequently, social psychology is often sent on the fool's errand of looking for psychological solutions to essentially political or economic problems with some small "psychological" components. Not only is it "politically naïve of social psychologists to suppose that racial prejudice or class conflicts, for example, have a purely psychological origin" (Turner, 1979) but it leads both those inside and those outside the profession to wildly unrealistic expectations about social psychology, to inappropriate objectives and to misplaced beliefs about the nature of applied social psychology and its contribution to social life.*

These misplaced hopes can, in part, be attributed to the general wish of social psychologists to be "visible", and also to the willing (or even initiatory) assistance given by the mass media (Thorngate, 1976). Exposure in such ways led to a lot of effort to cater to public whims and fashionable interests which, in turn, led to the creation of public expectations about social psychology's contribution and potential value in the realm of social issues. Prominent work on self-esteem and the learning of self-acceptance (Mehrabian and Ksionzky, 1974) would lead us in other contexts to assert that others' expectations about one's capacities can create whole strategies for social performance and that if performance and expectation consistently fail to match then depression, aversion to social encounters and lowered self-esteem are usually combined in a sense of worthlessness. It is also found (Dreyer, 1953; Hochbaum, 1953) that consistent failure to meet even unrealistic goals in competitive group tasks (for example, in the context of social psychology, competing for public funds or esteem) can be psychologically sapping. It is easy to imagine that ill-informed expectations, derived in part from the unwise or incautious generalizations and simplifications provided by social psychologists themselves, can leave a deep mark on the profession's general outlook.

Those versions of the crisis, then, that manifest themselves in a feeling of helplessness, inadequacy or dissatisfaction with social psychology's

---

* A different but interesting issue concerns the extent to which social psychology can contribute an explanatory analysis of the rise and fall of "political issues".

contribution to society may be attributed as much to faults in the disciples as to faults in the discipline. There has been a rather surprising immodesty in social psychologists' attempts to find themselves a role. Although one can understand the wish of social psychologists to be useful to society, one cannot applaud the mistaken belief that its *primary* objective is to solve or prevent for ever such political or high order and persistent problems as war, prejudice and divorce. More modest and no less exciting views of the potential contribution of social psychology to society could perhaps increase both the confidence and (because of a more useful product) the respectability of the profession. Whilst the ultimate problem is to persuade others to accept a social psychological account of a problematic activity, it is more likely that the benefits of such accounts will be obvious in relation to, say, counselling of maritally distressed partners in particular cases rather than in relation to the nature of marriage and divorce in general, for example.

Such a view of the origin of some versions of the crisis in social psychology amounts to saying that we have no good reasons for assuming that social psychologists are immune from the transitory influences and interests of their times (Innes and Fraser, 1971). Nor have we any good reasons to assume that the mood of the times does not affect research and thoughts about research in a number of important ways. Indeed what is surprising is that we have been surprised that the assumptions, methods and interests of U.S. psychologists are different from those in western Europe (Israel and Tajfel, 1972) or the U.S.S.R. (Andreyeva *et al.*, 1979). It is even more surprising that the observed differences are only infrequently attributed to some profound human similarity that simply manifests itself in a variety of ingenious ways in different contexts.

2. The place of social psychology in the academic system

The social psychologist has an unusual and unenviable role in many departments of psychology, often being identified by other colleagues as getting no further than common sense and, at best, "soft" science. Such views frequently lead to attacks on the status of the discipline of social psychology in meetings where departmental resources are distributed. What can we, as social psychologists, contribute to an understanding of the likely process here? First, that stigmatized individuals tend to become deviants, to leave the group, use other external reference groups, and cohere with other similar deviants (Schachter, 1951; Festinger, 1954). Secondly, that individuals often come to behave in ways consistent with the stereotype pre-existing in the minds of observers and to confirm that stereotype (Snyder et al., 1978) or even, when the impression in the observer's mind is seen to be negative, to overcompensate in ways that produce negative responses for other reasons (Farina et al., 1968). In general a group comes to perceive itself as categorically different from the rejecting source and to differentiate itself in a variety of ways from that source (Tajfel, 1978).*

With this in mind, we observe that social psychologists have tended to become interested in self-growth movements, to be concerned in illustrating through their textbooks the ways in which student experiences can be expanded, to engage in research on common-sense propositions, and to set up differentiating groups and movements in social psychology (e.g. SESP and SASP).

3. The structure of the profession and its outlets

A large amount of early work in social psychology concerned social networks, communication systems, attitude change, source credibility, and the influence of leaders. This ought to be relevant to the understanding of a number of structural and communication features of social psychology which affect the style of its activity and its relatively ponderous response to pressure for change. "Social psychology" is, of course, composed of the individuals who practise it and the groups or communication outlets that they establish in order to practise it. Groups have well-researched techniques for dealing with dissenters or revolutionaries, for encouraging orthodoxy of approach, style or assumptional framework and for socializing their members (Festinger, 1954; Festinger et al., 1950). Stroebe (1980) has given an impressive analysis of some of these socialization factors. However, there are other human, social pressures on the individual.

McGuire (1973) and Lubek (1976) have identified the various ways in which a relatively small group of individuals can influence the direction of growth in a discipline. The structure of the discipline is

---

* I am grateful to Barry McCarthy for the observation that "identification with the aggressor" is also a common response, manifesting itself in mindless technological sophistication, rabid experimentalism, and anti-sociological anecdotes.

such that research-funding committees, journal reviewers or editors, and publishers' consultants have considerable influence over the kinds of research that get support or wide circulation. Although it is true that such persons exert considerable control over the discipline, it does not dictate that the discipline takes one particular form unless all these powerful people are unanimous on all the issues; indeed, there are large numbers of journals, publishers and (to a lesser extent) funding agencies where one should find that neither unanimity nor uniformity is the general rule. However, this hope is naïve and misplaced: group pressures on the gatekeepers and indeed their very method of selection dictates, in practical terms, that they will be persons with similar backgrounds, research histories and socialization experiences.

There are, furthermore, some interesting hidden consequences of the specialization and selection of such gatekeepers. Naturally (it seems "natural" in the present social and political climate) journal editors are chosen from among those prominent in the profession, as are research-funding committees, presidents of psychological associations, thesis examiners, and publishers' consultants. Highly prominent individuals are likely to be approached to serve in several capacities at once and can then exert multiple influences on the discipline (Gergen, 1976b). One consequence is that the individuals become overworked in a variety of roles simultaneously, and one would presume that it becomes possible to do each job properly only by restricting oneself to an increasingly narrow set of concerns of research issues. It is to be expected that such persons would be referred the work of an increasingly specialized sort and hence exert a disproportionate influence over that area and the careers of those in it (much of whose work they will see often and in many capacities, Gergen, 1976b).

Specialization is possible in other ways also. For one thing it can lead (or has led) to the formal or informal creation of centres for particular sorts of work and to subgroups specializing in given topics. This has both advantages and disadvantages. Whilst it presumably creates fertile ground, increases brainstorming creativity and productivity, it may have the occasional detrimental effect of creating entrenched camps which take up precious literature space fighting one another in unconstructive ways (see Clore and Byrne, 1974, for a parable on this). By tending to remove the group from frequent external influence and separating it from other sorts of work it may, at the extreme, lead to mild forms of groupthink (Janis, 1972), derogation of other research groups, hostility, and precisely the closed-minded and sterile debates that are becoming more frequent in the literature.

4. Influences and constraints upon individuals

The increase in specialization and in work pressure presumably makes it increasingly difficult for individuals to keep up with the research and theoretical developments being made in areas other than their own or to cross-fertilize their own ideas with those available in other parts of the discipline (or in other disciplines). The overlooked consequence of this (or, rather, "unmentioned" since it bears on "teamwork") is that individuals need to place increasing reliance on review articles or texts to form the basis of their knowledge of other areas and are thus subject to the influence of any mild distortions of emphasis or inadequate qualification of general positions made by the review author(s). "Timely" review articles exert a disproportionate effect on the views held about an area, not simply, I suggest, because they serve to identify the faults and complexities in an area such that people are put off and lose confidence. I suspect that part of the reason is that they give outsiders an encapsulated view of an area which makes them feel that there is less urgency in a search for the details. It is easy to find examples in social psychology of mild or even gross distortions and inaccuracies about an area which seed themselves in the mind of the profession and perpetuate themselves (see, for example, the discussion of attacks on interpersonal attraction below). However, whilst it may anger us, it should not surprise us that social psychologists too show the tendency to abbreviate, summarize and lose detail that other humans do or to have a bias towards the easy view in the face of detailed statistical evidence (Tversky and Kahneman, 1974; Ross, 1977) or to the other sorts of convenient pluralistic ignorance (Shaver, 1975). Add to these the tendencies for humans on the whole to believe what they hear from a credible source (Hovland *et al.*, 1953), the findings of work on the spread of rumour (Allport and Postman, 1947), and the persistence of beliefs in the face of inconsistent or disconfirming evidence (Festinger *et al.*, 1956), and the selective attention that follows the definition of an attitude (Festinger and Carlsmith, 1959)—and a whole array of sobering thoughts is offered to us.

For these and other reasons, distortions and imbalances of view of an area may result and then become perpetuated because second-order (review or commentary) papers are easier to assimilate than first-order (original) papers. As an example, let us look at a frequent favourite for such treatment: interpersonal attraction (IPA) research. Gergen (1978a), McGuire (1980a), Eiser (1980), and Harré and Secord (1972) all choose this area to illustrate social psychology's weakness and it is instructive to examine the nature of the arguments put forward on their chosen ground—though I confess to the defensive human pressure that it is also my own chosen research area (Duck, 1973; 1977).

One general line of argument is that IPA research, as a representative of social psychology, makes too frequent use of general common-sense statements to guide its course and that it is thus obvious and uninformatively trivial. Harré and Secord (1972), Gergen (1978a) and Eiser (1980) are examples of those who take issue with IPA workers for basing their research on the common sense view that similarity is attractive. Gergen (1978a, p. 517) puts it thus: "a more or less well-established principle in contemporary social psychology ... found in virtually all the major texts of the field [is] that attraction to another person is a positive function of O's similarity to P.". Unfortunately, as those in the area have observed for more than ten years, this is *not* the proposition that IPA researchers believe to be true, nor is it the view of those workers whom Gergen cites in support of his observation (viz. Newcomb and Byrne). Byrne, for example, explicitly notes (Byrne and Lamberth, 1971, p. 66),

> Though the law of attraction is frequently misrepresented ... as dealing with similarity, it does in fact deal with the effect of reinforcement on attraction. The effect of similarity on attraction is a special case of the more general law and is not assumed to result from any qualities inherent in similarity.

Putting this differently, it is clear that, working from a general but oversimplified common-sense statement, social psychology (as represented in IPA) often takes common sense terms and expands them in a more ordered theoretical framework in which they take on both an altered significance and a greater precision. It is, regrettably, all too easy for this process to be *continually* misrepresented as a result of the human pressures and attributional or informational biases which preclude adequate detailed simultaneous familiarity with many areas of our subject.

A second line of attack which misuses similar reasoning is the claim that social psychology is contaminated by artificiality, by which is meant that it is too often exclusively laboratory based and the familiar example (used, for instance, by Eiser, 1980) is that IPA work involves studies of people who do not meet. Although a disclaimer is often added (e.g., "*much of* such work is artificial"), the disclaimer is subsequently ignored with considerable vigour—a typical simplificatory technique that is found in many human contexts. To assert that generalization is not possible from such studies is to dismiss without argument, or simply to disregard, the work that has extended the so-called hypothetical stranger studies to real-life contexts, used real-life strangers in face-to-face encounters with the same results, employed quasi-longitudinal studies of real-life friendships, or studied dating or married couples (e.g. in order, Byrne *et al.*, 1970; McCarthy and Duck, 1976, 1979; McWhirter and Jecker, 1967; Duck and Craig, 1978; Murstein, 1977).

More seriously, and more generally, such critical arguments fall into the trap of treating an empirical data base as equivalent to the generative hypothetical construct (Clore and Byrne, 1974; Turner, 1980). From the present perspective, however, it is important to recognize that the discipline has established norms, just as any group does, and these norms can operate perniciously against unbiased evaluation of experimental results. The important product of an experiment is not an approximation to some real-world observable event but an improvement in our real-world diagnosis (Turner, 1980), and this diagnosis in turn is accepted or rejected in relation to its plausibility, its persuasiveness with respect to the consensually determined criteria for acceptability as a contribution to the progress of the discipline. The influence of persuasiveness in such decisions is particularly important if one accepts McGuire's (1980a) point that *any* reasonable hypothesis will hold true under some circumstances: decisions between theories will then have to be made on the grounds of credibility and plausible persuasiveness alone.

One important component of such criteria concerns the extent to which results identify a limiting case for a general statement. Thus Gergen (1978a, b), again using the example of IPA, argues that research is insufficiently attentive to the limiting cases or cultural and historical embeddedness of many findings. Once again, however, the diversification of the discipline and specialization of areas leads to a misleading report of the study of limiting cases in IPA. Gergen's example is that, in studying the general proposition that attitude similarity is attractive, IPA workers have failed to distinguish between types of attitudes and opinions which may modify or limit the general proposition. This is inaccurate: Byrne *et al.* first made this very distinction in 1966 and their work has been built upon by, for example, Santee (1976) and McCarthy (1976). Indeed, Duck (1977) has indicated a theoretical perspective which incorporates these necessary and important distinctions into a general framework for explaining relationship growth.

Whilst one might suspect that some arguments for the existence of a crisis are not thorough in citation and are ill-founded in logic, we must ourselves be wary of making the illogical conclusion that the general critical position is therefore flawed. It is sufficient for the moment to see that some of its present supporting arguments are deficient or have some non-intellectual threads in them. However, one cannot be too sanguine that this will actually matter in the long run. It is likely that, given the present structure of the discipline and its outlets, the fallacious argument will continue to prosper and that hard-pressed social psychologists will continue to rely on the secondary, critical and mildly inaccurate sources rather than returning to the primary sources where the validity of the criticisms may be evaluated.

5. Fashionable influences on social psychology

Despite what we may wish to believe, there are many decisions in social psychology that are unlikely to be made purely on the basis of strict logic in a social vacuum, so, as social psychologists, we should not try to account for them purely as if they were. Examples are: the choice of a research area; the judgement of the value of given research; arbitration between competing theories; the rise and fall of ideas or reputations; the perception of relationships between theoretical constructs and empirical representation; and the style of reporting research to one's peers. Judgements about the evident logic, value or indeed the intuitive plausibility of a proposal are inevitably derived in part from norms and values of the surrounding culture, profession, department or research group ("the prefabricated verdict of social reality" in Steiner's (1974) elegant phrase). A whole wealth of social psychology research informs us about the details of such general influences, starting with Sherif (e.g. Sherif, 1936) and incorporating work on cross-cultural effects (Triandis, 1976) and on socialization (Danziger, 1971). If this were not so, then good ideas would, at all times and in all places and historical contexts, be patently and universally seen to be so, and they would be rapidly and generally diffused through the profession as deserving and useful notions.

However, good ideas may not catch on immediately and often lie dormant until a riper time or, in many cases, until a more "visible" person makes the same point. It would be useful to explore cases where the predominance of a theory may be partly attributed to (or aided by) the credibility, attractiveness or conference-style of the presenter, or to his or her place in the social and communicative network (Innes, 1980). Furthermore, we may observe instances where the inherent glamour of an idea may overcome interest in the relative frequency of its replications and replication failures, e.g. cognitive dissonance, an oft-cited contender for this unenviable role (Stroebe, 1980; Innes, 1980).*

A whole host of forces influences the choice of theories, the ways in which research areas blossom, flourish and wither, the establishment of reputations (and their subsequent effects on research), and so forth. Some analysis of these issues has already been offered in terms of fashion forces (Innes, 1980), group process loss—assuming social psychology to be like a group problem solving task on a vast scale (Stroebe, 1980), and sociological background (Backman, 1980). All of these emphasize the social or non-logical nature of such influences, and as an example we may note Innes' observation that, given the likelihood of simultaneous independent discoveries in social psychology, it is predictable that the better-known worker will be given most citation credit if he or she is ever involved in such a simultaneous discovery. A subsequent writer will merely need to note the advance and to quote a source for it. From the sources available, the subsequent writer is likely to select the most familiar name, which then becomes more often cited and hence more suitable for citation, and so on. This reinforced prominence is due, Innes suggests—in this sort of instance at least—as

---

* I am grateful to Robin Gilmour for the observation that there are many instances in psychology, and elsewhere, in which the popularity and social impact of an idea are unrelated to the quality (or even to the existence) of the data base from which it is ostensibly derived. Examples are found in the impact of the notions of maternal deprivation and of double bind. It might be argued that such ideas are, in large part, like functional myths and derive their effect not from some "truth in relation to facts" but from their neatness and utility in enabling people to handle better their cognitive or behavioural worlds (Gilmour, in preparation).

much to the fashion-like forces dictating selection of a reference as to the merit of the original article or theoretical statement.

Fashionable concerns in the community at large likewise feed into the research that is done by social psychologists and the predominant concerns of the time also make their appearance in psychologists' analyses. For example, the time is now ripe, but would not have been fifteen years ago, for discussions about democracy in the discipline, and some (e.g. Lubek, 1976) have pointed to the consequences for individuals of their place in the community of social psychologists. Indeed, some forms of statement of "the crisis" are instances of a general political feeling applied locally to our own discipline, as Lubek's (1976) discussion of the power issues in social psychology appears to be. Such reflections of the general mood of world opinion are likely to occur whatever the nature of the discipline and are structural, existential or democratic crises of a different nature from those that concern us here.

6. The nature and functions of decisions about social psychology?

Consideration of some of the above factors that impinge in real ways upon social psychologists as people prompts one to ponder on the true nature of the decisions that we take between theories (approaches, styles etc.) and our prevailing but implicit model of such decisions. As noted on p. 215 Totman (1979) has argued that the decisions taken between theories rarely, if ever, depend on the experimentation designed to decide between them. For Totman, experimental testing of hypotheses and theories is merely a convenient myth contrived by the profession to offer a so-called logical account for an essentially social progress.

The present analysis would press this point by urging that we recognize the significance of the fact that theories and decisions about them are discussed by individuals with certain sorts of background, in a social context, under significant kinds of psychological pressures or influences, and in a given academic structure. We might then well ask whether it is not (just?) the phenomena of social psychology itself but also the acceptance or rejection of its major theoretical tenets that lack transhistorical validity (Gergen, 1973). Given the analysis above and elsewhere (Stroebe, 1980; Turner, 1980) it seems an entirely open question whether even the same sorts of conclusions or theoretical propositions would be derived from or used to explain the same evidence by a social psychologist or a social psychological community enduring a different set of social psychological pressures, political circumstances and structural features in its discipline. But this itself simply extends the point that, even in the same set of circumstances, social psychologists usually disagree on the conclusions to be drawn.

In the present circumstances it has seemed feasible to explain part of the source for "the crisis" in terms of the psychological processes occurring within and between those concerned with it. One further extension of social psychological research is relevant here before we draw general conclusions against this background: an extension of work on conflict. Apfelbaum and Lubek (1976) analyse conflict in terms of "invisibles" (those without power or influence in the system) and the functions that struggle and conflict might serve for such individuals. Arguing that present research on conflict implicitly views it from the position of "the powerful", Apfelbaum and Lubek (1976) urge a shift in balance and suggest that "conflicts should ... be looked at as indicators of a certain 'state of society' and as an integral part of the dynamic processes by which society acts as the agent of its own transformation" (p. 89).

What about social psychology itself? Is it useful to see the conflict (crisis) in social psychology in these terms? The close links perceived by Apfelbaum and Lubek (1976) between conflict and identity are strikingly visible in social psychology. Perhaps social psychology is trying to refuse "the identity imposed upon [it] by the social system and by developing a new identity for [itself] become a vital part of ... society" (p. 85). Indeed, some have already viewed the crisis in similar terms (see above). Also striking in present debates is the assertion (for others as well as ourselves) of our very existence—although this is often obliquely stated in terms of mutual recognition of and by other disciplines. Conflicts (for Apfelbaum and Lubek) have *expressions* (of identity) and *functions* (communication, structuring of community views, creation of new identities). Perhaps their analysis applies as much to social psychology itself as to the other minority groups that they discuss and is another ingredient in the crisis. At any rate it is always worth bearing in mind that "the crisis" may have hidden functions for social psychologists and that these are independent of the methodological points on which it is often rested.

This section is, of course, not intended as an attack on the professionalism of the discipline but merely as a reminder that that professionalism is ever struggling against the "unprofessional" human tendencies on which we have to build the profession and which are presently far too little understood. It is also intended to indicate that social psychology has much to contribute to an understanding of the undercurrents of its continuing development through an analysis of itself in terms of its own subject matter. There are various properties of the community of social psychologists which, like those of any other community serve to focus or limit the freedoms and progress of individuals (see Stroebe, 1980, for a fuller analysis of other related issues). It is left open whether this is a good or bad thing, or whether the advantages outweigh any disadvantages.

C. NOT IN OUR SUBJECT, BUT IN OURSELVES?

Social psychologists are, like anyone else, people with personal histories and powerful socialization experiences. As individuals they have personal needs, motivations, changing moods, pressures, anxieties and all the other plastic influences of a human constituency. Just as Gergen (1978b) notes that subjects have at any one time confluences of different psychological factors impinging upon their decision to select one behaviour rather than another, so do social psychologists have multitudes of confluent pressures upon them, as individuals, as groups, and as a profession. One mistake in the arguments about "the crisis" is to regard the profession as having one mind, one past, one future, one present, one history, one style of approach, and so on. As Steiner (1974) observed: "Social psychologists have never spoken with a single voice about anything". Indeed, as has been seen, "the crises" of social psychology need better differentiation and clarification so that we can assess the coherence, interrelatedness and general significance of the different sorts of crisis.

1. Crises of theory?

There seems to be much less of a crisis—perhaps no crisis at all—if one rethinks the aims of social psychology in terms of several simultaneous purposes, not one single search for lasting, transhistorical truths. If one likes analogies, one stops thinking of a chaotic railroad full of engines hurling themselves at one another purposelessly and begins to rethink in terms of an ordered abundance of possible routes and destinations, some obtainable by parallel means or in connection with other routes. We should also note that comparisons of social psychology with other sciences are often put forward to depict goals rather than as warnings, whilst our own lack of progress is excused as due to our youthfulness as a discipline. It would, however be as well to remember that modern chemistry, for example, had as its youth a wild search for phlogiston and the elixir of life. It can, without restriction on social psychology's self-respect, be seen as *one* obvious task of social psychology to illuminate those things that are of temporary concern to a given society and to feed these illuminations back into the culture. This is one way that social psychologists can help to contribute to the renegotiation of social reality (Gergen, 1978b) without any pretence to be, by action of this sort, unravelling natural and enduring truths instead of culturally (or subculturally) embedded ones. Indeed it would be surprising if work on the social nature of Man—given the historical impermanence of its focus—*could* be other than a temporary illumination of that impermanence. However, one important part of such an enterprise is to identify and explore generalities that are culturally accepted at present and appear to have been so for a long time, but which are so general or limited as to be worthless illuminators of the detail of human experience (as, for example, a mountain of work on IPA has shown in the case of "similarity is attractive" or "opposites attract"). It is not a trivial enterprise to find the ways in which accepted general dogmas are unreliable or transhistorically and transculturally invalid (or perceived to be inapplicable). Indeed, an intention to increase understanding of the processes through which they are, or become, accepted as Truths is part of the proposal urged here in a more localized fashion.

2. Developing a data base: crisis of utility?

It need not be less exciting, less challenging, less difficult or ultimately less useful to aim lower and more specifically. One pressing need in all areas of social psychology is for a better descriptive base for the regular phenomena of social behaviour and a clearer picture of baseline data—but the task of establishing such a basic picture is as rich in challenge and complexity as it is necessary.

The call to take up such work has recently been made by a number of prominent workers in a variety of different areas. All of them point to the need for, and intricacy of, deriving such a base for assessing the ecological validity of laboratory experiments and for testing competing theories of psychological phenomena. For example, Bem and Funder (1978) have called for, and begun to assemble, a language of description for persons and situations, using a Q-sort technique to derive template-behaviour pairs for use in predicting individual behaviour in a given situation. Wheeler and Nezlek (1977) have started to illustrate the acquaintance process by recording and analysing the frequency and content of social interaction through use of subjects' own structured diaries of their social participation. Hinde (1979; in press) has delineated a basic typology upon which to found a description of personal relationships, giving suggested criterial dimensions for a taxonomy, whilst Huston et al. (in press) have set about providing a taxonomy of pathways to marriage and Rands and Levinger (1979) have depicted the different attitudes to relationships in different generations. All of these workers lend support to those who call for naturalistic studies with increased ecological validity, but it should be noticed that the impact of their work also addresses another point: that the regular and naturally occurring patterns of social behaviour are very poorly logged, let alone understood. We have failed to build up precisely those detailed records of normal patterns of social activity that would help us to identify the regularities that need to be explained and to assess the extents to which laboratory-based methods actually reflect those real-life regularities and frequently occurring events. Perhaps, by focusing on striking behaviour, laboratory studies actually exaggerate the contours of life, to which our theories are therefore more likely to give unrepresentative prominence.

The collection of inventories of regular patterns of social behaviour, maps of the frequencies of certain events, and records of the normal course of given familiar experiences provide researchers with a number of intriguing—but not daunting—methodological challenges. Yet solutions to these are likely to prove more useful in the long run than the suggestions that we restructure our high-level approach to social psychology, rethink our experimental style or eschew traditional and favourite methods such that we *fail* to record the base-rate data of human social interaction. These sorts of work are actually going to help research to deliver the goods: in developing social psychology we need more revolutionary empirical ants and fewer revolutionary stylistic grasshoppers.

3. Looking at ourselves: crisis of identity?

Equally, at another but related level, the exploration of the social psychological processes involved in hypothesis confirmation (Snyder, in press) taps a feature of human activity that is as fundamental to psychologists' explanations of human social behaviour as any discussion of the relative merits or limits of pure and applied research. For example, we cannot proceed properly with the conduct of social psychology until we know whether there is anything about human explanatory tendencies in general that systematically biases our styles of understanding human behaviour. I am thinking here of Monson and Snyder's (1977) point that experiments are systematically biased towards explanations of a type that reflect only one side of the actor-observer dichotomy. Equally relevant, however, is an observation built from Tajfel's (1978) important point that proper cross-cultural social psychology must be based on a good theory of (our own) culture: clearly, a part of the development of a social psychology of human behaviour at large requires the establishment of a clear understanding of ourselves as individuals doing social psychology, over and above the points noted earlier in this chapter. For instance we do not know and have not investigated the reasons why people choose to do social psychology nor do we understand fully the forces that act upon them when they do. Yet such insight is crucial to an understanding of whether, and in what ways, our theories of social behaviour at large are systematically biased by the psychological constituencies of those who produce these theories. We have all heard the criticism that too many social psychological experiments are performed on psychology students; it is also true that they are *all* performed by individuals who have chosen a career that puts them in a position to do experiments on other people and who are therefore a biased, self-selected sample. Snyder *et al.* (1978) have alerted us to present defaults of emphasis in cognitive social psychology and suggest that "theories in cognitive social psychology attend to the ways in which perceivers create the information that they process, in addition to the ways that they process that information". Let's start at home.

4. Relating to other departments: crisis of intellectual isolation?

The future development of social psychology will be based on an increasing methodological ingenuity, not only in those areas clarifying the activity of social psychologists themselves, but also in the constructive classification of social psychological processes occurring in the human activities traditionally researched from entirely other perspectives by other disciplines. Social psychologists do not, as yet, offer clear expositions of, for example, the social psychological antecedents of particular political actions, whether at the level of choice for a given act, in terms of the natures of political animals, or in relation to the interpersonal dynamics of the social perceptions and "power undercurrents" involved. Psychologists have researched such aspects of politics as dogmatism, authoritarianism, conservatism, and Machiavellianism. But surely we can contribute more to a field like politics than the usual thoroughly dismissable construction of a merely reliable test of, say, Machiavellianism, which a tribe of graduate students then proceeds to use as a handy independent variable in, say, the study of responses to Rorschach blots—entirely missing the point that such concepts could be used to explore the context and dynamics of political action. We should be more patient with sociologists who dismiss us as having nothing to say about politics. We have plenty to say once we recognize the follies of a mere dalliance with traitism and begin to attempt a more sophisticated analysis of the psychology of political activism, responses to structural unemployment, or inflation. Indeed although social psychological theory has borrowed heavily from economic terminologies and frameworks, it has not yet repaid the loan by means of, say, a psychological explanation for economic activity and beliefs. Government economists construct their hopes for the effects of particular economic policies on the basis of essentially psychological theories: they believe that individuals will respond uniformly and predictably in the light of certain economic circumstances. Presently part of the debate in one area of economics centres on whether people act in adaptive way (that is, that they adapt their expectations inductively on the basis of what has happened to the inflation rate in the past) or in a rationalist way (assuming a complex interaction of relatively predictable sets of variables relevant to the growth in the rate of inflation). Curiously, psychologists have not offered nor been asked for any help here in terms of the means that people might use to decide their actions in this sphere and how to spend their dwindling incomes. Yet policy-making economists and politicians continue to act on their own beliefs which, for all we know, may be as erroneous and simplified as the "common sense" belief in the proposition "similarity attracts".

5. The sound of the wrong hand clapping: crisis of practice?

Most areas of human *experience* are important but unexplored by social psychologists—or, significantly, by those whom we tend to think of as "proper" social psychologists—notwithstanding the concern of phenomenologists and humanistic psychologists over such issues. In the research mainstream, only recently has La Gaipa (1977), for example, attempted to discover what friendship actually means to people as a concept and as an experience; but clearly their expectations will affect their friendship behaviour and are thus relevant and significant in the explanation of it. Equally, only recently has attribution work turned to a general examination of felt social experience and its various types (Antaki and Fielding, in press); yet we know from introspection that such experiences are crucial influences on social behaviour. Equally although one observes in everyday interaction that certain central human emotions/states/feelings exert a powerful effect in social encounters, social psychologists cannot yet (indeed do not yet try to) explain them or the dynamics of their influence. What are the social psychological cognitive or interactional dynamics of shyness, modesty, arrogance, trustworthiness, maturity, honesty, reliability, efficiency, and courtesy? How are individuals' dynamic behaviours towards one another in social encounters affected by the making of these central judgements about others? What do people do when faced with these characteristics and how does it differ from their behaviour in the face of other characteristics? Similarly, one knows that rules for mannerly conduct are a central feature of human socialization; one also knows that people can acquire a repertoire of different levels of manners, employ them differently from time to time, gain different appreciation of them in different circumstances; but where are the thoroughgoing social psychological analyses of such central influences on human social contact, their dynamic effects in encounters, and their antecedents or consequences?

Whilst these characteristics might seem important to everyday conductors of human social activity, perhaps social psychologists just have a different or more sophisticated view of what is central to behaviour than the common man we seek to explain. Not so. Other workers (e.g. Gergen, 1978a) have arrived at a similar proposition from an entirely different set of arguments. True it is phrased differently, namely, that it is part of the job of social psychology to contribute to an understanding of human experience rather than of human behaviour. Can we doubt that it is part of the job of social psychology to illuminate those experiences that are embedded in a given time, culture, or set of attitudes? This, however, does not logically entail the view that *all* social psychological activity involves temporally embedded or transhistorically invalid inference. Nor does it mean that the whole enterprise of social psychology should be transformed or abandoned rather than complemented by methods and approaches with different emphases, merely because there are examples of findings that may be so bound. Part of the job of social psychology can be readily accepted as an attempt to discern for the present, or negotiate for the short-term future, a community of truths that are functional for a society *in the circumstances* and are useful *within the temporal bounds in which they are used*. In this context it is all too easy to forget the variety of levels at which humans conduct themselves and therefore the variety of occasions and purposes for which their "general truisms" are employed.

D. CONCLUDING REMARKS

Although it is frequently urged in general terms in social psychology that to search for a regnant, all-superseding theoretical style is misguided, the search through the undergrowth proceeds with a vigour of which any pioneer would be proud. However, McGuire (1980a) has shown that all theories capture varying degrees of truth and non-negligible amounts of falsity. He proposes a constructivist approach based on the view that "each of the different theories is right and that the empirical work reveals the conditions under which each is true". Independently, but in the same vein, Hinde (in press) makes a similar point in relation to the work on interpersonal attraction and urges us to give up attempts to prove one approach or paradigm right and another completely wrong or irrelevant. We must try to specify how far they overlap, how far they are dealing with the same phenomena at different levels of analysis, or different aspects of the same phenomena at the same level of analysis and can therefore be integrated. Just as this is true in the case of any single area of social psychology, so too is it true of the attempts to decide "the future" of social psychology in the present. The future development of social psychology lies at least partly in a clearer understanding of the past and present in terms of human social influences that have contributed their guiding hand to the intellectual growth of the subject.

We can help to understand the present of social psychology by looking at where we have come from and how we arrived. We have been almost too modest as psychologists: one might say we have not had the vanity to use social psychology itself to analyse our progress from "stage one" social psychology to where we are now. The choice of research topics, research methods and kinds of theorizing must have been affected by "psychological" influences of the sort we see operating on *other* people in laboratories; indeed some of us have maintained for a long time that the laboratory is generalizable to the home and the workplace. If we have been influenced by such things, let us admit it and try to come to terms with it. If social psychologists cannot sort out social psychological influences on their behaviour, who can?

ACKNOWLEDGEMENTS

I am very grateful to the following for their helpful and constructive discussions of the ideas in this chapter and for their useful comments on earlier drafts: Charles Antaki, Colin Brydon, Robin Gilmour, Barry McCarthy, Dot Miell, David K. Miell, and David O'Hare.

10
Towards Intellectual Audacity in Social Psychology

KENNETH J. GERGEN
Swarthmore College, Swarthmore

Pour les vaincre, Messieurs, il faut de l'audace, et encore de l'audace, toujours de l'audace.
George Jacques Danton
September 2, 1792

A. A dilemma solved and a crisis created	239
B. The decay of empiricism	246
1. The assumption of empirical evaluation	247
2. The assumption of accumulating knowledge	252
3. The assumption of application	255
C. Social psychology as an interpretative enterprise	258
1. Inquiry into interpretative forms	258
2. Generative theory and the cultivation of audacity	261
D. In conclusion	269

A. A DILEMMA SOLVED AND A CRISIS CREATED

We may begin with simple dilemma: if I see my good friends Ross and Laura approach each other at a social gathering, and Ross reaches out and momentarily touches Laura's hair, precisely what have I observed? What action has occurred before me? How am I to identify it? What does the action suggest about their relationship and the manner in which I should regard it if I wish to retain their friendship? Such dilemmas of identification are frequent; one might even conjecture that they are as numerous as there are discriminable social actions. And, such dilemmas *must* be solved, it would appear, in order for us to carry on effective interpersonal relations. How then, do we normally solve the essential problem of behavioural identification?

The problem is an especially vexing one, for it would appear that the action in itself can tell us little. We know only that Ross has engaged in a series of actions that might be described as "touching Laura's hair". Yet this level of description is virtually uninformative. What does it *mean* to engage in such an action? Of what interpersonal significance is the behaviour? This information is not contained in the action itself. Perhaps the most compelling solution to this dilemma lies in the employment of contextual indicators. We may locate the meaning of a given action by apprehending the manner in which others treat or define the action, whether in the past, present or future. Let us consider in this case the *retrospective context*, those events believed to define the action, but occurring prior to it. For example, if Ross informed me the week before that he was madly in love with Laura, this information would solve my dilemma. I could confidently view his action as a signal of affection or attraction. If in later interaction with Ross I were to treat it as such, and not as a signal of derision, Ross and I would presumably continue to maintain a smooth and unproblematic friendship.

Yet, we must expand the retrospective context. Ross's announcement of the previous week may not be the only contextual constituent. Suppose I also learned from Laura several days ago that she told Ross she didn't really believe he was a warm and affectionate sort of person. At this point we may doubt the initial conclusion that the act was a signal of affection. Rather, we might consider the possibility that it was an attempt on Ross's part to demonstrate that he is an affectionate person after all. In effect, the action is not quite so much an affectionate one as an act of self-presentation, or personal identification. Yet, consider the nasty bit of gossip to which I was just exposed: a mutual friend indicates that the lovers have recently had a serious quarrel in which Laura accused Ross of being a prime egotist who believes he can have any woman he likes. Laura has told him she wants nothing more to do with him; he is vulgar, insensitive and aggressive. With this new information, we may wish to reclassify the action. Perhaps it was an act of derision on Ross's part after all. Perhaps he was saying with this action that in fact he could have any woman he wanted, and that Laura would soon be his in spite of her abuse. Thus, to relate effectively with Ross at this point, it would be appropriate to treat the act as one of derision as opposed to attraction or self-presentation.

Yet, can one be so certain, after all, that derision is the proper identification of the action? Perhaps Ross was badly hurt by Laura's words and was making one last attempt to express his affection or to demonstrate finally that he was a most affectionate kind of person. More information is necessary to be confident. So far we have attended only to information based on the *retrospective context*. For additional information we must turn to the *emergent context*, that is, to relevant defining events that follow the action in question. For example, we immediately observe Laura smile and take Ross's hand. This reaction now relieves our doubts. Laura has clearly been touched by Ross's gesture, and feels contrite over the scolding she has administered. The stroking of the hair was a profound expression of affection after all. Or was it? Several minutes later, when we see Ross talking briefly with a friend, we notice that his posture and facial expressions are those of man who is very proud of himself. Perhaps the gesture was, after all, not so affectionate in itself, but his attempt at successful self-presentation. He is now quite pleased with himself because he has apparently succeeded. But the evidence is not yet complete. The following day we learn that Laura subsequently asked Ross if she could borrow his car to run an errand, and once the car was in her possession, she scraped its entire right hand side against a stone wall and thereupon abandoned the vehicle. At last, the mystery is solved. Laura saw that the stroking action was one of derision, yet treated it as an effective gesture in winning her love. This she did in order to gain Ross's confidence, whereupon she borrowed the car in order to damage it and thus avenge the derisive action.

A month later Ross and Laura are spied walking arm in arm....

Let us now collect several major propositions that may be derived from this turgid saga.

1. *The identification of any given action is subject to infinite revision.* As we are exposed to events from both retrospective and emergent contexts, our manner of identifying the present action is modified. Theoretically, this process is without limit. First, the range of past indicators is without evident bounds, for we must be prepared to account not only for all events in the lives of the individuals in question but also for all those events within the cultural history that shape current meanings. For example, in the case of Ross's life, if we learned that his feelings of affection were often fleeting, we might have been less inclined to view

the action in question as one of affection. With respect to the culture more generally, if we learned that public touching between opposite sex pairs was a culturally sanctioned signal of ownership or possession, we might hesitate in accepting the event as one of presentational proof of warmth.

It is also apparent that the relevance of one's life events or events within the cultural history may wax or wane according to our present manner of determining intelligibility. For example, events in Ross's early childhood may be viewed by the psychoanalytic theorist as relevant to the proper identification of the action in question (e.g. it could be a "reaction formation" expressing the opposite from the apparent emotion). However, the same early childhood events might not be viewed as relevant by one who is unschooled in this particular system of intelligibility. Similarly, if one determined the meaning of contemporary events from the standpoint of a cultural historian, Ross's actions may be interpreted very differently from one unfamiliar with this context and its implications for contemporary understanding.

The emergent context is similarly without anchor point. The present action is subject to continuous redefinition as further events take place. As we saw, the final action cited (that of the couple walking happily together) appeared to throw the "ultimate definition" once again into jeopardy. Yet, this latter event itself should scarcely be considered final. Nor are the future actions relevant to the definition in question, only those uniting the two individuals. Any further action on the part of any person may, if one possesses an appropriate system of intelligibility, be employed to reconstruct the meaning of the act in question. For example, if in the light of later social history we learned that this historical period was one of great superficiality in emotional expression, we might retrospectively discount the sincerity of Ross's action: perhaps it was simply a matter of artificial stylistics. We see, then, that identification of any given action is effectively open-ended.

2. *The anchor point for any given identification is not fundamentally empirical, but relies on a network of interdependent and continuously modifiable interpretations.* This second proposition amplifies the first. As we see, there is no obvious way in which one can satisfactorily identify any given action *in itself.* The action in question does not furnish any empirical touchstone for proper identification. One is thus forced to consider the context of events both preceding and following. Yet, to extend the analysis, we find that these events are *also* in need of

identification, and one must search the ever-unfolding context of events in order to determine their identity as well. For example, we were moved to interpret the stroking of Laura's hair as an expression of affection when we took into account Ross's previous declaration of love. Yet, the declaration itself is in need of interpretation. We must be certain that it is a declaration of affection rather than an attempt on his part to convince us of her ardour, for example, or perhaps an attempt at self-conviction, a whimsical gesture, an act of self-deception, or any number of other reasonable competitors. In order to determine which of the labels applies, we are again driven to consider the ever-unfolding context of events both retrospective and emergent.

Of course, events within these contexts are equally subject to the interpretative dilemma. Thus, we find that the single, critical identification is not fundamentally tied to any single set of observables; rather, the interpretation rests on a potentially immense array of interdependent interpretations. Further, any given interpretation is continuously subject to modification in light of a continuously altering context, and any event-interpretation occurring within the array may wax and wane in its relevance as intelligibility systems evolve over time. Thus the contextual array cannot be viewed as static but as in continuous and reverberating motion.

3. *Any given action may be subject to multiple identifications, no one of which is inherently superior.* Our third proposition extends the logic implied in our arguments thus far. In the initial example, we took the perspective of a single observer of a given action. However, this perspective is hardly sacrosanct and could be replaced by a virtual infinity of competitors. Each competitor might differ in (1) the range of events to which he or she is exposed, (2) the range of events deemed of relevance to identifying the action in question, (3) the system of intelligibility used to make sense of the present action in terms of the relevant context, and (4) the larger context of events on which the immediately relevant context depends for its interpretational support. Given the ultimate lack of an empirical touchstone on which to rest any given interpretation, we cannot easily argue for the superior validity of one form of explanation as opposed to another.

One may contest this view on two grounds. First, it could be countered that an explanation based on multiple contextual inputs is superior to one that rests only upon a few. Yet, on closer inspection this view fails to be convincing. At the outset, as the number of events believed relevant to a given identification increases in number, one does not move unproblematically towards clarity of definition. Rather, it would appear, one might anticipate increasing doubt in any given definition. As increasing numbers of events are considered, their contexts of interpretation appraised, and multiple interpretations are encountered in the behavioural reports of others, so confidence in any given interpretation might well be eroded. Thus, the most informed definition of any given action might be no definition at all. Although silence is philosophically defensible in this case, it does not enable us to solve the essential dilemma of behavioural definition. A second problem in seeking salvation through multiple indicators resides in the earlier argument that the number and range of events considered relevant to any given identification may vary from one individual to another: events that one observer views as particularly relevant to a given act, a second observer may see as insignificant. For example, many people would dispute the relevance of early childhood events to the proper definition of their adult actions. One person's attempt to increase the number of contextual inputs may be another person's exercise in inanity. Finally, since any given event may be subject to multiple interpretations, it should be possible for an observer to justify any given interpretation by reference to virtually any earlier contextual event. Once one has fixed on a given interpretation, increasing the number of events lends no additional strength to the interpretation. It merely demonstrates the conceptual agility of the observer in generating a veneer of consistency among interpretations.

One might also challenge the argument for equality among interpretations on the grounds that the actor's position is superior to any other. Although a full account cannot be given here, this rebuttal, too, falters upon inspection. First, we find that it cannot be sustained on grounds that the actor has access to a wider context of relevant events. As we have seen, increasing the range of events bearing on a given interpretation does not increase the validity of this interpretation. Also, it would not appear that the actor is necessarily privileged by virtue of his or her private access to internal experiences. In order to serve as a constituent of the interpretative context such experiences must themselves be identified. Presumably, one must be able to identify a given emotion, for example, in order to interpret a given behaviour as its expression. Yet, this emotional state (if we may presume the existence of such) is itself subject to the same fundamental dilemma of interpretation to which publicly observable events fall prey. To identify them one must ultimately refer to a contextual domain which is without limit and which may vary both from one individual to another and across time. It is to the vicissitudes of such internal identification that Schachter's classic work on emotions (Schachter and Singer, 1962), Nisbett's inquiry into mental processes (Nisbett and Wilson, 1977), and numerous studies of bias in self-attribution (Harris and Harvey, 1975; Langer and Roth, 1975; Luginbuhl et al., 1975; Mynatt and Sherman, 1975) have been devoted. As such work strongly suggests, internal identifications are subject to wide-ranging contextual influences, just as identifications of overt action. Internal identification, just as external, is in a continuous state of reconstruction (Gergen, 1977).

This is not to argue that *all* interpretations are equally valid. When terms of interpretation are tied closely to a given set of repeatable operations, their ambiguity is decreased. Thus, interpreting Ross' actions as "jumping in the lake", "performing a jeté en l'air", or "giving her a light" would be difficult to justify in our present case. In each instance, the terms of interpretation are tied to highly concrete actions that are repeated many times over in certain sectors of society and within specific contexts. Often interpretations at this level of abstraction are looked at as "data language", and the acts themselves must be reinterpreted at a more general level in order to understand their significance in social life (e.g. "his jumping in the lake was his way of *demonstrating his prowess* before the guests").

We have now posed a dilemma, that of how we go about identifying social action. We have formulated a tentative solution to the dilemma by elaborating on the manner in which both the retrospective and emergent context are employed in drawing tentative conclusions. Yet, although seemingly a problem in daily relationships, when extended its principles pose a critical challenge to the traditional conduct of sciences such as social psychology. When the implications of these arguments are examined, the positivist-empiricist programme for the sciences is placed in severe jeopardy. Alternative conceptions of the science are demanded. Below we shall first explore several critical implications of the present line of argument. Particular attention will be given to the traditional assumptions of (1) empirical evaluation, (2) the accumulation of knowledge and (3) the application of social psychological principles. We shall then turn to consider two major forms of scientific activity favoured by the present analysis. Attention will be given in this case to (1) the documentation of interpretative forms and (2) the generative capacity of social theory. We shall argue in the latter case that audacity may be among the chief criteria for the evaluation of social psychological theory.

B. THE DECAY OF EMPIRICISM

In his recent volume, *The Restructuring of Social and Political Theory*, Richard Bernstein presents a case for an "emerging new sensibility" within the social sciences, one that is currently fostering reconsideration of the epistemological and metaphysical suppositions on which the sciences are based and that may precipitate fundamental alterations in the definition, aims, and methods of the sciences. There is ample reason to believe that Bernstein is correct in his appraisal. Within sociology, for example, works by Gouldner (1970), Giddens (1976), and members of the "critical school" (cf. Birnbaum, 1971; Jay, 1973) have formed an active challenge to the traditional positivist-empiricist aims of the discipline. Such challenges are evident within political science, too (cf. Surkin and Wolfe, 1970; McCoy and Playford, 1969) and economics (Schackle, 1972). And, such ferment may also be discerned within general psychology: for example, Meehl's (1978) critique of contemporary modes of establishing knowledge, Cronbach's (1975) doubts concerning the cumulativeness and applicability of current research, Sarbin's (1977) argument for a contextualist orientation to psychology, Riegel's (1972) analysis of the social conditions favouring current developmental theory, Holzkamp's (1972) proposal for a critical psychology, and Neisser's (1976) argument for the fundamentally plastic character of cognitive processing.

In social psychology, the past decade has been one of bristling debate concerning the structure and aims of the discipline. Harré and Secord's (1972) proposal for an ethogenic orientation to social inquiry, critiques of the value base of traditional social psychology (Israel, 1972; Sampson, 1977, 1978; Apfelbaum and Lubek, 1976), analyses of the societal basis of social psychology theory (Buss, 1979), symposia and collective confrontations over the future of the discipline (cf. Armistead, 1974; Strickland *et al.*, 1976), critiques of method and systems of analysis (McGuire, 1973; Tajfel, 1972), arguments for the historical contingency of social knowledge (Gergen, 1973, 1976a), concerns with the fundamental unpredictability of social action (Scheibe, 1978), all contribute to a self-reflective *Zeitgeist* from which may be emerging a significant reconstruction of the field.

Although the present arguments are germane to much of this critical work, the aim of this chapter is not specifically to review or extend these previous treatments. Rather, it is to elucidate the single dilemma of behavioural interpretation, and the profound challenge thereby posed for traditional pursuits. Further, it is hoped that the present line of criticism will lend itself to the task of reconstruction in a way not precisely duplicated by other critiques. Many feel that the most urgent task currently facing the discipline is that of establishing alternative pursuits—means and ends for the day-to-day practice of social psychology. It is these interests that the latter arguments of the chapter will hope to serve.

Let us turn then, to examine three traditional mainstays of the positivist-empiricist programme in light of the interpretative dilemma posed above.

1. The assumption of empirical evaluation

Perhaps the chief assumption underlying contemporary research in social psychology is that general theoretical statements are subject to empirical evaluation. During the hegemony of logical positivism, the empirical validity of a given hypothesis was primarily linked to the frequency of its empirical confirmation. This line of thinking later became formalized in terms of the Bayesian concept of "antecedent probability". The greater the number of observed confirmations, the greater the antecedent probability that a given hypothesis is valid. Increments in the antecedent probability of a given hypothesis correspond to increments in "truth value". Although controversy continues, many feel this view has been supplanted by Popper's (1959) falsification theory. According to Popper, it is inappropriate to rest the validity of an hypothesis on the range of its confirmations. Any confirmation stands only as temporary support for a theory, as subsequent disconfirmations may always insubstantiate the theory. One can never complete the process of confirmation. More important in establishing the validity of a theory, argues Popper, is the extent to which it resists attempts at falsification. Thus, the scientist is invited to generate observations that prove inconsistent with a theoretical contention. Only those theories open to falsification through empirical observation are deemed scientific in character.

Both "confirmationist" and "falsificationist" positions have come under strong philosophic attack in recent years (cf. Kuhn, 1972; Feyerabend, 1975; Laudan, 1977), and neither of these traditional criteria for theoretical evaluation is now viewed as wholly satisfactory. Yet, it must also be realized that these more recent philosophic critiques are primarily concerned with the nature of long-term advances in the sciences. Little argument has been put forward against the desirability of comparing theoretical statements with observation. In this context, the present argument may prove disagreeably extreme. Yet, if we extend the line of thinking advanced earlier in this chapter, we see that in principle no given observation within social psychology may stand in an unequivocal relationship to a given theoretical statement. The extent to which any given datum either corroborates or falsifies a given theoretical statement is fundamentally ambiguous. Let us explore this doleful conclusion more fully.

At the outset, there is little reason to believe that social psychologists stand in a privileged relationship to the world of social activity such that their capacity to identify behavioural particulars is in any way superior to others. Scientists, too, must inevitably rely on the contextual meaning of social actions which, as we have seen, is without theoretical limit and allows continuous reconstruction of any given event. The acceptance of any given interpretation seems primarily dependent on a process of social negotiation as opposed to empirical test (Gergen and Gergen, 1978). Initial indication of the magnitude of this problem in social psychology is encountered in most textbook or handbook treatments of major concepts within the discipline. In spite of the decades of research on such issues as attitudes, prejudice, attraction, personality, intelligence, aggression, altruism, person perception, morality, equity, and cognitive dissonance, for example, one can scarcely find a definition for any of these concepts about which there is widespread agreement, one that ties the terms to concrete particulars or operations, or one that does not shift in implication from one treatment to another. Each of these fundamental theoretical terms remains in an ambiguous state, with the various lines of research that employ the term suggesting a range of possible meanings.

Let us extend the implications of this line of argument in two more specific directions. If the relationship between theoretical concepts and empirical exemplars is fundamentally ambiguous, no given finding will enable us to rule between competing theories. With conceptual skill each protagonist should be able to demonstrate how the opponent's empirical support is either not a clear test of his or her hypothesis or actually renders support for one's own theory or both. For purposes of illustration let us consider first the case of personal dispositions (that is, traits, attitudes, moral dispositions, habits, and the like). To clarify the present position it may be ventured that *virtually all operational measures of personal dispositions may be satisfactorily treated as measures of virtually any alternative disposition*. This is to say that any behavioural action purporting to measure achievement needs, dominance tendencies, sex role activity, authoritarianism, locus of control preferences, attitudes, a given level of moral development, or a habit of any kind, may be viewed as potential indicators of virtually any other dispositional construct. Responses said to be indicative of any one dispositional construct may be interpreted as exemplars of almost any other construct.

To explore this possibility in a concrete setting, undergraduate students were asked to select a trait that each felt was highly descriptive of self. A domain of twenty different theoretical dispositions was thus created. Each student was then exposed to four randomly selected items from a standardized and traditionally validated measure of the *need for social approval* (Crowne and Marlowe, 1964). The students were not informed as to the source of the items nor as to what they were purported to measure. Each student was then asked to demonstrate how *agreement* with each item would be an indication that one possessed the trait that each considered descriptive of him or herself. In effect, students were asked to explore the legitimacy of using each of the four items traditionally measuring approval needs as indicators of twenty wholly different traits.

In general, the students experienced little difficulty with this interpretative task. Agreement with the standard item "I always go out of my way to help others in trouble" could conveniently and compellingly be viewed as a measure of "conceit" (people who agree with this item clearly have a high opinion of themselves), "patience" (the patient person would appreciate the needs of others and would spare the time to help them), "perception of internal control" (people viewing themselves as in control would believe that they could effectively help others), "hostility" (hostile people would help another because in giving help they are demonstrating the other's inferiority), and so on. To press the illustration further students were subsequently asked to reconsider their interpretations of the response. Could they now find a legitimate reason for concluding that *disagreement* on each item was, in fact, a legitimate indicator of the trait disposition they had chosen for themselves. Again, the students responded to the challenge with relative ease. To return to the above example, people who indicated that they did *not* always go out of their way to help others in trouble were clearly indicating their "conceit" (conceited people are too self-centered to sacrifice themselves for others), "patience" (the patient person is one who believes that matters will work themselves out over time and that one should not interfere with others' lives), "perception of internal control" (those who believe in internal control will assume that others are in the best position to help themselves; to assert oneself in the situation is to threaten their control), and "hostility" (the hostile person dislikes others and therefore does not help them). All items selected for the illustration generally allowed such wide-ranging reinterpretations.

Of course, this is only a single illustration and is itself subject to many possible interpretations. However, the limits of the above assertion deserve careful consideration. What are the constraints, if any, on interpreting any dispositional response as an indicator of any alternative disposition as well as its opposite? If constraints can be located, what is their origin? For anyone concerned with the defence of an empirical science, such questions are of the first magnitude.

We may apply a similar line of argument to findings generated in the experimental domain. In general there is reason to believe that so long as the domain of concerns is similar, *virtually any experimental result developed as support for a given theory may be used as support for virtually any alternative theory*. The practice of annexing the empirical support established by a competing theory by either demonstrating how the competing theory may be translated into one's own, or how the empirical results are consistent with one's own, has long been common within psychology. Early learning theorists were quick to show how competing theories, such as the psychoanalytic, could be translated into the more "scientifically" appropiate language of learning theory (Dollard and Miller, 1950). Others have shown how both stimulus–response theories and cognitive–perceptual theories can subsume the empirical support gathered in the opposing domain. And, more recently, Lacey and Rachlin (1978) have argued that the claim of contemporary cognitive theorists for the superiority of cognitive theory over radical behaviourism (Fodor, 1975) is inappropriate. As they maintain, none of the behavioural exemplars cited by the cognitivists supplies unequivocal support for the cognitive orientation, nor is any beyond the explanatory power of the behaviourist.

To demonstrate the possibility of a thoroughgoing inter-translation of empirical results in social psychology, a dozen students in an advanced seminar were presented with a series of experimental findings typically used as essential support for seven different theoretical models in social psychology: dissonance theory, balance theory, Schachter's two-factor theory of emotion, self-esteem theory, social comparison theory, mere exposure theory, and equity theory. At random, each student was given four of the seven results and at the same time furnished with four randomly selected theories from the above list. Each theory was randomly matched to one of the four empirical results (excluding the possibility of linking a given theory with the data originally gathered in its support). The empirical results themselves were presented in observation language, and the students were asked how the randomly linked theory could explain the experimental results.

This exercise again suggested that compelling confirmation and falsification are chimerical goals for social psychology. With few exceptions the students accomplished the explanatory task with apparent ease. To consider only a single example—Adams and Jacobson's (1964) classic demonstration of equity theory—the students were told of the major conditions of the study. One group of subjects engaged in a proof-reading task were told they were being paid the wages of a well-trained professional proof-reader. Other groups were told that they would receive a rate of pay that was proper for someone with their skill. The first group subsequently demonstrated a higher degree of performance on the proof-reading task than the comparison groups. At the outset there was little difficulty in demonstrating how the result could be explained in dissonance theory terms, for as Adams initially realized, equity restoration could be viewed as a form of dissonance reduction. However, the students also saw how the results were consistent with Schachter's theory of emotion (subjects who were told they were receiving higher pay were more aroused by the knowledge and the arousal was channelled into task performance), balance theory (the task was positively linked to the high pay, and the high pay was positively linked to the subject, thus a positive link between the subject and the task could be forged by working hard), self-esteem theory (students receiving higher pay worked harder in order to retain the positive image of themselves symbolized by the high status wage), mere exposure theory (people are aroused by the unfamiliar, and the high pay condition was less familiar than the low pay condition; high pay subjects were thus more energized for the performance), and social comparison theory (subjects in the high pay condition were induced to compare their performance with that of professionals, and performed more diligently in order to reduce the discrepancy between themselves and the target).

Again, one may protest over the present interpretation of these findings, but it is difficult to discern what limits might be placed over such inter-translation of results from one theoretical domain to another. At the same time one can well appreciate why there are virtually no critical debates among competing theories in social psychology that have yet been decided on the basis of empirical evidence (Gergen, 1978a). Virtually no theory has been discarded as clearly falsified, and no theory sustained because of the clarity of its support or its robust resistance to falsification. From the present perspective there is little reason to suspect that empirically based decisions will ever occur.

2. The assumption of accumulating knowledge

As is readily apparent, if the validity of a given hypothesis about social interaction cannot readily be assessed through empirical means, there is little way in which the discipline can make good on the positivist-empiricist promise of accumulating knowledge. If one cannot falsify a given theory, thus eliminating incorrect theories, and if one cannot convincingly demonstrate the truth value of alternative theories or defend them empirically against challengers, then there is little way of emerging with superior knowledge, at least with respect to the traditional criterion of verisimilitude.

In this respect we must view the major generalizations contained within the traditional repositories of social psychological knowledge (the textbook, the handbook, the research monograph and the journal contribution) not as empirically based knowledge, nor as the results of an empirical winnowing process, but as representing the commonly favoured opinions of certain sub-cultures of the discipline. They represent "appropriate" or "reasonable" views of certain groups with vested interests in a particular conceptual vocabulary or intelligibility system. This is not to say that the concept of accumulation is irrelevant to social psychological knowledge, or that the textbooks or handbooks of today do not represent advances over previous treatments. As the conceptual weaknesses or ambiguities are elucidated within various theoretical domains, as alternative views or conceptual distinctions are developed, as research is mounted which challenges previous ways of thinking or pricks the public conscience, or as new means are found for increasing the accuracy of broad-scale social prediction, the attention paid to older work may be appropriately reduced. Advances may be generated primarily through criticism, novel theory generation, unsettling empirical findings, and new means of solving pressing problems within the society (Gergen, 1978a,b). However, advances are not generally to be found in the enhanced empirical validity or predictive power of contemporary theory as opposed to its predecessors.

Two implications of this line of thinking deserve attention. First, to the extent that empirical support is demanded, any theory may be sustained only so long as there is a community of agreement defining the appropriate way of interpreting the supporting data. Should a vocal critic or a dissident minority take an interest in challenging the existing interpretations of the supporting evidence, the theory can be debased. Thus, the social learning of aggression (Bandura, 1973) is placed at risk when one begins to ask whether such actions as striking a plastic doll, delivering shock to a person upon instruction in a learning experiment, or selecting a gun or a tank for play as opposed to building blocks or toy cars are "truly" aggressive acts. After all, when children strike a plastic doll after they have viewed a model doing so, are their actions aggressive, or are they simply copying the manner of *play* adopted by the model, demonstrating *acquiescence* to a socially desirable mode of responding, demonstrating *effectance*, manifesting *exploratory needs*, *showing off* to their peers, or any of a number of other equally intelligible possibilities? Similar questions can be raised about virtually any other measure of aggression. Thus, the viability of the social learning theory of aggression does not ultimately rest on the "data" collected on its behalf; rather, it depends in large measure on the capacity of the theorist to interpret a series of actions in a way that will be agreeable (or at least, not disagreeable) to members of the relevant sub-culture.

Finally, it is important to consider the inherent tendency towards conservatism in social psychology research implied by the present arguments. When any given research study is submitted for professional review, one of the major criteria by which it is typically evaluated is in terms of the availability of *alternative explanations*. Are there means of explaining the results other than those preferred by the investigator? If such alternatives are located, they are often used as grounds for rejection. As commonly argued, the research does not render unambiguous support for the underlying hypothesis. Yet, the task of locating alternative explanations is clearly one in which the dilemma of behavioural interpretation is paramount. Essentially the evaluator asks whether there are alternative interpretations of the actions (constituting either the independent or dependent variables) that threaten the interpretation favoured by the investigator. As the present analysis indicates, the number of alternative interpretations of any given action is virtually limitless. All action may be viewed as fundamentally ambiguous and open to a wide variety of interpretations, none of which is objectively superior.

In this light the fact that many investigations do succeed in passing the crucible of the "alternative explanation" becomes a matter of puzzlement. Ruling out cases in which the evaluator harbours vested interests in the favoured interpretation, along with cases of mental lassitude, it seems clear that those *investigations that fail to challenge commonsense assumptions regarding everyday life* will be favoured in the critical assessment over those which do not. Should the investigator's interpretation seem at odds with common sense, with what any "rational person" would conclude, then the research becomes a prime candidate for rejection. It becomes virtually incumbent on the evaluating agent, as a representative of a sane profession, to point out the "obvious alternative" interpretation. Deviant interpretations are thus relegated to oblivion. This rejection may be accompanied by a sense of self-righteousness, buttressed as it is by a view of proper scientific procedure. We now see that this view is a misleading one and that if steadfastly applied, little if any social psychological research could pass muster. As it now functions, the review process generally ensures that the scientific literature will not deviate markedly from "what every reasonable person" already knows.

3. The assumption of application

A third and final assumption central to the positivist-empiricist tradition is that the theories of the discipline, when properly corroborated, may be used for widespread social good. They may be employed in widely varied settings for purposes of prediction and control. Cartwright's recent tribute (1978) to the seminal work of Kurt Lewin captures the assumption, both as voiced by Lewin and as widely shared today:

> Lewin's treatment ... was premised on the assumption that every field of science must be primarily concerned with theory, since it is theory that illuminates the causal structure of the empirical world. [Lewin] then observed that, in social psychology, theory does more than advance knowledge, for it also provides the sort of understanding required for the solution of social problems. (p. 170)

It is largely on this basis that a common distinction is made between "pure" as opposed to "applied" social psychology, the former ostensibly generating sound principles of human interaction, and the latter employing such principles in the market place. And because this model casts the pure scientist in the role of "fount of knowledge", while the practitioner becomes the "exploiter of knowledge", the latter has generally failed to acquire high professional status within the discipline.

Yet, there are additional reasons for the obscurity of the practitioner within social psychology. Of particular interest is the fact that one is severely taxed to locate effective demonstrations that indeed social psychological theories do furnish the practitioner with a practical wedge for prediction and control. Varela (1975) is one of the very few to offer optimistic examples. Yet, if they are examined carefully, one soon realizes that his examples prove highly misleading: in no sense has the attempt been made to demonstrate systematically the superiority of one predictive model over another or to systematize the way in which one might proceed to make predictions. This is not to say that social psychological theory has no practical value. On the contrary, such theory may have immense value for the practitioner in such matters as broadening the scope of relevant considerations and enhancing intelligibility (Gergen and Basseches, in press). The value of basic theory, however, is not to be found in the realm of prediction and control.

It seems clear that the traditional dualistic model of a pure science and an applied science has outlived its value in the case of the social sciences, and must be replaced with an alternative conception (Gergen, 1973; Gergen and Basseches, in press). However, it is useful to consider briefly the problem of application in light of the interpretative dilemma posed above. As we have seen, theories in psychology do not rest on unambiguous evidential grounds; rather, when empirical support has been garnered for a theory, it can retain "support" only so long as there is a willing cartel to support a line of interpretation. Further, as we have seen, because of the inherent ambiguity of human action, it is exceedingly difficult to furnish empirical definitions of key theoretical terms, i.e. linkages connecting theoretical terms with ongoing social events. In effect, then, *social psychological theory furnishes the practitioner with a set of abstractions for which there are no unambiguous particulars*. There is no clear means of knowing how the theoretical terms may be linked to the ongoing processes in which the practitioner is immersed and thus no means of knowing how effective predictions can be made. If the practitioner is intent on "application", he or she must locate events that seem credibly related to the abstract terms. This search inevitably relies on the practitioner's inside knowledge of the common patterns of action and reaction within the application setting. In applying the theory, then, the practitioner is fitting the abstract theory to personal knowledge that he or she already possesses. The theory does not in this case furnish new knowledge; it primarily furnishes intelligibility to what is already known.

To illustrate, let us suppose an industrial psychologist in a manufacturing concern is given the task of increasing worker performance. Because many studies within the realm of equity theory (e.g. Walster *et al.*, 1978) suggest that the theory should be relevant to such problems, this theory is selected for application. The theory suggests that if workers' rewards are increased over what they believe to be equitable, their performance will then increase in order to achieve equity. How is this abstract theory to be realized within the factory setting? What constitutes an inequitable "over-reward" in this situation? The psychologist considers various possibilities. One might raise the hourly pay rate by 10% but the workers have been grumbling for several years that their pay increases did not equal the rate of inflation. An increase in the length of break periods is considered, but to extend these periods might only increase the periods of low concentration following such breaks. A decrease in the working hours is considered, but as the mass transportation system serving the vicinity only functions well during peak working hours, to shorten the day would only create difficulties in travelling. The investigator then remembers that the workers have long desired an athletics area that might be used during the lunch hour and after work. Perhaps they would perform more adequately if they were given this long-desired option. The advantage is not one which the worker anticipated or felt they deserved, therefore it might be considered an "over-reward" in equity theory terms.

At this point we can see that the theory has functioned primarily as a motivating device. The investigator has sorted through a variety of possibilities, discarding many not because of the theory but because of the psychologist's previous deep familiarity with the cultural ethos. Similarly, an option is selected not because the theory has informed the practitioner that it is an appropriate one but because the practitioner already knows through his immersion in the culture that this solution may be promising. At this point the theory serves as a justifying device that furnishes an increment in intelligibility to the decision. The theory thus prods the practitioner to search for conditions that may be made sensible in terms of the theory.

In sum, the interpretative dilemma poses fundamental and far-reaching problems for the traditional attempts to test hypotheses, accumulate knowledge and to enhance prediction and control in applied settings. In Chapter 8 Stroebe has raised the question of why the falsification model has so far failed to furnish us with empirically reliable theories. From the present standpoint, this failure can be importantly attributed to the essential problems in unambiguously linking theoretical terms to behavioural specifics, a problem that is intrinsic to our attempts at understanding social action from an abstract, analytic form. To be sure, the natural scientist is confronted with the dilemma of interpretation. However, inasmuch as the preponderance of natural science concepts is defined in terms of concrete operations, the problem of contextually based interpretation is far less severe. This is not to argue that if we adopt the operationist mode the social psychologist's problems would be at an end. For example, should the theorist define aggression solely in terms of a specific operation, such as pressing a shock button in a learning task, not only would the research lack generality to any other form of aggression, but the theoretical term itself would be trivialized. Further differences between the social and natural sciences with respect to the seriousness of the interpretative dilemma are treated elsewhere (Gauld and Shotter, 1977; Gergen, in press).

C. SOCIAL PSYCHOLOGY AS AN INTERPRETATIVE ENTERPRISE

> The formulation of experience which is contained within the intellectual horizon of an age and a society is determined, I believe, not so much by events and desires as by the basic concepts at people's disposal for analyzing and describing their adventures to their own understanding.
> Suzanne K. Langer
> *Philosophy in a New Key*

In recent years, expanding concern has been shown in the possibility of an interpretative social science (Birnbaum, 1971; Fay, 1976; Gauld and Shotter, 1977; Giddens, 1976; Radnitzsky, 1970; Taylor, 1971). Such a science would be chiefly concerned with conceptual transformations of social life. Rather than developing theories as mapping devices for a pre-existing reality—a view central to the positivist-empiricist orientation—theories would function to render experience intelligible, to "give meaning" to such experience. The theory is thus not constituted by a set of hypotheses to be verified or falsified: one cannot falsify the hypotheses that there are two kinds of gender, that people prefer equitable relationships, that situation and personality interact, or that behaviour is shaped according to reinforcement contingencies, any more than one can falsify the hypothesis that $4 \times 4 = 16$. Each of these "hypotheses" represents a conceptual construction, a form of interpretation that may or may not be used to negotiate the meaning of experience. From the present perspective there would appear to be two major forms of scientific activity favoured by the interpretative alternative to the traditional empiricist orientation. In particular we may consider the exploration of interpretative forms and the development of generative theory.

1. Inquiry into interpretative forms

Given the frequently close relationship between common forms of interpretation and social action, special importance may be attached to the systematic elucidation of such forms and their function within the culture. Ample precedent for this type of analysis exists within the so-called labelling tradition in sociology. Becker's (1963) analysis of deviance is perhaps a classic in this respect. In pointing to the self-protective way people label others as deviant, Becker sensitizes one to the potentially oppressive effects of the label. Much indebted to the work of Becker and his colleagues, the ethnomethodological tradition (Garfinkel, 1967) has stimulated wide-ranging inquiry into common rules of interpretation. Such study has frequently criticized the rules by which various subcultures generate the "common facts of social life". Cicourel's (1968) examination of the manner in which the juvenile justice system converts the immense complexity of an ever-shifting reality, into ordered units such as "offenses", "family units", "normal actions", "harmless behaviour", and so on, stands as a major contribution in this domain. Similarly, Kessler and McKenna's (1978) analysis of the conflicting rules for gender identification dramatically underscores the extent to which commonly shared and ontologically arbitrary rules of interpretation come to shape the "reality" of "two sexes". And Goffman's (1961) assessment of the ways in which the staff members of mental institutions teach inmates how to define themselves as "mentally ill" and the oppressive behavioural implications of this practice have played a powerful sensitizing role in the field of mental health.

Yet, in many ways the exploration of interpretative forms is struggling toward scientific respectability. In spite of the potential of such work, it has only begun to approach its full realization. The challenge of methodological rigour has yet to be confronted; investigators have seldom attempted systematic documentation or tried to extend the generality of their analyses across the social spectrum or across time. Compelling illustrations could be generated if advantage is also taken of both experimental and survey methodology. Indeed, much of the experimental research on the attribution of causality may be viewed as illustrating systematic variations in social interpretation (Kelley and Michela, 1980). The major difficulty with this latter work, however, is that it has sacrificed generality for concern with systematic variations. For example, it may be important to illustrate differential reliance on internal versus external attributions of causality in a variety of settings. However, that college students seem to make such distinctions under various conditions tells us little about the range and significance of such distinctions within the culture more generally.

Finally, inquiry into interpretative forms has suffered from an empiricist heritage in which the documentation of regularities is believed sufficient unto itself. Many studies of common-sense interpretation appear to view "fact gathering" as a reasonable endpoint for research, as if the accumulation of structured regularities might one day lead to a grand, theoretical synthesis. Two major difficulties with this view are immediately apparent. If forms of interpretation are subject to continuous change, both for a given individual and the society more generally, then such documentation is historically contingent. That is, it primarily gives us a glimpse into contemporary life, and is of questionable significance in terms of long-term utilization. Second, one must not be misled by the concept of "documentation" to the conclusion that the "forms under study" exist "out there" as public observables. To be sure, we may register sense data without interpretation, but to place sensory experience into a conceptual framework is also to engage in an interpretative act. To isolate or indicate a form is to engage in conceptual translation. The experience simply furnishes grounds for translation. In effect, the documentation process *creates* the "object of study", or the "meaning in use". When Cicourel (1968) demonstrates how the juvenile justice system divides the complexities of the world into "offences", "family units", and the like, he himself is reducing a complex and ever changing set of experiences to units such as "the juvenile justice system" and "rules of interpretation". And when Goffman (1961) demonstrates how the staff of mental institutions teach inmates a manner of self-interpretation, he is himself making a series of bold interpretations of exactly what is occurring in such settings. Inasmuch as the act of documentation is simultaneously one of creating social reality, one is again led to inquire into the purposes of the process. In what manner does such work gain significance? If long-term predictability is obviated, and one is creating meaning rather than objective description, then one must inquire into the function of the documentation process.

One major answer to such questioning lies in the capacity of the research to sustain a value position (Gergen, 1978b). That is, the inquiry may be viewed as significant to the extent that it champions a moral position in which one is invested. Each of the above-mentioned studies is quite powerful in this respect as each harbours a provocative prescription. For example, Cicourel's (1968) work challenges the working assumptions of the juvenile justice system and thereby the concept of justice itself. Goffman's (1961) work acts as a critique of the mental institution and its practices of oppressive humiliation. And Kessler and McKenna's (1978) research on gender interpretation opens the way to greater flexibility in sex-roles. In each case the research is based on vested valuational interests, and it thereby gains a cutting edge not shared by many other studies in the ethnomethodological or ethogenic traditions.

2. Generative theory and the cultivation of audacity

A second major role to be played by a science sensitized to its interpretative capacities is that of conceptual generativity. Theories of social behaviour may vary greatly with respect to their accord with dominant interpretative modes in society. Theories may reflect and support common-sense forms of interpretation on the one hand, or they may pose lethal challenges to these standards on the other. *The generative theory is one that challenges the guiding assumptions of the culture, raises fundamental questions regarding social life, fosters reconsideration of that which is "taken for granted" and thereby furnishes fresh alternatives for social action.* In effect, the generative theory is typically an audacious one, at times arousing irritation or derision, but when efficacious, stimulating debate, restoring sensitivity to ongoing experience, and opening new avenues for social action. Very little social psychology theory nurtured within the positivist-empiricist mode has been strongly generative in character, a fact that may largely be linked to positivist-empiricist practices themselves (Gergen, 1978b). Such practices generally lend themselves more to the substantiation than the challenge of common-sense interpretation.

Why should common-sense interpretation be challenged in this way? After all, such interpretation appears to form the basis for effective interaction within a culture. There are several important reasons for antagonistic theorizing. To begin let us consider Feyerabend's (1975) commentary on conventional ways of thinking about physical objects. As he points out,

> We typically say "the table is brown" when we view it under normal circumstances, with our senses in good order, but "the table seems to be brown" when either the lighting conditions are poor or when we feel unsure in our capacity for observation. This habit expresses the belief that there are familiar circumstances when our senses are capable of seeing

> the world "as it really is" and other equally familiar circumstances, when they are deceived. It expresses the belief that some of our sensory impressions are veridical while others are not. We also take it for granted that the material medium between the object and us exerts no distorting influence, and that the physical entity that establishes the contact-light carries a true picture. All these are abstract, and highly doubtful assumptions which shape our view of the world without being accessible to direct criticism. Usually, we are not even aware of them and we recognize their effects only when we encounter an entirely different cosmology: prejudices are found by contrast, not by analysis. (p. 31.)

From the present standpoint Feyerabend's example holds true for virtually any descriptive or explanatory statement concerning human interaction. All contain a host of unstated and questionable assumptions, and the prejudicial grounds for such assumptions may be realized primarily through contrast. Let us be more specific.

First, commitment to any given form of interpretation may truncate one's capacities for problem-solving. To the extent that patterns of human action are undergoing continuous and often unsystematic change, novel challenges to personal well-being are continuously encountered. Any given interpretation, whether of the fragmentary, common-sense variety or of the fully articulated science, furnishes but a single myopic view of such experience and a concomitant delimiting of problem solving modes. To think of the "nuclear family" as containing at least one member of each gender, for instance, is to reduce options for solving problems of marital incompatibility by expansion of the nuclear unit. A premium is thus to be placed on theory that may reduce the myopia of conventional theorizing; as one opens new theoretical vistas the options for adaptive action are increased. In addition to this reason for challenging common sense, every form of behavioural interpretation, whether informal or systematic, *serves as an implement of social control.* Common-sense understandings are often employed by people to sustain a social order in which they possess control. It is within this arena that theorists such as Habermas (1971), Apel (1967) and others in the critical tradition (e.g. Jay, 1973) have argued for *emancipatory theory.* When theoretical analysis reveals inconsistencies in the dominant conceptions of an oppressive society, such analysis may serve to free those who are victimized by these conceptions. Finally, on purely humanistic grounds, one may argue that *conventional interpretation limits the range of human potential.* As existing theories specify the range of "reasonable" actions, they also reduce the range of available interpersonal experiences, the range of human emotion, and the boundaries of imagination. As conventional theory is challenged, human potential may be enhanced.

This is not to argue that the theorist must always be working towards social disharmony or continuous conflict in society. One could envisage a society in which antagonism had become an accepted view of "the way things are" or should be. In this case, the audacious theory would be one demonstrating the possibility or desirability of unification. The point of audacious theorizing is not to create social conflict; rather it is to enhance choice through conceptual conflict.

Given these several rationales for generative theorizing, we must finally turn our attention to means of developing such theory. How can the manacles of common sense be broken and the theorist transcend "the facts as given"? The problem presents us with a special paradox: if one's understanding inevitably depends on existing interpretative modes, how can one engender interpretation that is alien to the existing modes? If "common sense" is employed as the instrument of understanding, how can one absorb an argument that violates "common sense"? Would such arguments not appear as patent nonsense? Let us consider, then, four avenues available for audacious theorizing, that is, styles of theoretical construction that may have generative potential. In each case we shall also indicate a relevant mechanism for overcoming the seeming inability of conceptual systems to absorb ideas that are antithetical to the system themselves.

1. *The articulation of minority group interpretation*

At perhaps the simplest level, an investigator may act on behalf of minority groups that do not share majority group perspectives or assumptions, and that simultaneously appear to be exploited by these perspectives. Frequently those who believe themselves to be oppressed by majority views share interpretative modes that have been neither fully articulated nor understood by members of the majority. By attempting to articulate these views, the social scientist may first galvanize the minority group by enabling it to achieve common understanding and secondly undermine or re-order the views of the majority.

Precisely this form of organized audacity has sparked the rise of most major social movements in recent American history. The black power movement, the anti-war movement, and the women's liberation movement, for example, are all indebted to individuals who have been close enough to the shared experiences of such groups to elaborate their assumptions and to redefine the world of human relations in such a way that the majority framework of interpretation was discredited. Although the vast majority of such interpretative efforts have not been undertaken within the social sciences, social psychologists have participated in significant measure. The attempt to redefine the motives of black ghetto rioters in such a way that they appear justifiable reactions to an oppressive society; the attempt to cast the anti-war protester as intelligent, hard-working, and of good character; and the attempt to redefine common heterosexual practices as prejudicial toward women have all served to fortify the groups in question and undermine existing views of the majority.

How are minority interpretations rendered intelligible to those who would otherwise view them as nonsense? At least one major mechanism would appear to be that of the *reconstituted referent*. That is, the social scientist in this case employs an already accepted form of conceptualization within majority culture and attaches it to a previously recognized form of activity (or person) with which it had not been previously associated. The scientist thus relies strongly on existing modes of understanding, but shifts the context of their usage. The majority culture already understands what it is to "react angrily to unjust frustration"; it is "common sense" that people would do so. The fact of "ghetto riots" is also recognized. What the social scientist does is to employ the two common-sense interpretations simultaneously, in a manner not previously practised. In this way minimal conceptual demand is made on the majority recipient. The components remain intact and only the context of usage is altered.

2. *Extension to the borders of absurdity*

A second means of achieving theoretical generativity is to extend an acceptable set of common-sense assumptions to the borders of absurdity, that is, a point at which the assumptions prove audacious but not offensively contrary. Perhaps the most dramatic example of this form of theorizing is furnished by Skinnerian behaviour theory. In its modest form, the theory captures many elements of common-sense reasoning. Most people would probably agree that environmental contingencies do have important effects on behaviour: obviously, people are responsive to reward and punishment. If such theoretical assumptions had been left unextended, behaviour theory might long ago have slipped into obscurity. Yet, Skinner has continued to elaborate and extend the interpretative bounds of the theory in ways that many consider audacious. First Skinner and his colleagues have demonstrated how the theory may encompass virtually *all* forms of human action. Further, the manner in which the theory may serve as the basis for a utopian society (Skinner, 1948) has been explicated, and demonstrations have been made of the way in which cherished ideals such as "freedom" and "dignity" stand in the way of achieving such utopian ends (Skinner, 1971). It is in just such arguments that the theory has become audacious and as a result has continued to play a highly catalytic role in intellectual and social life (e.g. Lacey and Rachlin, 1978).

Much contemporary social psychological theory *could* be extended in this manner. Such extension must perhaps await an eroding of the empiricist belief in theoretical testability; for as long as one's ideas move only minimally ahead of one's data base, little of challenging intellectual interest is likely to result. Dissonance theory (Festinger, 1957; Brehm and Wicklund, 1976) contained many elements of common sense (most people would probably agree that they prefer not to hold inconsistent ideas) but gained generative strength when it was argued that in the attempt to achieve consonance people will engage in irrational actions. However, the immense research effort devoted to verification (and falsification) of this claim virtually garrotted the theory in terms of generative potency. If less attention has been devoted to the ultimately futile attempt at empirical evaluation and a greater investment had been made in considering, for example, the use of dissonance in social control, the valuational implications of dissonance reduction, the class and educational biases reflected in the demand for dissonance reduction and the limitations of formal analytic processing implied by the theory, then the theory might continue to be of widespread interest. The rule–role orientation, capturing as it does many elements of common-sense interpretation (e.g. few would disagree that people frequently follow rules or play roles) has long been moribund in social psychology. However, in such pursuits as extending its metatheoretical implications to the point of threatening traditional empiricism in social psychology (Harré and Secord, 1972), examining its ethical implications, (Emmet, 1966) and showing how the orientation poses problems for traditional cognitive models (cf. Schank and Abelson, 1977), the intellectual vitality of the orientation has again been restored.

In contrast to the mechanism of reconstituting the referent for already existing assumptions, the present vehicle for enhancing generativity relies primarily on *extending the inherent logic of an existing set of assumptions*. Thus, in the Skinnerian case, one moves from the common-sense assumption that some activities are controlled by environmental contingencies to the audacious extreme: virtually all human interaction is controlled by environmental contingency. In the case of the rule–role orientation one moves from considering the assumption that behaviour is governed by rules to challenging the metatheoretical and ethical assumptions underlying commonly accepted alternatives. The recipient of such arguments is essentially moved by his or her commitment to a commonly accepted set of assumptions to positions initially unanticipated by this commitment.

3. *The search for antithesis*

One may also foster generative theory in searching for an intelligible antithesis to commonly accepted understandings. In arguing against a spiritualist account of the emergence of the human species, Darwinian theory served in this capacity at its inception. Sociobiologists have similarly attempted to replace social accounts of human institutions with genetic accounts and much useful controversy has resulted. In miniature form this orientation is often employed in experimental social psychology. Support for a given hypothesis stimulates others to propose an antithetical position for which support is then amassed. For example, a demonstration of the common-sense assumption that increased similarity has a positive effect on attraction has stimulated others to propose that increased similarity can produce the opposite effect. Yet, too often the generative capacity of the latter demonstration is diminished in the subsequent attempt by theorists to locate a common-sense rationale enabling both positions to be incorporated. One simply reverts to the position that under X conditions the phenomenon will be found but that under Y conditions its reverse will occur. Neither the original allegation nor its apparent reversal are beyond the common-sense understandings of the culture. Only occasionally does one find the leap to antithesis employed as a means of unseating the initial assumption. To propose a "fear of success" in the face of a commonly assumed belief that most everyone seeks success, to propose a search for intrinsic reward in the face of the behaviourist emphasis on extrinsic rewards, and to propose that spontaneous interaction is actually governed by a complex set of shared rules, all represent generative gains in contemporary theory.

However, ambitious attempts to sustain more general theories countervening current beliefs are much needed. For example, is it not possible to argue convincingly and extensively that most social behaviour reflects the individual's search for moral imperatives, that the vast share of human activity cannot accurately be accounted for by antecedent conditions but is based on spontaneously developed impulses, or that consciousness represents a form of ignorant onlooking of no consequence to human action? The elaboration of any one of these positions would contradict much that is widely accepted within the culture, and if the present analysis is correct, each should be capable of intelligible articulation.

Although the mechanisms of reconstituting referents and extending inherent logic may both be used to sustain an audacious antithesis, a third mechanism may play a more important role in the case of developing antitheses. In this case, prime reliance may be placed on the *reorganization of existing assumptions*, that is, the knitting together of previously held assumptions into a novel amalgam, which itself violates a set of major assumptions in the culture. Consider, for example, the argument that what appears to be spontaneity in interpersonal relationships is not in fact spontaneous but the result of highly constricting rules. If this position were applied to the unfolding of heterosexual relations, the theorist might make use of several component arguments, each of which would contribute to a convincing unity: (1) most heterosexual interaction appears to have a limited number of endpoints, so behaviour of the participants is not spontaneously varied but relevant primarily to these endpoints; (2) young people do not know how to achieve success in heterosexual relationships without exposure to peers, to television, the cinema, etc., so it makes sense that their behaviour in such relations is not spontaneous but a form of modelling; and (3) most people can tell us what forms of heterosexual activity are prohibited by the "rules of the game", just as they might in soccer or tennis, suggesting that they are indeed following rules in such relationships rather than acting spontaneously. The antithesis is sustained in this case by the theorist's search for a series of component arguments, each of which "makes sense" within itself and the combination of which serves to undermine the prevailing thesis.

4. *The search for alternative metaphors*.

Many commonly accepted explanations for human action are tied to prevailing metaphors within the culture: one frequently speaks of anger as explosive, of marriage as warfare, of heterosexual infatuation as disease, of friendship as bonding, of eating fully as piggishness, and so on. At times, such metaphors appear to have highly significant influences over social action. The metaphor of falling dominoes seemed to possess a mesmerizing influence over policy-making bodies of the United States during the 1960s: the fall of one nation to the Communists, it was believed, would cause the fall of its neighbour, and so on, with the eventual result of the collapse of democratic society. Such a theory could exist without the metaphor, but so convenient and compelling was the visual image, it could be argued, that very little attention was given to alternative perspectives. Similarly, it appears, many executives carry into the world of work the metaphor of the dog pack or the football match. To view their colleagues as out to maul or vanquish them (a conclusion favoured by such metaphors) can motivate a particularly brutal form of competitiveness that would be difficult to sustain in the absence of the metaphor.

Theories within the social sciences often employ metaphors as the central integrative mechanism. Lewin's field theory borrowed heavily from the image of electronic fields of activity in physics; dissonance and balance theories both employed the metaphor of bodily homeostasis; social exchange theory depends heavily on the metaphor of the marketplace; and so on. Although such metaphors have proved highly compelling, very little attention has been given to their use in unsettling common ways of thinking within the society, that is, to their generative capability. Should it not be possible to formulate alternative metaphors for the world of work, for example, such that the prevailing views are undermined? For instance, could one view work as a form of mutual entertainment in which various participants are performing for the delight of each other. Rather than a football field or a dog pack, is work not more like a circus? Perhaps one might consider work as a form of religious order in which participants are attempting to find spiritual significance in their investment, or as a form of dance in which the participants are attempting (with unequal success) to create beauty. In each case, the metaphor informs one of an alternative way of viewing the work experience and, in doing so, reduces the pervasive and potentially debilitating effects of the prevailing form.

Unlike the previous mechanisms for generative reinterpretation, the metaphor does not rely so much on concept manipulation as on *visual substitution.* The theorist attempts to create a novel visualization that may unify a range of diverse experiences. In many ways, this manner of unseating common knowledge may be very difficult. First, people commonly recognize the difference between metaphor and action (work is like a football match; it is clearly not the match itself), while it is not always so easy to distinguish between words and actions (e.g. to say "he hit me" is a form of verbal reification). Thus, the theorist who relies on metaphor asks others to join in what seems to be a form of make believe (Cohen, 1978). Secondly, to be effective, the theorist may have to rely on reconstituting multiple referents. To illustrate how the world of work is like a circus might require dozens of linking definitions: working interdependently is like a trapeze team; selecting one's clothing is like costuming; some people are high-wire experts while others are clowns. In many cases of theoretical transformation, such multiplicity in reconstituting referents is not required. In these ways, the use of metaphor as a generative device may be limited.

However, if a compelling metaphor can be effected, there is much to be gained. Metaphors often seem more accessible to cognition in daily relations than conceptual schemes: we can look at an individual and instantaneously see him or her as a clown, a lion tamer, or a bareback rider. The formal propositions of the theorist, on the other hand, often seem remote from the moment-to-moment fluctuation of daily relations, even for the theorist who has propounded them. The generative metaphor also lends itself to creative elaboration on the part of the recipient. After accepting the football match as an apt metaphor for the world of work, one can independently think of one's own resemblance to various heroes, or how certain individuals are captains or coaches and others are second-stringers. Such elaboration individualizes the metaphor and thus gives it a special potency.

CONCLUSION

This paper first attempted to elucidate a major problem both within social relationships and in the sciences themselves. The problem is essentially that of identifying instances of social action. As demonstrated, this problem is typically solved with reference to contextual indicators, which may precede, accompany, or follow the action in question. However, because such indicators are without theoretical limit and depend for their "validity" on social agreements concerning their relationships with each other, it may be concluded that the interpretation of social actions may be continuously reconstructed and that multiple and non-falsifiable interpretations may be brought to bear on any given action. As further demonstrated, when the traditional empiricist programme for the social sciences is viewed from this perspective, many of its key assumptions are eroded. We find little basis for the claim that theories may be evaluated with respect to empirical data, that knowledge accumulates, or that theoretical knowledge may be applied in the traditional manner. In this light, we turned to the central tasks for the discipline from the interpretative perspective. Two major possibilities were explored, the first centring on inquiry into common interpretative forms within the culture, and the second on undermining the prevalent forms at any given time. The latter task was termed *generative* because, in the questioning of assumptive bases, one enhances the possibility for alternative actions. The generative theory is one that places a special emphasis on theoretical audacity, and in the attempt to further such pursuits four essential mechanisms were sketched. Although the contours of an interpretative social psychology require further elaboration, such attempts would appear essential to the construction of a truly effective discipline.

ACKNOWLEDGEMENTS

Support for the preparation of the present chapter was furnished by a grant from the National Science Foundation (#7809393). Gratitude is also expressed to the Department of Psychology at Swarthmore College and to the Society for Experimental Social Psychology for their critical discussion of the arguments and to Mary Gergen, Andrew Ockwell, Barnett Pearce, Margaret Stroebe, and Wolfgang Stroebe for their appraisals of an earlier draft of the manuscript.

11
Prolegomena to a More Applied Social Psychology: towards a Critical Pragmatism

J. RICHARD EISER
*Institute of Psychiatry, University of London**

A. In the narrow street?	273
B. Clasping a shadow?	275
C. In an empty hut?	278
D. When he goes out ...	281
E. Nowhere for him to go?	285
F. Thorns and brambles?	289

> Flap, flap, the captive bird in the cage
> Beating its wings against the four corners.
> Sad and dreary, the scholar in the narrow street;
> Clasping a shadow he dwells in an empty hut.
> When he goes out, there is nowhere for him to go;
> Thorns and brambles block his every path.
>
> Tso Ssü

I do not know whether the scholar referred to in this poem was a classical Chinese equivalent of a social psychologist, but this picture of academic isolation is not so unfamiliar in our own time, nor so unimaginable a prospect for our own discipline, that we can afford to be complacent. In this chapter, I shall argue not only against complacency but also with as much conviction against any undue pessimism.

Although much social psychological research has been shaped by reliance on a limited set of paradigms, there exists a strong body of

---

*Now at the Department of Psychology, University of Exeter, England

theory which, while it may not necessarily deal with universal principles, is still sufficiently general and integral to encourage the hope that it will be applicable to real-life situations. Although such generality and applicability have sometimes been disputed, in my view most critics have ignored the fact that this body of theory is at best concerned with processes rather than products, i.e. with *how* people think and behave rather than with *what* they think and do under defined limiting conditions. Conclusions about processes can still be drawn even from some apparently artificial experiments, but the fact that an experiment uses an artificial situation does not necessarily mean that it is better controlled or more statistically rigorous than research conducted in the field. Social psychology can and should develop in a more applied direction, but should do so in a way that reflects and acknowledges the achievements that *have* been made, both in theory and in methodology.

Without a theoretical and methodological base, one cannot know which questions to ask or how to answer them. Yet within the universe of askable and answerable questions, some "matter" more than others. I would suggest that when confronted with a question that intrigues one personally, one should ask oneself what its practical implications are and not take it as a matter of pride, as some previous generations of scholars might have done, to assert airily that it has none whatsoever.

Pragmatic considerations should be regarded an an entirely proper part of social psychological thinking and practice. Indeed, a more pragmatic social psychology may, paradoxically, be theoretically more fertile and methodologically more flexible. At the same time, social psychology must maintain its orientation as a *critical* social science. It must look not only at social conditions but also at the possibilities of social change. It must identify the real social psychological issues involved in social problems and not just obediently accept the conventional or contractual definition of such "problems". Indeed, identifying the issues may often be one of the most important practical contributions that social psychologists can make.

Other chapters in this book discuss why social psychology has so far achieved less than it might—and perhaps ought to—have done. But the achievements of the past have still been real enough, even if social psychology now needs to change its tactics and adapt itself to new demands. In advocating a more applied social psychology, I am calling for such a change. Such a call is only sensible, though, if our discipline in fact offers perspectives, techniques and theoretical principles which can be applied, and are worth applying, to issues that really "matter". Let me therefore outline what I consider to be the kinds of perspectives, theories and techniques which social psychology has to offer and which suit it to a more applied role.

A. IN THE NARROW STREET?

Social psychology is not simply the study of human social behaviour; it is the study of social behaviour from a specific perspective, the psychological. This inevitably implies a selectivity and focusing of attention on certain kinds of questions at the expense of others. Some selective focus is fundamental to any distinctive discipline and is not in itself a cause for regret. What is regrettable is if members of different but related disciplines come to feel that it is not worth the effort of trying to communicate with each other because their perspectives are different. The important issue is not whether the psychological perspective is selective, but whether it is narrow and distorted in its selectivity.

In basic terms, social psychology aims to understand the part played in social behaviour by psychological processes such as (not in order of precedence) cognition, learning, perception, motivation, emotion and psychophysiology. Widely varying amounts of attention have been paid by researchers to the different kinds of processes. (Note that I am excluding "personality factors", which are not so much processes in their own right as empirical and theoretical generalizations concerning individual differences in the processes listed.) At the present time, most attention is paid to the role of cognitive processes subsumed under this general heading, and I, too, shall concentrate on the cognitive side, not because I feel that this is the only side that matters but because it is here that, so far, social psychology has made its major contributions and these have yet to be fully exploited in an applied context outside the laboratory.

It is often argued that because social psychology is so predominantly cognitive in orientation, it presents too narrow a view of man as an excessively rational decision-maker. There is both truth and overstatement in this accusation. Some of the most important applications of social psychology depend upon the concept of *bounded* rationality, and on the fact that individuals are selective and often biased in their interpretation of information. In other words, it is the *departures* from perfect rationality which are interesting from a theoretical and hence practical point of view. Yet other issues have tended to be neglected as a result. The relationship between psychophysiological processes (e.g. neurological, pharmacological, hormonal) and human social behaviour has barely been considered by social psychologists, apart from a few studies on drug effects and experiences and on the female menstrual cycle. Emotion also is a concept with which many social psychologists feel uneasy, whereas motivation is predominantly considered within an attribution theory framework (e.g. Weiner, 1970).

Consider, for example, some parts of the research on love and attraction. Love may be the single most important source of artistic inspiration, but it has hardly been the subject of many particularly stimulating experimental studies. The use of "simulated strangers", real or simulated computer matching, etc. has meant that the more emotional side of personal relationships has been hidden behind a paper mountain of measures of attitudinal similarity, physical attractiveness rated from facial photographs, and such like. Within such an approach, it is not too surprising to find workers who argue that romantic love is a *mis*attribution for the arousal caused by stress and frustration (Berscheid and Walster, 1974), a view criticized by Kenrick and Cialdini (1977).

On the other hand, the failure of many cognitively oriented social psychologists to deal convincingly with the effects of emotion and arousal does not mean that these effects can be safely ignored. Attraction ratings certainly seem to be influenced by arousing stimulus conditions (e.g. Dutton and Aron, 1974). Also, pharmacologically induced arousal, depending on its social context, has been widely recognized as a factor influencing cognitions and self-perceptions since the research of Schachter and Singer (1962). It is therefore all the more remarkable that one of the most tediously heated debates of recent years, the cognitive dissonance versus self-perception controversy, failed to look for direct evidence of one of the central tenets of dissonance theory, namely that "dissonance" produces arousal. Recent evidence that attitude-change effects consistent with dissonance theory depend upon a state of arousal attributable to the counter-attitudinal behaviour (Cooper *et al.*, 1978) is thus some of the most compelling in the literature. The influence of emotional arousal on social cognitive processes thus clearly needs further study. To understand either more fully, we must understand the relationships between them.

Other types of argument against the applicability of social psychology can also be rebutted. For example, social psychology is recently (perhaps validly) accused of being too individualistic, and hence providing too little insight into social behaviour within larger social groups. However, the fact that social psychology is, at present, highly cognitive does not prevent it from being applicable to a group context. Tajfel's (1978) theory of intergroup behaviour, for instance, is explicitly cognitive in its terminology and assumptions. Whereas social psychology should be more prepared to take societal factors into account, it is not the task of social psychology to provide an account of such factors. There are real and important questions concerning how societal factors affect the behaviour, decisions and perceptions of individuals within society, and social psychology is equipped to answer them.

A stronger version of this criticism is that it is misleading and naïve to assume that individuals *can* make free decisions about their own lives when their social conditions are constrained by political, economic or ethnic status. To this I would answer that one of the most persuasive ways of commenting on the inequalities that persist in society is to demonstrate how they constrain the expectations and aspirations of individuals and groups who are the victims of disadvantage or discrimination. Such expectations and aspirations are fundamental elements in any cognitive social psychological analysis of group membership and group behaviour.

In short, there are some directions in which the social psychological perspective could and should be broadened. However, even now, with its predominant preoccupation with cognition, this perspective is still broad enough to encompass very many important questions which merit empirical study.

B. CLASPING A SHADOW?

Theory is basic to scientific knowledge and inquiry, regardless of whether the problems of one's research are "fundamental" or "applied". In saying that social psychology should be more applied, therefore, I am not saying that it should be less theoretical; on the contrary, I suspect that it is often a lack of confidence in the validity of one's theories that holds many social psychologists back from applied research (see Chapter 4). This lack of confidence seems to stem partly from a belief that theoretical principles in social psychology are of limited scope and applicability. I feel that the issue here is one of the level of explanation at which one expects theories to operate. Most theories in social psychology can be looked at (1) in terms of specific empirical predictions (which are usually quite explicit); (2) in terms of the classes of variables to which they attach most importance; (3) in terms of their underlying assumptions concerning human social behaviour (which sometimes are not made explicit at all). Those critics who see social psychology as a hodge-podge of unrelated mini-theories are generally comparing these theories only at the first of these levels; as one moves to the second and third level, the family resemblances and common principles between different theories become more recognizable.

Most of the major topic areas of contemporary social psychology involve a consideration of processes of selecting, simplifying, categorizing, integrating, comparing and interpreting information. All these processes (or different names for a common process) reflect the fact that we live in a stimulus environment that is potentially very complex. If we viewed this complexity as purely random, planning and anticipation would be impossible; we could only react, and never act. Actions and decisions presuppose some (perceived) predictability of our environment. If we could never predict other people's behaviour, we would have no idea how we ourselves should behave towards them.

Consistency implies predictability, and predictability implies simplicity. The preference for balance in attitude organization can be seen as a preference for evaluatively simple cognitive structures (Eiser and Stroebe, 1972, pp. 182f), since balanced structures can be represented in terms of a uni-dimensional preference space, whilst imbalanced ones cannot. Uni-dimensionality in its turn implies that different pieces of information can be combined together to form a single composite index, which is to say that they can be further simplified into global assessments or single categories eliciting similar reactions. When the stimuli in question are other people it is a short step from here to real-life issues of stereotyping and prejudice (Tajfel, 1969).

Such categorization also involves evaluative comparison and there are many examples of the importance of such comparisons in social behaviour. The field of incomes policy and wage bargaining, for instance, is one where the choice of particular standards of comparison and their acceptability to the different parties lie at the crux of any negotiation. One judges outcomes as excessive, satisfactory or deficient, as deserved or undeserved, not on the basis of their absolute value, but in terms of their relationship to a standard of what would be equitable for people similar to oneself (Thibaut and Kelley, 1959; Berkowitz and Walster, 1976). Moreover, as Anderson (1976) has argued, this comparison is primarily interpersonal rather than intrapersonal in nature—one compares one's own outcomes and inputs with the outcomes and inputs of comparable others.

Such interpersonal comparison relates not only to the evaluation of mutual outcomes and inputs but also the interpretation of ambiguous stimulus situations. Thus in studies of bystander intervention, it appears that an individual may frequently rely upon the reactions of others as a valid basis for inference, even when the others are no better placed to interpret the situation than he is himself. The question "What is expected of me in this situation?" is translated into the normative question "What would other people, comparable to myself, do in this situation?". When one is surrounded by presumably comparable others, the answer seems simple: watch and see (Darley and Latané, 1970). Studies of group decision-making similarly emphasize the importance of processes of information exchange and integration (Lamm and Myers, 1970).

These different examples suggest that if we ignore, for the moment, the intricate foliage of social psychological theory, and instead take a bird's eye view of the wood, a pattern emerges that is anything but random. For better or worse, a clear family relationship is apparent among the different theoretical areas over which we have skimmed. The "model of man" implied is unmistakable. It is that of a processor and interpreter of information, seeking to be able to make quick, rough and ready decisions in complex and ambiguous situations. It is *not* a model of a rational decision-maker, if by rational one means in accordance with the principles of formal logic. Indeed, some of the most provocative research findings are those which demonstrate how human decision-making departs from perfect logical rationality (Tversky and Kahneman, 1974). However it is assuredly the model of a *pragmatic* decision-maker, someone who has to act, even without all the necessary information, who simplifies, even though this may mean ignoring relevant information, who assumes causal relationships, even when these cannot be tested in advance of the decision, and who, when frankly flummoxed, looks to others to find out what they would do.

C. IN AN EMPTY HUT?

Social psychology contains, then, a model of man which seems *a priori* rich in implications for application to social problems, but it could be claimed that there is little evidence that the established theories of social psychology have even a limited degree of generality as soon as one leaves the restricted and artificial confines of the experimental laboratory. Because so much research is laboratory-based, there would seem to be a very real danger that social psychology has or will become merely the science of social interaction in the laboratory. Artificiality is almost a defining feature of the laboratory experiment, and there is no problem in finding paradigms which impose "unreal" constraints on behaviour. However, it is by no means obvious what implications this artificiality has for the validity of our conclusions or how we should change our research methods as a consequence, if we wish to develop a more applied social psychology.

Reliance on a single experimental paradigm might be said to narrow our perspective and reduce the validity of our theories for either, or both, of two main reasons. Firstly, it may lead us to treat as fundamental "facts" findings which are contingent on limiting conditions which were not, and sometimes could not have been, varied within the paradigm. Secondly, it may lead us to limit the kinds of questions we ask to those which concern variables that can be easily manipulated or measured within the paradigm. We may be getting the wrong answers, or we may be asking the wrong questions. The first problem has probably received more critical attention, but the second is the more dangerous.

In many respects, the "wrong answers" argument is a weak basis for a critique of laboratory experimentation. One point that has to be appreciated before any constructive discussion can take place is the quite remarkable replicability of many, if not most, of the major experimental findings in the literature. Such replicability, moreover, can often be found across geographical, national and linguistic barriers, as well as over periods of a good many years. For the applied social psychologist, one problem with replicability over time is that once an experimental procedure becomes well enough known to become part of the "folklore" of social psychology (e.g. the Asch conformity experiment or, more recently, the Milgram obedience experiment), it becomes nearly impossible (at least with student subjects) to replicate the original situation, because one cannot replicate the naïvety of the original subjects' expectations or even their perception of the purpose of social psychology research generally. In other respects, though, there may be almost nothing the experimentalist likes more than the apparent failure to replicate an experimental finding. It implies the presence of limiting conditions which often may themselves be manipulated experimentally. It would not even be going too far to say that limiting conditions (or at least certain kinds of limiting conditions) are the lifeblood of the laboratory experiment.

The "wrong questions" problem is far more insidious in its influence. Professed interest in a socially relevant issue is no guarantee that the research one conducts around that issue will embody questions which are either particularly relevant or even particularly social. For instance, let us consider two large fields of experimental research—interpersonal attraction and co-operation and competition. Surely, one might say, the question of whether two people do or do not like each other is basic to almost any interaction one could imagine, and if one wants to do research which is clearly relevant to everyday social behaviour, one can hardly fail if one chooses the field of interpersonal attraction. If only things were that simple. One of the most staggering features of the attraction literature is the large proportion of published studies in which the people whose attraction to each other is supposedly being measured *never even meet*—often for the simple reason that one of them (the target person) does not even exist. Yet such paradigms have been used time and time again in an attempt to identify the antecedents of interpersonal attraction.

How could such an extraordinary situation come about? The answer is that the kinds of theoretical preconceptions prevalent, at least at the time such paradigms were first adopted, predisposed researchers to ask questions of the kind which did not require any actual interaction to take place. These preconceptions—based on a very *non*-cognitive interpretation of reinforcement principles—saw attraction as a response to reinforcing attributes of the target person. Most studies in this tradition simply represent attempts to vary such attributes experimentally, and just as in studies of animal conditioning, researchers have generally selected, from the vast array of reinforcers in principle available, a small handful which are procedurally convenient. Thus, similarity of responses to an attitude questionnaire and attractiveness of facial photographs became elevated, if one takes the results literally, to the status of the prime determinants of interpersonal attraction. The reason was that researchers (with a few notable exceptions) have simply failed to ask questions about other kinds of possible determinants and seem even to have forgotten that other considerations exist: the development of any relationship over time; perceptions by each person of their own and their partner's current satisfaction and future aspirations; sexual responsiveness and compatibility; patterns of verbal and non-verbal communication; congruence of the relationship in question with each partner's external social roles and relationships. These are questions which view the individual as an active participant rather than a passive receiver of reinforcements and pertain not only to first-year students waiting for their blind date but also apply through and beyond first encounters into life choices and commitments. They demand the study of real interactions and real relationships but for these very reasons they have been deliberately banished from the empty hut of the laboratory. This is where the influence of an experimental paradigm can be so insidious: it steers us towards the convenient questions and hides its bias beneath a cloak of replicability.

Next let us look at the field of co-operation and competition and the now unfashionable prisoner's dilemma game. We should not forget the glowing promises that accompanied the growth of experimental research in this area. War and peace, nothing less, were supposedly being studied through experimental analogue. We are more cautious now, but even so the reasons for regarding experimental games as socially irrelevant are not much sounder, if at all, than the reasons for once regarding them as socially relevant. Once again, concentrating on limiting conditions diverts our attention from the real problem, which is the assumption that co-operation and competition depend mainly on the reinforcement contingencies defined by the pay-off structure.

A limiting condition which undoubtedly *is* important is the set of rules defining the relative sizes of the pay-offs resulting from joint co-operation, unilateral competition, etc. Within the prisoner's dilemma game, the implications of a competitive move by one player are ambiguous in the information they give about the player's intentions—he could be acting in self-defence, or out of a wish to exploit (Kelley and Stahelski, 1970). This ambiguity may be removed by changing the format of the game (Miller and Holmes, 1975) with consequent effects on level of co-operation.

The finding that restricted opportunities for communication reduce co-operation (Wichman, 1970) may be related to the above problem, but seems to raise a broader issue as well. The experimental game, as typically played, is an anonymous interaction (again, often with only a simulated partner) encapsulated in time and space. The subjects interact with each other, and with the experimenter, in their roles as subjects and players; other possible roles have been excluded. Anything that allows for or encourages the subject to view the interaction as one which has interpersonal and role implications beyond those defined by the game itself may alter his construction of the situation and hence his behaviour. Many real-life encounters, perhaps especially those involving choices between co-operation and competition (at all levels), imply a conflict of possible roles and require a *choice* between roles. Many experimental situations, on the other hand, *impose* a specified role on the subject (or attempt to do so).

There are, however, some procedures which deliberately allow the possibility of identification with real-life roles within the experimental situation. Some of the experiments stemming from Tajfel's (1978) theory of intergroup behaviour provide examples of this. Other studies involve a direct conflict between a person's wider social obligations and his obligations as a subject to complete the experiment. Many experiments on reactions to emergencies fall into this category, but probably the clearest example is Milgram's (1974) obedience research.

In my view, then, experimental studies of interpersonal attraction using simulated strangers, and experimental gaming research on co-operation and competition are limited in their real-life applicability not merely because of certain "limiting conditions" but because the context of continuing role relationships, within which real-life attraction and co-operation occurs, has been excluded from the experimental situation and questions cannot be asked about it.

D. WHEN HE GOES OUT ...

This, then, is the crux of my argument: there are hosts of situations outside the laboratory, where controlled comparisons can be made and social psychological theories can be put to the test, yet where the problems of artificiality are avoided. I am not saying that any question which can be investigated inside the laboratory can be investigated as reliably and conveniently outside; but there are many questions which can be so investigated, and many also which would not normally even be raised within a laboratory context, but which are vitally important outside.

The conventional idea of a laboratory experiment is one which holds constant all variables other than those which the experimenter wishes to manipulate. Moreover, the strength of any manipulation is presumed to be constant across subjects within treatment conditions, so that variation between subjects within conditions in their responses to the manipulation can be treated as statistical error. I am not claiming that this ideal can be attained outside the laboratory. On the other hand, I doubt that it is ever attained by social psychologists, even with the most rigid laboratory procedures. For a start, an important departure from the ideal experimental model is the fact that subjects are often grouped together on deliberately non-random bases. One of the most frequent examples of this is the division of subjects into groups on the basis of some measure of attitude or personality, or on the basis of sex, race, or some such criterion. Such designs explicitly acknowledge the presence of a factor which is not strictly an independent variable in the sense that it can be varied completely independently of all other factors, but which none the less may relate to changes or differences in the dependent variables and may moderate the effects of experimental manipulations. Other designs acknowledge the presence of such factors implicitly, by non-random selection of subjects, as for example when subjects with deviant attitudes are excluded from studies on counter-attitudinal advocacy.

Another departure from the ideal model is the fact that subjects evidently differ in their interpretation of experimental situations. In itself this is not a cause for regret; on the contrary such differences in interpretation are precisely what a good social psychology experiment seeks to predict, measure and explain. What is implied, however, is again that the effects of any experimental manipulation on the dependent variables are mediated by the cognitive activity and personal attitudes of the individual subjects. Again, explicit recognition of this fact is made in designs where the "manipulation" consists of the explanatory instructions given to subjects and implicit recognition is given where subjects are excluded for suspicion or for guessing the experimental hypotheses.

So, even conventional laboratory experiments in social psychology are not "pure" experiments, but are far more like what Campbell and Stanley (1963) have termed "quasi-experiments". One is essentially making comparisons between groups or treatments and (in analysis of variance designs) using the variance within the group (or treatment) as the basis of one's error term. However, such "error variance" does *not* necessarily just reflect errors of measurement or chance. Instead much of what is called error variance is probably variance due to factors which the experimenter failed to control, either through oversight or because it was simply impracticable to attempt to do so. In other words, when we analyse the results of a social psychology experiment we are not really comparing the effects of a manipulated independent variable against chance, after controlling for other non-random sources of variation; what we are doing is comparing the predictive power of those variables on which we have some kind of grip with the total influence of other variables over which we have no grip at all. Experimental design in social psychology is thus fundamentally a pragmatic affair of seeing what is the best job that can be done with those factors which it is feasible to incorporate, rather than an aspiring to total control over everything but chance.

Viewed in this way, there is nothing essential to the social psychology experiment that restricts it to the laboratory. On the contrary, the field experiment is becoming an increasingly popular and persuasive part of social psychology methodology. There is insufficient space here to do justice to the large number of excellent field experiments that have already been conducted (see, for example, the collection by Bickman and Henchy, 1972). One only has to consider, though, how research on altruism has been advanced by field experiments, as well as how much of its initial inspiration was drawn from naturally occurring events. Laboratory experiments on bystander intervention require elaborate stage management, and it is not always easy to discern from experimental reports how credible the staged emergency was for the subjects, or indeed whether its credibility was constant over different conditions. Emergencies can be staged at least as convincingly in situations outside the laboratory, where subjects' behaviour can be recorded without their even knowing that they are subjects. Notable in this context is the series of studies conducted on the New York subway by the Piliavins and Rodin, which have looked at such variables as whether the victim appeared to be an invalid, or drunk, and black or white (Piliavin, *et al.*, 1969), whether he bled from the mouth after falling (Piliavin and Piliavin, 1972) or had a facial disfigurement (Piliavin *et al.*, 1975). There are also the studies reported by Darley and Latané (1970) on responses to requests for favours or information, as well as those by Dorris (1972) and by Langer and Abelson (1972) which show how norms of fairness and legitimacy can be brought into play by the way in which a request is phrased. All these studies leave some factors uncontrolled, but most laboratory studies in the area are no better controlled, and some may indeed have additional problems of confounding and evaluation apprehension.

And what of our theories? Does the fact that they are based on laboratory research render them inappropriate for an applied or more "real-life" context? There are those who would doubtless make such an assertion. Mixon (1972), for instance, following Harré and Secord (1972), argues that psychologists have traditionally concerned themselves only with performance, and not with the context of roles and rules in which such performance occurs. This assertion, however, neglects the fact that psychologists' main concern has not been with performance *per se* but with the cognitive and other processes underlying such performance. When one considers research on human attention, memory and perceptual discrimination, one finds rigorous experimental procedures, but also conclusions which are generalizable and useful in applied contexts. This generalizability rests on the fact that the conclusions are conclusions about *processes*. Even if psychologists have created experimental tasks which *seem*, at first sight, unlike anything encountered in normal life (e.g. tasks involving nonsense syllables), it is quite absurd to suggest that human beings have evolved a completely separate set of capacities for information processing which serve no function outside the laboratory. The same applies to how we process social information. Provided we do not delude ourselves into believing that all social psychology laboratory situations are direct analogues or simulations of real-life encounters, we can draw conclusions from laboratory research concerning how individuals deal with the information available to them and the problems posed by the experiment—conclusions not simply about the effects of specific variables on performance but more general conclusions about processes of social decision-making.

In attempting to apply models of social decision-making to real-life situations, however, pragmatic considerations again assume importance. Within the laboratory, one can study how individuals respond to highly complex combinations and sequences of information, but in real life, one is typically concerned with decision-making under conditions of uncertainty where individuals simply do not have all conceivably relevant information available to them (Bonoma, 1977). Over-sophistication of model-building, just like over-sophistication of experimental procedures, may not necessarily increase the practical utility or validity of one's research if it diverts attention away from simple questions which are of importance to any reasonable theory.

E. NOWHERE FOR HIM TO GO?

A more applied social psychology can retain its scientific authenticity in terms of both theory and method. But implicit in this argument is also a value judgement: that social psychologists *should* attend to questions which "matter" in the context of ordinary everyday social interaction outside the laboratory. As with most value judgements, in the end this reduces to a matter of personal conviction rather than any strictly logical argument. All I would say to those who reject this judgement is this: if you choose to attend to other questions, do not make this choice solely on the mistaken assumption that it is the only course to scientific respectability, or that more applied research is bound to be messier, either in method or in theory. To those who accept this judgement, let me tentatively suggest a few considerations to which future research might attend.

First and foremost, a more applied social psychology should be attentive to contemporary social change. It is quite misleading to think of the laboratory as the only place where changes in one variable can be related to changes in another; I have mentioned field experiments as a contrary example. However, it is often unnecessary to introduce deliberate manipulations into real-life situations in order to be able to observe such changes. Changes, indeed, are occurring all the time without any intervention by social psychologists. Sometimes changes take the form of an event affecting large numbers of people, for instance, a natural disaster, a strike, the closure of a factory, an election, a change in taxation or in the law. Sometimes changes can be spread over a longer period of time, such as the gradual weakening or growth of the economic base of a given region or industry, shifts in pattern of energy production and consumption, accumulation and dissemination of particular kinds of information (e.g. concerning the dangers of smoking), and shifts in patterns of child-rearing, population density, and the provision of housing, recreational and transport facilities.

The list could be expanded *ad infinitum*, but in any instance the implication for social psychology research is that a change in an identifiable environmental factor has taken place, which may have important repercussions on the lives of very large numbers of people, and the opportunity exists for studying such repercussions, and the psychological processes by which they are mediated. Of course, critics are bound to ask whether one has an "adequate control group". Sometimes they will be satisfied if we can gather data from another area unaffected by the specified event or long-term change; sometimes they will not be satisfied and will point to other obvious or imponderable differences between our "experimental" and "control" samples; sometimes we may simply have no control data at all. However, research questions *can* be asked, even though departures from conventional experimental design are undeniable. One very important safety net for such applied research is the fact that different individuals will almost certainly respond differently to such changes, and it can be of much more than academic interest to identify why this is so.

From this basic precept (that we should attend to social change) a number of more specific considerations follow. For instance, theories that deal with people's membership of social groups, and with relationships between groups, must take account of the fact that such membership and relationships can change, both gradually and suddenly. Tajfel's (1978) theory of intergroup relations represents a significant step in this direction, but a predominant concern (in the theory) with certain questions, such as the relationships between and within more and less privileged societal groups, should not detract attention from other kinds of groups, such as families, which are no less likely to change in terms of their internal and external relationships.

Another very important consideration is that, when we come to study questions of social information processing and decision-making in a changing environment, we must concern ourselves directly with how individuals and groups make judgements under conditions of uncertainty. There is a growing literature on this topic (Kaplan and Schwartz, 1975, 1977; Slovic *et al*., 1976, 1977; Tversky and Kahneman, 1974).

A specific example of judgement under uncertainty is the way jurors assess the guilt or innocence of a defendant. This is also a field where social psychology research can help identify and empirically examine some of the implicit assumptions underlying existing social practices and institutions. For instance, Kaplan (1977) has suggested that jurors do not typically start from a presumption that the accused is innocent, as assumed in law, but tend rather to estimate the probability of the accused's being guilty as closer to 50% before hearing other evidence. Judgements of guilt or innocence can also be influenced by the perceived consequences of a particular verdict. Kerr (1978) found that mock jurors were less likely to convict when the punishment for an offence was more severe.

The applicability of these and similar results, however, depends in part on two main considerations. First, the study of how *individuals* make judgements of guilt or innocence, whether before or after discussion with others, does not by itself give a complete account of how *juries* decide on a verdict; what is also needed is an understanding of the "social decision schemes" (Davis, 1973) used to translate a distribution of individual judgements into a single verdict. Secondly, as pointed out by Wells (1978), among the many variables investigated in experimental simulations of criminal trials, only certain kinds can be manipulated in real-life criminal cases (e.g. identification procedures), whereas others (e.g. personal characteristics of witnesses) cannot. Wells argues that research on variables of the former kind is potentially of greater practical value.

Another question is that of how individuals estimate the risks of possible future events. Tverky and Kahneman (1974) describe a number of heuristics or simplifying strategies which individuals use to cope with complex information but which can sometimes lead to marked errors especially with respect to estimates of probability. Notably, there are many situations where individuals will largely ignore statistical information concerning the base-rate probability of an event occurring and rely instead on intuitive heuristics.

For instance, the "gambler's fallacy" (an example of what Tversky and Kahneman call the representativeness heuristic) refers to the expectation that events presumed to be due to chance will occur in a sequence which itself *appears* random. The appearance of randomness, however, seems to depend on frequent alternations of events within a short time-span. Thus the occurrence of a "million-to-one" chance accident might lead to lessened vigilance against a repetition or to a reappraisal of prior probabilities.

Another important heuristic is that of "availability", whereby events which are more easily imagined or recalled tend to be perceived as more likely or frequent. Availability bias may be an important factor in decisions which require comparisons between different kinds of risks. Examples might be drawn from the field of energy policy, with regard to such government decisions as whether to place more emphasis on nuclear power or on energy production from fossil fuels, or from health decisions, where an individual might compare the easily pictured or recalled penalties of giving up smoking (e.g. putting on weight) with the remote, but potentially far more serious, risks of continuing. In an industrial context, certain kinds of risks of mechanical failure may be underestimated if it is difficult to imagine a particular component going wrong (Slovic *et al.*, 1976). Another interesting question is how far availability may be influenced by the media. In an evaluation of the effects of television violence on viewers in Toronto, Doob and Macdonald (1979) report that those who watched more television gave estimates of the relative probability of different kinds of crime which were more consistent with the representation of crime in television programmes than with true levels.

Ajzen (1977) has also identified what he calls a causality heuristic, according to which individuals will attend to statistical information only when it appears relevant to intuitive causal theories which they hold concerning the events in question. Attribution research has continually stressed the importance of people's "naïve" psychological theories about interpersonal behaviour, and it seems plausible that people will also hold naïve theories concerning factors which contribute to physical safety and danger in such diverse fields as medicine, nutrition, personal hygiene, pollution, transportation, and the various branches of engineering.

Another implication of the increased attention to social change is that social psychology will need to assign a much more central place in theory and method to the concept of time. The cognitive processes underlying social behaviour presumably need time for their full effects to become apparent, and the question of the durability of any such effects is very important for any attempt at application. It should also be remembered that the information on the basis of which social decisions are made may often become available to the people concerned only over an extended period of time. One of the most important restrictions imposed by the typical laboratory experiment is the need to complete it within a period which can be fitted into the timetables of student subjects. For instance, out of the host of studies which have produced attitude change as a result of some experimental manipulation, only a very small proportion have attempted any follow-up to determine the permanence, if any, of such effects. It is worth noting that, in spite of the current predominance of cognitive theory in social psychology, there is little direct consideration given to the relevance of memory processes for social behaviour.

F. THORNS AND BRAMBLES?

If social psychology is to become more applied, there are a number of obstacles to be overcome, as well as dangers against which one should be alerted. These fall generally under two headings—the organizational and the conceptual.

Among the organizational factors, the most important relate to the conditions of employment and funding for social psychologists doing applied research. University teaching departments tend to be organized among unidisciplinary lines, and often different departments in what are optimistically called "allied disciplines" are in direct competition for students and hence for faculty positions. Applied research, however, would seem to flourish in interdisciplinary settings, where different viewpoints can be brought to bear on a common problem. Somehow universities need to find an effective way of fostering interdisciplinary research in spite of entrenched disciplinary interests and without isolating research and teaching endeavours from each other.

Outside universities, the applied social psychologist may find himself doing research for a person or organization whose priorities and definition of the problem are different from his own. He may also come up against entrenched interest groups among other professional psychologists. Whereas the normal route into a career in social psychology is through a graduate research degree, in Britain at least a professional qualification (not a Ph.D.) is required for a graduate to practise as a clinical or educational psychologist. Since educational and clinical psychologists between them account for the vast majority of government-funded positions for psychologists outside universities, this has implications for the employment prospects of social psychology graduates. First of all, although it is easy to be a practising educational or clinical psychologist without doing any research, professional qualifications, rather than Ph.D.s or other research degrees, may be demanded of candidates for what are primarily research positions in educational or clinical fields. There are, however, many important research questions to be studied under the general headings of "the social psychology of education" or "the social psychology of mental health", and it would seem regrettable if trained *social* psychologists were not in position to study these.

Related to this is the difficulty that, because of the greater number and greater visibility of educational and clinical psychologists, research questions which are not specifically "educational" or "clinical" may be given to members of these two groups to solve. There is no reason, for instance, why a professional training in dealing with psychiatric patients should be regarded as either a necessary or sufficient condition of research competence in the more general field of the relationships of psychology to medicine and to physical health and illness. This is one very important area where social psychology has an immense amount to contribute. There are also many potential areas of social development research which have little necessary dependence on the specific training received by educational psychologists. Applied social psychologists may therefore find themselves, before too long, needing to argue strongly against over-rigid demarcation rules defining the areas of competence of psychologists in public service.

One factor which facilitates applied social psychological research, on the other hand, is the greater availability of research funds in general for projects of more recognizable practical relevance. This is not only because of the wider possible range of funding agencies but also because of preferences within a number of these agencies. This might be seen as unfair discrimination against more "basic" academic research, but "basic" academic research questions in social psychology can be studied at least as appropriately in applied settings. All that is needed is a greater responsiveness to contemporary social situations and a greater willingness to present the reasons for one's research in a way that is intelligible to people outside one's own discipline.

At one level, the applied social psychologist does not have to go in search of research questions—the questions come to him. But in this lies also one of the greatest dangers to applied research. If applied social psychology is to be based on a philosophy of critical pragmatism, rather than mere opportunism, it must retain the power to define questions in a meaningful way. This can be difficult—though not necessarily impossible—for social psychologists working in commercial or industrial settings, where their contract may be to answer questions specified by the client, but similar difficulties arise in research supposedly aimed at benefiting wider sections of society. The fact that one is studying "social problems" does not guarantee that one is asking questions about such problems which are meaningful from a social psychological point of view.

When faced with a "social problem", therefore, the social psychologist should ask the basic and sometimes almost heretical question "Why is this seen as a problem?" Usually, the answer will reveal a number of implicit assumptions about human nature and social behaviour which need to be directly confronted. This often applies where an environmental factor comes to be regarded as "obviously" detrimental to psychological development and functioning. One example is the concern with the sexual and violent content of television programmes. The identification of this as a problem for social psychological study does not appear to have been based on any pre-established empirical evidence that sex and violence on television have any damaging effects, but rather on a moral and/or aesthetic revulsion which may have led people to feel that such programmes *must* be psychologically damaging. Yet the questions of what counts as psychological damage and how this could be produced by television programmes are begged unless the social psychologist redirects attention to them. Another example is the concern with urban crowding, where it used to be assumed that crowding *must* be stressful. Theoretical and empirical advances have only been made in this field when social psychologists have refused to accept this assumption as a universal axiom, and have instead asked questions such as whether, why, where and for whom this is so (Baum and Epstein, 1978).

Then there is the wide class of "problems" which are defined not in terms of an identified environmental factor but in terms of the behaviour of particular groups or individuals. One may be asked what is "wrong" psychologically with certain kinds of deviants. There are many instances in many countries where assumptions of psychopathology are built into prevalent conceptions of, and recommendations for dealing with, various categories of "socially undesirable" persons, be they football hooligans, drug abusers, common criminals, terrorists, or political dissidents. Where a mere opportunist social technology might confine itself to assessing the effectiveness of certain "solutions", a critically pragmatic social psychology must start by examining the social psychological assumptions implicit in the presentation of a problem.

A theoretically and empirically based analysis of a problem must therefore precede any recommended solution. This is true whether one is studying the problem for oneself, for a commercial or industrial company, for a social or government agency, or for an individual client. Sometimes there may be no feasible solution until external circumstances alter, but even here a scientific analysis of the problem can have relevance to preparations for *future* practice. Sometimes possible solutions may be suggested, but on the basis of uncertain evidence. Here a scientific analysis can provide a basis for estimating the degree of such uncertainty in advance and for suggesting the conclusions to be drawn from the success or failure of any practical solution.

Social psychology is equipped both theoretically and methodologically to provide such scientific analyses of social problems, and to clear away some of the conceptual undergrowth that obstructs the progress of both research and practice. There may be thorns and brambles before us, but they need not block our way. Still less should they persuade us that we have reached the end of the road.

12
Social Psychology 2001: The Social Psychological Bases and Implications of Structural Unemployment

PETER KELVIN
Department of Psychology, University College, London

A. The protestant work ethic 295
B. A culture in transition 300
C. The social psychology of unemployment 308
D. The psychological limitations of leisure 310

I am not given to crystal gazing but the subject "Social Psychology 2001" provides the opportunity to discuss several issues which I believe to be crucial to the future of social psychology but which have received scant attention. The substantive problems arise from the generally accepted forecasts of high levels of unemployment or underemployment in the coming decades: most of the chapter will explore the social psychological implications of these predicted economic developments. To do this, however, raises conceptual and methodological issues. The conceptual issue is the need for an historical perspective, not as a discursive background but as an integral part of the body of evidence required to understand and predict certain classes of social psychology phenomena. In practice, social psychology is devoid of any systematic historical perspective. It comes closest to it in vague references to the importance of "cultural factors", but such serious attempts as have been made to examine these have only taken the form of "cross-cultural research", at the level of contemporaneity (cf. Jahoda, 1978): it has looked at similarities and differences *between* cultures separated in *space*, the historical origin of matters of interest being asserted, not explored. Yet in their essence "cultural" factors are historical factors: the study of history, especially of social and economic history, is itself fundamentally cross-cultural, *within* a given culture across *time*. The lack of such an historical perspective in social psychology is not just an academic nicety: it affects our efficacy and credibility as social psychologists. There are, of course, numerous "basic" social psychological processes which are not historical but "universal", for instance the basic processes of attitude change, of social comparison, or of the social construction of social reality. These can be assumed to be common to all mankind and to all times, because they derive from the nature of man as a species (Kelvin, 1970). However, there are other classes of social psychological phenomena, those characterized by their content rather than by their underlying process, that cannot be understood independently of their historical ("cultural") context. It is in connection with such phenomena, such industrial strife, race relations and international conflict, that social psychologists so often bewail their almost total impotence to influence the affairs of the "real" world. However, having no historical perspective we constantly misjudge the essential time-scale of our operations: as social psychologists in the real world we react rather than act. We are constantly faced with conditions and problems which are already well established and thus generally intractable, simply because we do not work sufficiently far ahead to take preventive, let alone creative, action. Yet we also know that the majority of significant social processes and problems build up over relatively long periods of time. In effect, while we should be in forestry, taking a long view of slow processes which we might help to shape, we find ourselves in market gardening, hoping at best to hoe up a little patch of this year's racial prejudice or to fertilize a bit of next year's industrial harmony. To become productive in the real world we have to think further into the future, not as inspired clairvoyants but as rational (and credible) forecasters. To that end, however, we need to look further and more systematically into the past—not because the past lends itself to simple extrapolation but because it is essential to an understanding of our own time, which in turn is providing the conditions of the future.

The methodological problems are considerable but not insurmountable, and they are greater for us than they need be for our successors, if only we ourselves begin to provide the foundations for them. The central problem is the nature of the evidence for an historical perspective in social psychology. In one way or another this will, of course, be "archival" rather than "direct"—but greater use of archival material has already been strongly advocated as a potentially valuable source of non-reactive measures (Webb *et al.*, 1966; Sales, 1973). The difficulty in our time is that we ourselves have access only to material which, from a social psychological standpoint, has survived merely by chance and which is often little more than incidentally illuminating. What we should do for our successors, as economists have done for generations (and who is more influential?), is to build up a body of systematic records of social psychological data, at least some of which is collected with a view to its potential value in the future as well as the present. There is no reason whatever why we should not do for attitudes and behavioural norms what economists have done for wages and prices. Indeed it would be invaluable to an understanding of our age if, for instance, there had been records of systematic, periodically replicated studies of attitudes towards the unemployed, or reflecting the Protestant Ethic generally, even if only from the early nineteenth century. As it is, we do not even have systematic and integrated records from the 1930s, when public opinion surveys began. If I have one wish for Social Psychology 2001, it is that it will have come to terms with its need for historical perspectives, and its consequent need to invest in the creation of records.

The rest of this chapter will be concerned with the social psychological implications of one particular and foreseeable set of social circumstances: structural unemployment. I believe that we cannot begin to understand and forecast these without an historical perspective. This chapter has therefore also become a tentative exercise in the application of historical considerations to social psychological problems.

A. THE PROTESTANT WORK ETHIC

The turn of the millennium will in retrospect mark the end of our particular culture, and the quite valid reasons for this—that is, the phenomena and processes which will come to justify this future historical convention—will provide much of the context and content of the social psychology of those years. I do not anticipate either cataclysm or paradise on New Year's Day 2001. There will be nothing fundamentally new that day and nothing that in principle we do not know now; for the basic truth is that we are already participant observers of our own final years, gradually becoming participant observers to quite another time. We are coming to the end of the age of the Protestant Ethic, which has shaped Western cultures these last four to five hundred years. Its origins preceded the Reformation, though its full attitudinal effects did not reach maturity until the nineteenth century, and although these origins lay in Europe (and were there associated with the rise of capitalism), it spread far beyond Europe and remains at the root of socialist economies. It lies at the base of all industrial systems, because its distinctive character, whenever and wherever it developed, was a distinctive attitude to *work*. Thus if we remove the specifically religious component of the Protestant Ethic (however crucial it may have been initially), in essence that ethic transformed work from something which was necessary into something which was virtuous—and then made a necessity of virtue. As a result, work came to be (or at least came to be presented as) of central significance to the life of the individual, to the informal as well as formal organization of society, to the development of industry and, ultimately, to the political state—whatever its politics. It was that *attitude* to work which distinguished this period from the Middle Ages; for the Industrial Revolution, though its achievements and social consequences were dramatic, was itself the product of that work ethic, its fruition, not its cause.

It is this age of the Protestant Ethic which is now coming inexorably to its close, through processes which from a social psychological standpoint were always inherent in it. Our culture is therefore not just undergoing one of its periodic variations on a basic theme (as it did with, for example, the growth of modern industry). It is coming to a close in the fundamental sense that the age which will follow will be as different from our own age as it was from the Middle Ages. The root of the difference between ourselves and our heirs will be the inevitable difference between us and them in attitudinal terms, specifically in attitudes about the function of work in our respective lives and therefore about the role of work and the concept of work in our respective cultures. Whether or not it is deliberately planned, the next age will be an age of widespread unemployment. Either large proportions of the potential work-force will be unable to find employment, or there will be systematic underemployment and hours of work will be reduced rather than the numbers working. In either case, there will be less work, and work will therefore lose many of the central connotations it has carried in the last five hundred, and particularly the last two hundred years. The one thing that the Protestant Ethic cannot survive is structural unemployment or systematic underemployment, because these affect not merely a specific industry but the structure of society itself. Work and idleness are morally significant only when the individual can choose between them, or at the very least can be perceived to be able to choose between them. When unemployment becomes structural at the global level, the crucial element of choice on which morality depends is lost.

I can hear the objections, conceptual and empirical. "He is confusing 'employment' and 'work'." But one can be working without being employed. Or "technology may lead to a rise in the number of unemployed and for many people the working week or working day may well be shorter, but the greater part of mankind will still spend a substantial portion of its life 'at work'." To some extent this is true, but for very good social and psychological reasons which I shall explain throughout this chapter it will not retard the demise of the Protestant Work Ethic. That demise now has its own psychological momentum. Even so, we need to consider these two objections briefly.

To tackle first the conceptual objection, there is the very real problem of how to define unemployment, which is not synonymous with "being without work". This question of definition is not merely a semantic nicety but has important practical implications: the way in which a society defines unemployment not only reflects but also shapes its attitudes toward it. Furthermore, since unemployment constitutes an administrative as well as a social problem for the modern state, governments and their bureaucracies have vested political and administrative interests in formulating their various definitions. These definitions therefore differ, not only at different times but also between states. The nuances between being "unemployed" and "not working" do not appear to enter either into administrative consideration or into that other fount of modern definitions, the mass media. For our purposes here, therefore, I have decided to adopt (and slightly adapt) the refined common sense version offered by Garraty:

> Unemployment means "the condition of being without some socially acceptable means of earning a living", and the unemployed are persons capable of labor, [probably] in need of its rewards, but idle without regard

to their willingness to work. (Garraty, 1978, p. 10; the "probably" is mine.)

The second (empirical) objection is historically quite justified. The Luddites of the nineteenth century also feared massive unemployment through the growth of technology, and were proved misguided. More recently, since the earliest days of automation in the late 1940s and early 1950s, the potential replacement of men by machines has been seen either as a threat to jobs or as a promise of more leisure, for better or worse, according to taste (e.g. Arendt, 1958). In the event, boom or recession, times of high or low employment cannot be and have not been directly attributed to automation. Therefore, although the advent of microprocessors may greatly expand the range of future automation, precedent suggests that this need not *of itself* lead to large-scale unemployment. Consequently, it may justly be argued that if the application of microprocessors does indeed create millions of jobless—rather than merely higher productivity and a better quality of life—the fault will lie within ourselves. From which, in turn, we may argue this: *unemployment attributable to the development of microprocessors should not be seen as a cause of the end of the Protestant Ethic but as a symptom of its terminal stage.*

To understand the social psychological bases and implications of structural unemployment it is essential to look at the Protestant Ethic and its course, from a social psychological standpoint, albeit inferentially. The concept of the Protestant Ethic is of course itself an invention, developed by Weber to account for the social and economic changes wrought by capitalism (Weber, 1904–1905; 1976). The central thesis is that the Puritan wing of English Protestants, in particular, held two beliefs very firmly. First, that labour is ordained by God, in the sense of "If any would not work, neither should he eat". Secondly, that all of us have a "calling" of divine origin and that successful achievement within that calling makes us pleasing in the sight of God. Work is thus enjoined on the good Christian as an integral part of his faith and salvation, and manifest success in one's calling becomes a symbol of that salvation. However, material success is not to be valued for its own sake or used to avoid subsequent work; rather wealth should create opportunities for more work. Hence the earlier argument that unemployment following the introduction of a new manufacturing process is a symptom not a cause of the end of the Protestant Ethic; according to that ethic the benefit of new technologies should be expressed in the creation of new jobs, not in more leisure or unemployment. The ethic would have utterly rejected the notion that the efficiency of machines should lead to leisure or worklessness among men.

In terms of what actually happened the crucial psychological factors were a compound of the tendency of motives to become functionally autonomous (Allport, 1937) and of social comparison processes (Festinger, 1954). In its "pure" form, the Protestant Ethic treated the acquisition of goods and wealth as a *means* for funding further endeavour, but from its very beginnings it contained an element of ambiguity in that evidence of success in one's calling was regarded as the outward sign of one's good standing in the eyes of the Lord. Psychologically it would therefore not be surprising if for many of those who grew up in that ethic, wealth as a means became transmuted into wealth as an *end*—in the sense that wealth and its attendant possessions became proof of success in one's calling, not least to oneself.

If we now bear in mind that the deeply religious will probably have been quite few in number, though great in influence, we can readily identify the processes whereby wealth as a means became generally transformed into an urge for the acquisition of possessions as an end. For, given the stress put on success in one's calling, how could such success be evaluated? Among the truly devout the sheer sense of the intensity and range of one's activities may well have been sufficient, a feeling no doubt akin to purely secular job-satisfaction. For the great majority, however, it is not unreasonable to assume that so tenuous an attribute as success was assessed in terms of the social reality which emerges from social comparison processes (Festinger, 1954). Recourse to social comparisons may not have been crucial during the early history of the ethic: the salience of social comparison processes must, I think, depend considerably on opportunities for social mobility, and social mobility remained fairly restricted until at least the end of the eighteenth century. The Industrial Revolution, however, did provide the economic conditions for a marked increase in social mobility—in terms of the social reality of success based on the economic reality of expanding industrial wealth. Material possessions simply lend themselves more readily and unequivocally to social comparisons than personal qualities. However, once underlying attitudes shift so that the concern is with possessions as the sign of success (rather than with work as the essence of one's calling) we move into a world in which goods are more important than work and productivity becomes more important than employment. Very simply, where the desire is for goods, the demand is for low prices in relation to high incomes, and the productivity of machines becomes less costly than the labour of men. This may not be a universal law of nature, but it is certainly a valid empirical generalization for our time. It is the position which we have reached in practice, but we have hardly begun to explore its potential consequences. We are essentially in a period of transition between awareness and understanding.

B. A CULTURE IN TRANSITION

To understand the social psychological implications of structural unemployment at the present time therefore, it is essential to distinguish between transition and ambiguity. A period of transition is a period of ambiguity, such that sometimes ambiguity causes transition and sometimes transition causes ambiguity. It is not a trivial question to ask of any particular set of circumstances which is the predominant direction of causality. On the contrary, it is only to the extent to which we can answer that question that we can identify the origin of any change as primarily within men or within their conditions. Conditions may change and, in doing so, be in transition; but they are never, *qua* conditions, ambiguous. Ambiguity does not reside in nature but in ourselves. Thus when an individual finds himself in what (to him) is an ambiguous situation, he may seek to change it in order to resolve that ambiguity and he may thereby induce a transition; or he may find himself in a period of transition which is not of his own making and which creates ambiguity for him where previously he had felt certainty.

Given this distinction between transition and ambiguity, and the relation between them, I suggest that we are first and foremost in a period of *transition* in our conditions, which is only beginning to give rise to the ambiguities which over the next few decades will generate social and psychological problems—and change. I cannot "prove" the validity of this suggestion: I can only take you through illustrations and discussion.

> "What does he do?" remains the most illuminating question to ask about someone met for the first time. It is illuminating precisely because a man's or a woman's work, or the fact that they do not need to or cannot work,

is indicative of so much else about their social situation and their likely life experiences ... An occupation is a socially recognised set of work activities ... It therefore implies ... a place in the social division of labour. (Brown, 1978, pp. 55, 56.)

Brown's basic assertion is that a person's work is crucial for his or her position and standing in society and, at least by implication, for his or her self-concept. Conversely, to be out of work, in the sense of unemployed, constitutes not merely a financial but also, and perhaps more painfully and more significantly in psychological terms, a social and personal loss. Telling and often poignant evidence for this comes from the case studies of Marsden and Duff—and I quote from different cases recorded in 1972:

> Well it makes you feel a bit guilty. If you're an able-bodied man, you're just leeching, aren't you? Poncing, or whatever you like to call it, on society. (p. 124.)

> My children don't have free school meals. It's a silly thing, I know, but, well, you don't want to send the kids off to get free meals, you know what I mean? You don't want them to be different. (p. 135.)

> And if you can't find any work to do, you have the feeling you're not human. You're out of place. You're so different from all the rest of the people around you that you think something is wrong with you. (p. 63.)

> Sometimes when I'm walking around the town I wear this old B.R.S. [British Road Services] coat that I've picked up, and then it's surprising, I feel just like everybody else. (p. 157.)

The fieldwork from which these quotations were taken was carried out in 1972 and published in 1975. It is perhaps significant that 1972 was also the year in which Tavistock Publications first issued the translation of *Marienthal*, the classic study of an unemployed community conducted in 1930 by Jahoda, Lazarsfeld and Zeisel, which, after its initial impact in the 1930s, had lain dormant for some forty years. After the "recoveries" of the 1950s and the "expansions" of the 60s, the early 70s, even before the Six-Day War and the "energy crisis" saw some signs of concern about possibly large-scale unemployment.

The crucial difference between Jahoda's *Marienthal* and Marsden and Duff's *Workless* is that the people of Marienthal constituted a community, whereas those in *Workless* were individuals, only a few of whom knew each other. In both studies, though many years apart, the psychological effects of unemployment, while still harsh, seem to be less damaging for those who felt themselves to be members of a community or group than for individuals. However, the two themes which dominate throughout Marsden and Duff are of the unemployed as the exception in his social setting, especially his *sense* of being an exception, and the implications of that for him. There can be no clearer tribute to the continued efficacy of the Protestant Ethic amongst most of these men than their reaction to being out of work: they did not regard themselves simply as exceptions in a statistical sense, as momentary quirks of some objective pattern of probability of working; they saw themselves as that most promising material for social psychological study, the deviant and stigmatized. They saw themselves as "poncing" on society, or wondered what others thought of them while they joked; they did not want their children to suffer by association; there was at least one case of that classic attempt to avoid stigma by "passing", by wearing a British Road Services coat. The assumptions which underlay these reactions and feelings in 1972 were fundamentally those of the Protestant Ethic. And let me admit now to a purposive deception (which I shall not repeat): the penultimate quotation identified as p. 63, which lies so harmoniously amidst the rest, does not come from Marsden and Duff but from Bakke's *The Unemployed Man*, published in 1933. There seems to be little evidence here, then, of any ambiguity concerning the work ethic, nor any sign of transition across forty years.

Yet for some time there has also been growing up, in parallel, a literature which has concerned itself with the decline, in some form, of work. The loss of quality of life through the loss of quality of work, which is often one aspect of automation, preoccupied Hannah Arendt in *The Human Condition*, 1958. In 1963 a collection of articles was published under the telling title *Work and Leisure: A Contemporary Social Problem* (Smigel, 1963). The following examples are from 1977 and 1978:

> In more immediate and more practical terms, work itself appears to be shedding some significance in our lives. The simple equation between work and production is no longer obvious; machines, rather than human effort, produce goods ... There is also some worrying negative evidence concerning the declining significance of work. We hear more about leisure, sometimes as a reward ... sometimes as a major social problem. (Anthony, 1977; 1978 edition, p. 9.)

> The irrational tendency of so many of the unemployed of the thirties to blame themselves for their unfortunate condition ... is fast disappearing among the unemployed of the seventies. The Germans are supposedly an especially work-oriented people, but during the recession of 1975 a

reporter interviewing large numbers of idle German workers ... wrote "The loss of dignity that used to accompany the loss of a job has been remedied." (Garraty, 1978, pp. 251–252.)

The different attitudes and behaviour exemplified on the one hand in Marsden and Duff and in Brown, and on the other hand in Anthony and Garraty, reflect a period of transition in which two very different sets of attitudes coexist within society. Although it is conceivable that individuals will quickly come to hold one view rather than another, all that we, as social psychologists, know of the diffusion of opinions and attitudes suggests that the prevalence of both attitudes within society will give rise to ambiguity and ambivalence among individuals. The resolution of these uncertainties will produce a culture very different from our own.

There have of course been fluctuations in employment throughout recorded history, but in our time we are, I think, faced with a wholly new situation. Until the present the relation between manpower, productivity and the cost of production has generally been reasonably close. "If any would not work, neither should he eat" has mostly been valid for all except special castes, such as priests and military aristocracies, and often for those too. The fact that a relation between work and productivity was demonstrable (even if the distribution of rewards was unfair) may itself have made it easier to hold reasonably clear attitudes towards work and employment. That is speculation; what is certain is that although attitudes towards the workless differ very sharply as between the Middle Ages and, say, as from the sixteenth century, those attitudes were, until recently, quite clear. The official morality of the Middle Ages enjoined charity and care for the poor, and the poor included the workless, until labour shortages after the Black Death (1349) caused some concern over the work-shy. Furthermore, feudalism gave the serf the protection of his lord in hard times. This official morality may not always have found expression in action, any more than the later Protestant Ethic always produced hard work, but it was the morality endorsed by the still very powerful Church. Perhaps particularly important from our standpoint today the beggar, who was often in our terms simply "unemployed", had a recognized status as such in society, and it was a significant and in its way respected status. In the Middle Ages, the opportunity to give to the poor was as important a means to salvation as the opportunity to work became a means to salvation under the Protestant Ethic. The poor did of course continue to be regarded as the proper recipients of the proper exercise of charity, and many Protestant Sects have from their beginnings given devoted service to the needy. Nevertheless, from the sixteenth century onwards a distinction was made increasingly articulate between the poor and what were frequently called sturdy beggars: the poor were the old and the sick, particularly of one's own parish; sturdy beggars were strong, fit people, apparently fully able to work but unwilling to do so, who often wandered over the countryside, becoming a charge on whatever parish they alighted. The poor were given some relief; sturdy beggars were not only denied support but for the next three centuries were also subject to punishments, often of great severity. In British history the pattern of attitudes, perhaps to the present day, is exemplified in an article of the Poor Law of Elizabeth I: subvention is to be made from public funds to provide work, especially for the young:

> Also to the intent youth may be accustomed and brought up in labour and work, and thus not like to grow up to be idle rogues, and to the intent also that such as be already grown up in idleness and so be rogues at this present, may not have any excuse in saying that they cannot get any service or work. (18 Eliz. I, c. 3. *Statutes of the Realm*, Vol. IV, Part I, pp. 610–613, 1575/6.)

This is similar to the modern Job Creation Programme: beneath the archaic language the sentiments are recognizably modern and of the essence of the Protestant Ethic. Indeed, in Britain during most of the period between Elizabeth I and Elizabeth II the position of the able-bodied unemployed deteriorated, perhaps particularly under the Poor Law Amendment Act of 1834, until the massive unemployment at the end of the nineteenth century and, no doubt, the growth of the trade unions and the Labour Party produced the beginnings of more supportive legislation which reflected the beginning of a change of feeling. But note that where the Middle Ages had an accepted place for the unemployed *within* the mainstream of society, the Protestant Ethic inherently *excluded* the unemployed from society and created that sense of deviance which so affected the people studied, just a few years ago, by Marsden and Duff. And now consider this:

> And far from seeing reduced unemployment figures we should prepare for the day when they could reach the ten million mark! Now what does one do with ten million able-bodied men and women who need to experience the satisfaction of a job well done if life is to have any real meaning?

Here is a tremendous problem which no amount of dole money can solve
... Perhaps we need a "Use It" human energy campaign to run parallel
with our "Save It" natural energy one. Plus revolutionary thinking on
wages and hours.

Despite the ending these are not the words of a revolutionary demagogue, nor those of a social worker, priest, or firebrand academic. They come from the Editorial of the October 1978 issue of *Do-It-Yourself— The Home Improvement Magazine*, and it is precisely their source in that publication which makes them significant. This magazine is one of the two biggest and most influential of their genre in the United Kingdom, with an estimated readership of $2\frac{1}{2}$ million. The genre itself is in essence the late twentieth century descendant of the large self-improvement literature of the aspiring members of the Victorian working and lower middle classes. It is a magazine whose readership consists predominantly of ordinary citizens within the broad middle range of our society. Above all it consists of people who may be partly motivated by the economies of "do-it-yourself", but for whom there is also great satisfaction in the work, and in the sheer sense of independence which comes from making one's own things and being able to carry out one's own repairs. All of which—economy, work, independence—are the core values of the Protestant Ethic; and however much it may surprise some of these readers to learn it, that is what they are the heirs of and witness to.

Here, therefore, we have a magazine whose appeal is to the present day grassroots of the Protestant Ethic—and it advocates acceptance of the possibility of widespread unemployment. Descended as it is from that ethic, it looks at the situation in terms of the satisfactions of work rather than in terms of leisure, but that is in a sense a detail. More fundamentally and significantly, the article reflects recognition that the unemployed (as I shall call them) consist of increasing numbers of ordinary people—with as much right to a place in society as other ordinary people. To use the language of an earlier age: a readership which not long ago would have had scant time for sturdy beggars is in effect advised to adopt attitudes towards the workless which have far more in common with those found in the Middle Ages than at any time since.

Thus a host of items (all relevant to the concerns of the social psychologist), many of which are in themselves perhaps quite trivial, provides evidence of a process of change in the most basic assumptions of our present culture. The outcome of that change will be the acceptance of being unemployed as an essentially normal rather than deviant condition, like maternity or retirement rather than like poncing or recidivism. With this will come financial provision for the unemployed at levels comfortably above subsistence; and the acceptability of unemployment and the provisions for the unemployed will greatly reduce the significance and status attached to work. Before I explore the social psychological processes which underlie this transition, it is necessary to examine two alternative outcomes and give reasons for discounting them.

At first sight it could reasonably be argued that on the contrary we shall in fact evolve a two-tier society of the employed and of the unemployed; that the gap in living conditions between them will be as wide and as brutal as any in the long history of differences between rich and poor; that even so the employed will resent the contributions they will have to make to maintain the unemployed; that they will justify their resentment by continuing to attribute responsibility for his unemployment to the unemployed individual himself; and that they will thus be able to discount him by treating him as a deviant. It would be unwarranted and foolish to dismiss the possibility of this alternative, but I think it unlikely. Historically, the overtly unemployed have always been among the "lower orders" of society, the "higher orders" absorbing their jobless more or less unobtrusively by using their wealth to underwrite the pursuits and occupations of "gentlemen" (and sometimes "ladies"), or indeed by deliberately fostering a "leisure class" (Veblen, 1899/1953). Today there are still the disadvantaged poor (Rutter and Madge, 1976), and some of the well-to-do still support idle offspring.

Much more crucial in our time, however, is that broad middle range of workers, who as a class are essential to any industrial society but who as individuals have become vulnerable to structural unemployment through technological change; these include not only skilled workers and technologists but also managers and public servants, teachers and research workers. *Their* vulnerability to unemployment has brought the possibility of unemployment within the compass of almost everyone. In doing so it has made the development of a two-tier society much less likely: at the simplest level, too many people would have too many connections on both sides to allow persistent confrontation. More fundamentally, it will become morally and politically increasingly difficult to be "tough" with the unemployed. Their number will be too large, their range of backgrounds and occupations will be too wide, and they will be too representative of the normal population to be treated as deviant; nor will they feel themselves to be deviant, for that very reason. That alone will mean that on political (as well as economic) grounds, the subvention of the unemployed will have to enable them to lead essentially normal lives: "deviants" may often submit to being economically disadvantaged; a large body of often able people who regard themselves as "normal" is unlikely to do so. The unemployed will therefore have to be maintained at a level which is "comfortable"—not only by some absolute objective criteria but also in comparison with their employed fellows.

> It may well be that in the next 10, 15, or 20 years we will have a new philosophy towards unemployment. We may have to move away from the Protestant work ethic ... We have to pass on the benefits of increased productivity "reasonably equally" not just to the workforce but to the workforce that no longer work. (Mr. James Prior, M.P., then British Conservative Spokesman on Employment. Quoted in *The Guardian*, 22nd March, 1979.)

If this turns out to be the case, as I have argued it will, it will inevitably reduce the significance of work, at least in the sense of occupation or job; and the significance of work would similarly be reduced in conditions of widespread underemployment. In strictly quantitative terms, for a substantial proportion of ordinary people work will simply not take as large a slice of their lives; it will therefore not be so central to their self-concept as work is for most people today.

The counter-argument is that precisely because there will be less work, what work there is will be more significant. It is essential to avoid sentimentality: the nature of a vast array of jobs is sheer drudgery or dull routine, and often it is both. Moreover, since drudgery and routine are partly in the eye of the beholder, these attributes of work belong to many an executive and managerial job, not only to operating a machine or to labouring: the literature on man's alienation from work of every kind cannot all be fantasy (e.g. Anthony, 1977). For very many individuals, the significance of their work and the satisfaction they get from it do not stem from the nature of that work as a task but from its social and psychological concomitants. These aspects of work, and the social and psychological problems that arise from unemployment, will be the main issues for the last section. Very many people will be able to live quite happily without doing the tasks demanded by their work. So, in effect, work will not be economically essential; to be unemployed will not be socially deviant; the proportion of one's life spent on work will, for many people, be much reduced; and the nature of that work would not be missed by many. As a generalization, which may not apply to everyone but is likely to be valid for most, the significance of work is bound to decline.

C. THE SOCIAL PSYCHOLOGY OF UNEMPLOYMENT

I have so far discussed a number of symptoms and discussed in general terms their aetiology and likely future course. What we are seeing is a shifting of attitudes: for centuries the Protestant Ethic had led the unemployed to be rejected; structural unemployment is making them acceptable. If as social psychologists we had instituted systematic records of attitudes like those economists keep of wages and prices, I believe we would be able to trace this change systematically over time, in terms of shifts of latitudes of rejection and acceptance with respect to the unemployed (Sherif and Hovland, 1961). As it is, the looser evidence of the kind which I have cited must suffice. This then provides reasonable, if not conclusive grounds for asserting that a fundamental change of attitudes is taking place which constitutes a change in the social status of the unemployed: to be unemployed is ceasing to be automatically "deviant" and stigmatized, and is increasingly becoming compatible with being a "normal", respectable member of society, entitled to be treated as such. However, this is simply to describe happenings which can and will continue to be quite readily observed. The more long-term task of social psychology, is to go beyond the description of discrete observable particulars in order to trace and explain the processes which underlie and link them. To this end it is necessary to bring together several psychological theories which are not often found in each other's company—yet are most helpful to one another: adaptation level theory, self-perception theory, symbolic interactionism, reference group theory and attribution theory.

The shift from rejection to acceptance of the unemployed and the concomitant change in their status are basically an adaptation level phenomenon. Since about 1970 there has not only been a rise in the actual number of unemployed but also considerable attention has been drawn to unemployment by the mass media, by trade unionists, and by politicians. Furthermore, both in fact and in public discussion, unemployment is no longer predominantly associated with manual work but has become conceivable in all kinds of occupations. In other words, there has been an actual increase in the probability of encountering, or at least knowing of, someone like oneself who is or is about to become redundant. This, and the dissemination of news about unemployment can be assumed to have increased the subjective and perceived probabilities of unemployment for everybody, including for "someone like myself". Thus people have become adapted to the possibility of unemployment among "ordinary" people like themselves. In terms of self-perception theory (Bem, 1972), the higher the perceived or subjective probability of one's own potential unemployment, the greater should be the relevance and salience of the term "unemployed" as one of the potential labels for one's self-descriptions. From a symbolic interactionist standpoint (e.g. Hewitt, 1976), inasmuch as we define ourselves as others define us, the higher subjective probability of one's possible unemployment increases the sense that, one of these days perhaps, one is going to be seen as one of the unemployed; and it also increases the sense that at least some of those who are important to one, some of those most salient to one's self-definition, may themselves be, or become, unemployed. But of course, once one adapts to the possibility of unemployment so that to be unemployed is compatible with one's membership and reference groups, to be unemployed inevitably ceases to be deviant (and *pari passu* work loses some of its salience to one's self-definition). Note, finally, a link between, on the one hand, subjective probabilities and adaptation level processes and, on the other hand, attribution processes. From the standpoint of an observer (and often also from that of the affected individual), when the perceived probability of unemployment is low, responsibility for it will tend to be attributed to the individual (locus of control will be perceived to be internal); as the perceived probability of unemployment increases, so responsibility for it will tend to be attributed to the situation (locus of control will be perceived to be external). What is happening in our time is precisely such a shifting of the attribution of responsibility for being unemployed from the internal personal level to the external situational level. As I suggested at the beginning, this is not so much a cause as a manifestation of the end of the Protestant Ethic. The term "structural" in connection with unemployment is not only descriptive but itself also symptomatic: our culture is in a period of profound transition during which its most basic assumptions of several centuries are being modified to the point of losing their validity, and alternatives have yet to emerge.

D. THE PSYCHOLOGICAL LIMITATIONS OF LEISURE

The art of science is to identify unforeseen consequences in foreseeable events. The probable outcome which I have presented so far, which is foreseeable without undue difficulty, may be summarized thus: there may be intermittent tensions concerning "scroungers", "drop-outs", or whatever might be the fashionable words for "idle rogues", but the shift towards the acceptance of the unemployed will continue. In practice this will mean that they will be maintained financially at levels which are "comfortable", they will not be seriously disadvantaged materially, and they will not feel themselves to be deviant socially. This in turn will gradually but inexorably reduce the significance of work. The longer term consequences will, of course, be so numerous and complex that no one individual could have the knowledge and skill to describe them. I shall therefore conclude by confining myself to examining only one problem, which in principle falls within the competence of social psychologists and which warrants more systematic research than has been devoted to it so far. To what extent can activities of leisure replace the psychological needs currently met by work—even if in many respects one does not like one's work?

The central issue is poignantly expressed in two quotations, one from an unemployed man, the other from a man facing retirement:

> The next time you see a *lot of fellows* standing and watching *a gang* laying a pavement or putting up a house, just ask yourself how much fun it is to stand and watch other men at work. (Bakke, 1933, p. 64; my italics.)

> I'll miss my friends out there; and mostly I'll miss just not working. Every time I look at the clock I'll think: I should be just starting work, or finishing, or doing this or that ... Even on vacation now ... I get tired just sitting around. (Friedmann and Havighurst, 1954, p. 29.)

Similar reactions to being out of work can be found in any study of people without jobs (e.g. Jahoda *et al.*, 1933/1972; Marsden and Duff, 1975; Millham, 1978). They reflect a sense of loss and of two profound needs arising from it. First there is the need not to feel an isolated individual among just an unstructured "lot of fellows", but to belong to a group, a "gang", whose relationships are meaningfully structured by their work. It is the *social structure* created in performing the task, not the task itself (say, shovelling sand) which is the crucial and envied aspect of being at work. Psychologically, what is lost in losing one's job or retiring, is not the job itself but the sense of belonging to a group whose members are for some purposes interdependent and committed to one another, even if they do not particularly like each other, or their job. Belonging to a working group simply provides a structure for a significant proportion of one's social life. Secondly, having to turn up for work, and so the doing of it, effectively structures both our time and our activities; and within quite broad limits it is not critical psychologically just how strictly one keeps to time and to the order of activities. A job provides structure *psychologically* inasmuch as it specifies what *should* be the case, which then acts as a framework for evaluating what *is* the case.

Foreseeing an age of widespread unemployment or at least underemployment, many social scientists have looked to leisure activities as the alternative to work. Very typical of this approach are Weiss and Riesman: "It is a political and economic problem to ensure that leisure be the consequence of technological developments, and not simply unemployment." (Weiss and Riesman, 1963, p. 168.) Psychologically, however, the problem is that leisure is not just an alternative to work but rather its opposite. Perhaps because for the vast majority of people work is a necessity, they regard it as a fact of life and as real. To work is therefore to live in the real world; in contrast the pursuits of leisure, which are part of one's private life, often constitute a private world, sometimes even a fantasy world. This is not only a distinction made by ordinary folk: it permeates the foundations of professional psychology. There is the reality principle, the mode of behaviour of stable and mature people, who show that they are stable and mature not least by their ability to hold a job. There is socialization, whereby the individual learns to fit into his society: a central aspect of this is the acquisition of so-called sound work-habits, the teaching of which is one of the basic aims of education. In rehabilitation many a therapist may indeed be most pleased when his patient takes a more active part in social or leisure activities—but the criterion of being fully rehabilitated is the return to work. For psychologists as well as for ordinary people, the whole man is the working man; not just the busy person, who could be a patient, or a child, or even, for some, just a jobless housewife—but someone who is "out there in the real world holding down a job". *Overtly* we may, as psychologists, often seem particularly concerned with the problems which arise for the satisfaction of the individual's personal internal needs; *fundamentally* we attach much greater significance to his ability to cope with the demands of external reality. Maturity, stability, social and psychological soundness—all attributes which are central to the social psychological status of an individual, not least in his own eyes—are defined in terms of the capacity to meet such external demands: and singly the outstanding and most influential criterion of the ability to cope with life is the ability to cope with work.

This special social and psychological significance which is attached to work as the test which defines the mature and sound individual is, of course, itself to some extent a product of the Protestant Ethic. Consequently, if this ethic is losing its influence as a basic assumption of our society and, more crucially, if I am broadly correct in saying that the unemployed will cease to be regarded as deviant but will be equitably provided for, then that will indeed soften the distinction which we now make between leisure and work. However, although the decline of the Protestant Ethic may soften the distinction, much of it will remain, since its roots are very much deeper. Basically, leisure activities allow for the expression and development of *individual* interests and potential, but they are only rarely able to replace the *social* psychological structure and function of work-role relationships. In contrast to most work, many leisure activities do not involve any social contact at all; some may provide for informal social relations, in parallel, at the level of an associated club; only a very few depend on, and therefore create, interdependence in the activity itself, with the commitment which this entails to The Team or The Group. Examination of leisure activities shows that they are combinations of four basic characteristics in a 2×2 matrix: independent activities, such as reading; interdependent activities, like tennis or acting; self-contained activities, which can be begun and finished satisfyingly in any one session; and committed activities, which of their essence extend in time (Kelvin, 1979). The matrix (with typical examples) looks like this:

	Self-Contained	Committed
Independent	Reading Painting	Gardening Astronomy
Interdependent	Tennis Chess	Team sports Amateur acting Voluntary work

There are of course problem cases which do not fit neatly: the chess team, the gardening co-operative, the once-a-year football team or jumble sale. Nevertheless, the matrix provides a useful framework for an analytic classification of leisure activities from a social psychological standpoint and elicits that it is only in one cell of the matrix that we find activities which demand approximately the social psychological condition of a structure of work–role relationships, namely the committed interdependent set. On inspection, these activities seem to appeal to relatively few people, and this raises the central issue of the importance of *appeal*: it is of the essence of leisure activities that they are freely chosen—because they appeal and only for as long as they appeal. It is because of this that no leisure activities, not even the committed interdependent ones, carry quite that crucial conviction of being real which is associated with being in a job and doing something as a job, day after day because, as it were, "that's how things are". There always remains with respect to leisure activities that subtle but critical distinction between the amateur or volunteer and the professional, whereby even the same task may be leisure for one individual and work for another. The difference on which that distinction is based is, in the final analysis, that between filling one's leisure as one wants to and fulfilling one's work role as one has to, and the further feeling that the world and life have structure, comes precisely from the sense of having to meet demands other than just one's own.

The practical problem, therefore, is to try to identify possible sources of structure under industrial conditions in which the demand for labour is relatively low. The first and very important point to note here is that while the demand for labour may become much lower than it has been for most of the last two hundred years, for the foreseeable future it will only be *relatively* lower. Given that our adaptation level is to around $6 \pm 2\%$ of unemployment, the possibility of 25% conjures up the vision of the vast number of unemployed, at the cost of forgetting that 75% of the workforce will still be at work, and will have to be there, if society is to function. The most immediate problems which will arise will not be manifestly psychological but, in the first instance, political and economic. The putative 25% level of unemployment would create the demand and the political force for the "comfortable" basic financial support for the unemployed which I suggested earlier. This would then make many a worker wonder why he or she should bother to stay at work. The "rational" approach, which for a very long time ahead could avoid most of the social and psychological problems of unemployment, would be work sharing: we would then not talk in terms of unemployment at 25% or 7 million jobless, but in terms of a 25% drop in the demand for labour to be somehow distributed across the workforce as a whole. However, there are limits to the interchangeability of skills and the mobility of people, and there is likely to be quite widespread resistance to sharing by those at work on grounds of a perceived threat to their earnings. Industrial management is also likely to resist a large workforce, partly because of the problems of the distribution of shared working and partly, at least in the United Kingdom, because of the considerable capitation costs imposed by traditional government policies. However, the brutal fact is that a reduction in the demand for labour has to be paid for, whether through taxation to maintain the full-time unemployed, or through sharing the substantial amount of work which will remain to be done for a very long time. Looked at quite coolly, once productivity ceases to be directly related to human effort the problems of production will increasingly give way to problems of distributing its benefits; from that perspective, taxation and work sharing are largely alternative methods for distributing income as the demand for labour declines.

From a social psychological standpoint, however, there could scarcely be a more profound difference between a response to structural unemployment which takes the form of taxation and one which takes the form of work sharing. Taxation easily becomes a disincentive and a source of resentment, and except for taxes to discourage "bad habits", I cannot think of any psychologically positive function of taxation. Work sharing may also initially cause resentment, and it would be unrealistic and foolish to underrate this. Potentially, however, it offers three very important social psychological advantages. First, it keeps the largest possible number of individuals at work and thereby gives them both the benefits of structure to their lives and the flexibility of more time to pursue their leisure. Secondly, it provides a means for distributing income which can quite easily be seen to be reasonably equitable. Thirdly, it will therefore reduce potential resentment, particularly during a transition period, over apparent arbitrariness about who gets work and who gets what for not working.

I distinguished earlier between two main classes of problems within social psychology: those concerned with basic or "universal" processes, such as attitude change or the construction of social reality, and those which arise as social psychological aspects of the particular issues of a given culture over a certain period of its history. We shall probably study basic processes in 2001 much as we do now, unless some revolutionary technological or conceptual breakthrough utterly transforms the discipline. To attempt to foretell *how* we shall do our work twenty-odd years from now cannot be better than crystal-gazing, but I think we can reasonably anticipate *what* will concern us, at least within the domain of problems which are of an historical nature.

What we therefore most need as social psychologists is to *think* and *plan ahead* very much more than we have done traditionally, and to do so we need to initiate records. The high probability of widespread and lasting structural unemployment is precisely the kind of problem which needs that long-term approach if, as social psychologists, we are to make a practical contribution to society. We should, for example, *now* begin to collect systematic records on the concepts of, say, work, unemployment, work sharing, leisure, and of attitudes towards them, so that we can trace changes over time as unemployment rises (and falls) or as information about various forms of work sharing is disseminated. Although the practical problems of work sharing would be formidable and may indeed be insurmountable because of the co-operation which would be involved, *in principle* systematic empirical work should be undertaken to study the effects of different patterns of shared working, not least on family and social life. I have cited important advantages of work sharing over taxation, and these might lead governments to impose work sharing as, after all, they impose taxes; but research might show that, at this point in time, people are more ready to accept the imposition of higher taxes than of fellow workers. The reader may continue with his or her own list. My point is simply this: most of the significant *practical* problems of a society, such as those of structural unemployment for us now, have their basis in history and take their course over historical periods of time; if, as social psychologists, we wish to make constructive contributions to the handling of such problems, rather than just to apply at best first aid to the wounds they inflict, we have to learn to take an historical perspective—backwards and forwards. To this end we need to devise, collect and keep our records. That is a contribution which *we*, in 1980, can begin to make to coping with structural unemployment and to the work of social psychology 2001.

ACKNOWLEDGEMENT

Some of the work reported in this chapter forms part of a larger research project supported by a grant (HR 6182) from the Social Science Research Council.

Endpiece: Valedictory for a Young Social Psychology

ROBIN GILMOUR

When the original plan for this book was drawn up, the contents list started with "Causes for pessimism" and ended with an "Obituary for a young social psychologist". As one of the contributors pointed out, this was a somewhat contradictory presentation of material for a book intended to be a positive and constructive contribution to the subject—unless it was to be construed as the expression of a covert death-wish. Were we, in fact, so thoroughly infected by some of the various strains of pessimism periodically epidemic through social psychology that our intentions in producing the book were to be sabotaged from the outset?

That query certainly gave us, as they say, to think. One immediate outcome was the reorganization of the volume contents, not to effect a kind of cosmetic surgery but to reflect what was on consideration a renewed determination to produce that "positive and constructive contribution", coupled with an even stronger belief that such a contribution was actually possible.

The more long-term outcome was to make us as social psychologists think rather more carefully about the positive elements in our development and to focus us even more sharply and critically on them. As editors, too, there was a marked effect in that we became more sensitized to that aspect (among others) of the chapters as they came in. The results, in the event, were most satisfactory: the various authors separately and together, do demonstrate that positive and constructive contributions to the development of social psychology are realistically possible and proceed to provide cogent analyses of the nature and location of such contributions.

That we found producing this volume such a stimulating and

encouraging task reflects not merely our commitment to it and the ability and enthusiasm of our contributors (though these are also significant), it also reflects very positively on the subject. The variety and quality of the different contributions should impart a strong sense of the positive value of the discipline that produced them—even when they are critical of that discipline. It is heartening when social psychologists can take such effective evaluative stock of their past and present activities, can be more self-aware in terms of process as well as product, and can build on that to enhance the development of their subject.

It is perhaps not too fanciful to hope that the reader finds the experience of reading this book to act as a kind of reaffirmation of faith in the value and importance of social psychological endeavour. This could then be considered to be one significant kind of justification in presenting this book.

Social psychology has often been described as a young science, and at best the term has been used in an exculpatory way. When that happens it makes one wonder when the subject is going to grow up. The answer we would like to give, and would like this book to be seen as giving to that question, is "now". We believe that in the present volume the contributors have provided more than adequate justification for taking such a position. To pursue the growth metaphor, it might perhaps be useful to view recent upheavals and crises as the later symptoms of adolescence (for instance, as has been suggested, as crises of identity) which signal approaching adulthood. The abilities which we trust are now amply demonstrated in this volume, to take stock, to learn from past experience, to be self-monitoring, and to plan meaningfully ahead, are all indicative of maturity. If this analysis holds true, we can properly claim that social psychology has come of age and the next decades promise to be exciting ones.

References

Abelson, R. P., Aronson, E., McGuire, W. J., Newcomb, T. M., Rosenberg, M. J. and Tannenbaum, P. H. (eds.) (1968). *Theories of Cognitive Consistency*. Rand-McNally: Chicago.
Adams, J. S. and Jacobson, P. R. (1964). Effects of Wage Inequities on work quality. *Journal of Abnormal and Social Psychology*, **69**, 19–25.
Aderman, D. (1969). Effects of anticipating future interaction on the preference for balanced states. *Journal of Personality and Social Psychology*, **11**, 214–219.
Adorno, T. W., Frenkel-Brunswick, E., Levinson, D. J. and Sanford, R. N. (1950). *The Authoritarian Personality*. Harper and Row: New York.
Ajzen, I. (1977). Intuitive theories of events and the effects of base rate information on prediction. *Journal of Personality and Social Psychology*, **35**, 303–314.
Ajzen, I. and Fishbein, M. (1975). Bayesian analysis of attribution processes. *Psychology Bulletin*, **82**, 261–277.
Akutagawa, R. (1952). *Rashomon and other stories*. Liverright: New York.
Albert, H. (1975). *Traktat über die kritische Vernunft*. Mohr and Siebeck: Tübingen.
Alexander, N. and Knight, L. (1971). Situated identities and social psychological experimentation. *Sociometry*, **34**, 65–82.
Allport, G. W. (1937). *Personality: a Psychological Interpretation*. Holt, Rinehart and Winston: New York.
Allport, G. W. (1961). *Pattern and Growth in Personality*. Holt, Rinehart and Winston: New York.
Allport, G. W. and Postman, L. (1947). *The Psychology of Rumor*. Holt: New York.
Anderson, N. H. (1976). Equity judgements as information integration. *Journal of Personality and Social Psychology*, **33**, 291–299.
Andrews, F. M. and Withey, S. B. (1976). *Social Indicators of Well-being*. Plenum Press: New York.
Andreyeva, G. M., Bogomolova, N. N. and Petrovskaya, L. A. (1978). (Russian Text about Western social psychology.) Moscow State University Press: Moscow.
Antaki, C. and Fielding, G. (in press). Research on ordinary explanations. In: Antaki, C. (ed.). *The Psychology of Ordinary Explanations of Social Behaviour*. Academic Press: London and New York.
Anthony, P. D. (1977). *The Ideology of Work*. Tavistock: London.

Apel, K. O. (1967). *Analytic Philosophy of Language and the 'Geisteswissen Schaften'*. D. Reidel: Dordrecht, Holland.

Apfelbaum, E. and Lubek, I. (1976). Resolution versus Revolution? The theory of conflicts in question. In: Strickland, L. H., Aboud, F. E. and Gergen, K. J. (eds). *Social Psychology in Transition*. Plenum: New York.

Arendt, H. (1958). *The Human Condition*. University of Chicago Press: Chicago.

Argyle, M. (1964). *Psychology and Social Problems*. Methuen: London.

Argyle, M. (1972). *The Social Psychology of Work*. The Penguin Press: London.

Argyle, M. (1975). *Bodily Communication*. Methuen: London.

Argyle, M. (1976). Personality and social behaviour. In: Harré, R. (ed.). *Personality*. Blackwell: Oxford.

Argyle, M. (1978). *The Psychology of Interpersonal Behaviour*. Penguin Books: Harmondsworth.

Argyle, M. (1979). Social behaviour as a function of situations. In: Ginsburg, G. P. (ed.). *Emerging Strategies in Social Psychological Research*. Wiley: London.

Argyle, M., Furnham, A. and Graham, J. A. (in press). *Social Situations*. Cambridge University Press: Cambridge.

Argyle, M., Gardner, G. and Cioffi, F. (1958). Supervisory methods related to productivity, absenteeism and labour turnover. *Human Relations*, **11**, 23–45.

Argyle, M. and McHenry, R. (1970). Do spectacles really increase judgements of intelligence? *British Journal of Social and Clinical Psychology*, **10**, 27–29.

Armistead, N. (1974). *Reconstructing Social Psychology*. Penguin Books: Harmondsworth.

Aronson, E. (1966). The psychology of insufficient justification: An analysis of some conflicting data. In: Felman, S. (ed.). *Cognitive Consistency*. Academic Press: New York and London.

Aronson, E. (1972). *The Social Animal*. W. H. Freeman: San Francisco.

Aronson, E., Blaney, N., Stephan, C., Sikes, J. and Snapp, M. (1978). *The Jigsaw Classroom*. Sage Publications: Beverley Hills, Calif.

Aronson, E. and Carlsmith, J. M. (1963). Effect of severity of threat on the valuation of forbidden behaviour. *Journal of Abnormal and Social Psychology*, **66**, 584–588.

Atkinson, J. W. (1964). *An Introduction to Motivation*. Van Nostrand: Princeton, N.J.

Backman, C. W. (1976). Symbolic interactionism: some reinforcement from psychology. Paper presented at the annual meetings of the Pacific Sociological Association, San Diego, Calif.

Backman, C. W. (1979a). Epilogue: A New Paradigm. In: Ginsburg, G. P. (ed.). *Emerging Strategies in Social Psychological Research*. Wiley: London.

Backman, C. W. (1979b). Social Norms. In: *Encyclopedia of Psychology in the 20th Century*. Kendler Verlag: Zurich.

Backman, C. W. (1980). Promises unfulfilled: on the premature abandonment of promising research. In: Gilmour, R. and Duck, S. W. (eds). *The Development of Social Psychology*. Academic Press: London.

Bakke, E. W. (1933). *The Unemployed Man: a social study*. Nisbet: London.

Bandura, A. (1973). *Aggression: A social learning analysis*. Prentice Hall: Englewood Cliffs, N.J.
Bandura, A. (1977). *A Social Learning Theory*. Prentice Hall: Englewood Cliffs, N.J.
Bandura, A. and Walters, R. H. (1963). *Social Learning and Personality Development*. Holt, Rinehart and Winston: New York.
Barber, B. (1968). The functions and dysfunctions of 'fashion' in science: A case for the study of social change. *Mens en Maatschappij*, **43**, 501–514.
Barlow, N. (ed.) (1958). *The Autobiography of Charles Darwin 1809–1882*. Collins: London.
Baum, A. and Epstein, Y. M. (eds) (1978). *Human Response to Crowding*. Erlbaum: Hillsdale, N.J.
Beaman, A. L., Barnes, P. J., Klentz, B. and McQuirk, B. (1978). Increasing helping rates through information dissemination: Teaching pays. *Personality and Social Psychology Bulletin*, **4**, 406–411.
Becker, H. S. (1963). *Outsiders: Studies in the Sociology of deviance*. Free Press: New York.
Bem, D. J. (1964). An experimental analysis of beliefs and attitudes. Doctoral dissertation, University of Michigan: Ann Arbor, Michigan.
Bem, D. J. (1965). An experimental analysis of self persuasion. *Journal of Experimental Social Psychology*, **1**, 199–218.
Bem, D. J. (1972). Self-perception theory. In: Berkowitz, L. (ed.). *Advances in Experimental Social Psychology*, Volume 6. Academic Press: London and New York.
Bem, D. J. and Funder, D. C. (1978). Predicting more of the people more of the time: assessing the personality of situations. *Psychological Review*, **85**, 485–501.
Bem, D. J. and McConnell, H. K. (1970). Testing the self-perception explanation of dissonance phenomena: On the salience of premanipulation attitudes. *Journal of Personality and Social Psychology*, **14**, 23–31.
Berger, B. M. (1960). How long is a generation? *British Journal of Sociology*, **11**, 10–23.
Berkowitz, L. (1962). *Aggression: A social psychological analysis*. McGraw-Hill: New York.
Berkowitz, L. and Walster, E. (eds) (1976). *Advances in Experimental Social Psychology*, Volume 9. *Equity Theory: Toward a General Theory of Social Interaction*. Academic Press: New York and London.
Berlyne, D. E. (1969). Laughter, humor and play. In: Lindzey, G. and Aronson, E. (eds). *Handbook of Social Psychology*, Volume 3. Addison-Wesley: Reading, Mass.
Bernstein, R. J. (1978). *The Restructuring of Social and Political Theory*. University of Pennsylvania Press: Philadelphia.
Berscheid, E. and Walster, E. (1974). A little bit about love. In: Huston, T. L. (ed.). *Foundations of Interpersonal Attraction*. Academic Press: New York and London.
Berscheid, E. and Walster, E. H. (1978). *Interpersonal Attraction* (2nd Ed.). Addison-Wesley: Reading, Mass.

Bettelheim, B. and Janowitz, M. (1964). *Social Change and Prejudice*. Free Press: New York.
Bickman, L. and Henchy, T. (eds) (1972). *Beyond the Laboratory: Field Research in Social Psychology*. McGraw-Hill: New York.
Birnbaum, N. (1971). *Toward a Critical Sociology*. Oxford Press: New York.
Blake, R. R. and Mouton, J. S. (1965). A 9.9 approach for increasing organizational productivity. In: Schein, E. H. and Bennis, W. G. (eds). *Personal and Organizational Changes through Group Methods*. Wiley: New York.
Blank, T. O. (1978). Two social psychologies: is segregation inevitable or acceptable? *Personality and Social Psychology Bulletin*, **4**, 553–556.
Blumstein, P. W. (1973). Audience machiavellianism, and tactics of identity bargaining. *Sociometry*, **36**, 348–365.
Bonoma, T. V. (1977). Business decision making: Marketing implications. In: Kaplan, M. F. and Schwartz, S. (eds). *Human Judgement and Decision Processes in Applied Settings*. Academic Press: New York and London.
Brehm, J. W. (1956). Postdecision changes in the desirability of alternatives. *Journal of Abnormal and Social Psychology*, **52**, 384–389.
Brehm, J. W. and Cohen, A. R. (1962). *Explorations in Cognitive Dissonance*. Wiley: New York.
Brehm, J. W. and Wicklund, R. (1976). *Perspectives on Cognitive Dissonance*. Erlbaum: Hillsdale, N.J.
Brenner, M. (1978). Doctoral Dissertation, University of Oxford.
Brenner, M., Marsh, P. and Brenner, M. (1978). *The Social Contexts of Methods*. Croom-Helm: London.
Brickman, P. (1978). Is it real? In: Harvey, J. H., Ickes, W. J. and Kidd, R. F. (eds). *New Directions in Attribution Research*, Volume 2. Erlbaum: Hillsdale, N.J.
Brickman, P., Coates, D. and Janoff-Bulman, R. (1978). Lottery winners and accident victims: Is happiness relative? *Journal of Personality and Social Psychology*, **36**, 917–927.
Briskman, L. B. (1972). Is a Kuhnian analysis applicable to psychology? *Science Studies*, **2**, 87–97.
Broadbent, D. E. (1971). *Decision and Stress*. Academic Press: London and New York.
Brock, T. C. and Balloun, J. L. (1967). Behavioral receptivity to dissonant information. *Journal of Personality and Social Psychology*, **6**, 413–428.
Brown, G. A. (1975). Microteaching: research and developments. In: Chanan, G. and Delamont, S. (eds). *Frontiers of Class-room Research*. N.F.E.R.: Slough.
Brown, J. M., Berrien, F. K. and Russell, D. L. (1966). *Applied Psychology*. Collier MacMillan: London.
Brown, R. (1965). *Social Psychology*. Free Press: New York.
Brown, R. (1978). Work. In: Abrams, P. (ed.). *Work, urbanism and inequality in U.K. society today*. Weidenfeld and Nicolson: London.
Bruner, J. S. (1975). The Ontogenesis of Speech Acts. *Journal of Child languages*, **2**, 1–19.
Bruner, J. (1978). Address to Social Psychology Workshop, Oxford University.

Burke, K. (1945). *A Grammar of Motives*. Prentice-Hall: New York.
Burnstein, E. (1969). An analysis of group decision involving risk. *Human Relations*, **22**, 381-395.
Burnstein, E. and Vinokur, A. (1977). Persuasive argumentation and social comparison as determinants of attitude polarization. *Journal of Experimental and Social Psychology*, **13**, 315-332.
Buss, A. R. (1974). Psychology's future development as predicted from generation theory. *Human Development*, **17**, 433-459.
Buss, A. R. (1975). The emerging field of the sociology of psychological knowledge. *American Psychologist*, **30**, 988-1002.
Buss, A. R. (1979). *Psychology in Social Context*. Irvington Press: New York.
Butler, D. E. and Rose, R. (1960). *The British General Election of 1959*. Mac-Millan: London.
Byrne, D., Ervin, C. R. and Lamberth, J. (1970). Continuity between the experimental study of attraction and real-life computer dating. *Journal of Personality and Social Psychology*, **16**, 157-165.
Byrne, D. and Lamberth, J. (1971). Cognitive and reinforcement theories as complementary approaches to the study of attraction. In: Murstein, B. I. (ed.). *Theories of Attraction and Love*. Springer: New York.
Byrne, D., Nelson, D. and Reeves, K. (1966). The effects of consensual validation and invalidation on attraction as a function of verifiability. *Journal of Experimental Social Psychology*, **2**, 98-107.
Campbell, D. T. (1963). Social attitudes and other acquired behavioural dispositions. In: Koch, S. (ed.). *Psychology: A Study of a Science*, Volume 6. McGraw-Hill: New York.
Campbell, D. T. (1969). Reforms as experiments. *American Psychologist*, **24**, 409-429.
Campbell, D. T. (1970). Natural selection as an epistemological model. In: Naroll, R. and Cohen, R. (eds). *A Handbook of Method in Cultural Anthropology*. Natural History Press: Garden City, New York.
Campbell, D. T. (1973). Natural selection as an epistemological model. In: Naroll, R. and Cohen, R. (eds). *Handbook of Method in Cultural Anthropology*. Columbia University Press: London.
Campbell, D. T. (1975). On the conflicts between biological and social evolution and between psychology and moral tradition. *American Psychologist*, **30**, 1103-1126.
Campbell, D. T. and Stanley, J. C. (1963). *Experimental and Quasi-Experimental Designs for Research*. Rand-McNally: Chicago.
Campbell, D. T. and Stanley, J. C. (1968). Experimental and quasi-experimental designs for research on teaching. In: Gage, N. L. (ed.). *Handbook of Research on Teaching*. Rand-McNally: Chicago.
Canter, D., Breaux, J. and Sime, M. (in press). *Human Behaviour in Fires*. Building Research Establishment, Current paper.
Carlsmith, J. M., Collins, B. E. and Helmreich, R. L. (1966). Studies in forced compliance: I. The effect of pressure for compliance on attitude change

produced by face-to-face role playing and anonymous essay writing. *Journal of Personality and Social Psychology*, **4**, 1–13.

Carnegie, D. (1936). *How to Win Friends and Influence People*. Simon and Schuster: New York.

Cartwright, D. (1973). Determinants of scientific progress: The case of research on the risky shift. *American Psychologist*, **28**, 222–231.

Cartwright, D. (1978). Theory and practice. *Journal of Social Issues*, **34**, 168–180.

Cartwright, D. (1979). Contemporary social psychology in historical perspective. *Social Psychology Quarterly*, **42**, 82–93.

Child, I. L. (1973). *Humanistic Psychology and the Research Tradition*. Wiley: New York.

Cicourel, A. V. (1968). *The Social Organization of Juvenile Justice*. Wiley: New York.

Clarke, D. (1975). The use and recognition of sequential structure in dialogue. *British Journal of Social and Clinical Psychology*, **14**, 333–339.

Clarke, D. (1979). The Linguistic Analogy, or When is a Speech Act Like a Morpheme? In: Ginsburg, G. P. (ed.). *Emerging Strategies in Social Psychological Research*. Wiley: London.

Clegg, C. W., Jackson, P. R. and Watt, T. D. (1977). The potential of cross-lagged correlation analysis in field research. *Journal of Occupational Psychology*, **50**, 177–196.

Clore, G. L. and Byrne, D. (1974). A reinforcement-affect model of attraction. In: Huston, T. L. (ed.). *Foundations of Interpersonal Attraction*. Academic Press: New York and London.

Coch, L. and French, J. R. P. (1948). Overcoming resistance to change. *Human Relations*, **11**, 41–53.

Cohen, T. (1978). Metaphor and the cultivation of intimacy. *Critical Inquiry*, **5**, 3–12.

Coleman, J. S., Katz, E. and Menzel, H. (1957). The diffusion of an innovation among physicians. *Sociometry*, **20**, 253–270.

Cook, S. W. (1970). Motives in a conceptual analysis of attitude-related behavior. In: Arnold, W. J. and Levine, D. (eds). *Nebraska Symposium on Motivation*. University of Nebraska Press: Lincoln.

Cook, T. D. and Campbell, D. T. (1976). The design and conduct of quasi-experiments and true experiments in field settings. In: Dunnette, M. D. (ed.). *Handbook of Industrial and Organizational Research*. Rand-McNally: New York.

Cooper, J., Zanna, M. P. and Taves, P. A. (1978). Arousal as a necessary condition for attitude change following induced compliance. *Journal of Personality and Social Psychology*, **36**, 1101–1106.

Crane, D. (1969). Fashion in science: Does it exist? *Social Problems*, **16**, 433–440.

Cronbach, L. J. (1975). Beyond the two disciplines of scientific psychology. *American Psychologist*, **30**, 116–127.

Crowne, D. P. and Marlowe, D. (1964). *The Approval Motive*. Wiley: New York.

Danziger, K. (1971). *Socialization*. Penguin: Harmondsworth.
Darley, J. M. and Latané, B. (1968). Bystander intervention in emergencies: Diffusion of responsibility. *Journal of Personality and Social Psychology*, **8**, 379-383.
Darley, J. M. and Latané, B. (1970). Norms and normative behavior: Field studies of social interdependence. In: Macaulay, J. and Berkowitz, L. (eds). *Altruism and Helping Behavior*. Academic Press: New York and London.
Darwin, C. (1859). *The Origin of Species*. J. Murray: London.
Darwin, C. (1871). *The Descent of Man*. J. Murray: London.
Darwin, C. (1872). *The Expression of the Emotions in Man and Animals*. D. Appleton and Co.: London. Reprinted, 1965, by the University of Chicago Press (page references in the text are to this edition).
Dashiell, J. F. (1935). Experimental studies of the influence of social situations on the behavior of individual human adults. In: Murchison, C. (ed.). *Handbook of Social Psychology*. Clark University Press: Worcester, Mass.
Davis, J. H. (1973). Group decision and social interaction. *Psychological Review*, **80**, 98-125.
Dawkins, R. (1976). *The selfish gene*. Oxford University Press: Oxford.
Deutsch, M. and Hornstein, H. A. (1975). *Applying Social Psychology*. Erlbaum: Hillsdale, N.J.
Diamond, S. S. and Morton, D. R. (1978). Empirical landmarks in social psychology. *Personality and Social Psychology Bulletin*, **4**, 217-222.
Do-It-Yourself: The Home Improvement Magazine. October, 1978.
Dollard, J., Doob, L. W., Miller, N. E. and Sears, R. R. (1939). *Frustration and Aggression*. Yale University Press: New Haven.
Dollard, J. and Miller, N. E. (1950). *Personality and Psychotherapy*. McGraw-Hill: New York.
Doob, A. N. and Macdonald, G. E. (in press). Television viewing and fear of victimisation: Is the relationship causal? *Journal of Personality and Social Psychology*.
Doob, L. W. (1947). Behavior of attitudes. *Psychological Review*, **54**, 135-156.
Dorris, J. W. (1972). Reactions to unconditioned cooperation: A field study emphasizing variables neglected in laboratory research. *Journal of Personality and Social Psychology*, **22**, 387-397.
Dreyer, A. (1953). Behaviour in a Level of Aspiration situations as affected by group comparison. Ph.D. Thesis, University of Minnesota.
Duck, S. W. (1973). *Personal Relationships and Personal Constructs: a study of friendship formation*. Wiley: London.
Duck, S. W. (1977). *The Study of Acquaintance*. Teakfield (Saxon House): London.
Duck, S. W. and Craig, R. G. (1978). Personality similarity and the development of friendship: a longitudinal study, *British Journal of Social and Clinical Psychology*, **17**, 237-242.
Dutton, D. G. and Aron, A. (1974). Some evidence for heightened sexual attraction under conditions of high anxiety. *Journal of Personality and Social Psychology*, **30**, 510-517.

Duval, S. and Wicklund, R. A. (1972). *A Theory of Objective Self Awareness.* Academic Press: New York and London.

Eibl-Eibesfeldt, I. (1973). *Der Vorprogrammierte Mensch.* Molden: Vienna.

Eiser, J. R. (1980). Prolegomena to a more applied social psychology: towards a critical pragmatism. In: Gilmour, R. and Duck, S. W. (eds). *The Development of Social Psychology.* Academic Press: London and New York.

Eiser, J. R. and Stroebe, W. (1972). *Categorization and Social Judgement.* Academic Press: London and New York.

Ekman, P. (1974). *Darwin and Facial Expression.* Academic Press: New York and London.

Elms, A. C. (1975). The crisis of confidence in social psychology. *American Psychologist*, **30**, 967–976.

Emmet, D. (1966). *Rules, Roles and Relations.* Beacon Press: Boston.

Endler, N. S. and Magnusson, D. (1976). *Interactional Psychology and Personality.* Hemisphere: Washington.

Erdelyi, M. H. (1974). A new look at the new look: Perceptual defense and vigilance. *Psychological Review*, **81**, 1–25.

Erikson, E. H. (1963). "Eight stages of man" Chapter 7 in *Childhood and Society.* (2nd Ed.). Norton: New York.

Erikson, E. H. (1968). *Identity, Youth and Crisis.* W. W. Norton: New York.

Fairweather, G. W. *et al.* (1969). *Community Life for the Mentally Ill.* Aldine: Chicago.

Farina, A., Allen, J. G. and Saul, B. B. B. (1968). The role of the stigmatised person in affecting social relationships. *Journal of Personality*, **36**, 169–182.

Farr, R. M. (1978). On the varieties of social psychology: An essay on the relationships between psychology and other social sciences. *Social Science Information*, **17**, 503–525.

Farr, R. M. (1980a). Homo socio-psychologicus. In: Chapman, A. and Jones, D. (eds). *Models of Man.* British Psychological Society: Leicester.

Farr, R. M. (1980b). Homo loquens in social psychological perspective. In: Giles, H., Robinson, P. and Smith, P. (eds). *Social Psychology and Language.* Pergamon Press: London.

Fast, J. (1970). *Body Language.* Pocket Books: New York.

Fay, B. (1976). *Social Theory and Political Practice.* Holmes and Meier: New York.

Festinger, L. (1950). Informal social communication. *Psychological Review*, **57**, 271–182.

Festinger, L. (1954). A theory of social comparison processes. *Human Relations*, **7**, 117–140.

Festinger, L. (1957). *A Theory of Cognitive Dissonance.* University Press: Stanford.

Festinger, L. and Carlsmith, J. M. (1959). Cognitive consequences of forced compliance. *Journal of Abnormal and Social Psychology*, **59**, 203–210.

Festinger, L., Gerard, H., *et al.* (1952). The influence process in the presence of extreme deviates. *Human Relations*, **5**, 327–346.

Festinger, L., Riecken, H. W. and Schachter, S. (1956). *When Prophecy Fails:*

A social and psychological study of a modern group that predicted the destruction of the world. University of Minnesota: Minneapolis.

Festinger, L., Schachter, S. and Back, K. (1950). *Social Pressures in Informal Groups.* Harper: New York.

Feyerabend, P. (1975). *Against Method.* NLB: London.

Fishbein, M. and Ajzen, I. (1975). *Belief, Attitude, Intention and Behavior.* Addison-Wesley: Reading, Mass.

Fleming, D. (1967). Attitude: The history of a concept. *Perspectives in American History*, **1**, 287–365. Published by the Charles Warren Center for Studies in American History, Harvard University.

Fodor, J. A. (1975). *The Language of Thought.* Crowell: New York.

Freedman, J. L. and Sears, D. (1965). Selective exposure. In: Berkowitz, L. (ed.). *Advances in Experimental Social Psychology*, Volume 2. Academic Press: New York and London.

French, J. R. P., Jr. and Raven, B. (1959). The bases of social power. In: Cartwright, D. (ed.). *Studies in Social Power.* Institute for Social Research, University of Michigan: Ann Arbor.

Fried, S. B., Gumper, D. C. and Allen, J. C. (1973). Ten years of Social Psychology: Is there a growing commitment to field research? *American Psychologist*, **28**, 155–156.

Friedlander, E. R. and Havighurst, R. J. (1954). *The meaning of work and retirement.* University of Chicago Press: Chicago.

Fromkin, H. L. (1972). Feelings of interpersonal undistinctiveness: An unpleasant affective state. *Journal of Experimental Research in Personality*, **6**, 178–185.

Gadenne, V. (1976). *Die Gultigkeit Psychologischer Untersuchungen.* Kohlhammer: Stuttgart.

Gambrill, E. G. (1977). *Behavior Modification: Handbook of Assessment, Intervention, and Evaluation.* Jossey-Bass: San Francisco.

Garfield, E. (1978). The 100 most cited SSCI authors, 1969–1977. *Current Contents*, **32**, 5–11.

Garfinkel, H. (1967). *Studies in Ethnomethodology.* Prentice Hall: Englewood Cliffs, N.J.

Garfinkel, H. (1972). Studies of the routine grounds of everyday activities. In: Sudnow, D. (ed.). *Studies in Social Interaction.* Free Press: New York.

Garraty, J. A. (1978). *Unemployment in History: Economic thought and public policy.* Harper and Row: London, New York.

Garvey, W. D. and Griffith, B. C. (1971). Scientific communication: Its role in the conduct of research and the creation of knowledge. *American Psychologist*, **26**, 349–362.

Gauld, A. and Shotter, J. (1977). *Human Action and its Psychological Investigation.* Routledge and Kegan Paul: London.

Gergen, K. J. (1973). Social psychology as history. *Journal of Personality and Social Psychology*, **26**, 309–320.

Gergen, K. J. (1976a). Social psychology, science and history: A rejoinder. *Personality and Social Psychology Bulletin*, **2**, 373–383.

Gergen, K. J. (1976b). The power structure in social psychology. In: Strickland, L. H., Aboud, F. E. and Gergen, K. J. (eds). *Social Psychology in Transition*. Plenum: New York.
Gergen, K. J. (1977). The social construction of self-knowledge. In: Mischel, T. (ed.). *The Self in Psychology*. Blackwell: London.
Gergen, K. J. (1978a). Experimentation in social psychology: a reappraisal. *European Journal of Social Psychology*, **8**, 507–527.
Gergen, K. J. (1978b). Toward generative theory. *Journal of Personality and Social Psychology*, **36**, 1344–1360.
Gergen, K. J. (in press). *Regenerating Social Knowledge*. Plenum Press: New York.
Gergen, K. J. and Basseches, M. (in press). The potentiation of social knowledge. In: Saks, M. and Kidd, R. F. (eds). *Advances in Applied Social Psychology*, Volume 1, Academic Press: New York and London.
Gergen, K. J. and Gergen, M. M. (1977). Attribution in the context of social explanations. In: Gorlity, H., Meyer, W. V. and Weiner, B. (eds). *Bielefelder Symposium Uber Attribution*. Klett-Cutta:Stuttgart.
Gibson, J. J. (1968). *The Senses Considered as Perceptual Systems*. George Allen and Unwin: London.
Giddens, A. (1976). *New Rules of Sociological Method*. Basic Books: New York.
Gilmour, R. (in preparation). Theory as functional myth.
Ginsburg, G. P. (ed.) (1979). *Emerging Strategies in Social Psychological Research*. Wiley: New York.
Glassman, R. B. (1973). Persistence and loose coupling in living systems. *Behavioural Science*, **18**, 83–98.
Goffman, E. (1961). *Asylums*. Doubleday: New York.
Goffman, E. (1969). *The Presentation of Self in Everyday Life*. Allen Lane, The Penguin Press: London.
Goffman, E. (1970). *Strategic Interaction*. Blackwell: Oxford.
Gorer, G. (1955). *Exploring English Character*. Cresset: London.
Gouldner, A. W. (1970). *The Coming Crisis in Western Sociology*. Basic Books: New York.
Green, R. G. and Quanty, M. B. (1977). The Catharsis of Aggression: An evaluation of a hypothesis. In: Berkowitz, L. (ed.). *Advances in Experimental Social Psychology*. Volume 10. Academic Press: New York and London.
Greenwald, A. G. (1975). On the inconclusiveness of "crucial" cognitive tests of dissonance versus self-perception theories. *Journal of Experimental Social Psychology*, **11**, 490–499.
Habermas, J. (1971). *Knowledge and Human Interest*. Beacon Press: Boston.
Hackman, J. R. and Morris, C. G. (1975). Group tasks, group interaction process and performance effectiveness: A review and proposed integration. In: Berkowitz, L. (ed.). *Advances in Experimental Social Psychology*, Volume 8. Academic Press: New York and London.
Hagstrom, W. O. (1965). *The Scientific Community*. Southern Illinois University Press: Carbondale.
Halpin, A. W. and Winer, B. J. (1952). *The Leadership Behavior of the Airplane Commander*. Ohio State University: Columbus.

Harlow, H. F. (1958). The nature of love. *American Psychologist*, **13**, 673–685.
Harré, R. (1977). Friendship as an accomplishment: An ethogenic approach to social relationships. In: Duck, S. W. (ed.). *Theory and Practice in Interpersonal Attraction*. Academic Press: London and New York.
Harré, R. (1980). Making social psychology scientific. In: Gilmour, R. and Duck, S. W. (eds). *The Development of Social Psychology*, Academic Press: London and New York.
Harré, R. and Secord, P. (1972). *The Explanation of Social Behaviour*. Blackwell: Oxford.
Harris, B. and Harvey, S. H. (1975). Self-attributed Choice as a function of the consequence of a decision. *Journal of Personality and Social Psychology*, **31**, 1013–1019.
Harris, R. J. (1976). The uncertain connection between verbal theories and research hypotheses in social psychology. *Journal of Experimental Social Psychology*, **12**, 210–219.
Harvey, J. H. and Smith, W. P. (1977). *Social Psychology: An attributional approach*. Mosby: St Louis.
Hastorf, A. H. and Cantril, H. (1954). They saw a game: A case study. *Journal of Abnormal and Social Psychology*, **49**, 129–134.
Heidegger, M. (1962). *Being and Time*. Harper and Row: New York. (German edit., 1927.)
Heider, F. (1946). Attitudes and cognitive organization. *Journal of Psychology*, **21**, 107–112.
Heider, F. (1958). *The Psychology of Interpersonal Relations*. Wiley: New York.
Helmreich, R. (1975). Applied Social Psychology: The unfulfilled promise. *Personality and Social Psychology Bulletin*, **1**, 548–560.
Hendrick, C. (1977). *Perspectives on Social Psychology*. Erlbaum: Hillsdale, N.J.
Hendrick, C. and Jones, R. A. (1971). *The Nature of Theory and Research in Social Psychology*. Academic Press: New York and London.
Hewitt, J. P. (1976). *Self and Society: A symbolic interactionist social psychology*. Allyn and Bacon: Boston.
Himmelweit, H. T., Oppenheim, A. N. and Vince, P. (1958). *Television and the Child*. Oxford University Press: Oxford.
Hinde, R. A. (1979). *Towards understanding relationships*. Academic Press: London and New York.
Hinde, R. A. (in press). The bases of a science of interpersonal relationship. In: Duck, S. W. and Gilmour, R. (eds). *Personal Relationships*. Academic Press: London and New York.
Hochbaum, G. M. (1953). Certain personality aspects and pressures to uniformity in a social group. Ph.D. Thesis, University of Minnesota.
Hogan, R. T. and Emler, N. P. (1978). The biases in contemporary social psychology. *Social Research*, **45**, 478–534.
Hollander, E. P. (1978). Applied social psychology: problems and prospects. Paper to 19th International Congress of Applied Psychology at Munich.
Holzkamp, K. (1976). *Kritische Psychologie*. Fischer Taschenbuch Verlag: Hamburg.

Holzkamp, K. (1977). Die Uberwindung der wissenschaftlichen Beliebigkeit psychologischer Theorien durch die Kritische Psychologie. *Zeitschrift für Sozialpsychologie*, **8**, 1–22.

Homans, G. C. (1961). *Social behaviour: Its elementary forms*. Harcourt Brace Jovanovich: New York.

House, J. S. (1977). The three faces of social psychology. *Sociometry*, **40**, 161–177.

Hovland, C. I. (1959). Reconciling conflicting results derived from experimental and survey studies of attitude change. *American Psychologist*, **14**, 8–17.

Hovland, C. I., Janis, I. L. and Kelley, H. H. (1953). *Communication and Persuasion*. Yale University Press: New Haven.

Hovland, C. I., Lumsdaine, A. A. and Sheffield, F. D. (1949). *Experiments on mass communication*. Princeton University Press: Princeton.

Hovland, C. I. and Rosenberg, M. J. (eds) (1960). *Attitude Organization and Change*. Yale University Press: New Haven.

Hsu, F. K. (ed.) (1971). *Kinship and culture*. Aldine: New York.

Hull, C. L. (1952). *A Behavior System*. Yale University Press: New Haven.

Huston, T. L., Cate, R., Fitzgerald, N. and Stump, C. S. (in press). The development of premarital relationships: towards a typology of pathways to marriage. In: Duck, S. W. and Gilmour, R. (eds). *Developing Personal Relationships*. Academic Press: London and New York.

Huston, T. L. and Levinger, L. (1978). Interpersonal attraction and relationships. In: Rosenzweig, M. R. and Porter, L. W. (eds). *Annual Review of Psychology*, Vol. 29. Annual Reviews: Palo Alto, Calif.

Hyman, H. H. and Sheatsley, P. B. (1954). The authoritarian personality: A methodological critique. In: Christie, R. and Jahoda, M. (eds). *Studies in the scope and method of "The Authoritarian Personality"*. Free Press: New York.

Innes, J. M. (1973). The utility of a citation index as a measure of research ability in psychology. *Bulletin of the British Psychological Society*, **26**, 227–228.

Innes, J. M. (1978). Collaboration and Productivity in social psychology. Unpublished MS., University of Adelaide.

Innes, J. M. (1980). Fashions in social psychology. In: Gilmour, R. and Duck, S. W. (eds). *The Development of Social Psychology*. Academic Press: London and New York.

Innes, J. M. (in press). Social psychological approaches to the induction and alleviation of stress: Influences upon health and illness. In: Stephenson, G. and Davis, J. H. (eds). *Progress in applied social psychology*. Wiley: London.

Innes, J. M. and Fraser, C. (1971). Experimenter bias and other possible biases in psychological research. *European Journal of Social Psychology*, **1**, 297–310.

Insko, C. A. and Schopler, J. (1972). *Experimental Social Psychology*. Academic Press: New York and London.

Insko, C. A., Songer, E. and McGarvey, W. (1974). Balance, positivity, and agreement in the Jordan paradigm: A defense of balance theory. *Journal of Experimental Social Psychology*, **10**, 53–83.

Insko, C. A., Worchel, S., Folger, R. and Kutkus, A. (1975). A balance theory interpretation of dissonance. *Psychological Review*, **82**, 169–183.

Israel, J. (1972). Stipulations and construction in the Social Sciences. In: Israel, J. and Tajfel, H. (eds). *The Context of Social Psychology*. Academic Press: London and New York.

Israel, J. and Tajfel, H. (1972). *The Context of Social Psychology: A critical assessment*. Academic Press: London and New York.

Ittelson, W. H., Proshansky, H. M. and Rivlin, L. G. (1970). The environmental psychology of the psychiatric ward. In: Proshansky, H. M. *et al.* (eds). *Environmental Psychology*. Holt, Rinehart and Winston: New York.

Izard, C. E. (1971). *The Face of Emotion*. Appleton-Century-Crofts: New York.

Jahoda, G. (1978). Cross-cultural perspectives. In: Tajfel, H. and Fraser, C. (eds). *Introducing Social Psychology*. Penguin Books: Harmondsworth, Middlesex.

Jahoda, G. (1979). A cross-cultural perspective on experimental social psychology. *Personality and Social Psychology Bulletin*, **5**, 142–148.

Jahoda, M., Lazarsfeld, P. F. and Zeisel, H. (1972). *Marienthal: The sociography of an unemployed community*. Tavistock: London.

Janis, I. L. (1968). Attitude change via role playing. In: Abelson, R. P. *et al.* (eds). *Theories of Cognitive Consistency*. Rand-McNally: Chicago.

Janis, I. L. (1972). *Victims of Group Think: A psychological study of foreign policy decisions and fiascoes*. Free Press: New York.

Janis, I. L. and Gilmour, J. B. (1965). The influence of incentive conditions on the success of role playing in modifying attitudes. *Journal of Personality and Social Psychology*, **1**, 17–27.

Janis, I. L., Kaye, D. and Kirschner, P. (1965). Facilitating the effects of "eating-while-reading" on responsiveness to persuasive communication. *Journal of Personality and Social Psychology*, **1**, 181–185.

Janis, I. L. and Mann, L. (1977). *Decision Making*. Free Press: New York.

Jaques, E. (1951). *The Changing Culture of a Factory*. Tavistock: London.

Jaspars, J. M. F. (1978). Determinants of attitudes and attitude change. In: Tajfel, H. and Fraser, C. (eds). *Introducing Social Psychology*. Penguin Books: Harmondsworth.

Jay, M. (1973). *The Dialectial Imagination*. Heinemann: London.

Jensen, U. J. (1971). Conceptual Phenomenalism. *Monist*, **56**, 250–275.

Jones, E. E. (1979). The rocky road from acts to dispositions. *American Psychologist*, **34**, 107–117.

Jones, E. E. and Gerard, H. B. (1967). *Foundations of Social Psychology*. Wiley: New York.

Jones, E. E. and Nisbett, R. E. (1971). *The Actor and the Observer: Divergent perceptions of the causes of behaviour*. General Learning Press: New York.

Jones, M. (1952). *Social Psychiatry: A study of therapeutic communities*. Tavistock Publications: London.

Jordan, N. (1953). Behavioral forces that are a function of attitude and cognitive organization. *Human Relations*, **6**, 273–287.

Kaplan, M. F. (1977). Judgement by juries. In: Kaplan, M. F. and Schwartz, S. (eds). *Human Judgement and Decision Processes in Applied Settings*. Academic Press: New York and London.

Kaplan, M. F. and Schwartz, S. (eds) (1975). *Human Judgement and Decision Processes*. Academic Press: New York and London.

Kaplan, M. F. and Schwartz, S. (eds) (1977). *Human Judgement and Decision Processes in Applied Settings*. Academic Press: New York and London.

Katz, D. (1960). The functional approach in the study of attitudes. *Public Opinion Quarterly*, **24**, 163–204.

Katz, D. et al. (1951). *Productivity, Supervision and Morale among Railroad Workers*. Institute for Social Research: Ann Arbor, Michigan.

Katz, D. (1967). Editorial, *Journal of Personality and Social Psychology*, **7**, 341–344.

Katz, D. (1972). Some Final Considerations about Experimentation in Social Psychology. In: McClintock, C. G. (ed.). *Experimental Social Psychology*. Holt, Rinehart and Winston: New York.

Katz, D. and Braly, K. W. (1958). Verbal stereotypes and racial prejudice. In: Maccoby, E. E., Newcomb, T. M. and Hartley, E. L. (eds). *Readings in Social Psychology*, (3rd Ed.). Holt, Rinehart: New York.

Katz, E. and Lazarsfeld, P. F. (1955). *Personal Influence*. Free Press: New York.

Keat, R. and Urry, J. (1976). *Social Theory as Science*. Routledge and Kegan Paul: London.

Kelley, H. H. (1967). Attribution theory in social psychology. In: Levine, D. (ed.). *Nebraska Symposium on Motivation*, Volume 15.

Kelley, H. H. and Michela, J. L. (1980). Attribution theory and research. *Annual Review of Psychology*, **31**, 457–501.

Kelley, H. H. and Stahelski, A. J. (1970). Social interaction basis of co-operators' and competitors' beliefs about others. *Journal of Personality and Social Psychology*, **16**, 66–91.

Kelley, H. H. and Thibaut, J. W. (1969). Group problem solving. In: Lindzey, G. and Aronson, E. (eds). *Handbook of social psychology*, (Rev. ed.). Addison-Wesley: Reading, Mass.

Kelly, G. A. (1955). *Psychology of Personal Constructs*. (2 volumes). Norton: New York.

Kelman, H. C. (1968). *A Time to Speak: On human values and social research*. Jossey-Bass: San Francisco.

Kelvin, P. (1970). *The Bases of Social Behaviour: An approach in terms of order and value*. Holt, Rinehart and Winston: London and New York.

Kelvin, P. (1979). A memorandum on leisure. Prepared for the Joint SSRC Sports Council Panel on Leisure and Recreation Research. Mimeograph.

Kelvin, P. (1980). Social psychology 2001: the social psychological bases and implications of structural unemployment. In: Gilmour, R. and Duck, S. W. (eds). *The Development of Social Psychology*. Academic Press: London and New York.

Kenrick, D. T. and Cialdini, R. B. (1977). Romantic attraction: Misattribution versus reinforcement explanations. *Journal of Personality and Social Psychology*, **35**, 381–391.

Kent, G. G., Davis, J. D. and Shapiro, D. A. (1978). Resources required in the reconstruction of conversation. *Journal of Personality and Social Psychology*, **36**, 13–22.
Kerckhoff, A. C. and Davis, K. E. (1962). Value consensus and heed complementarity in mate selection. *American Sociological Review*, **27**, 295–303.
Kerr, N. L. (1978). Severity of prescribed penalty and mock jurors' verdicts. *Journal of Personality and Social Psychology*, **36**, 1431–1442.
Kessler, S. J. and McKenna, W. (1978). *Gender: An ethnomethodological approach*. Wiley: New York.
Klein, L. (1976). *A Social Scientist in Industry*. Gower: London.
Kluckhohn, F. R. (1965). Dominant and variant value orientations. In: Kluckhohn, C. and Murray, H. A. (eds). *Personality in Nature, Society and Culture*, (2nd Ed.). Alfred A. Knopf: New York.
Kogan, N. and Wallach, M. A. (1964). Risk-taking as a function of the situation, the person, and the group. In: Mandler, G. *et al.* (eds). *New Directions in Psychology*. Volume 3. Holt, Rinehart and Winston: New York.
Kuhn, T. S. (1962). *The Structure of Scientific Revolutions*. University of Chicago Press: Chicago.
Lacey, H. and Rachlin, H. (1978). Behaviour, cognition and theories of choice. *Behavioralism*, **6**, 177–202.
La Gaipa, J. J. (1977). Testing a multi-dimensional approach to friendship. In: Duck, S. W. (ed.). *Theory and Practice in Interpersonal Attraction*. Academic Press: London and New York.
Lakatos, I. (1970). Falsification and the methodology of scientific research. In: Lakatos, I. and Musgrave, A. (eds). *Criticism and the Growth of Knowledge*. Cambridge University Press: Cambridge.
Lambert, W. W. and Weisbrod, R. (eds) (1971). *Comparative Perspectives on Social Psychology*. Little, Brown: Boston.
Lamm, H. and Myers, D. G. (1978). Group-induced polarization of attitudes and behavior. In: Berkowitz, L. (ed.). *Advances in Experimental Social Psychology*, Volume 11. Academic Press: New York and London.
Langer, E. J. (1978). Rethinking the role of thought in social interaction. In: Harvey, J. H., Ickes, W. J. and Kidd, R. F. (eds). *New Directions in Attribution Research*, Volume 2. Erlbaum: Hillsdale, N.J.
Langer, E. J. and Abelson, R. P. (1972). The semantics of asking a favor: How to succeed in getting help without really dying. *Journal of Personality and Social Psychology*, **24**, 26–32.
Langer, E. J. and Roth, J. (1975). Heads I win, tails it's chance: The illusion of control as a function of the sequence of outcomes in a purely chance task. *Journal of Personality and Social Psychology*, **32**, 951–955.
Latané, B. and Darley, J. (1970). *The Unresponsive Bystander: Why doesn't he help?* Appleton-Century-Crofts: New York.
Laudan, L. (1977). *Progress and its problems: Towards a theory of scientific growth*. University of California Press: Berkeley, Calif.
Lazarus, R. S. and Monat, A. (eds) (1977). *Stress and Coping*. Columbia University Press: New York.

Lerner, M. J. (1975). The justice motive in social behavior. *Journal of Social Issues*, **31**, 1–20.
Lévi-Strauss, C. (1963). *Structural Anthropology.* (Translated by Jacobson, C. and Schoepf, B. G.) Basic Books: New York.
Levinger, G., Senn, D. J. and Jorgensen, B. W. (1970). Progress toward permanence in courtship: A test of the Kerckhoff–Davis hypotheses. *Sociometry*, **33**, 427–443.
Levy, L. H. (1961). Anxiety and behavior scientists' behavior. *American Psychologist*, **16**, 66–68.
Lewin, K. (1926). Untersuchungen zur Handlungs and affektpsychologie. *Psychologisches Forschung*, **7**.
Lewin, K. (1936). *Principles of topological psychology*. McGraw-Hill: New York.
Lieberman, M. A. (1976). Change induction in small groups. In: *Annual Review of Psychology*. Annual Reviews: Palo Alto, Calif.
Lieberman, M. A., Yalom, I. D. and Miles, M. B. (1973). *Encounter Groups: First Facts*. Basic Books: New York.
Linder, D. E., Cooper, J. and Jones, E. E. (1967). Decision freedom as a determinant of the role of incentive magnitude in attitude change. *Journal of Personality and Social Psychology*, **6**, 245–254.
Lindzey, G. and Aronson, E. (1968). *Handbook of Social Psychology*. (2nd Ed.). Addison-Wesley: Reading, Mass.
Lofland, J. (1976). *Doing Social Life*. Wiley: New York.
Lorenz, K. (1966). *On Aggression*. Harcourt, Brace and World: New York.
Lorge, I. and Solomon, H. (1955). Two models of group behavior in the solution of eureka type problems. *Psychometrika*, **20**, 139–148.
Lubek, I. (1976). The power structure in social psychology. In: Strickland, L. H., Aboud, F. E. and Gergen, K. J. (eds). *Social Psychology in Transition*. Plenum Press: New York.
Luginbuhl, J. E., Crowne, D. H. and Kahan, J. P. (1975). Causal attributions for success and failure. *Journal of Personality and Social Psychology*, **31**, 86–93.
Lunn, J. A. (1968). Empirical techniques in consumer research. In: Pym, D. (ed.). *Industrial Society*. Penguin Books: Harmondsworth.
McCall, C. J. and Simmons, J. L. (1966). *Identities and Interactions*. Free Press: New York.
McCarthy, B. (1976). Agreement and friendship: affective and cognitive responses to attitudinal similarity-dissimilarity among same-sex friends. Ph.D. thesis, University of Lancaster.
McCarthy, B. and Duck, S. W. (1976). Friendship duration and responses to attitudinal agreement-disagreement. *British Journal of Social and Clinical Psychology*, **15**, 377–386.
McCarthy, D. and Duck, S. W. (1979). Studying friendship: experimental and role-playing techniques in testing hypotheses about acquaintance. *British Journal of Social and Clinical Psychology*, **18**, 299–307.
McClelland, D. C. (1975). *Power: The Inner Experience*. Halstead: New York.

McClelland, D. C. and Winter, D. G. (1969). *Motivating Economic Achievement.* Free Press: New York.
McClintock, C. G. (1972). *Experimental Social Psychology.* Holt, Rinehart and Winston: New York.
McCoy, C. and Playford, J. (eds) (1967). *Apolitical Politics: A critique of behavioralism.* Crowell: New York.
McDonagh, E. L. (1976). Attitude changes and paradigm shifts: Social psychological foundations of the Kuhnian thesis. *Social Studies in Science,* **6,** 51–76.
McGinnies, E. (1948). Emotionality and perceptual defense. *Psychological Review,* **56,** 244–251.
McGrath, J. E. (1978). Small Groups Research. *American Behavioral Scientist,* **21,** 651–674.
McGuire, W. J. (1966). The current status of cognitive consistency theories. In: Feldman, S. (ed.). *Cognitive Consistency.* Academic Press: New York and London.
McGuire, W. J. (1967). Some impending reorientations in social psychology: Some thoughts provoked by Kenneth Ring. *Journal of Experimental Social Psychology,* **3,** 124–139.
McGuire, W. J. (1968). Personality and susceptibility to social influence. In: Borgatta, E. F. and Lambert, W. W. (eds). *Handbook of Personality Theory and Research.* Rand-McNally: Chicago.
McGuire, W. J. (1969). The nature of attitudes and attitude change. In: Lindzey, G. and Aronson, E. (eds). *The Handbook of Social Psychology,* Volume 3. Addison-Wesley: Reading, Mass.
McGuire, W. J. (1969). Theory-oriented research in natural settings: The best of both worlds for social psychology. In: Sherif, M. and Sherif, C. W. (eds). *Interdisciplinary Relationships in the Social Sciences.* Aldine: Chicago.
McGuire, W. J. (1971). The guiding theories behind attitude research. In: King, C. W. and Tigert, D. J. (eds). *Attitude Research Reaches New Heights.* American Marketing Association: New York.
McGuire, W. J. (1972). Attitude change: The information-processing paradigm. In: McClintock, C. G. (ed.). *Experimental Social Psychology.* Holt, Rinehart and Winston: New York.
McGuire, W. J. (1973). The Yin and Yang of progress in social psychology. *Journal of Personality and Social Psychology,* **26,** 446–456.
McGuire, W. J. (1974). Psychological motives and communication gratification. In: Blumler, S. G. and Katz, E. (eds). *The Uses of Mass Communications.* Sage: Beverley Hills.
McGuire, W. J. (1975). Creative Hypothesis Formation: Can It Be Described? Invited lecture, Society of Experimental Social Psychology, Purdue University, West Lafayette, Indiana.
McGuire, W. J. (1980a). The development of theory in social psychology. In: Gilmour, R. and Duck, S.W. (eds). *The Development of Social Psychology.* Academic Press: London and New York.
McGuire, W. J. (1980b). The probabilogical model of cognitive structure in

attitude change. In: Petty, R., Ostrom, T. and Brock, T. (eds). *Cognitive Responses in Persuasion*. McGraw-Hill: New York.

McPhail, P., Ungoed-Thomas, J. R. and Chapman, H. (1972). *Moral Education in the Secondary School*. Longman: London.

McPhail, P., Middleton, D. and Intram, D. (1978). *Moral Education in the Middle Years*. Longman: London.

McWhirter, R. M. and Jecker, J. (1967). Attitude similarity and inferred attraction. *Psychonomic Science*, **7**, 225–226.

Machiavelli, N. (1950). *The Prince and Other Discourses*. Random House: New York.

Maines, D. R. (1977). Social Organization and Social Structure in Symbolic Interactionist Thought. In: Inkeles, A., Coleman, J. and Smelser, N. (eds). *Annual Review of Sociology*, Volume 3. Annual Reviews: Palo Alto: Calif.

Mann, F. C. (1957). Studying and creating change: a means to understanding social organization. *Research in Industrial Human Relations*, **17**, 146–167.

Mannheim, K. (1952). *Essays on the Sociology of Knowledge*. Routledge and Kegan Paul: London.

Mannheim, H. and Wilkins, L. T. (1955). *Production Methods in Relation to Borstal Training*. H.M.S.O.: London.

Mark, M., Cook, T. D. and Diamond, S. S. (1976). Fourteen years of social psychology: A growing commitment to field experimentation. *Personality and Social Psychology Bulletin*, **2**, 154–157.

Marsden, D. and Duff, E. (1975). *Workless: Some unemployed and their families*. Pelican books: Harmondsworth, Middlesex.

Marsh, P., Rosser, E. and Harré, R. (1978). *The Rules of Disorder*. Routledge and Kegan Paul: London.

Marston, B. J. (1976). Trait attribution to a described action as a function of changes in salient information. *Journal of Research in Personality*, **10**, 245–255.

Maslow, A. H. (1954). *Motivation and Personality*. Harper: New York.

May, P. R. A. (1968). *Treatment of Schizophrenia*. Science House: New York.

Mead, G. H. (1934). *Mind, Self and Society*. University of Chicago Press: Chicago.

Mead, G. H. (1936). *Movements of thought in the Nineteenth Century*. University of Chicago Press: Chicago.

Meehl, P. E. (1967). Theory testing in psychology and physics. *Philosophy of Science*, **34**, 103–115.

Meehl, P. E. (1978). Theoretical risks and tabular asterisks: Sir Karl, Sir Robert and the slow progress of soft psychology. *Journal of Consulting and Clinical Psychology*, **46**, 806–834.

Mehrabian, A. and Ksionzky, S. (1974). *A Theory of Affiliation*. Lexington Books: Lexington.

Meltzer, L. (1972). Applied, applicable, appealing and appalling social psychology. Seminar at Oxford and other Universities.

Merton, R. K. (1957). Priorities in scientific discovery. *American Sociological Review*, **22**, 635–659.

Merton, R. K. (1968). The Matthew effect in science. *Science*, **159**, 56–63.
Milgram, S. (1974). *Obedience to Authority*. Tavistock: London.
Miller, D. T. and Holmes, J. G. (1975). The role of situational restrictiveness on self fulfilling prophecies: A theoretical and empirical extension of Kelley and Stahelski's Triangle Hypothesis. *Journal of Personality and Social Psychology*, **31**, 661–673.
Miller, J. (1978). *The Body in Question*. Cape: London.
Miller, N. E. and Dollard, J. (1941). *Social Learning and Imitation*. Yale University Press: New Haven.
Millham, S., Bullock, R. and Hosie, K. (1978). Juvenile unemployment: a concept due for recycling. *Adolescence*, **1**, 11–24.
Mills, J. (1968). Interest in supporting and discrepant information. In: Abelson, R. *et al.* (eds). *Theories of Cognitive Consistency*. Rand-McNally: Chicago.
Mischel, W. (1968). *Personality and Assessment*. Wiley: New York.
Mixon, D. (1971). Behaviour analysis treating subjects as actors rather than organisms. *Journal for the Theory of Social Behaviour*, **1**, 19–31.
Mixon, D. (1972). Instead of deception. *Journal for the Theory of Social Behaviour*, **2**, 145–178.
Monson, T. C. and Snyder, M. (1977). Actors, observers and the attribution process. Towards a reconceptualisation. *Journal of Experimental Social Psychology*, **13**, 89–111.
Morawski, J. G. (1979). The structure of social psychological communities: A framework for examining the sociology of social psychology. In: Strickland, L. H. (ed.). *Soviet and Western Perspectives in Social Psychology*. Pergamon Press: Oxford.
Moscovici, S. (1972). Society and theory in social psychology. In: Israel, J. and Tajfel, H. (eds). *The Context of Social Psychology*. Academic Press: New York and London.
Moscovici, S. (1976). *La Psychoanalyse, son Image et son Public*. (2nd Ed.) Presses Universitaires de France: Paris.
Moscovici, S. and Zavalloni, M. (1969). The group as a polarizer of attitudes. *Journal of Personality and Social Psychology*, **12**, 125–135.
Mulder, M. (1971). Power equalization through participation. *Administrative Science Quarterly*, **16**, 31–38.
Mullins, N. C. (1973). *Theories and Theory Groups in Contemporary American Sociology*. Harper and Row: New York.
Murchison, C. A. (ed.) (1935). *Handbook of Social Psychology*. Volumes 1 and 2. Clark University Press: Worcester, Mass.
Murray, H. S. *et al.* (1938). *Explorations in Personality*. Oxford University Press: New York.
Murstein, B. I. (1977). The stimulus-value-role (SVR) theory of dyadic relationships. In: Duck, S. W. (ed.). *Theory and Practice in Interpersonal Attraction*. Academic Press: London and New York.
Myers, C. R. (1970). Journal citations and scientific eminence in contemporary psychology. *American Psychologist*, **25**, 1041.

Mynatt, C. and Sherman, S. J. (1975). Responsibility attribution in groups and individuals: A direct test of the diffusion of responsibility hypothesis. *Journal of Personality and Social Psychology*, **32**, 1111–1118.
Neisser, V. (1976). *Cognition and Reality*. W. H. Freeman: San Francisco.
Nisbett, R. E. and Ross, L. D. (1980). *Human Inference: Strategies and shortcomings*. Prentice-Hall: Englewood Cliffs, N.J.
Nisbett, R. E. and Wilson, T. D. (1977). Telling more than we can know: Verbal reports on mental processes. *Psychological Review*, **84**, 231–259.
Orne, M. (1962). On the social psychology of the psychological experiment: With particular reference to demand characteristics and their implications. *American Psychologist*, **17**, 776–783.
Osgood, C. E. and Tannenbaum, P. H. (1955). The principle of congruity in the prediction of attitude change. *Psychological Review*, **62**, 42–55.
Pagano, D. F. and Katahn, M. (1972). Construct validity, disconfirming evidence and test-anxiety research. *Journal of Personality*, **40**, 137–148.
Paige, J. M. (1975). *Agrarian Revolution*. Free Press: New York.
Pepitone, A. (1976). Toward a normative and comparative biocultural social psychology. *Journal of Personality and Social Psychology*, **34**, 641–653.
Phillips, D. L. (1973). *Abandoning Method: Sociological Studies in Methodology*. Jossey-Bass: San Francisco.
Piaget, J. (1928). *Judgement and Reasoning in the Child*. Harcourt, Brace and World: New York.
Piliavin, I. M., Piliavin, J. A. and Rodin, J. (1975). Costs, diffusion and the stigmatized victim. *Journal of Personality and Social Psychology*, **32**, 429–438.
Piliavin, I. M., Rodin, J. and Piliavin, J. A. (1969). Good Samaratanism: An underground phenomenon? *Journal of Personality and Social Psychology*, **13**, 289–299.
Piliavin, J. A. and Piliavin, I. M. (1972). Effect of blood on reactions to a victim. *Journal of Personality and Social Psychology*. **23**, 353–361.
Popper, K. R. (1934). *Die Logik der Forschung*. Julius Springer Verlag: Vienna.
Popper, K. R. (1959). *The Logic of Scientific Discovery*. Hutchinson: London.
Popper, K. R. (1963). *Conjectures and Refutations*. Routledge and Kegan Paul: London.
Powers, W. T. (1978). Quantitative analysis of purposive systems: Some spadework for the foundation of scientific psychology. *Psychological Review*, **85**, 417–435.
Price, D. J. de Solla (1962). *Science since Babylon*. Yale University Press: New Haven.
Price, D. J. de Solla (1970). Citation measures of hard science, soft science, technology and nonscience. In: Nelson, C. E. and Pollock, D. K. (eds). *Communication among Scientists and Engineers*. Lexington: Lexington, Mass.
Price, D. J. de Solla and Beaver, D. de B. (1966). Collaboration in an invisible college. *American Psychologist*, **21**, 1011–1018.
Prior, J. (1979). Address quoted in *The Guardian*, 22nd March, 1979.
Prus, R. C. (1975). Resisting designations: An extension of attribution theory into a negotiated context. *Sociological Inquiry*, **45**, 3–14.

Radnitzky, G. (1970). *Contemporary Schools of Metascience*. Scandinavian University Books: Gotenburg, Sweden.
Rands, M. and Levinger, G. (1979). Implicit theories of relationship: An inter-generational study. *Journal of Personality and Social Psychology*, **37**, 645–661.
Rapoport, R. H. (1960). *Community as Doctor*. Tavistock: London.
Rescher, N. (1978). *Scientific Progress*. Basil Blackwell: Oxford.
Rich, A. R. and Schroeder, H. E. (1976). Research issues in assertiveness training. *Psychology Bulletin*, **83**, 1081–1096.
Richardson, J. T. (1977). Conversion and Commitment in Contemporary Religion. *American Behavioral Scientist*, **20**, entire issue.
Riecken, H. W. (1962). A program for research on experiment in social psychology. In: Washburne, N. F. (ed.). *Decisions, Values and Groups*, Volume 2, Pergamon Press: New York.
Riecken, H. W. (1965). Research Developments in the Social Sciences. In: Klineberg, O. and Christie, R. (eds). *Perspectives in Social Psychology*. Holt, Rinehart and Winston: New York.
Riegel, K. F. (1972). Time and change in the development of the individual and society. In: Reese, H. (ed.). *Advances in Child Development and Behavior*, Volume 7. Academic Press: New York and London.
Ring, K. (1967). Experimental social psychology: some sober questions about some frivolous values. *Journal of Experimental Psychology*, **3**, 113–123.
Rodrigues, A. (1967). Effects of balance, positivity and agreement in triadic social relations. *Journals of Personality and Social Psychology*, **5**, 472–476.
Rokeach, M. (1973). *The Nature of Human Values*. Free Press: New York.
Rommetveit, R. (1976). On the architecture of intersubjectivity. In: Strickland, L. H., Aboud, F. E. and Gergen, K. J. *Social Psychology in Transition*. Plenum Press: New York.
Rosch, E. (1977). Human categorization. In: Warren, N. (ed.). *Advances in cross-cultural Psychology*, Volume 1. Academic Press: London and New York.
Rosenberg, M. J. (1965). When dissonance fails: On eliminating evaluation apprehension from attitude measurement. *Journal of Personality and Social Psychology*, **1**, 28–42.
Rosenberg, M. J. (1970). The experimental parable of inauthenticity: Consequences of counter attitudinal performance. In: Amtrobus, J. S. (ed.). *Cognition and Affect*. Little Brown: Boston.
Rosenshine, B. (1971). *Teaching Behaviours and Student Achievement*. N.F.E.R.: Slough.
Rosenthal, R. (1966). *Experimenter Effects in Behavioral Research*. Appleton-Century-Crofts: New York.
Rosenzweig, S. (1933). The experimental situation as a psychological problem. *Psychological Review*, **40**, 337–354.
Ross, H. H., Campbell, D. T. and Glass, G. (1970). Determining the social effects of a legal reform: the British "Breathanalyser" crackdown of 1967. *American Behavioral Science*, **13**, 493–509.

Ross, L. (1977). The intuitive psychologist and his shortcomings: Distortions in the attribution process. In: Berkowitz, L. (ed.). *Advances in Experimental Social Psychology*, Volume II. Academic Press: New York and London.
Rubin, Z. (1973). *Liking and Loving*. Holt, Rinehart and Winston: New York.
Rutter, M. and Madge, N. (1976). *Cycles of disadvantage*. Heinemann: London.
Ryle, G. (1949). *The Concept of Mind*. Hutchinson: London.
Sagatun, S. J. and Knudsen, J. H. (1977). The Interactive Effect of Attributor Role and Event on Attributions. Paper presented at the annual meeting of the American Sociological Association, Chicago, Ill.
Sales, S. M. (1973). Threat as a factor in authoritarianism: an analysis of archival data. *Journal of Personality and Social Psychology*, **28**, 24–57.
Samelson, F. (1974). History, origin myth and ideology: Comte's 'discovery' of social psychology. *Journal for the Theory of Social Behaviour*, **4**, 217–231.
Sampson, E. E. (1977). Psychology and the American ideal. *Journal of Personality and Social Psychology*, **35**, 767–782.
Sampson, E. E. (1978). Scientific paradigms and social values: Wanted—a scientific revolution. *Journal of Personality and Social Psychology*, **36**, 1332–1343.
Sanders, G. S. and Baron, R. (1977). Is social comparison irrelevant for producing choice shifts? *Journal of Experimental Social Psychology*, **13**, 303–314.
Sandowsky, A. M. (ed.) (1972). *Social Psychology Research: Laboratory-Field Relationships*. Free Press: New York.
Santee, R. T. (1976). The effect of attraction on attitude similarity as information about interpersonal reinforcement contingencies. *Sociometry*, **39**, 153–156.
Sarbin, T. (1977). Contextualism: A world view for modern psychology. In: Landfield, A. W. (ed.). *Nebraska Symposium on Motivation*, Volume 24. University of Nebraska Press: Lincoln.
Sarup, G. (1978). Historical antecedents of psychology: The recurrent issue of old wine in new bottles. *American Psychologist*, **33**, 478–485.
Scaife, M. (1979). Observing infant social development. In: Ginsburg, G. P. (ed.). *Emerging Strategies in Social Psychological Research*. Wiley: London.
Schachter, S. (1951). Deviation, rejection and communication. *Journal of Abnormal and Social Psychology*, **46**, 190–207.
Schachter, S. (1959). *The Psychology of Affiliation*. Stanford University Press: Stanford.
Schachter, S. (1964). The interaction of cognitive and physiological determinants of emotional states. In: Berkowitz, L. (ed.). *Advances in Experimental Social Psychology*, Volume 1. Academic Press: New York and London.
Schachter, S., Silverstein, B., Kozlowski, L. T., Perlick, D., Herman, C. P. and Liebling, B. (1977). Studies of the interaction of psychological and pharmacological determinants of smoking. *Journal of Experimental Psychology: General*, **106**, 3–40.
Schachter, S. and Singer, J. E. (1962). Cognitive, social and physiological determinants of emotional state. *Psychological Review*, **69**, 379–399.
Schackle, G. L. S. (1972). *Epistemies and Economics*. Cambridge University Press: Cambridge, England.

Schank, R. C. and Abelson, R. P. (1977). *Scripts, Plans, Goals and Understanding*. Wiley: New York.
Scheff, T. J. (1967). A Theory of Social Coordination Applicable to Mixed Motive Games. *Sociometry*, **30**, 215-234.
Scheibe, K. (1978). The psychologist's advantage and its nullification. *American Psychologist*, **33**, 869-881.
Schlenker, B. R. (1974). Social psychology and science. *Journal of Personality and Social Psychology*, **29**, 1-15.
Schlenker, B. R. (1977). On the ethogenic approach: Etiquette and revolution. In: Berkowitz, L. (ed.). *Advances in Experimental Social Psychology*, Volume 10. Academic Press: New York and London.
Schwartz, S. H. (1968). Words, deeds, and the perception of consequences and responsibility in action situations. *Journal of Personality and Social Psychology*, **10**, 232-242.
Scott, M. B. and Lyman, S. M. (1968). Accounts. *American Sociological Review*, **33**, 46-62.
Scott, W. A. (1974). Inter-referee agreement on some characteristics of manuscripts submitted to the JPSP. *American Psychologist*, **29**, 698-702.
Secord, P. F. and Backman, C. W. (1974). *Social Psychology*, (2nd Ed.) McGraw-Hill: New York.
Seligman, M. E. P. (1975). *Helplessness*. W. W. Freeman: San Francisco.
Shaver, K. G. (1975). *An Introduction to Attribution Processes*. Winthrop: Cambridge, Mass.
Shaw, M. E. (1932). A comparison of individuals and small groups in the rational solution of complex problems. *American Journal of Psychology*, **44**, 491-504.
Sherif, M. (1936). *The Psychology of Social Norms*. Harper and Row: New York.
Sherif, M. and Hovland, C. I. (1961). *Social Judgement*. Yale University Press: New Haven, Connecticut.
Shields, N. (1977). "Attribution processes in natural settings: A critique and an alternative." Paper presented at the annual meeting of the American Sociological Association, Chicago, Ill.
Short, J., Williams, E. and Christie, N. (1976). *The Social Psychology of Telecommunications*. Wiley: London.
Shotter, J. (1975). *Images of Man in Psychological Research*. Methuen: London.
Shulman, A. D. and Silverman, I. (1972). Profile of social psychology: A preliminary application of reference analysis. *Journal for the History of Behavioural Science*, **8**, 232-236.
Sigall, H. and Page, R. (1971). Current stereotypes: A little fading, a little faking. *Journal of Personality and Social Psychology*, **18**, 247-255.
Simonton, D. K. (1975). Sociocultural context of individual creativity: A transhistorical time-series analysis. *Journal of Personality and Social Psychology*, **32**, 1119-1133.
Skinner, B. F. (1948). *Walden Two*. Knopf: New York.
Skinner, B. F. (1971). *Beyond Freedom and Dignity*. Vintage Books: New York.
Slovic, P., Fischhoff, B. and Lichtenstein, S. (1976). Cognitive processes and

societal risk taking. In: Carroll, J. S. and Payne, J. W. (eds). *Cognition and Social Behavior.* Erlbaum: Hillside, N.J.

Slovic, P., Fischhoff, B. and Lichtenstein, S. (1977). Behavioral decision theory. *Annual Review of Psychology,* **28**, 1–39.

Smigel, E. D. (1963). *Work and leisure: a contemporary social problem.* College and University Press: New Haven, Connecticut.

Smith, M. B. (1972). Is Experimental Social Psychology Advancing? *Journal of Experimental Social Psychology,* **8**, 86–96.

Smith, M. B. (1974). *Humanizing Social Psychology.* Jossey-Bass: San Francisco.

Snyder, M. (1974). The self-monitoring of expressive behavior. *Journal of Personality and Social Psychology,* **30**, 526–537.

Snyder, M. (in press). Seek and ye shall find: testing hypotheses about other people. In: Higgins, E., Herman, C. and Zanner, M. (eds). *Social Cognition: The Ontario symposium on personality and social psychology.* Erlbaum: Hillsdale, N.J.

Snyder, M. and Swann, W. B. (1978). Behavioral confirmation in social interaction: From social perception to social reality. *Journal of Experimental Social Psychology,* **14**, 148–162.

Snyder, M., Tanke, E. D. and Berscheid, E. (1977). Social perception and interpersonal behavior: On the self-fulfilling nature of social stereotype. *Journal of Personality and Social Psychology,* **35**, 656–666.

Sofer, C. (1970). *Men in Mid-Career.* Cambridge University Press: Cambridge.

Sommer, R. (1969). *Personal Space.* Prentice-Hall: Englewood Cliffs, N.J.

Spock, B. (1957). *Baby and Child Care.* Pocket Books Inc.: New York.

Star, S. A., Williams, R. M. and Stouffer, S. A. (1958). Negro infantry platoons in white companies. In: Maccoby, E., Newcomb, T. M. and Hartley, E. L. (eds). *Readings in Social Psychology.* Holt: New York.

Staub, E. (1979). *Positive Social Behavior and Morality,* Volume 2, *Socialization and Development.* Academic Press: New York and London.

Steiner, I. D. (1966). Models for inferring relationships between group size and potential group productivity. *Behavioral Science,* **11**, 273–283.

Steiner, I. D. (1970). "Perceived freedom". In: Berkowitz, L. (ed.). *Advances in Experimental Social Psychology,* Volume 5. Academic Press: New York and London.

Steiner, I. D. (1972). *Group Process and Productivity.* Academic Press: New York and London.

Steiner, I. D. (1974). Whatever happened to the group in social psychology? *Journal of Experimental Social Psychology,* **10**, 94–108.

Strickland, L. J., Aboud, F. E. and Gergen, K. J. (eds) (1976). *Social Psychology in Transition.* Plenum Press: New York.

Stroebe, W. (1975). European social psychology today. Paper given at the Annual Meeting of the Society of Experimental Social Psychology, Lafayette, U.S.A.

Stroebe, W. (1977). Ahnlichkeit und Komplementaritat der Bedurfnisse als

Kriterien der Partnerwahl: Zwei spezielle Hypothesen. In: Mikula, G. and Stroebe, W. (eds). *Sympathie, Freundschaft und Ehe*. Huber: Bern.
Stroebe, W. (1979). The level of social psychological analysis: A plea for a more social social psychology. In: Strickland, L. H. (ed.). *Soviet and Western perspectives in social psychology*. Pergamon Press: Oxford.
Stroebe, W. (1980). Process loss in social psychology: Failure to exploit? In: Gilmour, R. and Duck, S. W. (eds). *The Development of Social Psychology*. Academic Press: London and New York.
Stryker, S. (1977). Developments in two social psychologies: Toward an appreciation of mutual relevances. *Sociometry*, **40**, 145–160.
Suls, J. M. and Miller, R. L. (eds) (1977). *Social Comparison Processes*. Wiley: New York.
Surkin, M. and Wolfe, A. (eds) (1970). *An End to Political Science*. Basic Books: New York.
Swingle, P. G. (1976). Critique: On 'Resolution versus Revolution?' In: Strickland, L. H., Aboud, F. H. and Gergen, K. J. (eds). *Social Psychology in Transition*. Plenum Press: New York.
Tajfel, H. (1969). Cognitive aspects of prejudice. *Journal of Social Issues*, **25**, 79–97.
Tajfel, H. (1972). Experiments in a vacuum. In: Israel, J. and Tajfel, H. (eds). *The Context of Social Psychology*. Academic Press: London and New York.
Tajfel, H. (ed.) (1978). *Differentiation between Social Groups: Studies in the social psychology of intergroup relations*. Academic Press: London and New York.
Tajfel, H. (1978). Interindividual and intergroup behaviour. In: Tajfel, H. (ed.). *Differentiation between Social Groups*. Academic Press: London and New York.
Taylor, C. (1971). Interpretation and the sciences of man. *Review of Metaphysics*, **25**, 4–51.
Thibaut, J. W. and Kelley, H. H. (1959). *The Social Psychology of Groups*. Wiley: New York.
Thomas, E. J. and Fink, C. F. (1961). Models of group problem solving. *Journal of Abnormal and Social Psychology*, **63**, 53–63.
Thorngate, W. (1976). Possible limits on a science of social behaviour. In: Strickland, L. H., Aboud, F. E. and Gergen, K. J. (eds). *Social Psychology in Transition*. Plenum Press: New York.
Thorngate, W. (1976). Must we always think before we act? *Personality and Social Psychology Bulletin*, **2**, 31–35.
Thurley, K. and Wirdenius, H. (1973). *Supervision: A Reappraisal*. Heinemann: London.
Thurstone, L. L. (1929). Theory of attitude measurement. *Psychological Bulletin*, **36**, 222–241.
Tomkins, S. S. (1959). *Affect, Imagery, Consciousness*, Volume I. *The Positive Affects*. Springer: New York.
Tomkins, S. S. (1963). *Affect, Imagery, Consciousness*, Volume II. *The Negative Affects*. Springer: New York.
Tomkins, S. (1978). Script theory: Differential magnifications of affects. In:

Cole, J. K. (ed.). *Nebraska Symposium on Motivation*. University of Nebraska Press: Lincoln.

Torode, B. (1976). The revelation of a theory of the world as grammar. In: Harré, R. (ed.). *Life Sentences*. Wiley: London and New York.

Totman, R. (1979). The myth of experimentation in social psychology. Paper to Social Psychology Section of BPS, Guildford, September.

Triandis, H. C. (1976). Social Psychology and Cultural Analysis. In: Strickland, L. H., Aboud, F. E. and Gergen, K. J. (eds). *Social Psychology in Transition*. Plenum Press: New York.

Trites, D. K. *et al.* (1970). Influence of nursing-unit design on the activities and subjective feelings of nursing personnel. *Environment and Behaviour*, **11**, 303–334.

Trivers, R. L. (1971). The evolution of reciprocal altruism. *Quarterly Review of Biology*, **46**, 35–57.

Trotter, W. (1919). *Instincts of the Herd in Peace and War*. (2nd Ed.). Fisher Unwin: London.

Trower, P., Bryant, B. and Argyle, M. (1978). *Social Skills and Mental Health*. Methuen: London.

Turner, J. C. (1980). Some considerations in generalising experimental social psychology. In: Stephenson, G. and Davis, J. (eds). *Progress in Applied Social Psychology*, Volume I. Wiley: London.

Tversky, A. and Kahneman, D. (1973). Availability: a heuristic for judging frequency and probability. *Cognitive Psychology*, **5**, 207–232.

Tversky, A. and Kahneman, D. (1974). Judgement under uncertainty: Heuristics and biases. *Science*, **185**, 1124–1131.

Varela, J. A. (1971). *Psychological Solutions to Social Problems*. Academic Press: New York and London.

Varela, J. A. (1975). Can social psychology be applied? In: Deutsch, M. and Hornstein, H. A. (eds). *Applying Social Psychology*. Wiley: New York.

Veblen, T. (1963). *The Theory of the Leisure Class*. Allen and Unwin: London.

Veroff, J. (1968). Social motivation. *American Behavioral Scientist*, **21**, 709–730.

Wall, T. D. and Lischeron, J. (1977). *Worker Participation*. McGraw-Hill: London.

Walker, N. (1976). *Behaviour and Misbehaviour*. Blackwell: Oxford.

Walster, E. H., Walster, G. W. and Berscheid, E. (1978). *Equity: Theory and Research*. Allyn and Bacon: Boston.

Webb, E. J., Campbell, D. T., Schwartz, R. D. and Sechrest, L. (1966). *Unobtrusive Measures: Non-reactive Research in the Social Sciences*. Rand-McNally: Chicago.

Weber, M. (1976). *The Protestant Ethic and the Spirit of Capitalism*. Allen and Unwin: London.

Weiner, B. (1970). New conceptions in the study of achievement motivation. In: Maher, B. (ed.). *Progress in Experimental Personality Research*, Vol. 5. Academic Press: New York and London.

Weiner, B. (1974). *Achievement Motivation and Attribution Theory*. General Learning Press: Morristown, N.J.

Wells, G. L. (1978). Applied eyewitness—testimony research: System variables and estimator variables. *Journal of Personality and Social Psychology*, **36**, 1546–1557.
Wheeler, L. and Nezlek, J. (1977). Sex differences in social participation. *Journal of Personality and Social Psychology*, **35**, 742–754.
Whorf, B. L. (1965). *Language, Thought and Reality*. M.I.T. Press: Cambridge, Mass.
Whyte, W. F. (1957). *The Organisation Man*. Penguin Books: Harmondsworth.
Wichman, H. (1970). Effects of isolation and communication on cooperation in a two person game. *Journal of Personality and Social Psychology*, **16**, 114–120.
Wicklund, L. A. (1974). *Freedom and Reactance*. Wiley: New York.
Wicklund, R. A. (1975). Objective self-awareness. In: Berkowitz, L. (ed.). *Advances in Experimental Social Psychology*, Vol. 8. Academic Press: New York and London.
Wiess, R. J. and Riesman, D. (1963). Some issues in the future of leisure. In: Smigel, E. O. (ed.). *Work and Leisure*. College and University Press: New Haven, Connecticut.
Williams, E. P. and Raush, H. L. (eds) (1969). *Naturalistic Viewpoint in Psychological Research*, Holt, Rinehart and Winston: New York.
Wilson, E. O. (1975). *Sociobiology*. Harvard University Press: Cambridge, Mass.
Wilson, E. O. (1978). *On Human Nature*. Harvard University Press: Cambridge, Mass.
Winch, R. F. (1958). *Male Selection: A Study of Complementary Needs*. Harper: New York.
Wispel, L. G. and Thompson, J. N. (1976). The war between the words: Biological versus social evolution and some related issues. *American Psychologist*, **31**, 341–347.
Wundt, W. (1874). *Lectures on Human and Animal Psychology*. Translation from the second German edition by J. E. Creighton and E. B. Titchener. Swan Sonnenschein & Co.: London.
Wundt, W. (1904). *Volkerpsychologie. Erster Band: Die Sprache*. Erster und Zweiter Teil. Verlag von Wilhelm Engelmann: Leipzig.
Wundt, W. (1916). *Elements of Folk Psychology*. Authorised translation by L. Schaub. George Allen & Unwin: London.
Xhignesse, L. V. and Osgood, C. E. (1967). Bibliographic citation characteristics of the psychological journal network in 1950 and in 1960. *American Psychologist*, **22**, 779–791.
Young, R. M. (1966). Scholarship and the history of the behavioural sciences. *History of Science*, **5**, 1–51.
Zadny, J. and Gerard, H. B. (1974). Attributed intentions and informational selectivity. *Journal of Personality and Social Psychology*, **10**, 34–52.
Zajonc, R. B. (1966). The development of social psychology. In: *Social Psychology: An Experimental Approach*. Wadworth: Belmont, Calif.
Zajonc, R. B. (1968). The attitudinal effects of mere exposure. *Journal of Personality and Social Psychology*, **9**, 1–27.

Zimbardo, P. G. (1973). The psychological power and pathology of imprisonment. In: Aronson, E. and Helmreich, R. (eds). *Social Psychology*. Van Nostrand: New York.

Zuckerman, M. (1974). The sensation seeking motive. In: Maher, B. A. (ed.). *Progress in Experimental Personality Research*. Academic Press: New York and London.

AUTHOR INDEX

ABELSON, R. P., 61, 66, 144, 265, 284
Aboud, F. E., 246
Adams, J. S., 251
Aderman, D., 185
Adorno, T. W., 17, 67, 152
Ajzen, I., 64, 151, 158, 288
Akutagawa, R., 9
Albert, H., 189
Alexander, N., 168, 174
Allport, G. W., 15, 223, 299
Anderson, N. H., 277
Andrews, F. M., 15
Antaki, C., 235
Anthony, P. D., 302, 303, 307
Apel, K. O., 262
Apfelbaum, E., 229, 246
Arendt, H., 302
Argyle, M., 84, 85, 87, 88, 89, 96, 97, 99, 173
Armistead, N., 27, 165, 246
Aronson, E., 61, 144, 176, 186, 187
Atkinson, J. W., 20

BACKMAN, C. W., 170, 174, 175, 176, 215, 227
Bakke, E. W., 302, 310
Balloun, J. L., 185
Bandura, A., 28, 71, 253
Barber, B., 141
Baron, R., 145
Baum, A., 291
Becker, H. S., 259
Bem, D. J., 63, 119, 120, 145, 153, 182, 232, 309
Berger, B. M., 160

Berkowitz, L., 199, 277
Berlyne, D. E., 68
Berrien, F. K., 92
Berscheid, E., 70, 173, 233, 274
Bettelheim, B., 66
Bickman, L., 283
Birnbaum, N., 246, 258
Blake, R. R., 101
Blank, T. O., 170
Blumstein, P. W., 173, 175
Bonoma, T. V., 285
Brehm, J. W., 186, 187, 265
Brenner, M., 49, 172
Brickman, P., 19, 21, 23
Briskman, L. B., 155
Broadbent, D. E., 141
Brock, T. C., 185
Brown, G. A., 93
Brown, J. M., 92
Brown, R., 152, 300–301
Bruner, J., 35, 174
Burke, K., 42
Burnstein, E., 145
Buss, A. R., 161, 246
Butler, D. E., 92
Byrne, D., 222, 224, 225, 226

CAMPBELL, D. T., 12, 15, 16, 86, 122, 127, 149, 156, 161, 183, 197, 223, 283
Canter, D., 94
Cantril, H., 9
Carlsmith, J. M., 186, 187
Carnegie, D., 102
Cartwright, D., 24, 145, 218, 255

Child, I. L., 145
Cicourel, A. V., 259, 260
Clarke, D., 48, 175
Clegg, C. W., 86
Clore, G. L., 222, 225
Coch, L., 100
Cohen, A. R., 187
Cohen, T., 269
Coleman, J. S., 99
Collins, B. E., 187
Cook, S. W., 90
Cook, T. D., 156
Cooper, J., 274
Crane, D., 138
Crowne, D. P., 249

Danziger, K., 226
Darley, J. M., 11, 141, 175, 277, 284
Darwin, C., 111, 113–129
Dashiell, J. F., 152
Davis, J. H., 287
Dawkins, R., 198
Deutsch, M., 82, 99
Diamond, S. S., 167
Dollard, J., 55, 66, 68, 71, 250
Doob, A. N., 288
Doob, L. W., 68
Dorris, J. W., 284
Dreyer, A., 219
Duck, S. W., 216, 224, 225, 226
Dutton, D. G., 274
Duval, S., 116, 158

Eibl-Eibesfeldt, I., 198
Eiser, J. R., 224, 225, 276
Ekman, P., 119, 135
Elms, A. C., 215
Emler, N. P., 143, 157
Emmet, D., 265
Endler, N. S., 97
Erdelyi, M. H., 156
Erikson, E. H., 16, 20, 21, 69
Evreinov, N., 33, 46

Fairweather, G. W., 91
Farina, A., 221
Farr, R. M., 113, 116, 123, 125
Fast, J., 98
Fay, B., 258
Festinger, L., 72, 119, 153, 187, 193, 213, 221, 223, 258, 265, 299
Feyerabend, P., 189, 248, 261–262
Fingarette, H., 33
Fink, C. F., 183
Fishbein, M., 64, 151, 158
Fleming, D., 121
Fodor, J. A., 251
Fraser, C., 143, 160, 220
Freedman, J. L., 185
French, J. R. P., 23
Fried, S. B., 172
Friedman, E. R., 310
Freud, S., 32
Fromkin, H. L., 139
Funder, D. C., 232

Gadenne, V., 183
Gambrill, E. G., 71
Garfield, E., 144, 157
Garfinkel, H., 173, 259
Garraty, J. A., 297–298
Garvey, W. D., 149
Gauld, A., 34, 214, 215, 258
Gerard, H. B., 82, 214
Gergen, K. J., 5, 10, 127, 170, 177, 181, 203, 213, 215, 222, 224, 225, 228, 230, 231, 236, 245, 246, 248, 252, 253, 254, 255, 256, 259, 260, 261
Gergen, M. M., 248
Gibson, J. J., 30
Giddens, A., 246, 258
Gilmour, R., 227
Ginsberg, G. P., 172
Glassman, R. B., 139
Goffman, E., 42, 116, 120–121, 217, 259, 260, 261
Gorer, G., 94
Gouldner, A. W., 246

AUTHOR INDEX

Green, R. G., 67
Greenwald, A. G., 145, 203

HABERMAS, J., 262
Hackman, J. R., 155
Hagstrom, W. O., 191
Halpin, A. W., 87
Harlow, H. F., 19
Harré, R., 27, 43, 84, 96, 181, 203, 213, 215, 216, 224, 226, 246, 265, 284
Harris, B., 245
Harris, R. J., 155, 202
Harvey, J. H., 62, 245
Hastorf, A. H., 9
Heidegger, M., 54
Heider, F., 154, 213
Helmreich, R., 178, 187
Henchy, T., 283
Hendrick, C., 165, 172, 174, 213, 214
Hewitt, J. P., 309
Himmelweit, H., 84
Hinde, R. A., 232
Hochbaum, G. M., 219
Hogan, R. T., 143, 157
Hollander, E. P., 82
Holzkamp, K., 181, 182, 203, 246
Homans, G. C., 154
Hornstein, H. A., 82, 99
House, J. S., 177, 178, 215
Hovland, C. I., 85, 141, 151, 154, 223, 308
Hsu, F. K., 19
Hull, C. L., 55
Huston, T. L., 232
Hyman, H. H., 152

INNES, J. M., 143, 147, 148, 150, 159, 160, 220, 227
Insko, C. A., 82, 182, 185
Israel, J., 181, 214, 215, 220, 246
Ittelson, W. H., 94
Izard, C. E., 198

JAHODA, G., 177, 294
Jahoda, M., 301, 310
Janis, I. L., 176, 182, 188, 191, 214, 222, 223
Jaques, E., 84, 100
Jaspars, J. M. F., 92
Jay, M., 246, 262
Jensen, U. J., 32
Jones, E. E., 30, 62, 80
Jones, M., 90
Jordan, N., 185

KAHNEMAN, D., 23, 158, 214, 223, 276, 286, 287
Kaplan, M. F., 286, 287
Katz, D., 67, 87, 141, 158, 164, 213
Katz, E., 99, 138, 139, 149
Keat, R., 34
Kelley, H. H., 62, 153, 154, 189, 259, 277, 280
Kelly, G. A., 20, 216
Kelman, H. C., 6
Kelvin, R. P., 218, 294, 312
Kenrick, D., 274
Kent, G. G., 175
Kerckhoff, A. C., 186
Kerr, N. L., 287
Kessler, S. J., 259, 261
Klein, L., 102
Kluckhohn, F. R., 19
Knight, L., 168, 174
Kogan, N., 142
Kuhn, T. S., 13, 140, 155, 193, 194, 248

LACEY, H., 251, 265
La Gaipa, J. J., 234
Lakatos, I., 186
Lambert, W. W., 177
Lamberth, J., 224, 225
Lamm, H., 277
Langer, E. J., 24, 245, 284
Latané, B., 11, 141, 175, 277, 284
Laudun, L., 248

AUTHOR INDEX

Lazarus, R. S., 64
Lerner, M. J., 16
Lévi-Strauss, C., 23
Levinger, G., 186, 232
Levy, L. H., 148, 152
Lewin, K., 6, 153
Lieberman, M. A., 98, 177
Linder, D. E., 185, 188
Lindzey, G., 82, 87, 127, 144
Lischeron, J., 84, 88
Lofland, J., 172
Lorenz, K., 198
Lorge, I., 183, 187
Lubek, I., 221, 228, 229, 246
Luginbuhl, J. E., 245
Lunn, J. A., 92
Lyman, S. M., 175

McCall, C. J., 175
McCarthy, B., 221, 225, 226
McClelland, D. C., 69, 88
McClintock, C. G., 82
McConnell, H. K., 182
McCoy, C., 246
McDonagh, E. L., 143
McGinnies, E., 156
McGrath, J. E., 164, 165
McGuire, W. J., 55, 57, 61, 71, 72, 74, 92, 144, 151, 170, 182, 197, 213, 215, 221, 224, 225, 236, 246
McHenry, R., 85
McKenna, W., 259, 261
McPhail, P., 104
McWhirter, R. M., 225
Machiavelli, N., 9
Magnusson, D., 97
Maines, D. R., 176
Mann, F. C., 101
Mann, L., 176
Mannheim, K., 100, 160
Marlowe, D., 249
Marsden, D., 301-303, 304, 310
Marsh, P., 43, 96, 172
Marston, B. J., 214
Maslow, A. H., 15

May, P. R. A., 91
Mead, G. H., 129-135, 158
Meehl, P. E., 155, 156, 157, 246
Mehrabian, A., 219
Meltzer, L., 83
Merton, R. K., 149, 191
Milgram, S., 48, 281
Miller, D. T., 280
Miller, J., 105
Miller, N. E., 55, 66, 68, 71, 250
Millham, S., 310
Mills, J., 185
Mischel, W., 49, 99
Mixon, D., 48, 284
Morawski, J. Y., 192
Moscovici, S., 6, 45, 85, 145
Mulder, M., 89
Mullins, N. C., 153
Murchison, C. A., 126
Murray, H. S., 15
Murstein, B. I., 225
Myers, C. R., 149, 277
Mynatt, C., 245

Neisser, U., 246
Nezlek, J., 232
Nisbett, R. E., 16, 30, 156, 245

Orne, M., 156, 216
Osgood, C. E., 144, 147, 154

Pagano, D. F., 152
Paige, J. M., 17
Pepitone, A., 198, 199
Phillips, D. L., 147
Piaget, J., 21, 23
Piliavin, I. M., 283, 284
Pilliavin, J. A., 283, 284
Playford, J., 246
Popper, K. R., 182, 183, 184, 185, 186, 189, 190, 193, 195, 247
Postman, L., 223
Powers, W. T., 66
Price, D. J. de S., 143, 147, 149-150

Prior, J., 307
Prus, R. C., 169, 174, 176

RADNITZKY, G., 258
Rands, M., 232
Rapoport, R. H., 91
Rescher, N., 155
Rich, A. R., 90
Richardson, J. T., 177
Riecken, H. W., 156, 164
Riegel, K. F., 246
Ring, K., 164, 167
Rodrigues, A., 185
Rokeach, M., 15
Rommetveit, R., 175
Rosch, E., 191
Rose, R., 92
Rosenberg, M. J., 142, 145, 185, 187
Rosenshine, B., 93
Rosenthal, R., 6
Rosenzweig, S., 156
Ross, H. H., 86, 223
Ross, L., 214
Roth, J., 245
Rubin Z., 16
Rutter, M., 306
Ryle, G., 131

SAGATUN, S. J., 169, 174
Sales, S. M., 138, 295
Samelson, F., 158
Sampson, E. E., 159, 198, 246
Sanders, G. S., 145
Santee, R. T., 226
Sarbin, T., 246
Sarup, G., 158
Scaife, M., 174
Schachter, S., 118–119, 153, 159, 192, 193, 198, 221, 245, 274
Schackle, G. L. S., 246
Schank, R. C., 66, 265
Scheff, T. J., 168
Scheibe, K., 247
Schlenker, B. R., 181
Schwartz, S. H., 175

Scott, M. B., 175
Scott, W. A., 147
Secord, P. F., 176
Seligman, M. E. P., 17
Shaver, K. G., 223
Shaw, M. E., 202
Sherif, M., 151, 153, 193, 226, 308
Shields, N., 174
Short, J., 94
Shotter, J., 27, 34, 214, 215, 258
Shulman, A. D., 146
Sigall, H., 158
Simmons, J. L., 175
Simonton, D. K., 160
Skinner, B. F., 265
Slovic, P., 286, 288
Smigel, E. D., 302
Smith, M. B., 166, 167, 170, 182, 195, 200
Snyder, M., 24, 158, 173, 221, 233
Sofer, C., 100
Sommer, R., 94
Spock, B., 102
Stanley, J. C., 86, 156, 183, 283
Star, S. A., 90
Steiner, I. D., 23, 176, 183, 187, 196, 198, 200, 226, 230
Strickland, L. J., 246
Stroebe, W., 186, 196, 198, 200, 201, 202, 214, 221, 227, 228, 230, 276
Stryker, S., 170, 215
Surkin, M., 246
Swingle, P. G., 200

TAJFEL, H., 84, 199, 201, 218, 221, 233, 246, 275, 276, 281, 286
Tanke, E. D., 173, 233
Taylor, C., 258
Thibaut, J. W., 154, 277
Thomas, E. J., 183
Thompson, J. N., 195
Thorngate, W., 156, 219
Thurley, K., 87
Thurstone, L. L., 151
Tomkins, S. S., 66, 198

Torode, B., 48
Totman, R., 215, 228
Triandis, H. C., 177, 226
Trites, D. K., 94
Trivers, R. L., 19
Trotter, W., 158
Trower, P., 90
Turner, J. C., 213, 219, 225, 228
Tversky, A., 23, 158, 214, 223, 276, 286, 287

URRY, J., 34

VARELA, J. A., 9, 255
Veblen, T., 306
Veroff, J., 16, 20
Vinokur, A., 145

WALL, T. D., 84, 88
Walker, N., 34
Walster, E., 70, 274, 277
Walters, R. H., 28
Webb, E. J., 295
Weber, M., 298
Weiner, B., 69, 274

Weisbrod, R., 177
Wells, G. L., 287
Wheeler, L., 232
Whorf, B. L., 191
Whyte, W. F., 99
Wichman, H., 281
Wicklund, R. A., 64, 116, 158, 265
Wilson, E. O., 19, 70, 198
Wilson, T. D., 156, 245
Winch, R. F., 186
Winter, D. G., 88
Wirdenius, H., 87
Wispé, L. G., 197
Withey, S. B., 15
Worchel, S., 182, 185
Wundt, W. 111–130

XHIGNESSE, L. V., 144, 147

YOUNG, R. M., 158

ZADNY, J., 214
Zajonc, R. B., 10, 37
Zimbardo, P. G., 176
Zuckerman, M., 65

SUBJECT INDEX

ABSURDITY, 264–266
Accounts, 32ff, 43f
Action, psychology of, 30f
Adaptation level, 308f
Agent, person as, 38f
Aggressor, identification with, 72, 221
Ambiguity, 300
Applied social psychology, 37, 81–106, 177f, 255ff, 271–292
Approval, need for social, 249
Archival records in social psychology, 295ff
Artificiality, 278
Attitudes, 121–123
Attribution, 164ff, 169, 288, 308f

BALANCE, 276
Biased scanning hypothesis, 182
Black Death, 303

CASE STUDIES, 49f
Categorization, 276
Cohort analysis, 158ff
Common sense, and social psychology, 11
  intuitive theories, 185, 261–262
Communication, 193, 221–223
Comparison, social, 277, 299f
Competition, 280–281
Conflict, 229–230
  see also Competition
Comformity pressures, 194
Consensus, 195ff
Constructs, 34f
Constructivism, 74ff, 76f

Context for explanation, 239–246
  Emergent context, 241
  Retrospective context, 240–241
Co-operation, 280
Crisis in social psychology, 5, 83, 212, 229, 239f
  Crisis of identity, 217, 233
  Crisis of intellectual isolation, 215, 233–235
  Crisis of practice, 215, 235–236
  Crisis of spirit, 5, 7
  Crisis of theory, 215, 230–231
  Crisis of utility, 215, 231–233
Critical rationalism, 182, 183ff, 187ff
Cross-cultural psychology, 293–294
  see also Culture
Culture, 19, 36, 48, 112f, 126f
  and meaning, 36
  as a factor in psychology, 19f

DEMAND CHARACTERISTICS, 216
Developmental psychology, 21f
Deviants, 192, 220–221, 307, 308
Diffusion of research, 143ff

ECOLOGICAL VALIDITY, 232
Economics and psychology, 15f, 219, 234
Ego defence, 67
Emotions, 11, 113–123, 198, 235, 274
  and evolution, 117f
Empirical content of theories, 184, 190, 247f, 253
Empiricism, 74f, 77ff, 156f, 245, 246ff
Environmental design, 94f

Equity theory, 256
Erikson's theory, 16f, 21f
Ethogenics, 42ff, 44ff, 173f, 176, 246
Experimentalism, 27, 126f
  attacks on, 27, 28f, 214
  decline of, 179
  method in, 33, 196, 200
  see also Methodology
Explanations, alternative, 254

FADDISM, 157ff, 163, 164, 165ff, 178, 202, 226ff
  see also Fashion
Falsificationism, 182, 184ff, 247f, 251, 252, 257, 265
Fashion, 226–228
  see also Faddism
Fashion forces, 151f
Fear of success, 266
Fires, escaping from, 94
Futures of social psychology, 207–318

GATEKEEPERS, 224
Generative theory, 39, 71f, 261–269
Genetic factors in behaviour, 197ff, 200
Gestalt theory, 62f
Gestures, 112, 131f
Groups,
  norms, 193
  problem solving in, 187ff
  process loss in, Chapter 8, esp. 182ff, 190f, 203f
  productivity of, 188f, 190ff
  small group research, 164ff, 176ff
  see also Intergroup behaviour
Groupthink, 222

HANDSHAKE, 35
Hermeneutics, 44
Human concerns, 5ff, 18
  see also Social psychology

INDUSTRIAL CONSULTANCY, 82, 100f
Intergroup behaviour, 89ff, 199f, 275, 286
Interpersonal attraction (IPA) 224–226, 231, 274, 279
Interpretation,
  forms of, 258–261, 276
  minority, 263f
  see also Explanations
Interpretation of action, 239ff

JAMES-LANGE THEORY, 121

LABORATORY EXPERIMENTS, 5f, 30f, 85, 156, 165f, 172, 278ff, 281, 282–285
Labour, division of, by scientists 187f
Language, 112, 129
Leadership, 87, 164ff
Leisure, 310f
Lewin's field theory, 64
Linguistics and psychology, 40ff
Love, 274

MANAGERS, 88f
Mass Media, 91f, 219
"Matthew effect", 149
Meaning, 44, 62, 131f
Metaphors, 267–269
Methodology, 200
  attacks on, 213–215
  see also Experimentalism

NETWORKS, 150ff
Non-verbal communication, 175
Norms, 175, 193

"PASSING", 302
Pluralistic ignorance, 223
Politics and psychology, 15f, 219, 234

Poor law, 304
Positivist philosophy, 30f, 33, 34f, 75f
Power, 69
Prisoner's dilemma, 154, 280–281
Process loss, *see under* Groups
Protestant work ethic, 295–316
Psychodynamics, 45f

RACIAL ATTITUDES, 89f
Rationality, bounded, 273
Recruitment, of psychologists, 191
Reference group, 308f
Reference systems, 149ff
Research, factors in choice of, 272, 289–290
 fun-and-games, 167
 trivialization of, 166
Reward structure in social psychology, 163
Roles, 174
Role theory, 69

SCRIPT, 66
Self as object, 115–136
Self perception, 115, 119–136, 308–309
SESP (Society of Experimental Social Psychology) 195, 221
Social behaviourism, 129–136
Social comparison, 277, 299
Social control, 191
 see also Conformity pressures
Social dimension, 29
 to psychological concepts, 31f
Social movements, 263
Social problems, 6, 22, 82, 219, 291–2
 see also Research, factors affecting choice of

Social psychology,
 aims of, pp5ff
 and common sense, 11f
 and Human Concerns, 5ff, 14ff, 20f
 and Sociology, 138f
 and wisdom, 12f
 as a science, 10f
 as culturally mandated outlook, 8ff
Social skills, 87, 90ff
Socialization, 174f
 of psychologists, 190–191
Sociology and psychology, 167ff
Social-structural variables, 198f
Stigma, 302, 308
Symbolic interactionism, 308ff

T-GROUPS, 82, 97
Taxonomic priority thesis, 31f
Teamwork, 217, 223
Theories, 53
 affective growth theories, 68ff
 as thinking, 53–54
 classification of, 55ff, 58, 59ff
 cognitive stability theories, 60ff
 cognitive growth theories, 63ff
 systems theories, 71
 testing of, 203
 see also Falsification
Transition, 300

UNEMPLOYMENT, 293–316

VERIFIABILITY, 202, 204, 265

WAR, 199
 Second World, 6, 82, 165
 Six-day, 301